BOREDOM, ARCHITECTURE, AND SPATIAL EXPERIENCE

BOREDOM, ARCHITECTURE, AND SPATIAL EXPERIENCE

Christian Parreno

BLOOMSBURY VISUAL ARTS
LONDON • NEW YORK • OXFORD • NEW DELHI • SYDNEY

BLOOMSBURY VISUAL ARTS
Bloomsbury Publishing Plc
50 Bedford Square, London, WC1B 3DP, UK
1385 Broadway, New York, NY 10018, USA
29 Earlsfort Terrace, Dublin 2, Ireland

BLOOMSBURY, BLOOMSBURY VISUAL ARTS and the Diana logo are trademarks of
Bloomsbury Publishing Plc

First published in Great Britain 2021
Paperback edition first published 2022

Copyright © Christian Parreno, 2021

Christian Parreno has asserted his right under the Copyright, Designs and Patents Act, 1988, to be identified as Author of this work.

For legal purposes the Acknowledgements on p. ix constitute an extension of this copyright page.

Cover design by Namkwan Cho
Cover image © Nicolo Sertorio / Getty Images

All rights reserved. No part of this publication may be reproduced or transmitted in any form or by any means, electronic or mechanical, including photocopying, recording, or any information storage or retrieval system, without prior permission in writing from the publishers.

Bloomsbury Publishing Plc does not have any control over, or responsibility for, any third-party websites referred to or in this book. All internet addresses given in this book were correct at the time of going to press. The author and publisher regret any inconvenience caused if addresses have changed or sites have ceased to exist, but can accept no responsibility for any such changes.

A catalogue record for this book is available from the British Library.

Library of Congress Cataloging-in-Publication Data
Names: Parreno, Christian, author.
Title: Boredom, Architecture, and Spatial Experience / Christian Parreno.
Description: London; New York: Bloomsbury Visual Arts, 2021. | Outgrowth of the author's thesis (doctoral)–Oslo School of Architecture and Design, 2017, under the title: Boredom as Space: Episodes of Modern Architecture. | Includes bibliographical references and index. |
Identifiers: LCCN 2020038483 (print) | LCCN 2020038484 (eBook) |
ISBN 9781350148130 (hardback) | ISBN 9781350213647 (paperback) | ISBN 9781350148147 (pdf) |
ISBN 9781350148154 (ePub) | ISBN 9781350148161
Subjects: LCSH: Architecture–Psychological aspects. | Boredom.
Classification: LCC NA2540. P445 2021 (print) | LCC NA2540 (eBook) | DDC 720.1—dc23
LC record available at https://lccn.loc.gov/2020038483
LC eBook record available at https://lccn.loc.gov/2020038484

ISBN: HB: 978-1-3501-4813-0
PB: 978-1-3502-1364-7
ePDF: 978-1-3501-4814-7
eBook: 978-1-3501-4815-4

Typeset by RefineCatch Limited, Bungay, Suffolk

To find out more about our authors and books visit www.bloomsbury.com and sign up for our newsletters.

CONTENTS

List of Illustrations — vii
Acknowledgments — ix
Preface — x
Foreword
   by Iain Borden — xi

Introduction: Boredom as Architecture — 1

1 A Component of Modernity — 9

Part 1 Differential Distances

2 Fascination and Aversion — 17
3 Søren Kierkegaard's Babylonian Tower — 23
4 Catherine Gore and Charles Dickens: Idle Restlessness/Restless Idleness — 29
5 Blunting and Jading — 41
6 Coney Island, Misleading Structures — 47

Part 2 Circular Trajectories

7 A Unity of Disarray — 57
8 Martin Heidegger's Urge to Be at Home — 69
9 Oran, the Capital of Boredom — 77
10 International Style Confusions: Sigfried Giedion — 87
11 Los Angeles, Flat Enough — 101

Part 3 Extended Thresholds

12 Potential Architectures — 115
13 Andrew Benjamin's Antithesis to Boredom — 127
14 Boredom in *Domus* — 131
15 Servitude and Liberalism: Russell Kirk — 147

Contents

16	Charles Jencks, Rem Koolhaas, and the Generic	157
17	Jorge Silvetti and Sylvia Lavin: Unamused Muses and Lying Fallow	171
Epilogue: Architectures of Boredom		183
Notes		189
Bibliography		237
Index		253

ILLUSTRATIONS

4.1	Frontispiece and title page of *Women as They Are, or the Manners of the Day*, volume 1. London: Henry Colburn and Richard Bentley (1830).	31
4.2	Frontispiece and title page of *Women as They Are, or the Manners of the Day*, volume 2. London: Henry Colburn and Richard Bentley (1830).	32
4.3	Cover of the first instalment of *Bleak House*. London: Bradbury & Evans (March 1852).	35
4.4	Frontispiece and title page of *Bleak House*. London: Chapman & Hall (1853).	36
6.1	The main promenade of Luna Park during daytime, from "Boredom," *The Independent Magazine* (August 8, 1907), 312.	48
6.2	Luna Park at night, from "Boredom," *The Independent Magazine* (August 8, 1907), 315.	49
9.1	Oran from the fort of Santa Cruz (1930). Photograph by M. Lavina.	78
9.2	Maison du Colon (c. 1940). Unknown photographer. Courtesy of the Musée de l'Histoire vivante—Montreuil.	81
10.1	Press release for the symposium "The International Style—Death or Metamorphosis?" (1961). Archives of American Art, Smithsonian Institution. Architectural League of New York records, 1880s–1974; 1960 League-Sponsored Functions and Events. Box 88. Folder 39, "New Forces in Architecture," 1960–1.	90
10.2	Invitation to the cocktail reception and dinner for the symposium "The International Style—Death or Metamorphosis?" (1961). Archives of American Art, Smithsonian Institution. Architectural League of New York records, 1880s–1974; 1960 League-Sponsored Functions and Events. Box 88. Folder 39, "New Forces in Architecture," 1960–1.	91
10.3	Press release titled "Outspoken Briton Dislikes U.S. Architecture" (March 24, 1961). Douglas Putnam Haskell papers, 1866–1979 (bulk 1949–64), Avery Architectural & Fine Arts Library, Columbia University.	93
10.4	"Architecture—Fitting and Befitting," excerpts of the speeches delivered by Philip Johnson and Reyner Banham at the symposium "The International Style—Death or Metamorphosis?" *Architectural Forum* (June 1961), 86–7.	95
11.1	First page of "Los Angeles: The Ecologies of Evil." *Artforum* (December 1972), 67. © *Artforum*.	109
14.1	First spread of "Boredom," *Domus* 605 (April 1980).	139
14.2	Second spread of "Boredom," *Domus* 605 (April 1980).	141
14.3	Third spread of "Boredom," *Domus* 605 (April 1980).	143

Illustrations

15.1 Construction of parking behind City Hall, Cleveland (1973). Photograph by Bernie Noble, from the Cleveland Press Collections. Courtesy of the Michael Schwartz Library Special Collections, Cleveland State University.   150
15.2 Aerial photo of Poletown General Motors plant, Detroit, Michigan (1986). BL004030. Michigan Bell Telephone Company Photographs, Bentley Historical Library, University of Michigan.   152
16.1 Graph of the Ivan Illich Law of Diminishing Architecture (2002). Courtesy of Charles Jencks.   159
16.2 First spread of "How Big is Bad?" *The Architectural Review* (August 2002). Courtesy of *The Architectural Review*.   161

Every effort has been made to obtain necessary permissions for the publication of copyright protected images. Should there be certain cases that have been overlooked, please contact the publisher so that any missing or inaccurate information can be corrected in future editions.

ACKNOWLEDGMENTS

At the onset, I anticipated that the study of boredom, architecture, and spatial experience would be isolating. Yet many people have contributed and accompanied this work, acting as two families. The first is the academic. Thanks to Mari Lending and Iain Borden, this project found a beginning, a process, and a conclusion; their support has been immensely generous. This clan includes the inspiring faculties of the Oslo School of Architecture and Design, The Bartlett School of Architecture, the University of California, Los Angeles, and Universidad San Francisco de Quito. Mari Hvattum, Erik Langdalen, and Sylvia Lavin deserve special mention, as does Lenore Hietkamp, whose input during the revision for publication added clarity to an otherwise diffuse theme of investigation. The second family comprises my parents, siblings, Peter, relatives, and friends. Despite my esoteric ramblings and constant distractedness, they have remained my most enthusiastic supporters.

My gratitude to all of you.

PREFACE

My concern with boredom and architecture began in the spring of 2008. Amidst the agitated routine of an international architectural firm in Covent Garden, in Central London, and the looming possibility of dedicating a lifetime to corporate production, I reflected on the surrounding fixation with the interesting and spectacular. My musings guided me toward boredom, the opposite of the fullness and excitement sought in the design of buildings that is fostered by economic agents and validated by the media. If the search for stimulation eludes canons and favors originality and innovation, then boredom is to be avoided. Yet boredom is that condition of inhabitation which interlaces the habits of architects with the qualities of their designs, the experience of users, and the reception of the public, charged with ideological nuances. As I concluded then, and which continues to be valid today, in the world of commercial architecture, the ability to create form prevails, turning the practice of the discipline into a rapidly changing field where the new is soon outmoded and the old serves as a stylistic pattern book. Within this labyrinthine frame, boredom constitutes a point of access into the disaffection with what already exists, driving the ideation of what has not been imagined yet.

These initial thoughts, hesitantly pursued but illuminating, led me down a path of researching and writing about boredom, its development and many expressions, and how it is understood in our relationship with the built environment. Since spatial experience colors our lives and casts our spatiality, which become forces in the production of architecture, boredom reveals our modernity, questioning our individuality as well as our physical and existential interconnectedness with the world. With these considerations, I employ the condition as a historical and theoretical discourse; the aim of this book is to explore the non-physical and ambiguous implications of edifices, the parallel spaces they generate, and the multiple temporalities they embed.

FOREWORD
Iain Borden

Boredom has too often received a bad press. As Christian Parreno points out early on in this comprehensive study, boredom has almost always been associated with some of the most negative qualities of our modern (and not so modern) life, such as being apathetic, dreary, dull, jaded, monotonous, and world weary. And yet, as this book shows in its historical arc from ancient Greece to the present day—and following intellectual thought from Hippocrates through Thomas Aquinas to Søren Kierkegaard, Martin Heidegger, and Albert Camus—boredom has always been an essential part of the human condition. Surely then, it must be relevant to architecture, that most social and spatial of the arts, and which is plugged in to the very heart of our urban existence. Must not boredom be considered as an intrinsic part of the built environment?

Rarely has boredom been identified as part of architecture—at least not explicitly. Instead, nearly all of architectural writing, be it critical, historical, theoretical or journalistic, has tended to pursue that other grand narrative of human endeavor, the one that follows the trajectory of all that is innovative, exciting, simulating, and—above all—interesting. Architects, in the end, tend to design a different building with every commission, rarely preferring to repeat an earlier design. So surely it is this imperative to change, to alter, to invent, that architectural study should follow.

Well, yes, and of course that is right. But there are limits to this dynamic trajectory, or rather it might be better to say that there are hidden complexities and other essential components. In his seminal essay "The Metropolis and Mental Life" of 1903, the great German sociologist Georg Simmel writes of the "neurasthenia" of modern life, of the onslaught of visual, social, and informational stimuli that threaten to overpower and to consume the urban citizen. And so, Simmel contends, modern individuals have to adopt a "blasé" attitude, a form of indifference to the world and to people around them, as a way to cope with, filter, and survive the demands of everything that is interesting, and which demands their attention.

In this sense, boredom is the necessary counterpoint to stimulation and interest, the inevitable and necessary moment at which that which once was interesting becomes tired and hackneyed, an instance of stasis in which the city dweller can pause, switch off and breathe ... before the next stage of stimulation takes off. Boredom is at once a stage of respite, a moment of critical reflection, and a launch pad for something born anew. It is the car crash that provides the necessary moment of near death after a passage of high-speed intoxication, but out of which new life emerges.

And here we arrive at the most surprising—perhaps we should say interesting—aspect of boredom, and which the commanding exposition of this book tellingly explores.

Foreword

This is the notion that boredom is far more than just a juncture of down time amid the otherwise irrepressible surge of modernity; it is also in itself a way of encountering architecture in a creative and meaningful manner. In this remarkable and stimulating journey, Parreno shows us—in his engagements with the likes of Sigfried Giedion, Le Corbusier, Philip Johnson, Reyner Banham, Charles Jencks, Rem Koolhaas, Sylvia Lavin, and Jorge Silvetti—how boredom is not just a condition to be avoided, a kind of warning against inactivity, but a central feature of our spatial and mental encounters with architecture, all of which are modulated both individually and historically.

INTRODUCTION
BOREDOM AS ARCHITECTURE

"In the beginning was boredom, commonly called chaos," declares the eccentric antihero of *Boredom*, a novel by Alberto Moravia. Published in 1960, at the apex of mid-twentieth-century modernism, it portrays boredom as both antecedent to any deity and constituting a space to be designed, for "God, bored with boredom, created the earth, the sky, the waters, the animals, the plants, Adam and Eve." Far from providing stasis, the exhaustion with what already exists endlessly surfaces, again and again, to structure the architecture of civilizations, "the great empires—Egyptian, Babylonian, Persian, Greek and Roman— rose out of boredom and fell again in boredom"; along with their religions, geographies, and socioeconomic contracts, "the boredom of paganism gave rise to Christianity; that of Catholicism to Protestantism; the boredom of Europe caused the discovery of America; the boredom of feudalism kindled the French Revolution; and that of capitalism, the revolution in Russia."[1]

As an implacable force responsible for all changes caused by human intervention, boredom explains—and incites—transgression and creativity. This power, Moravia implies, resides in its capacity to look to the past and the future with equal indifference, providing a critical stance. Fredric Jameson, in his diagnosis of the cultural logic of late capitalism, asserts that this structural position, of a lingering now, is a "very useful instrument with which to explore the past, and to stage a meeting between it and the present."[2] Likewise, amidst the questionings of existentialism, Emil Cioran concludes that in the definition of one's own history, "no matter what you do, the starting point is boredom, and the end self-destruction."[3] After exhausting the celebrated, becoming bored with the classical and the canonical, one can turn to what has been forgotten and has not been preserved—the non-survivors that did not qualify for posterity because, at the moment of their evaluation, they were deemed to be boring.

Though historically specific, boredom figures in this chronology as a modern condition of architecture that rejects the offerings of the surroundings. It is a disruption of outer and inner dwelling. Drawing attention since the late nineteenth century, in studies of philosophy, psychology, and psychoanalysis, the interdependence between boredom and milieu reveals a preference for distraction caused by the incapacity of individuals to maintain interest and concentration. The condition, acknowledged by all but remaining elusive, encompasses a simultaneity of sentiments and thoughts that entails an involuntary deficit of meaning. In contrast to melancholy and depression, it exists beyond psychological and physiological states because of its involvement with the qualities of the immediate environment, combining perceptions of space and time.[4] Despite these important attributes and connotations, boredom has not been incorporated into the study of the experience and discipline of architecture—neither as a construct to contextualize its structures nor as a reference by which to understand its spatiality.

Pliable Omnipresence

An investigation of boredom and architecture inevitably entails three fundamental questions. First, to what extent and under which circumstances are inhabitants willing to respond to their built environment? Second, which architectural configurations are significant? And third, how does the condition transform into obliteration and construction? Boredom itself, however, cannot provide definite answers, since it impedes the identification of what to demand of the world, distrusting the capacity of the world to ignite desire. When desire irrupts, the desire for desire causes confusion and discomfort; Maine de Biran wants to be somewhere else soon after reaching a previously coveted destination: "having left Paris ... I arrived at Grateloup on the third of February ... In Paris I complained of the bustle there; here I complain of the lack of it. ... Where is the balance point and how to find it?"[5] Unlike a convex formation that covers many other emotions and intellectual responses, boredom acts as a vessel that constantly changes shape according to its content—transient, completely lacking, replete—susceptible to infinite portrayals.[6] Semantically, this plasticity is evident in the extent of possible synonyms: anhedonia, apathy, arid, banal, blasé, burn-out, chatter, cliché, cloying, discontent, disinterest, drag, dreary, dry, dull, fatigue, flatness, hackneyed, humdrum, inane, inactive, indifferent, insipid, jaded, jejune, languor, lassitude, listless, monotony, mundane, platitude, prosaic, repetitious, sameness, satiation, soporific, stagnant, sterile, stultifying, surfeited, tiresome, tedium, torpor, trivial, uniform, uninteresting, weariness, and world weary. Many sayings also suggest paralysis and suffering, navigating from one dimension to another: "bored silly," "bored to distraction," "bored to tears," "bored stiff," and the ominous "bored to death."[7]

These adjectives, nouns, and aphorisms designate the everyday as the realm of boredom, in complex and indissoluble connection with modernity. Friedrich Schlegel, in erudite Romanticism, insinuates that the condition suffocates: "both in their origins and effects, boredom and stuffy air resemble each other ... usually generated whenever a large number of people gather together in a closed room."[8] In turn, Maurice Blanchot responds that "boredom is the everyday become manifest." If boredom is the moment when the uneventful, insignificant, and unnoticed move to the fore, dependent upon architecture, then it composes the fabric that organizes habit but loses the capacity to be perceived—"thus held by boredom in boredom, ... just as carbon dioxide accumulates in a closed space where too many people find themselves together."[9] The condition, a lasting mood rather than a fleeting sentiment, is collective but contributes to social fragmentation and the withdrawal from communal memory. A malady that accompanies the suspension of traditional forms of positive engagement, boredom is "an atrophy of experience" that permeates every inhabitable space, preferring the fissures that abscond from functional planning and from which waiting is established—the marker of invariable monotony.[10]

Yet boredom does not belong to any architecture in particular. It can emerge in the domestic—minimal and modest—and the monumental—convoluted and grandiose. If seen through boredom, architecture presents not as a physical realm demarcated by edifices but as relationships and operations, in constant adjustment. When it connects tangible designs with intangible forms, the condition becomes a topos in philosophical enquiry, rendered through metaphors, allegories, and metonymies of buildings and spatial occupation—ungraspable and entropic, contrary to the defined boundaries, precise and pure, usually associated to modernism. Martin Heidegger, with phenomenological intention, portrays boredom as "a silent fog" that "draws back and forth," impairing vision and orientation and leading the sufferer to the edge of a groundless abyss.[11] Walter Benjamin also represents it meteorologically, through the cycles of weather that stir up the residues of the metropolis and confront its regulated territories, as when the rain hits the streets of Paris and dust invades and transforms the arcades, leaving them gray and "without accent."[12] For both, boredom is an opaque and diluted agent that blankets everyone and everything, paradoxically unveiling the muffled sameness of modernity.

A Long Essay

Rather than being an exhaustive analysis, this book is a long essay, interdisciplinary in approach. This strategy resonates with the unclear location of boredom and its capacity to articulate the emotional and rational with the physical and immaterial. Because of the suppleness of the condition, its study ought to focus not on its multiple configurations but on the situations that allow its rise, recognizing its resistance to fixed definitions while assuming that some of its attributes can be incommunicable. The midpoint of boredom cannot be arrived at without swerving; a circling around is therefore required, similar to an epistemological meandering that pursues an unquantifiable circumstance of inhabitation. Boredom is ambiguous and ambivalent—local and foreign, familiar and uncanny, neutral and critical—and capable of not only remaining in the superficial and diving into the existential but also coalescing rather than dividing.

Including this imponderable character, and due to the lack of studies on the infiltration of boredom in architecture, this exploration begins with the emergence of the English term *boredom* in the nineteenth century and extends to the first decade of the twenty-first century. Since the condition transpires in those parts of the world that are guided by ideals of modern progress, the focus is on the boredom that emanated in Western Europe, particularly the United Kingdom, the center of the Industrial Revolution, and proliferated in the United States. Although in the globalized world, boredom accompanies modernity as an indispensable constituent—to be modern is to be bored—it presents nuances related to local development; Henri Lefebvre notes, "people are more bored in advanced countries like the USA and Sweden than they are in Africa or Yugoslavia, or even in this dear old France of ours," while "the Soviets or the Chinese... haven't time to get bored, to get bored you need leisure... Those good people are workers, they produce; they are told that production is synonymous with satisfaction."[13]

History and theory are the methods of this long essay. History reconstructs events that indicate the advent and transformations of boredom, in interrelation with the reigning ideologies, hence communicating experiences that convey distinctive comprehensions of architecture. Theory permits the consideration of philosophical elaborations on boredom, from an architectural standpoint, and the imagining of numerous ways of organizing space.[14] Both logics follow the historiography of Fernand Braudel and the Annales School, in which non-grandiose incidents of cultural, political, and emotional life are linked together to identify overarching trends and patterns of behavior.[15] In addition, cycles of capitalist transformation, as formulated by Nikolai Kondratieff, Ernest Mandel, and Carlota Pérez, contextualize boredom as the propellant for creation and consumption.[16] The economic cycle of prosperity, recession, depression, and improvement, lasting approximately fifty years, results in political and social upheaval and cultural peaks defined by technological innovation—the steam engine and the textile industry in 1815, steel and heavy engineering in 1873, electricity and mass production in 1918, and information technology and telecommunications in 1971.

Within these phases, objects of study unfold chronologically, a series of episodes that illustrate boredom as an ongoing story of varied architectures. Following Søren Kierkegaard, Martin Heidegger, and Andrew Benjamin, for whom the textual and the literary constitute the closest and most direct entrance into boredom, these episodes dissect written and spoken evidence.[17] Literary works—novels and essays—are concerned with the provision of narratives and meaning, and they thus facilitate the enquiry into boredom, while evading the aesthetical determinism of visual symbolism. This type of written material features semantic repetition, elliptical phrases, and associative words that together describe seemingly abstruse circumstances of distance and direction, in private and public spheres. Another category of evidence comprises architectural theory, history, and criticism—books, chapters of volumes, articles in specialized magazines, and lectures, as well as interviews with Charles Jencks, Rem Koolhaas, Sylvia Lavin, and Jorge Silvetti. In these instances, boredom is an indictment of architecture. Aligned with the relationality of the condition and its potential for inspiring change, the elaborations stem from interpretation, departing from particular cases to isolate causes and speculate on effects. Both kinds of evidence—literature and theory of architecture—are treated in the chapters as primary, denoting that architecture can be written as a text and expressed orally, and positioning the practice of theorizing architecture as integral to the field. In their progression from the poetic and fictional to the prosaic and factual, these episodes themselves resemble the criticality of boredom and resonate with the split attention and free association of memories and thoughts that color modernity.

Although the source material was originally produced in German, French, Italian, Danish, and other languages, it is unraveled through the understanding of the English word *boredom*, procuring unity. Unavoidably, those main sources are supplemented by numerous quotes, anecdotes, and allusions. The mixture of tones and references demonstrates the ubiquity, multiplicity, and haziness of the condition, revealing its need for architecture, by which it decisively persists but subtly morphs according to the arrangement of the surroundings.

Differential Distances, Circular Trajectories, and Extended Thresholds

To survey the presence of boredom in modern architecture, and to interlace its many aspects, this book employs three conceptual frameworks that are conceived as corresponding parts: "Differential Distances," "Circular Trajectories," and "Extended Thresholds." Each depicts boredom as a structure with particular spatial qualities that possess a twofold advantage. Boredom transgresses issues of form and function, entanglements of authorship, and appraisals of value; it also unveils the political, cultural, and socioeconomic forces behind architectural production. The condition not only accompanies the development of the era, as a historical incident, but also moves from the individual to the social and communal, as a hybrid and a nexus, simultaneously precise and general, abstract and concrete.

The first part, "Differential Distances," traces the experiential aspects of boredom in its nascent phase—a qualifier of the encounter with architecture during the consolidation of modernity in the nineteenth century. In response to the social and cultural variations derived from the first and second cycles of capitalist advance, the condition—unsolicited but fascinating—emerges as a discord between interiority, the space of ideas and sentiments, and exteriority, the space of the world and society. In *Either/Or* (1843), Kierkegaard argues that modernity is defined by the awareness that the interrelation between these two spaces, their processes and outcomes, does not need to become public; since self-reflectivity guides everyday life, the individual can respond to outer demands while keeping inner circumstances private. By extension, and to oppose the Hegelian mediation of dualities, Kierkegaard identifies two modes of living—the aesthetical and the ethical, the either/or that cannot be separated or fused into a different entity. Within this fulcrum, boredom dwells in the aesthetical as a threat to enjoyment and beauty; demonic, even, for it hinders proximity to the spiritual, being "the root of all evil" but with "such power to set things in motion" as the potential for a field lying fallow to be fertile again.[18]

Uncovering the spatiality embedded in boredom, this part contains three episodes. The first, "Catherine Gore and Charles Dickens: Idle Restlessness/Restless Idleness," examines two novels that contributed to the naming and popularization of the condition. In *Women as They Are, or The Manners of the Day* (1830) by Gore, boredom—one of the earliest records of the term—accompanies the routine of wealthy females, preoccupied with activity despite the uniformity of their confinements.[19] Similarly, in *Bleak House* (1852–3) by Dickens, boredom belongs to aristocratic women, caught in the conventions of society but devising manners to move among men and in the openness of the city, trying to attain transcendence. The second episode is "Blunting and Jading" and presents these effectual concepts as prototypes of boredom, capable of explaining the continuous change in the forms and canons of beauty of the built environment, elaborated respectively by Heinrich Wölfflin and Adolf Göller. In *Renaissance and Baroque* (1888), Wölfflin avows that the form of buildings fluctuates because the sensibility of architects and users diminishes with the progression of any period, shifting from early to late stages of stylistic evolution. Göller conceived an almost identical formulation in "What Is the Cause of Perpetual Style Change in Architecture?" (1887), distinguishing a process of exhaustion in which the appreciation of buildings grows from small beginnings only to climax and decline, reaching a state of fossilization. The third episode, "Coney Island, Misleading Structures," looks into "Boredom" (1907) by Maxim Gorky. In this article, the condition is a collective affection, palpable within the amusement park. Despite his admiration for the "fantastic city of fire" by night and the "delicate white structures" by day, the author identifies boredom as the intoxicating aftermath of an architecture that promises fulfilling joy but only delivers vacuous entertainment.[20]

The second part of this book, "Circular Trajectories," investigates how boredom became normalized as an index of the predicaments of twentieth-century architecture. Experienced within the third and fourth cycles of capitalism, the condition turns cyclical, beginning in the individual and moving to the surroundings only to return to the origin, with new and critical information. In *The Fundamental Concepts of Metaphysics* (1929–30), Heidegger explicates boredom as homesickness, which urges the return to the wholeness of home; the whole is the world and the world is home. In modernity, being out of home is aggravated due to the Cartesian fixation with certainty that disregards religious beliefs and elevates consciousness, turning the "I" into the undisputed foundation of philosophical questioning. To reincorporate the questioner, Heidegger employs moods—conditions arising from the I—as structures linking to the surroundings.

The relationship between boredom and the modern built environment is expanded through three episodes. The first, "Oran, the Capital of Boredom," provides an account of the condition in "The Minotaur, or the Stop in Oran" (1939) by Albert Camus. He describes the Algerian town as "the capital of boredom," "besieged by innocence and beauty," with "very ugly constructions" that diminish the presence of nature by presenting their back to the ocean.[21] Rather than being a realm of possibility, Oran is a space of unending waiting and conformist absurdity, where the Minotaur reigns, inflicting an all-pervading state of torpor, without poetry or humor. The second episode is "International Style Confusions: Sigfried Giedion." In the introduction to the fourth edition of *Space, Time and Architecture* (1941), called "Architecture of the 1960's: Hopes and Fears," added in 1961, Giedion identifies "confusion and boredom" as the prevailing sentiments of mid-twentieth-century architecture. To make this diagnosis, he refers to the symposium "The International Style—Death or Metamorphosis?," arranged by the Architectural League of New York in the spring of the same year, challenging the premise that the International Style was a "style" that had "grown thin."[22] Both the dismissal of style and the recognition of boredom can be traced to the speeches that Philip Johnson and Reyner Banham delivered at the event, marketed by the organizers as a confrontation between practice and theory as well as between the United States and the United Kingdom. The third episode, "Los Angeles, Flat Enough," delves into *Los Angeles: The Architecture of Four Ecologies* (1971) by Banham. As the most spacious city in the world, Los Angeles provides ideal conditions by which to inspect the formation of a settlement based upon the excitement for the new and its complement, the inexorableness of boredom. To trace the fundamental qualities of Los Angeles, Banham identifies "four ecologies" that compose a multi-layered system of topological relations; across these, boredom percolates as a non-gravitational force, neither centrifugal nor centripetal, which consolidates a homogeneous field of suspension.

The third and final part, "Extended Thresholds," focuses on boredom as a requirement for creativity. The postmodern search for variety in the late twentieth and early twenty-first centuries, centered on the contention of Francis Fukuyama that "history has ended" and only boredom remains, emerges during the fifth cycle of economic prosperity and decline. Moreover, in "Boredom and Distraction: The Moods of Modernity" (2005), Andrew Benjamin, construing "Boredom, Eternal Return" of *The Arcades Project* (1927–40) by Walter Benjamin, poses boredom as inherent to modernity. It is a mood that informs the actions of the network of the "mass individual."[23] With unpredictable consequences, boredom provides a threshold of awaiting; passing through its in-betweenness allows forming, evolving, and becoming, omitting utopias and preconceived versions of the future and elevating the condition to a state of latency, ripe with the potential to act upon the desire to experiment—the moment after negative stimulation but before the positive need to create.

In four episodes, this part enquires into the role of boredom in the production of postmodern architecture. The first, "Boredom in *Domus*," expounds on the "Forum" section of the Italian magazine *Domus* that was published in April 1980. Under the direction of Alessandro Mendini, this Forum juxtaposed short entries by Hermann Grosser, Fulvio Irace, Allan Kaprow, Nam June Paik, Pierre Restany, and the editorial team. Coherent with the postmodern critique of the architect as the autocratic figure of genius, the multiple contributions focus on the possibilities of interrelation, the concurrence of dissimilar personalities, and the potential of open endings, favoring the use of literary references. The second episode, "Servitude and Liberalism: Russell Kirk," analyzes "The Architecture of Servitude and Boredom" (1982). In this essay, Kirk alleges that the American and British built environments of post-World War II are "wondrously boring"—a failure of the governing liberal ideologies and their disregard of religious beliefs, moral values, and social distinction. To him, "featureless," "grim," and "unskilfully constructed" architecture marks political domination and the lack of significance of those who are forced to occupy it, fostering subjugation and unrest.[24] The third episode is "Charles Jencks, Rem Koolhaas, and the Generic." In the 1970s, Jencks formulated the Ivan Illich Law of Diminishing Architecture, relating the size of buildings to levels of boredom: the bigger the project the less its quality of design and construction. This architecture is exemplified by the "dumb box typology"—big, neutral, and iterated globally—an expression of the principles of the corporations that propel their speculative construction and are historically rooted in modernism and its connection with capitalism. Describing architecture with the same qualities in the 1990s, Koolhaas rescues the generic as the opportunity for respite; façades covered in reflective glass as well as interiors artificially controlled to offer comfort, the zone of zero disturbance, propound architecture as a setting rather than as an object demanding primary attention. Finally, the fourth episode, "Jorge Silvetti and Sylvia Lavin: Unamused Muses and Lying Fallow," elaborates on how the condition is used to evaluate architecture as a discipline. In a Walter Gropius Lecture at Harvard University Graduate School of Design, titled "The Muses are Not Amused, Pandemonium in the House of Architecture" (2002), Silvetti distinguishes four trends in the architectural conceptions of the 1990s: programism, thematization, blobs, and literalism—all pretentious due to their incapacity for being culturally relatable. Their false innovation had produced fleeting styles and unstimulating conditions for any further development. Some ten years later, in "Lying Fallow" (2013), Lavin diagnosed the direction of the efforts of the discipline of the 2000s as actually boring. However, boredom in architecture is tendered as dormancy before innovation, a historical occasion for the reconsideration of how the built environment should be conceived.

The epilogue, "Architectures of Boredom," collapses the previous frames—"Differential Distances," "Circular Trajectories," and "Extended Thresholds"—to redefine the condition as an individual, social, and communal experience: "I'm bored," "they're bored," and "we're bored." Through attending architectures and complexities, these modes of boredom reveal its extensiveness, moving across all the strata of the production and experience of the modern built environment. Without being totalizing and stifling, the condition surfaces as flexible and diverse, subtle and dynamic, with a sensibility that favors neutrality and enforces the identification of the contradictory; boredom questions rather than validates, bringing into relief episodes of change in architecture.

CHAPTER 1
A COMPONENT OF MODERNITY

Among the many histories of boredom, Aldous Huxley offers a concise genealogy in "Accidie" (1920), comprising literary fragments by a variety of authors.[1] The essay presents the condition, modern in character and pervasive, as a separating factor in the timeline of Western civilization—a pre- and post-boredom world. As a proto-boredom, *acedia* surfaces in the medieval period, breaking from similar notions popular in antiquity, including the lack of determination of desire venerated through Eros, the irritation with mundane repetition of ἄλυς, and the displeasure with boundaries implied by *horror loci* and *taedium vitae*.[2] The term derives from the Greek *kedos*, meaning "to care," and the negative prefix *a-*, denoting absence and connoting lack of attention, which anticipates the crisis of faith of secularization. Although framed by towns and the early control of the countryside, acedia is a spiritual malaise, independent from the physical environment. Borrowing from Evagrius Ponticus, Huxley portrays it as a *daemon meridianus*—"a fiend of deadly subtlety," pestering monks who wander in open deserts or rest in closed monasteries in the heat of midday, and so diminishing their capacity to pray and work.[3] Importantly, acedia is committed rather than suffered. As a personal failure, it is manifested in "tardiness," "coldness," "undevotion," and "sadness," condemning those who have sinned to find "everlasting home in the fifth circle of the Inferno."[4] As a public weakness, the condition establishes a bond between the offenders, forming a community based on guilt and practices of penance. In the "Parson's Tale" (c. 1390) of *The Canterbury Tales* by Geoffrey Chaucer, acedia prevents redemption by being contrary to the experience and demonstrations of the joy caused by being close to God, operating as a disjunction between heaven and earth, or as an unsuccessful escape from the material realm due to the demands of the body. For Huxley, echoing the warnings of Thomas Aquinas about the power of acedia to induce irrepressible misery "on account of the flesh utterly prevailing over the spirit," if atonement does not enact change, the condition leads to despair, with the risk of suicide.[5]

In the Renaissance, *melancholy* ousted acedia. Originally diagnosed by Hippocrates in the fifth century BC as an excess of black bile, it is a malfunction that produces fear and despondency, emphasizing individual needs. Unlike the exclusively negative character of its predecessor, melancholy entails creativity by promoting inspiration and the reconsideration of the nearby circumstances. Huxley cites *The Anatomy of Melancholy* (1621) by Robert Burton, which eclectically identifies the origins of the condition in lack of movement or erroneous orientation. It impedes the meaningful approximation to the environment—"as long as he or she or they are idle, they shall never be pleased, never well in body and mind, ... offended with the world"—and therefore enforces the ideation of remedies that are based on active rectification through the avoidance of inadequate spaces: "if the seat of the dwelling may not be altered, yet there is much in choice of such a chamber or room, in opportune opening and shutting of windows, excluding foreign air and winds, and walking abroad at convenient times."[6]

In eighteenth-century Britain, melancholy branched into *spleen*, also as a corporeal ailment but with added overtones particular to its cultural context. In "The Spleen" (1737) by Matthew Green, which Huxley mentions, the condition is poetically described as a convulsion of the nerves caused by small particles in the blood, derived from the "stormy" qualities of certain locations.[7] In a systematic manner that alternates measures to improve the body with instances of entertainment, the impurities could be cleaned through a regimen of "a moderate diet," "laughter," "reading," "the company of young ladies," "exercise," and the abstention of "passions," "drinking," and the company of "Dissenters and missionaries, especially missionaries."[8] Without spiritual allusions, Green's remedy focuses on enjoyment, dynamism, and exploration, advocating for the poised combination of hedonism and asceticism—a maxim of the Georgian and Regency eras. The recommendation echoes the contemporaneous theories of the sublime in which the monotony of the quotidian covers and counterbalances existential anxiety and terror. Surpassing the physiological basis of melancholy and anticipating the popular character of boredom, the spleen constitutes a refusal to engage with the unattainable and a preference to linger within the ordinary, insisting on temporary distractions.[9]

In parallel, *ennui* became prevalent in Europe during Romanticism, expanding the creative qualities of melancholy by denoting the existence of intangible dimensions. According to Huxley, ennui is more complicated and dangerous than acedia—"a mixture of boredom, sorrow and despair." Opposed to the associations with the daily routine of melancholy and spleen, ennui is aspirational, "an essentially lyrical emotion, fruitful in the inspiration of much of the most characteristic modern literature," epitomized in the writings and sensibility of Charles Baudelaire.[10] Also known as the *mal du siècle*, the condition is fundamentally negative, stifling and elitist, without possibility of recovery but with limitless modes of expression.[11] Huxley asserts that ennui marks "the triumph of the meridian demon" of acedia, and signals the consolidation of modernity and the eagerness to be "anywhere out of the world," an ambiguity of being in one particular place yet wanting to be in another.[12]

The problem of existential inhabitation finds its mundane but "respectable and avowable" counterpart in *boredom*, popular in Britain since the mid-nineteenth century. For Huxley, the French Revolution (1789–99) created a fertile ground that introduced and nurtured the condition across Europe, aided by secular and materialist interpretations of existence that displaced the belief in religious salvation and the possibility of transcendence. The overpowering processes of capitalism led to the speculative accrual of wealth, the desecration of nature, and the loss of communal values, starting a process of disenchantment in which all expectations of meaning depend on individual experience. Moreover, the Industrial Revolution (c. 1760–1840) mechanized and divided time into regular segments that ordered everyday life and imposed predictable sequences of work and leisure, amidst processes of intense urbanization and the rise of the architecture of commodity—without symbolism, at once concrete and abstract. As a mode of being rather than a spiritual or physical disorder, boredom found its space in the city, "with a certain pride"; "habituated to the feverish existence of these few centers of activity, men found that life outside them was intolerably insipid. And at the same time they became so much exhausted by the restlessness of city life that pined for the monotonous boredom of the provinces, for exotic islands, even for other worlds—any haven of rest."[13]

Spatial Etymology

As Huxley implies, boredom did not come into existence when the word was coined. Instead, it surfaced progressively with the need to articulate and explore the experience of modernity; the mechanisms of progress, including capitalism, industrialization, secularization, rationalization, and urbanization, demanded new vocabulary. From the equivalents in the main languages in Europe, two groups of terms can be distinguished according to their chronological distance. The older ones, which remain close to their origins, relate boredom to bodily feelings and undesirable emotions. In the thirteenth century, the French *ennui* and the Italian *noia* emerged from the Latin *inodiare* to denote a sentiment of annoyance and the action of making something hateful. In the sixteenth century, the Spanish *aburrimiento*, from the Latin *abhorrēre*, "to abhor," and the Portuguese *tedio*, from the Latin *tedium*, "tiresomeness," became prevalent in their capacity to convey physical exhaustion. In the late seventeenth century, the Slavic languages adopted cognate versions of the onomatopoeic *ky* to allude to the loneliness and generic qualities of the cuckoo.[14] And since the eighteenth century, the Swedish *tristess* and the Norwegian *kjedsomhet* designate states of sorrow and the absence of appreciation, both derived from Latin. Newer expressions include the German *Langeweile* and the English *boredom*, both with specific associations to the modern experience. The first surfaced in the early eighteenth century to indicate an extended time of waiting, and the second followed to suggest an extreme condition of intolerability to the surroundings.

According to *The Oxford English Dictionary*, the etymology of *boredom* is uncertain; its meaning refers to "the state of being bored; tedium, ennui."[15] The term transpired from the combination of the verb or substantive *bore* and the suffix *-dom*, from Old English. While the latter forms nouns that denote domains or general conditions, the former has two possible origins. The first suggests the figurative use of "to perforate," probably as a result of a forgotten anecdote.[16] This sense can be traced further to two variations. One derives from the Old English *borian*, which indicates the action of drilling a solid with an auger or gimlet, with an active and masculine tone, as in puncturing. The other stems from Aryan roots and the Latin *forāre*, meaning "to cut" or "to pierce" in order to generate something new, with a passive and feminine character, as in ploughing. In the late eighteenth or early nineteenth century, these two modes of creating a void fused into *boredom* as an indication of a repetitive movement that creates annoyance as well as emptiness.[17] Conversely, the second possible origin of *bore* is linked to the French *bourre* and *bourrer*, signifying "padding" and "to stuff, to satiate."[18] All these possible meanings contradict each other, but they conceptualize of boredom as an ambiguous space, completely full but entirely hollow, capable of germinating from multiplication as well as from subtraction—from too much and from too little.

Although *The Oxford English Dictionary* dates the first public register of *boredom* to the publication in 1852–3 of the periodicals containing *Bleak House* by Charles Dickens, the word appears earlier, both in his private letters and in literary work by other writers. For instance, on July 27, 1851, in correspondence with his secretary H. W. Wills, Dickens employed *boredom* to expose his preoccupation with the effects on the visitors of the contentious architecture of the Crystal Palace.[19] He found the design for the Great Exhibition in London by Joseph Paxton as disquieting, a response that opposed the prevailing excitement for a structure viewed as a sign of accelerated progress: "My apprehension—and prediction—is, that they will come out of it at last, with that feeling of boredom and lassitude (to say nothing of having spent their money) that the reaction will not be as wholesome and vigorous and quick, as folks expect."[20] The same understanding of boredom as an infliction of the environment is present in the first and third volumes of *Women as They Are, or The Manners of the Day*, a novel by Catherine Gore, published in 1830. In this story, which depicts the gentility and etiquette of the British high society during the Regency era, boredom accompanies the everyday life of Lady Lilfield, a character in dimensional movement despite the monotony of her surroundings.

As Dickens and Gore evince, the boring and the interesting necessitate one another. The adjective *interesting* appeared at the same time as *to bore* in the late eighteenth century.[21] It stemmed from the verb *to interest*, which entered the English language in the thirteenth century to replace the Latin *interesse*, meaning "to be *inter* or between" other phenomena, signaling the possibility of involvement.[22] Unlike the idea of objective importance, the modern definition of the interesting entails subjectivity, based on the uniqueness of individual experience and contrary to the lack of response that typifies boredom. In terms of occupation, the interesting indicates a positive existence in a space of nothingness or an object of difference in a space of sameness, with a privileged position. In the same way that absence depends on presence, "the interesting" depends on "the boring," since "the boring" is "the not interesting."[23] Nonetheless, the two conditions do not form a dichotomy, but rather engender a reciprocal relationship characterized by negativity and positivity, a circular scale of value that moves seamlessly from tiredness and tedium to vitality and enthusiasm.

Around Desire, in Abstract Space

In addition to the structural connection with that which is noteworthy and stimulating, boredom establishes an interrelation with desire as it constitutes an imprecise yearning; Roland Barthes remarks, it is "bliss seen from the shores of pleasure."[24] Rather than defining limits or residing fixedly in one location, the condition is a void, with enough space to accommodate endless but always fruitless possibilities. By establishing doubt in the determination of desire, boredom turns into undefined desire, or the desire for desire that forces the individual to dwell involuntarily in a realm of absence.[25] In relation to the built environment, the sense of longing and aspiration that surfaces while experiencing boredom transforms the perception of architecture as an object to one in which architecture establishes frames of existence. If buildings and spatial instances gain authority from their appreciation through experience and use, then the potential of their objective qualities lies in the capacity to suggest rather than to dictate.

In this manner, boredom interrogates the capacity of design and technology to satisfy desire. In a drawing titled "Appeal to the Europeans," part of the utopian projects of *Alpine Architecture* (1919), Bruno Taut reacts against functionalism because of its insufficient materialism, the boredom that it imposes, and its close connection to the politics of war:

> But / have use- / ful things brought us / happiness? – Incessant / utility and futility: / comfort, ease, /—fine dining, / education—knives, / forks, railway / trains, lavatories and / not to forget ~ ~ ~ / cannons, bombs, / murder implements! / Merely desiring utility / and comfort / without a higher / idea is bore- / dom / causes quarrelling, million times over.[26]

Anticipating Le Corbusier, who declares that architecture is "a product of happy peoples and a thing which in itself produces happy peoples," Taut avows that the only redemption from the suspended animation of boredom is designing and constructing—creating new environments for the pleasure of inhabiting them.[27] As part of this endeavor, technology ought to contribute to the realization of beauty rather than only provide efficiency and utility. Accordingly, the fantastic structures of *Alpine Architecture*—always in proximity to mountains, rivers, and forests—create opportunities of experience, in opposition to the infinity and homogeneity of mathematical space that reject individual perception. To morph the neutral into the characterful and to demonstrate that the use of technology does not need to derive into the predictable, Taut employs geometry, treating it as an instrument without content and only significant in its capacity to establish relations of space, to propose diversity and substance through architecture. In this ambit, boredom would only emerge if space is conceived without spatiality; as Erwin Panofsky observes through the elaborations of Ernst Cassirer, "visual space and tactical space are both anisotropic and unhomogeneous in contrast to the metric space of Euclidean geometry: 'the main directions of organization—before-behind, above-below, right-left—are dissimilar in both physiological spaces.'"[28] Equally, the operations of perspective flatten experience by negating the relationships between "bodies and intervening space ('empty' space), so that the sum of all the parts of space and all its contents are absorbed into a single 'quantum continuum.'"[29] For Panofsky, rectilinear perspective defines the predominant understanding of space in the modern era—infinite, neutral, systematic, and uniform—in contrast to the curved perspective of antiquity—discontinuous, relative, and impossible to universalize.

To Henri Lefebvre, the abstraction of space becomes unequivocally evident in the modern built environment.[30] Instead of producing conditions for lived experience, twentieth-century architecture and urban planning created functionalist architecture that perpetuated boredom. In "Notes on the New Town" (1960), he distinguishes two types of boredom according to the historical development of Navarrenx, a medieval town, and Mourenx, a settlement enlivened after the discovery of natural gas in the 1950s. The first type belongs exclusively to Navarrenx, always boring due to the idleness and slow pace of life there, "vegetating and emptying"; this boredom is pre-modern, "soft and cosy . . . like Sundays with the family, comforting and carefree . . . life was *lived* there." The second type is modern, present in both towns. In Navarrenx, the incessant construction of the new and the selective preservation of the old had turned the city into a wasteland, invaded by cars, lorries, and industrial noise; this moment "is just boring, the pure essence of boredom." In Mourenx, everything is functional. State capitalism had succeeded in its efforts to provide "well planned and properly built" tower blocks, "machines for living in." However, there "everything is almost a hundred per cent redundant," easy to comprehend; "the text of the town is totally legible, as impoverished as it is clear, despite the architects' efforts to vary the lines." The clarity and hermetic resolution of the techno-architecture of Mourenx mark the triumph of material development, but expose the modern built environment as a space devoid of naturalness— "Will people be compliant and do what the plan expects them to do, shopping in the shopping centre, asking for advice at the advice bureau, doing everything the civic centre offices demand of them like good, reliable citizens?"[31]

Without being able to provide an answer, although aligned with the etymology of the term as a space in which the identification of what is longed for is interrupted and thus is infused with creative latency, Lefebvre recognizes boredom as "pregnant with desires, frustrated frenzies, unrealized possibilities." The condition directs attention to dormant richness and instigates ingenious action and radical transgression against modern abstraction; "it is waiting like the cake is waiting when there's butter, milk, flour and sugar."[32]

PART 1
DIFFERENTIAL DISTANCES

CHAPTER 2
FASCINATION AND AVERSION

Boredom, an indissoluble component of excitement rather than its distant opposite, defined the spaces of the nineteenth century. Fernand Braudel describes this era as "at once sad, dramatic and marked by genius," and Robert Heilbroner concludes that the "huge self-confidence and ebullience" of the time was permeated by a mood of "panic and pain."[1] The unpleasant conditions of urban everyday life, its social unrest, and the recurrent wars emerged, as did moments of virtuosity in scientific discoveries, technological progress, and political affairs. Attendant upon this process, consistent throughout Western Europe, a cultural homogeneity followed cycles of economic prosperity and recession. The Industrial Revolution propelled international markets, credit, and the accumulation of capital, generating financial and banking opportunities, supported by governmental investment and policies that facilitated the planning and execution of projects of architecture and infrastructure, including transportation systems. By initiating rapid movement, railways and roads spread a civilization of wellbeing and communication, which boosted industrial and commercial nodes. Framed by the conceptions of the geometrized universe of René Descartes and the abstract space of Isaac Newton, the materialism of science, industrialization, and technology became the forces of change by which the theoretical developments of the previous hundred years were put into practice, and which also informed new architecture. Western Europe thus became tightly interwoven, involved in transnational cooperation and aware of the existence of multiple realms—pre-modern and modern, physical and intangible, each with their own sensibility.

Yet the division between the experience of the outward world and the occurrences of inner life is not exclusive to modern development. Such a disunion can be traced to the Christian theology that separates body and flesh from spirit and soul. For Blaise Pascal, the space of humanity is detached from the space of God by boredom, a differential distance that disturbs the center of gravity of the individual. Boredom imposes severance, creating voids through superficial diversions and temporary pleasures that deceivingly attempt to provide existential meaning with tautological material; abundant in the modern era, fashionable forms of entertainment force fullness and maximize the gap between the opposites that ought to be mediated. Pascal notes that the subsequent repletion propels a flight from reality that inevitably leads to a fall, of two types. If the flight remains within the existing boundaries, idleness and stagnation become an intolerable state of rest and imprisonment, which turns into isolation and disengagement from the public sphere. If the flight aspires to surpass what already exists, restlessness and fidgeting become impatience and anxiety, a change that promotes disobedience in the search for transcendence—"a man who has enough to live on, if he knew how to dwell with pleasure in his own home, would not leave it for sea-faring or to besiege a city."[2]

Because boredom was considered a moral failure and therefore had to be avoided and kept concealed, the threat of its experience nurtured the capacity for living actively and consciously in the emotional and private while responding to the corporeal and collective. This double mode of inhabitation grew into an essential trait of being modern that informed the constructs and constructions of the nineteenth century. To Braudel, the introspection of this period magnified humanity by appealing to "both study and action" and supporting the production of knowledge and systems of belief through the transformation of nature.[3] As a result, the simultaneity of interiority and exteriority brought experience into question; for Georg W. F. Hegel, boredom impairs the ability to find significance in any occupation of space, because it causes lethargy and drowsiness, as if the sufferer would be enraptured by "the regular motion of a cradle, a monotonous singing, or the murmuring of brook."[4]

During boredom, the spaces of the world and sentiments and thought are flattened. They become interchangeable and therefore inadequate for any endeavor toward individuation or engagement. Echoing the rhythmic cadence of boredom depicted by Hegel, Arthur Schopenhauer maintains that boredom is the opposing shore of pain, the emptiness between them occasionally spanned by the oscillation of an inverted pendulum. Both borders define the possibilities of experience—"each of these two poles stands in a double antagonism to the other, external or objective, and inner or subjective." For the philosopher, the tendency to occupy one side or the other depends on material wealth; those living in poverty battle pain due to deficiency, and those dwelling in affluence face boredom due to surplus. The responses are directly proportionate to the degree of mental dexterity. The more the mind is cultivated, "the less room it leaves for boredom," and the less it is learned, the more room is vacant for the superficial.[5] Coinciding with Pascal, Schopenhauer avows that the condition can be diagnosed in the "continual panting after excitement" that results from the efforts to obtain recognition, luxuries, and extravagances. In his view, to disguise boredom, "the people need *panes et circenses*. . . . Just as need and want are the constant scourge of the people, so is boredom that of the world of fashion."[6]

As the condition morphed, late in the nineteenth century, boredom helped critique the significance of Western civilization. Observing the recurrence of the sequences of nature and social development, Friedrich Nietzsche affirms that the condition is not only inevitable—"against boredom the gods themselves fight in vain"—but also necessary, "permitting chaos to remain chaos and will to power the configuration of chaos."[7] Rather than being a factual verdict, boredom configures a literal meta-structure responsible for the organization of constancy and change. Its repetition interrogates intention: "'Do you desire this once more and innumerable times more?' . . . [H]ow well disposed would you have to become to yourself and to life to *crave nothing more fervently* than this ultimate eternal confirmation and seal?"[8] Punctuated by moments of disparity, the consistency of monotony permits the detection of human agency, thus promoting dynamic sensibilities and active modes of dwelling. For Nietzsche, boredom acts as a cohesive and permanent force in the task of discovery and creation; without it, everything would remain equally inchoate.

Ruminating on these conceptualizations and metaphors, this first section of the book focuses on the nascent experience of boredom in the nineteenth century, as a condition of distance between interiority and exteriority. After an overview of the initial cycles of capitalist prosperity and decline, the episodes that follow move from the analytical to the critical. The aim is to study the spatial nature of boredom while surveying its ambiguities and ambivalences, contributing to the understanding of modernity through the emotional awareness of the users of architecture.

Cycles of Boredom

Because it can be a projection of a long temporal scale, boredom can organize historical periodization, distinguishing phases with cultural, scientific, and technological expressions aligned to economic development, with positive and negative instances. Like waves, these cycles refute the antecedent trajectory, but they nevertheless build from preceding forces, as if their actors become bored with what has already been achieved and so begin to procure what has not been constructed yet. According to Nikolai Kondratieff, research and intellectual thinking are invigorated before an economic period begins its ascent, in intervals of approximately fifty years. These innovations are applied in the following stage due to the time that it takes to disseminate them, restructure the system of fabrication, and popularize their application. As a rule, financial growth is accompanied by social upheaval and radical change in everyday life, encouraging exteriority and relations with the world. When the downward episode begins again, the production of scientific knowledge replaces technological consumption, favoring not only interiority and self-reflection but also the discard of the unnecessary.[9] In both cases, moods and sentiments transpire as definers of variation; for Heilbroner, economic "boom and crash" are accompanied by corresponding "euphoria and despair," a succession that characterizes the course of capitalism.[10]

While most commodities have a short or medium commercial life, architecture and infrastructure occupy a full cycle, or even several. The realization of edifices and land planning depends on technological advancement, monetary resources, and skilled labor. Due to these requirements, the built environment is marked by the availability of materials as well as by the training of architects, who are influenced by media and academia that circulate, homogenize, and validate information and conceptual reasoning. In the nineteenth century, the conventions of architecture—drawings with measurements, placed in an infinite and objective space, supported by the neutrality of perspective—not only steadily accelerated construction but also informed industrial growth. They provided consistency in the discipline and encouraged building standardization.

First Cycle

In Britain, the first wave began to rise in the late 1780s and early 1790s, reaching the highest point between 1810 and 1817, at the end of the Regency era and the apex of the

Industrial Revolution. It was heralded by the technological inventions financed by profits from the cotton industry.[11] Based on the observations by Max Weber that the production and consumption of textiles dominated the material past of the West, Braudel suggests that the cycle of excitement and boredom in the realm of fashion provided the economic force to ignite the modern era: "first came the age of linen (Charlemagne was dressed in something like canvas); then the age of wool; then the age of cotton—or rather a craze for cotton—in the eighteenth century." This trend, both popular and aspirational, organized the architecture of factories and the consolidation of urban centers—"bound up with the Indian, African and American trade, and with the traffic in black slaves, cotton was established in or around the great colonial ports such as Liverpool and Glasgow."[12]

Framed by these economic interests that fostered functionalism, the systematized and mechanized making of fabrics displaced artisans and their values, exchanging tradition for immediacy. Fashion necessitated designers and specialists, housed in industrial buildings for monotonous production. As early as 1761, the *Encyclopédie* described the silk factories in Lyon as structures where "one worker does only one single thing, which he will do all his life, while another does something else; hence everyone performs his given task promptly and well."[13] The same system was applied in the construction industry, supported by the patent of Portland cement (1824), a low-cost material that fueled the use of concrete, mortar, and stucco and the production of cast-glass plates (1848). In addition, architectural imagery began to be informed by the functionalism and aesthetics of technical contraptions and the machinery of heavy industry. These included the steam locomotive (1824), the turbine (1824–7), the harvesting machine (1831), the automobile (1831), the electromagnetic and Morse telegraphs (1832–7), the electric boat (1834), the paddle-wheel steamboat (1836), the steam pump (1840), the rotary press (1846), the use of water for drilling (1846), the sewing machine (1847), and the laying of cables (1848).

According to Braudel, the creation and popularization of this equipment were accompanied by Romantic angst. As part of the economic downturn after 1817 and the reconsideration of the initial enthusiasm for the French and Industrial Revolutions, a joyless sensitivity encouraged the emergence of political liberalism that supported a rising propertied class, the business aristocracy, and bourgeoisie, and consolidated the State as the governmental system. During this economic deflation, the interest in the role of the individual in society and the everyday experience of the city became central, turning interpersonal relations and conditions of inhabitation into the predominant themes of cultural manifestations and scholarly study. Furthermore, novel vocabulary was coined to describe this environment; not only did *boredom* and *interesting* surface in popular parlance, but also terms such as *industrial, industrialist, proletariat, mass, socialism, socialist, capitalist, capitalism, communist,* and *communism*.[14]

Unlike the connection that Pascal and Schopenhauer made, between boredom and the wealth of the elite, in actuality the condition became a characteristic of the masses— the modern category for the poor and exploited. In the *Communist Manifesto* (1848), published at the lowest moment of the first economic recession, Karl Marx and Friedrich

Engels identify a conflict of social classes due to differences in the material conditions that determine opportunities for attaining meaning in everyday life.[15] The struggle of the underprivileged is intensified by the impositions of capitalism, making the experience of workers partial and disconnected from the overall system; "in the factory we have a lifeless mechanism which is independent of the workers, who are incorporated into it as living appendages... even the lightening of the labour becomes an instrument of torture, since the machine does not free the worker from the work, but rather deprives the work itself of all content." With the aim to maximize output, factories installed the disciplined methods of the assembly line, which validated the linear regularity of mechanical operations as the official rhythm of modernity. For Marx, the resulting boredom turned into a political strategy of subjugation and servitude that was organized by the reigning economy and supported by promethean myths of progress. The fabrication and consumption of "ready-mades" nurture "fantasies of a *locus communis*," a unifying space as "dry and boring" as repetitive labor.[16]

Second Cycle

The curve of another economic cycle began in 1850 and peaked between 1870 and 1875, with the expansion furthered by foreign investment, the export and import of manufactured goods, and the development of local architecture, all shaped by the implementation of technological innovations from the previous recession. Sponsored by the revenues of the textile industry, the production of iron and steel allowed not only the construction of the railway system in Europe but also the use of metallic structures and standardized architectural components, epitomized by the Crystal Palace for the Great Exhibition of 1851 in London. Because capitalism required faster and more efficient production, buildings were erected with elements easy to transport and iterate, endorsing sameness. In addition, commissions from public authorities and private clients replaced religious and aristocratic patrons. This contributed to the growth of programs related to mechanical and industrial fabrication, commerce, banking, entertainment, and mass housing—in or around urban nodes of high economic value.

The downward swing began in 1875 and lasted until 1893, before the heyday of British imperialism and finance capital, which extended into the early twentieth century. During this period, characterized by the free competition of industries, several inventions heralded the mass consumption of electricity in the cycle that was to follow. These included the dynamo (1870), the direct-current electrotransmitter (1877), the electric transformer (1882), and the Sprengel vacuum pump (1895). At the same time, transportation and communication systems benefited from the gas motor (1876), the electric telephone (1877), the Westinghouse air brake (1879), the electric railroad (1880), the electric streetcar (1881), the first successful dirigible (1884), gasoline engines (1885), the wireless telegraph (1892), the Diesel motor (1893), the first airplanes (1895), and the tandem steam engine (1898). Systems and devices that particularly favored the development of construction methods and the rise of the construction industry were the drill press (1875), the Thomas method of steel production (1878), electric welding and forging (1881, 1889), the electric hoist (1887), photoelectricity for lighting (1887), and electric iron melting (1892).

From these technologies arose an interest in the experiential effects of the built environment, which prompted scientific attempts to quantify emotional responses. In a brief letter to *Nature*, titled "The Measure of Fidget" (1885), Francis Galton maintains that the agitation and impatience of "bored attendants" at "tedious meetings" could be mathematically and geometrically assessed. How an audience moves in relation to architectural elements, such as columns and furniture, indicates the degree of attention to the surroundings. When intent, "each person forgets his muscular weariness and skin discomfort, and he holds himself rigidly in the best position for seeing and hearing," keeping the body equidistant from others. But when bored, "individuals cease to forget themselves and they begin to pay much attention to the discomforts attendant on sitting long in the same position," swaying uncoordinatedly from side to side.[17] For Galton, the corporeal reaction in space constitutes a way of detecting physiological conditions, from those receiving information as well as from those imparting it. Acknowledging that science was not yet able to quantify precisely this phenomenon, he foresees a future in which the frequency, amplitude, and duration of fidgeting—a distinctive symptom of boredom—could be positively grasped in the same way that optometry measures sight in order to improve it.

However, in parallel to these developments, social conditions deteriorated due to the rise of unemployment and the worsening of labor environments. The surplus of European workers who had migrated from the peripheries to urban centers during the previous moment of expansion—replenishing the industrial sector, with low remuneration—journeyed to North America, outweighing the flow of population within Europe. This occurrence not only created favorable circumstances for the emergence of political labor movements in the 1880s and 1890s, but also contributed to the expansion of international influence. Exporting their dual mode of inhabitation, in simultaneous but unconnected interiority and exteriority, the immigrants carried with them the naturalized rhythm of fascination with excitement and aversion to boredom that resulted in more cycles of prosperity and recession.

CHAPTER 3
SØREN KIERKEGAARD'S BABYLONIAN TOWER

In "Spleen" (1869), Charles Baudelaire—the poet of modernity—describes boredom as a "damp and small" room below ground level, similar to a "tremendous jail."[1] The room is aesthetically unmodern, even counter-modern, but it is a modern space. Dark and inward focused, sealed against the openness of the urban realm, it is empty, without external references or symbolic points of orientation, defining a neutral territory that signals something beyond itself. As an enclosure with identified but unstable limits, boredom is closer to the notion of architecture as space than to architecture as form.

Before Baudelaire, writing from the self-confinement of his apartment in Copenhagen,[2] Søren Kierkegaard affirmed that what defines being modern is the capacity to act in the spheres of the outward world while actively inhabiting inwardness, in heightened self-awareness.[3] In *Either/Or: A Fragment of Life* (1843), the philosopher questions, and eventually negates, the premise that "the outward is the inward, the inward the outward"—a formulation derived from his interpretation of the idealism of Hegel.[4] If experience is defined by the interrelation between the characteristics of the physical environment and the intricacies of ideas and sentiments, then those components are not equivalent. To illustrate their difference, Kierkegaard refers to the case of Marie Beaumarchais, a character from *Clavigo* (1774) by Johann von Goethe. When her lover leaves, "she sinks helplessly into the arms of the environment," but "she need have no fear of boredom, she can keep herself busy"; although "her exterior is calm and peaceful ... her heart is not the incorruptible being of a quiet spirit, but a restless spirit's fruitless occupation."[5] The failure to avoid boredom looms with the disclosure of inwardness to outwardness, as if the condition would be a funnel between these two spaces. However, the locus of boredom lies not in-between but rather in exteriority, and the function of that exteriority is to denote the separation from its immaterial counterpart, as an ailment that commences in the surroundings and contaminates the body.[6]

To demonstrate how these realms coexist, in parallel and so in a modern way, Kierkegaard elaborates on moods and emotions, arguing that they cannot be transposed to the physical world. Whereas the manifestation and purge of inner feelings in antiquity was achieved through catharsis, the modern individual requires an impenetrable space that does not have to be displayed; "the reason is of course to be found in the fact that in the ancient world subjectivity was not fully conscious and reflective. Even though the individual moved freely, he still depended on substantial categories, on state, family, and destiny." The new sentiments require an innermost recess that permits their oscillatory movement, vaulting from limit to limit but never breaking any boundary, since they are inexpressible. With the exception of boredom, which is presented as exclusively modern,

Kierkegaard contrasts the updated adaptions of desire, eroticism, sorrow, despair, and other feelings to their original versions. For instance, Greek love "is according to its own lights essentially faithful just because it is of the soul," as Eros was not the god of sensuality but of inward love extended to exteriority. Its recent variation is embodied in the absolute faithlessness of Don Giovanni, the protagonist of the eponymous opera (1887) by Wolfgang Amadeus Mozart, who seduces and loves not one but all. Modern desire, which is driven by the idea of representation introduced by Christianity, and which is similar to boredom, entails separation; Kierkegaard writes, "if one paints the ceiling of a room so that it is entirely covered with figures, such a ceiling presses down on us, as the painter says. If, lightly and quickly, one puts just a single figure on it, this ceiling seems higher. Such is the relation between desire and the desired."[7]

Inwardness discloses abstraction and rationality as unfeasible and unreal because interiority cannot be reconciled with the regulations of exteriority. Instead, moods and emotions are only evidence of emotional and intellectual events, articulating actions and reactions in the outward world and transforming "either/or" into a single vocable. The two conjunctions "belong inseparably together and should therefore be written as one word, seeing that together they form an interjection which I shout at mankind."[8] Accordingly, Kierkegaard relates the outward spheres to the aesthetic and the inward realm to the ethical and religious; not being mutually exclusive, both spaces pollute each other with their values and sensitivities. In *Either/Or*, the aesthetic and the ethical are incarnated in two characters, the protagonists of the two parts that were originally published as separated volumes.[9] In the first section, "Containing the Papers of A," Johannes is the aesthete who finds life boring due to his incapacity to identify a sole object of attention: the world is about excess. A hyperactive plotter, he passes the time organizing convoluted plans to avoid or postpone boredom, occupying inwardness with the aim of amusing and controlling his outward existence and thus turning life into a playful act.[10] In the second part, "Containing the Papers of B: Letters to A," Vilhelm responds to Johannes by insisting that the beauty and meaning of life reside in long-term rituals that might appear as boring but that cultivate tradition and continuity: the world is about scarcity. A sedate thinker, he relates to the surroundings through the practices of the law and habits of marriage, experiencing exteriority as a source of reflection that furnishes interiority. Rather than providing a formal description, Kierkegaard compares boredom to a bad type of eternity, without surprises or expectations, like a moment of stasis in which the future is either uncertain or undesired, although raising the suspicion that a better environment can be constructed. As a temporal condition, experience is slowed—"time passes, life is a stream, people say, and so on. I haven't noticed it. Time stands still and I with it." As a spatial instance, perception is altered—"I lie stretched out, inert; all I see is emptiness, all I live on is emptiness, all I move in is emptiness." Combining the temporal and the spatial, boredom resembles a spider plummeting down a void—"it sees always before it an empty space in which it cannot find a footing however much it flounders."[11]

For Kierkegaard, boredom uncovers the impossibility of Hegelian mediations since it cannot be opposed to excitement or any other sentiment to create a synthesis; nor can it materialize itself, though it informs itself. In architecture, design is not limited to a single principle because its nature is "too essential to provide sufficient contingency, too accidental to provide an essential ordering," and thus boredom is connected to the medium but it does not reduce the medium to an instrument. However, the medium, infused by boredom in the modern era, allows architecture "to speak" and define a vocabulary that "penetrates the form" while at the same time "the form penetrates the matter." In non-boring architecture—the canonical and the classic—this flow establishes an "immortal friendship" that does not run out of material for dialogue. In boring architecture—the purely poetic and the frivolous—form overburdens matter and asphyxiates it with extremes, such as "knick-knacks and trifles, so much so that the natural conception of a cool hall of great figures of individual distinction disappeared altogether, and the pantheon became a junk-room instead." As Kierkegaard suggests, boredom in architecture is exposed by the desirability of repetition. If a building is "abstract," then its medium must be "abstract and impoverished," unable to provide variations and therefore having no possibility of iteration; its reproduction leads to the exhaustion of the same. If a building is "concrete," then its medium must be "concrete and rich," therefore inviting repetition in order to explore its suggestions; its reproduction leads to the vigor of difference.[12]

Defining Outward Spheres

In *Either/Or*, boredom is an agent of the demonic, comprising all that impedes access to interiority and that lingers in the outward and aesthetic; it is the trivial and vacuous. The demonic conspires with boredom—"the root of all evil" but with "such power to set things in motion"—in two manifestations to avoid profound change and to encourage the creation and showcasing of the novel and banal.[13] The first, a functional approach, is when the demands of exteriority meet the requests of interiority accurately and immediately, without igniting further desire or motivation. The second, a tactic of alienation, is when these two spaces cannot be connected and the distance between them increases. In both cases, the individual remains within the proximate boundaries of the material world, immersed in its processes; the experience of boredom intensifies the focus on the outward spheres—altered and rarefied by being the only frame of existence—represented in the conventions of society and the territories of the urban and public.[14]

Due to the prevalence of boredom in modernity, the majority of the population behaves either following the formalities of tradition or according to the codes of the interesting, discounting inner convictions and thus enacting rather than genuinely acting. To Kierkegaard, "they never use the freedoms they do have but demand those they don't have; they have freedom of thought, they demand freedom of speech."[15] Another contradiction within society is that boredom appears as an alibi; the public admission of being bored maximizes an inner state—incontestable and impossible to verify—to denounce the civic and cultural rules of the outward world as lacking in significance.[16] Because shared codes remain external, they impose egotism, the need for distraction, and secular apprehensions as well as the consumption of prefabricated dispositions, unoriginal attitudes, and institutionalized faith.[17] With the aim to postpone "as far as possible that point at which one suspects the movement is circular, that point where repetition begins," the interesting is in unremitting production:

> The gods were bored so they created man. . . . Adam was bored alone, then Adam and Eve were bored in union, then Adam and Eve and Cain and Abel were bored *en famille*, then the population increased and the peoples were bored *en masse*. To divert themselves they conceived the idea of building a tower so high it reached the sky. The very idea is as boring as the tower was high, and a terrible proof of how boredom had gained the upper hand.[18]

The tower that reached the sky, the Babylonian tower, is the archetype of boredom. As an expression of the modern ethos, it is repetitious and predictable, ambitious but destined to failure. With a strict formal language that conveys a totalitarian message and impedes the tendering of the unexpected, the structure only challenges its materiality in terms of gravity and its temporality by its potential to become a ruin. Against this determinism, the aesthete opposes the proposal of the Danish government to improve the economy by enforcing savings. As an alternative, he recommends taking "out a loan of fifteen millions yet use it not to pay our debts but for public pleasure," by which corresponding architecture would secure a culture of enjoyment: theatres, promenades, parks, and even cemeteries, free for all and thereby eliminating ordinary preoccupations. The new structures would not only avoid boredom through the creation of the iconic and the promotion of entertainment, but also turn Copenhagen into a creative polis—"another Athens." By attracting "the greatest artists, actors and dancers," "men of wealth would all settle in this city," including "the Shah of Persia and the King of England." If the project fails or the money runs out, the aesthete suggests kidnapping the Shah and "sell[ing] him to the Turks," in the name of the construction of an adventurous and extravagant land.[19]

The aesthete admits that Copenhagen is populated by "those who bore themselves"—"the elect, the nobility"—and "those who bore others"—"the plebeians, the mass, the endless train of humanity." The latter group represents the generic person, "busy in the world" and laboring to become "Mr Anybody, a tiny little pivot in the machinery of the corporate state"—"one acquires a title, and in it is contained all the consistency of sin and evil. The law one is then in thrall to is equally boring, whether promotion is rapid or slow."[20] To escape this fate of regular unoriginality, the aesthete prescribes variation, because "change is what all who are bored cry out for." Compared to indispensable agricultural crop rotation after a field has lain fallow, the method promotes the crossing of borders and the experience of different environments, from the suburban to the city, from the local to the global, and from the physical to the immaterial, augmenting the distance between destinations; "one is tired of living in the country, one moves to the city; one is tired of one's native land, one travels abroad; one is *europamüde*, one goes to America, and so on; finally, one indulges in a dream of endless travel from star to star."[21]

By deduction, "the whole secret lies in arbitrariness." The inhabitation of spaces, where the parameters of closure and enclosure are undefined, avoids that which can become foreseeable, instead promoting enjoyment derived from uncertainty, revelation, and wonder—"you see the middle of a play, read the third part of a book." To encourage the accidental, two practices are advised. One is the conscious balance between remembering and forgetting, which locks memories in order to liberate them later, in a haphazard fashion; this habit not only intensifies and actualizes the past, but also promotes the rediscovery of the present as buoyant and potentially engaging, surpassing the actual. Another practice is the observation of previously unnoticed details, which requires the examination of every surrounding feature to the point of sensory exhaustion; Johannes is an example of this recommendation, with his anecdote of an academic who insisted on lecturing him at every opportunity. Incapable of absconding himself from these encounters, he realized that the professor perspired profusely when he spoke. From then on, Johannes turned every meeting into amusement by encouraging heated discussions, not for their scholarly content but because of the spectacle of watching "how the pearls of sweat gathered on his brow, then joined in a stream, slid down his nose, and ended hanging in a drop at the extreme tip of it."[22]

Acknowledging Inwardness

For Kierkegaard, inwardness is impossible to represent. It is an immaterial space where everyone dematerializes, disembodies, and is validated by self-consciousness, although susceptible to boredom if that self-consciousness turns self-referential—"the boring signify ... the self-enclosed." This intimacy does not emerge solely from intellectual or emotional activity, since it can derive from a response to the phenomena of the outward spheres; nonetheless, only the liberation from the aesthetic world allows inner transfiguration and movement. In inwardness, the dimension of the ethical, "what matters is *nil ad ostentationem, omnia ad conscientiam*" (nothing for appearances, everything for conscience).[23]

Unlike the aesthete who is absorbed by the immediacy of moods, the ethicist acknowledges them but not in order to satisfy their requests; "he is not inside the mood, he is not the mood itself, he has mood and has the mood in him." The aesthete passes the time and experiments, as a stranger in the world, whereas the ethicist lives in time and commits, as a component of the world. The boredom of the outward spheres is a sign of material progress but of regress of values and beliefs. Modernity provides conventions and innovations that are uncritically implemented by the aesthete but interpreted by the ethicist, who "remains in the multiplicity and yet preserves the secretiveness," and "so only when life is regarded ethically does it acquire beauty, truth, meaning, substance; only when one lives ethically does one's own life acquire beauty, truth, meaning, security; and only in the ethical view of life can self-directed or other-directed doubts about the meaning of life be put to rest."[24]

Resonating with the remembrance of strolling with his father inside their bourgeois apartment, pretending to be in exciting places but having as reference only the reflection of an endless row of apartment buildings, Kierkegaard presents the architecture of the domestic interior as the material echo of inwardness, in contrast to the uncanniness of the urban exterior. Although the façades of houses and residential blocks appear similar and repetitive, how their interior is equipped and occupied distinguishes them from each other; to the philosopher, "the outer is the object of our observation, but not of our interest." By extension, the wrapping membranes of buildings are significant "not as an expression of the inner but like a telegram telling of something hidden deep within"— "we pass one another in the street, the one person looks like the other, and the other just like anyone else, and only the experienced observer suspects that, in that head, there lives a lodger who has nothing to do with the world, but lives out his lonely life confined to quiet domesticity."[25]

Despite the fenced character of interior architecture, it provides a certain spaciousness that eases respiration, "a flowing back of what had first flowed out." Equally, inwardness provides freedom in everyday life. Different from "fearful monotony" and "the perpetual sameness in the dreadful still life of married domesticity," home is the space of familiarity and good habits that rhythmically organize meaningful occupation. As an ethical call, inwardness encourages the construction of a place in the world, the space of vocation "where you should concentrate all your activity." For Kierkegaard, this achievement facilitates transcendence to the religious, the space of the infinite and eternal that, unlike the aesthetical and ethical, lies "not behind either/or but ahead of it."[26]

CHAPTER 4
CATHERINE GORE AND CHARLES DICKENS: IDLE RESTLESSNESS/RESTLESS IDLENESS

Stendhal employs "Ennui," translated as "Boredom," to title two chapters of *The Red and the Black* (1830), modernizing the elevated connotations of the French expression as a condition closer to the mundanity of its English counterpart.[1] In the psychological novel, although the word denotes slowness, haziness, and paucity of sharpness, referring to the exhaustive efforts of an agent that fails to cause any effect, it also indicates encounters and findings. In chapter 6, Julien Sorel, the protagonist, is found by Mdme. de Rênal at the doorstep of her house; he is in tears, afraid of crossing the threshold and entering a home that is not his own for the first time. In chapter 59, Mathilde de la Mole, Julien's then-fiancée, discovers an ongoing correspondence between her beloved and Mdme. de Fervaques, a widowed socialite. Through Julien, Stendhal playfully but with gravity manipulates the outcome of these emotional and social struggles by controlling the capacity to sustain "the air of boredom."[2] The dominant character is the one who cannot be amused by others, since anyone who pleases and concedes interest is counted as inferior. Whereas in the first case Mdme. de Rênal appears victorious because Julien exposes his vulnerability, in the second Mathilde de la Mole is defeated by confessing jealousy. The letters sent by Mdme. de Fervaques, which Julien considers repetitive and unimportant and leaves unopened, are the result of "the boredom of a mode of life whose ambitions were concentrated on impressing the public without her having at heart any real faculty of enjoyment for that kind of success."[3] Similarly, the crisis of desire of Mathilde de la Mole unveils boredom not only as a condition of the privileged but also as a cause of transgression, inciting impetuous and impish behavior. Movement from idleness to restlessness, from the public to the private, and from exteriority to interiority occurs when Julien occupies the Rênal residence, and an opposite movement occurs when Mathilde exposes her sentiments.

As portrayed by Stendhal, both complexions of boredom entail dissimilar modes of inhabitation that also emerged and were consolidated in nineteenth-century Britain. These spatialities, infused with the belief in progress, can be detected in two works that popularized the use of the term—*Women as They Are, or the Manners of the Day* (1830), by Catherine Gore, and *Bleak House* (1852–3), by Charles Dickens. In the novels, restlessness and idleness are symptomatic. Restlessness emerges as the vigorous need for action in order to attempt meaning, and idleness as the debilitated aptitude for initiating such efforts. Comprising layers of different profiles of activation and decline, they can be concomitant although in different dimensions. Idleness can occur in the corporeal, enforcing physical inactivity but provoking mental dysphoria; inversely, restlessness can keep the individual in constant bodily movement but with paused emotional and intellectual processes, waiting to be reactivated. Comparable to Kierkegaard's either/or, the idleness and restlessness of boredom articulate a conjunction that cannot be separated, an ambiguity of two orders—idle restlessness/restless idleness.[4]

In Gore and Dickens, these variations are difficult to name due to their newness. The stories of *Women as They Are* and *Bleak House* mobilize boredom as the cause of critical events that indicate the existence of something beyond their factual details, with multiple tones and configurations. To expose the nebulous, imprecise, and varying experience, both authors construct relationships, coalescing architecture and the idiosyncrasies of the protagonists, without formal explanations.

Idle Restlessness

Women as They Are (Figures 4.1 and 4.2) is an early work by Catherine Gore, a prolific writer who produced more than sixty novels, journal articles, plays, and lyrics of popular songs, procuring commercial success to support her family.[5] Published in 1830 and comprising three volumes, it is a quintessential "silver fork novel"—a best-seller narrating the intricacies of the aristocratic Regency (1811–20), and its aftermath.[6] Rather than providing a psychological analysis or an examination of cultural memory, *Women as They Are* entertains through humorous and extensive parallel plots, consciously designed to appear superficial and pleasing, dedicated to a wide audience of every status.[7] It is composed in constant present tense, with meticulous descriptions of the surroundings, referring to important streets, upper class neighborhoods, sites where people gathered, and fashionable shops in London. The exclusive clubs in St. James Street, the Mesdames Hobson and Jobson store on Charlotte Street in Fitzrovia, and the imposing mansions of Harley, Wimpole, and Welbeck—"of Oriental Portland Place, and its immediate purlieus, which bear so singular a character of sameness and monotony"—frame lengthy dialogues between characters of equal rank. Like the encircling architecture, their language is contrived and unspontaneous, plagued by almost identical metaphors and epigrams, polysyllables and expressions in French. The regular rhythm reveals preoccupations with aesthetics, class boundaries, status, and social acceptance, all conveying a nostalgia for the customs of the past that implies dissatisfaction with the present. As such, this rhetorical strategy, of an eternal tradition unwilling to unfold into a future of radical difference, contributes to its passive criticality. The novel lingers in the domestic spaces destined for female occupation only to render satirically, from afar, the domains of their male counterparts, diagnosing—"the court-yard was handsomely paved, and of immense extent; but it was only calculated to reveal and unite in one offensive focus, all the mysteries of the domestic offices, and all the disorder of the stable-yard, which modern taste so carefully recedes from observation"—and curating, "the only feature which counterbalanced, on a first view, these striking errors of design, was a stately grove of ancient and magnificent trees."[8]

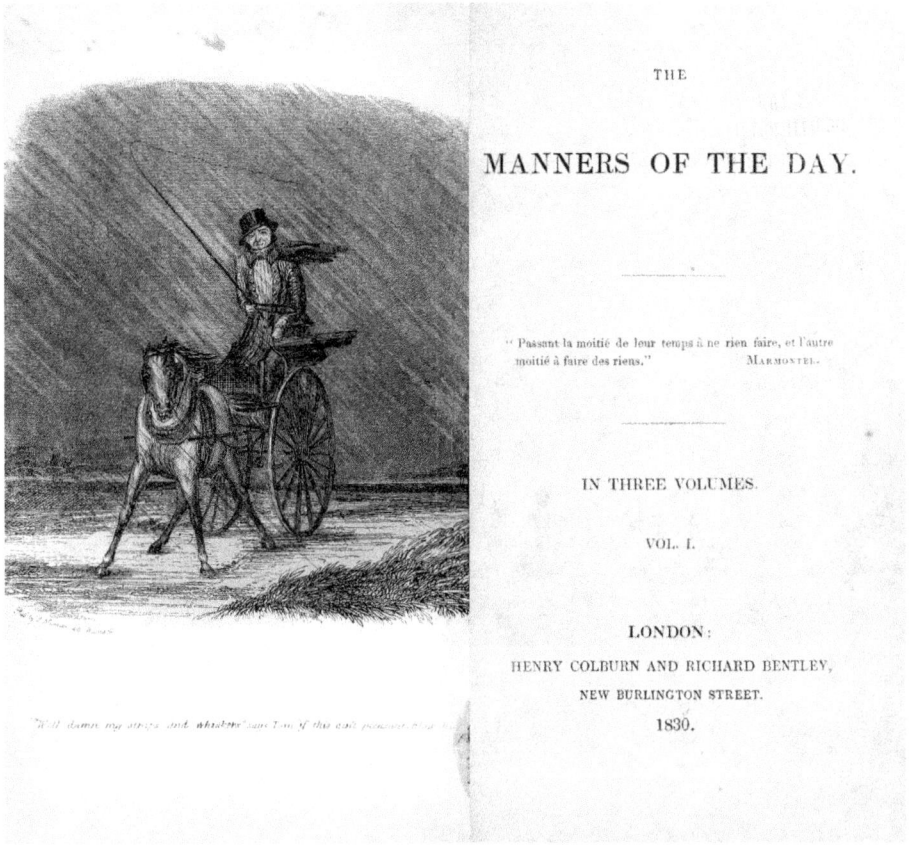

Figure 4.1 Frontispiece and title page of *Women as They Are, or the Manners of the Day*, volume 1. London: Henry Colburn and Richard Bentley (1830).

Rather than being aligned with the approaching Victorian concern with emotional truth, the female characters constitute pretense, constructions elaborated without interiority, assembled through decorative surfaces. Qualifying the architecture, ornament abounds, in docile and binding interaction with the presence of women. Their convoluted garments become one with the draped furniture and surrounding walls covered with paintings and stucco reliefs, as choreographed but interchangeable components of a theatrical scenography. In the background, constantly reminded of their inability to participate in the world of knowledge and the economy of value, women behave submissively; they must be attractive and mute, tranquil and demure. Since every action is calculated, without opportunity for impulse, norms become decisive, and repetitious canons of deportment procure homogeneity and predictability. Aided by conduct guides mostly authored by men, including *Sermons to Young Women* (1767) by James Fordice, *A Father's Legacy to his Daughters* (1774) by John Gregory, and *An Enquiry into the Duties of the Female Sex* (1797) by Thomas Gisborne,[9] every woman of importance follows, in

Figure 4.2 Frontispiece and title page of *Women as They Are, or the Manners of the Day*, volume 2. London: Henry Colburn and Richard Bentley (1830).

dress, conduct, and conversation, the example of Queen Charlotte, the wife of George III, who raised thirteen children:

> "The late Lady Willersdale, my dear, was said to have the finest jewels at the court of the late king. She was always remarkably well received,—a great favourite of Queen Charlotte, who had so few favourites."
>
> ...
>
> "And your sister really showed so much character—so much nerve—for her's was a very trying predicament. She wrote me in answer—and it was a very sensible, well-worded letter,—just such a one as I could show the Worsleys—she wrote me that she had always held the example of her late Majesty a mirror of domestic virtue; and that as Queen Charlotte had made it her rule to discourage vice by receiving no divorcee at her court, she felt herself under the necessity of declining Mrs. Meynell's visits at Beech Park! Now that is what I call character—presence of mind."[10]

Bored Women and Dull Men

Boredom is evident in the habits of women; their everyday survival requires an interminable battle against sameness. Similar to the function of the silver fork novel as a source of emotional catharsis rather than of intellectual reflection, their practices were directed to control and improve emotions. Soon after the publication of *Women as They Are*, an anonymous appraisal in *The Edinburgh Review* presented it as a "respectable specimen" of "light reading."[11] Although regretting its triviality, the reviewer applauds the eloquence of the writer who "never sinks into dulness [*sic*]" and insists on the portrayal of "good moral values," firmly maintaining that the free time at women's disposal is a privilege that allows them to lead observant rather than active lives, with "greater delicacy of taste and feeling" and with "a moral sense not blunted and debased by those contaminations to which men are exposed."[12] With their stress on the "attributes of the heart," these assertions insinuate not only that the achievement of perfect domesticity ought to entail existential satisfaction, but also that the misstep of acknowledging boredom carries social condemnation.[13]

Communicating boredom tactfully, as a possible act of subversion, Gore pairs the neologism not with the main characters, Lady Danvers and Lady Willersdale, but with secondary ones. In the first volume, Lady Lilfield enacts the condition.[14] Sister to Lady Danvers, she is exemplary—"strict in her own conduct"—residing eight months of the year in Beech Park, a suburb of Durham. During "her pastoral seclusion," she gossips on every possible occasion and writes prose, "in undetected tautology," about "her London importance—her court dress—her dinner parties—and her refusal to visit the Duchess." During her stay in London, she makes it her duty "to bore" her social acquaintances with chronicles of the countryside: "the history of the new Beech Park school-house—of the Beech Park double dahlias—and of the Beech Park privilege of uniting, in an aristocratic dinner party, the abhorrent heads of the rival political factions—the *Bianchi e Neri*—the houses of Montague and Capulet of the County Palatine of Durham."[15] Although Lady Lilfield is perceived as a "very charming woman" by "her respectable clan of dinner-giving baronets and their wives," she has no role in public matters "among those men of the world, who know the world like men." A "weed in the nobler field of society," she embodies the futile and the prosaic. Gore renders her almost acquiescent, barely moving from one space to another, framed by doors and windows that allow her to look to the outside but not inhabit it. The pieces of furniture, in conservatories, living rooms, and drawing rooms, configure a restrained but safe space where women in similar conditions barely engage with each other, attempting to surpass "the wide chapter of colloquial boredom" by silently outlining a shared intimacy.[16] Echoing Gore's marginal position in the literary milieu of the period, Lady Lilfield observes and records the details of her surroundings, being a repository of information rather than an executor, in the dilemma of living and transmitting a previously unrevealed condition.

In the third volume, boredom is not exclusive to any character but surfaces in a relational manner, depending on two or more agents. During a session of nattering, a female socialite condemns the possibility of Barton Daly or William Daly as suitors for

Florence, her daughter. She foresees that a marriage with either man would cause "insufferable boredom."[17] Even though Barton is labeled as "the most ratiocinacious being that ever bestowed its tediousness on mortal ears" and William as "a literary log," the sufferer would have been Florence, who "would have stagnated into a black letter and a dead letter," victim of the judiciousness of the first and the academicism of the second. Disregarding both, the mother advocates for Henry Mitford, due to his capacity to balance, or obliterate, the emotional expressions of the bachelorette; "he will bring her down from the skies when she affects to be too ethereal; and rouse her when she is indolent."[18]

Like Barton and William, the men of *Women as They Are* can be boring and can experience boredom, but their condition is not identified as such. Instead, they can be *dull* and experience *dullness*. Unlike *boring* and *boredom*, these terms do not denote absence or connote failure, designating presence but with limited influence, close to the neutrality of the banal. The dullness of men is validated as an expression of their virtuous temperament and cerebral dynamism. Sir Herbert Gray, the husband of one of the sisters of Lady Lilfield, is portrayed as "a dense dull man" due to his "up-right intentions and sobriety of conduct"; his demeanor is dictated by his unrestricted interiority, expressed in his "ill-timed vivacity," "a tenacity about his preserves" and "severity with his tenants." This moral soundness leads him to prosecute "a juvenile offender for paring a turnip in a field" and to exert unduly "his might and right as a commissioner of the roads."[19] Since dullness is not considered an offence, he is entitled to decide whether or not to explore his surroundings—how and when—with freedom of action.

For Gore, despite the dissimilar connotations, boredom and dullness constitute privileges.[20] Because physical needs are fulfilled, idleness ensues, which in turn propels restlessness and the search for activities to pass the time. Informing and conditioning the dwelling of the wealthy spaces of early nineteenth-century England, boredom is parochial and fashionable, private and public, domestic and social, reliant on the environment but not exclusive of any particular configuration. It operates in interiority and exteriority, as a dual formation that became the basis for the emerging bourgeoisie.

Restless Idleness

Not long after the publication of *Women as They Are*, the values of the Regency turned into negative references in the Victorian era (1837–1901). The inactivity and lack of political commitment of the upper classes constituted questionable and even condemnable circumstances that accounted for the economic decline of 1815. As Dickens narrates in *Bleak House* (Figures 4.3 and 4.4), the boredom of the patrician life became a pervasive manifestation of moral and political corruption; replicating Gore, the condition is a negative affection of two noblewomen, Lady Dedlock and cousin Volumnia.[21] The first is the protagonist whose secret drives the plot. She is restless, in physical and dimensional transition, from the urban, material, vogueish, and elitist to the suburban, moral, timeless, and popular—"to-day she is at Chesney Wold; yesterday she

Figure 4.3 Cover of the first instalment of *Bleak House*. London: Bradbury & Evans (March 1852).

Figure 4.4 Frontispiece and title page of *Bleak House*. London: Chapman & Hall (1853).

was at her house in town; to-morrow she may be abroad, for anything the fashionable intelligence can with confidence predict." Her cousin Volumnia is a supporting character who echoes the traditions of culture. She is idle, emotionally and intellectually stagnant, with predictable reactions and repetitive behavior, always adorned with "an indiscreet profusion in the article of rouge, and persistency in an obsolete pearl necklace like a rosary of little bird's-eggs. In any country in a wholesome state, Volumnia would be a clear case for the pension list."[22] Like centers of contagion from which boredom disperses centrifugally, their contrasting traits inform their spatial occupation, extending to the spaces they inhabit. Lady Dedlock attempts to conquer existential validation through the active exploration of spaces beyond her immediate limits, in anxiety; cousin Volumnia is preoccupied with maintaining any remnants of the past through dwelling passively in her surroundings, with contentment.

In the novel, *boredom* appears six times, and is capitalized three times, articulating velocity of movement and spatial symbolism. Because boredom is related to promptness and action as well as to slowness and stasis, the dynamism of Lady Dedlock alternates with the lassitude of cousin Volumnia, in rhythmic sequence. And because it is combined with natural phenomena, such as wind, coldness, dusk, and dawn, boredom creates an atmosphere of opacity and entropy, opposed to modern sanitation.[23] The condition has multiple formations, surfacing as an unbalanced locus, an exasperating malady, and a portentous dragon.

Bleak Houses

Bleak House was written and published serially, in nineteen monthly instalments between March 1852 and September 1853, each containing three or four chapters, with the exception of the last, which included eight. They were printed as thirty-two-page pamphlets, accompanied by two illustrations by Hablot Knight Browne, known as Phiz. The fragmentary format and regular pace of publication required parallel plots and thus a careful consideration of the effect of each episode. To increase expectation and sustain the attention of readers, avoiding boredom, Dickens charged each chapter with suspense.[24]

Following the same modular and scalar principle, the novel is constructed through metaphors that comment on England, the "bleak house" that everyone occupies. Within this all-encompassing domain, other "bleak houses" of different complexities and sizes coexist, in organic interrelation.[25] Within the institutional and official, the Court of Chancery is the setting for the proceedings of the Jarndyce and Jarndyce litigation, the long-running case of a moneyed testator with several wills. The building is perpetually surrounded by fog and mud—"the raw afternoon is rawest, and the dense fog is densest, and the muddy streets are muddiest, near that leaden-headed old obstruction, appropriate ornament for the threshold of a leaden-headed old corporation"— accommodating an archaic system of governance drowning in conventions, different to democracy, progress, and efficiency.[26] Within the residential and private, Chesney Wold, the countryside home of Baronet Leicester Dedlock in Lincolnshire, constitutes an anachronistic fortress of the aristocracy, a container with elaborated interiors, isolated from the city. Despite the wealth of its owner, the building is in decay due the inclement rain and its unmanageable size: "the hot-water pipes that trail themselves all over the house, the cushioned doors and windows, and the screens and curtains, fail to supply the fires' deficiencies, and to satisfy Sir Leicester's need." And within the urban and social, Tom-all-Alone's, the most derelict neighborhood in London imagined by the author, marks the tenement for the poor where architectural façades determine an accidental but active public sphere, in efforts of survival. It is full of fractures, with residual spaces and unhealthy interstices—"on the banks of the stagnant channel of mud which is the main street of Tom-all-Alone's, nothing is to be seen but the crazy houses, shut up and silent."[27] While inane restlessness reigns in the Court of Chancery, constant idleness persists in Chesney Wold; the bureaucracy of the hegemony and the ceremonies of the gentry configure analogous realms, in status quo. Yet in between the ill edifices of Tom-all-Alone's, inventiveness surfaces as both restlessness and idleness, in unpredictable exchange.

Irrespective of the architecture and location, climatic conditions are common to all "bleak houses." Dickens, with homogenizing intention, connects the deterioration of the Dedlock state with the insalubrity of the London slum by the weather that also covers the ineffective procedures of Chancery. In Victorian England, rain does not bring fertility but rather erodes the ground; "the rain is ever falling, drip, drip, drip, by day and night ... The weather is so very bad ... that the liveliest imagination can scarcely apprehend its ever being fine again." The downpours, inclement and seemingly perpetual, force everyone to inhabit interior spaces, with closed doors and windows, breathing stifling air, as in a state of imprisonment. Within this damp scenario, the idyllic home is nonetheless a feasible construction. After marrying Dr. Allan Woodcourt, Esther Summerson, the secret child of Lady Dedlock, moves to the only balanced house in the story, where the fog disperses, deluges stop, and the mud dries. Proper for the emerging middle classes, it is located in the outskirts, connected to the city through public infrastructure, with a front garden, a backyard, and architecture that promotes reflection and conformity as components of morality—"I was sitting out in the porch of all places, that dearly memorable porch.... 'The moon is shining so brightly, Allan, and the night is so delicious, that I have been sitting here, thinking.'"[28]

Once as a Locus, Malady, Confinement, and Curiosity, and Twice as a Dragon

In chapter 12, "On the Watch" (fourth instalment, June 1852), Boredom, capitalized, is a locus. After vacationing in Paris, the Dedlocks return to Chesney Wold, since "the clipped trees and the statues in the Palace Garden," "the performing dogs and wooden horses" in the Elysian Fields, the windows of the "gloomy Cathedral of Our Lady," as well as "dancing, love-making, wine-drinking, tobacco-smoking, tomb-visiting, billiard, card and domino playing, quack-doctoring, and much murderous refuse, animate and inanimate" proved to be as boring as drizzly England. Although the elite await the return of Lady Dedlock to be informed about the latest trends in continental Europe, her stay in the French capital deepens her inhabitation in Boredom. Flanked by "desolation" and "the clutch of Giant Despair," its territory is incessantly redefined by the promotion of demands that cannot be satisfied.[29] False promises of fulfillment are malleable boundaries that swell and vary according to temporary needs and reigning norms; to Lady Dedlock, the object of permanent desire is elusive.

For Dickens, the lack of determination of boredom pollutes. It is an unnecessary component of the air, emitted by the values of religion and social hierarchy—part of ordinary rituals. In chapter 28, "The Ironmaster" (ninth instalment, November 1852), boredom emerges as a vaporous malady. While idling in the living room after dinner, cousin Volumnia compliments Lady Dedlock for recruiting Rosa, a young maid. In turn, the mistress credits Mrs Rouncewell, the housekeeper, for the hiring, which gives rise to a lengthy conversation about her family and her grandson, who is in love with the adolescent girl. The comments and questions of cousin Volumnia invade Chesney Wold, occupying its hollow spaces, masking the boredom of the infected interiors only to impose further boredom upon those around her; "'My Lady, whose chronic malady of boredom has been sadly aggravated by Volumnia this evening, glances wearily towards the candlesticks and heaves a noiseless sigh.'" When the son of Mrs Rouncewell, an ironmaster from Northern England, requests to remove the maid from the house so she can be educated in a modern manner, everyone is briefly entertained by the news—"not a cousin of the batch but is amazed to hear from Sir Leicester, at breakfast time, of the obliteration of landmarks, and opening of floodgates, and cracking of the framework of society, manifested through Mrs. Rouncewell's son."[30]

As in the case of Rosa, the difference between where the individual is and where the individual wants to be tests the offerings of the environment, disclosing discomfort and the consequent need for variation. In chapters 53, "The Track" (sixteenth instalment, June 1853), and 56, "Pursuit" (seventeenth instalment, July 1853), boredom is the inertia that incites movement. In the first episode, a debilitated man rests on a daybed, "casting sofa-pillows on his head . . . in a prostration of boredom," unclear if he suffers due to immobility, if the condition has produced disability or if the condition is cause and effect. As if merged with the supporting furniture, he is part of the background, yawning and iterating the same monosyllable in every conversation: "'Vayli,'—being the used-up for 'very likely.'" In the second instance, boredom provokes cousin Volumnia, "with some virulence," to investigate the house, which "changes not externally, and hours pass before its exalted dullness is disturbed within."[31] Her exploration leads to the discovery of the secret child of Lady Dedlock and the consequent apoplexy of the Baronet. Finding herself exposed, the mistress runs away from Chesney Wold, without destination, prompting an extensive search for her during a winter night. Their boredom, arising from an incapacity for movement, is abandoned for transgressive action, with the possibility of turning to the world with renewed drive.

However, following Victorian Romanticism, the cycle of exhaustion and vitality of boredom is futile. It opposes morality, industrialism, and progress due to its exaggerated solipsism, beginning and ending in the bored individual. In chapters 58, "A Wintry Day and Night" (eighteenth instalment, August 1853), and 66, "Down in Lincolnshire" (nineteenth instalment, September 1853), boredom morphs into a menacing dragon not native to England, allegorical of the addictive effects of opium. The Oriental figure pesters cousin Volumnia, following her to every room of Chesney Wold to impose somnolence, nervousness, and disquiet—she, "being one of those sprightly girls who cannot long continue silent without imminent peril of seizure by the dragon Boredom, soon indicates the approach of that monster with a series of undisguisable yawns." Aiming to keep "the dragon at bay" and thus contain her tendency to "bird-like hopping about and pecking at papers," cousin Volumnia reads to Sir Dedlock, another sufferer of the turmoil initiated by boredom and in need of palliative care.[32] As preys of the fiend, their faculties become affected; the immobility of the Baronet and the meanderings of cousin Volumnia intensify their identity.

Modern Ambiguity

For Gore, boredom belongs to the elite, who experience it as a peripheral condition that defines cultural and economic relations, separating society. For Dickens, it can be suffered by everyone, as an emotional ailment that informs movement and describes inertia, uniting society. To both, boredom constitutes a protest enacted by female characters of ostensible unimportance. In *Women as They Are*, Lady Lilfield exposes the everydayness of monotony due to male dominance; in *Bleak House*, Lady Dedlock and cousin Volumnia are justified victims of a system of false values.[33] While in the idleness of fully decorated rooms they can ascertain neither identity nor desire, in the restlessness of the metropolis they cannot focus on any object of significance. Molding their sensibilities and syncopating moments of waiting, boredom directs inhabitation. The collisions due to busyness, searches and travels, suspicious visits, gossip and bureaucratic encounters are all signs of the flow of emotion and thought, an internalized architecture in conflict with the external world due to the need to assume prescribed roles.

In the formative consumer society of England, the boredom with tradition stimulated the consumption of anything considered interesting, organizing the modern fixation with renewal. As anticipated by Gore and depicted by Dickens, the fashionable is not subversive, but rather it is what permits the system to stay the same.[34] The search for difference elevated the city—typified by London, equally celebrated and condemned—as the nucleus of experience. Within this space, *Women as They Are* and *Bleak House* absorb boredom as a field of action in which the occupancy of architecture exposes the capacity of living in parallel dimensions—tangible and intangible, invigorating and stultifying.[35]

CHAPTER 5
BLUNTING AND JADING*

In 1934, Otto Fenichel, making a psychosomatic diagnosis, compared a bored person to someone who has forgotten a name and inquires about it from others—from the environment. The psychoanalyst observed that this disorder has a "physiological foundation, namely that of the damming-up of libido"; in his view, during boredom the outward world is rejected, leading to "introversion and fantasy-activity." Far from being passive, the condition is a dynamic mechanism of defense, operational and even aggressive, "characterized by the coexistence of a need for activity and activity-inhibition."[1] This elaboration departed from one of the earliest definitions of modern boredom, formulated in 1903 by Theodor Lipps. The philosopher-cum-psychologist described the condition as "a feeling of displeasure due to a conflict between a need for intensive psychological activity and lack of stimulation."[2]

The influence of Lipps in the work of Heinrich Wölfflin and Adolf Göller is evident in their adoption of the theory of empathy. This connection suggests that Lipps's ideas on boredom might have informed Wölfflin's and Göller's conclusions on perceptual exhaustion and architectural change—all three shared the assumption that boredom is not only a negative condition but also a force that compels experimentation. In the second part of *Renaissance and Baroque* (1888), entitled "The Causes of the Change in Style," Wölfflin argues that architectural styles fluctuate because the sensibility of individuals becomes "blunted"; forms cease to "exert their charm, so that the too-often-seen was no longer effective and that jaded sensibilities demanded a more powerful impact," forcing architecture to vary.[3] Göller formulated an almost identical explanation in "What Is the Cause of Perpetual Style Change in Architecture?" (1887). The response to this question explores a process of "jading" in which the perception of buildings grows from "small beginnings" to a crescendo only to decline and reach a state of "fossilization and indifference"; every architectural form "appears, shuffles through every guise from one style to another, and disappears, perhaps to return after hundreds of years."[4] In both accounts, the empathic response to architecture is typified by boredom, which becomes more intense as form loses its power to impress.

Modern Subjectivity

Boredom can start, develop, and end in inwardness, acting as a capsule that differentiates but also isolates and enforces estrangement. Georg Simmel, writing at the same time as Lipps, and in agreement with him as well, affirms that the apathetic nature of the modern subject is historically shaped by concerns about meaning in relation to the physical circumstances of the quotidian reality—"with every crossing of the street, with the tempo and multiplicity of economic, occupational and social life."[5] If optimum material surroundings are not achieved, then fragmentation and inner conflict emerge; yet if no purpose in life is identified, then material conditions become void and irrelevant. In modernity, boredom increases due to the loss of absolute values and ideals, previously provided by mythical, religious, and long-term interpretations of life, which informed inhabitation and the assembly of architecture.

At the end of the nineteenth century, psychology challenged philosophical and metaphysical accounts of subjectivity.[6] Mental pathologies were diagnosed, with therapeutic intentions, as the result of the efforts of individuals to calibrate the stimuli of the metropolis. The naming of *hyperesthesia*, *lassitude*, *neurasthenia*, and other types of protective reactions helped not only to normalize boredom but also to promote the study of the sequels of urbanization. The work carried out by interdisciplinary scholars—including Lipps, Wölfflin, and Göller—combined aesthetics and psychology to reincorporate emotion and reason, propounding a corporeal faculty capable of reflection and generating knowledge. Unlike the post-Galilean view of the body as mechanical, this proposal, based on the immediacy of the "eye, feelings, and imagination" working in combination with "the spirit of a whole, warm living being," paved the way to conceptualizations of space as a mediatory agent between the environment and the projection of the entirety of the users of architecture.[7] In this relationship, boredom surfaces interstitially as a circumstance that requires the reconsideration of the nature of attention, concentration, and distraction as well as of the sequence of individual–space–architecture. Since experience is dependent on the conditions of the body, perception is a non-arbitrary extension of the physical dimension; if the corporeal is affected, then spatial awareness is altered. For Lipps, the capacity for projection constitutes engagement:

> The more reality, that means the more force, depth and inner congruity the individual has, or in other words the more the world consciousness releases itself into his reality—and we could say the more I, in every sense of the word, "experience" and accept that experience as truth—, the more everything experienced is a participation in the World-Me continuum and all apperceptions are a turning to its message and the message-bearing World-Me, then all the more will the individual become liberated from his isolation.[8]

As such, architectural creation becomes a vehicle of emotional rhythms. Aesthetic apprehension is "dependent upon the attribution of life" and space is susceptible to being perceived "only inasmuch as it is space which has been given life."[9] This extension of the individual in the outward world is the notion of empathy, or *Einfühlung*, promulgated by Friedrich and Robert Vischer.[10] Their theorizations focus on the mechanisms of the brain to interpret artistic creations; sentiments are understood as "unifying and contractive," capable of unraveling the outside world. *Einfühlung*, which means "in-feeling" or "feeling-into," refers to the unconscious projection of "one's own bodily form—and with this also the soul—into the form of the object." For instance, "the compressed or upward striving, the bent or broken impression of an object fills us with a corresponding feeling of oppression, depression, or aspiration, a submissive or shattered state of mind."[11] Similarly, if the individual encounters a small object, then the response is a feeling of feebleness, and if the individual encounters a large form, then sensations of grandeur are experienced.[12]

Empathy thus surpasses the direct architectural transposition, translation, or representation of emotional or intellectual processes. Instead, being associative, personal, and three-dimensional, it gestures to the flux between the inwardness and the outwardness of the individual, with space operating as the connective tissue that mediates both. For Lipps and R. Vischer, the qualities of the human body determine the way "we read our emotions and our personalities into the objects of the world."[13] This physiognomic interpretation comes into question when blunting and jading—conditions that engender a deficit of meaning—arise as disconnecting agents in the physicality experienced by the body and the immateriality perceived by the mind.

Expressive Blunting and Perpetual Jading

Wölfflin and Göller had an interest in the potential of psychology to explain the basic processes of inhabitation. They reduced architecture to form to explore why its configurations evolve, conceptually anticipating mid-twentieth-century laboratory experiments in which individuals were confined in minimal compartments to measure their resistance to boredom. Aware of each other's views, Wölfflin concentrated on the analysis of the causes of this phenomenon, while Göller constructed a law to explain its effects. Despite the innovative nature of these arguments, their preoccupation with classical and canonical principles as the source of aesthetic pleasure in architecture, mainly beauty, remained distant from any reference to modern notions, including boredom.[14]

As an art historian, Wölfflin emphasized creativity and the physical experience of being in contact with art. To him, perception exceeds the recording "of what is seen" and becomes instead "a reformation of the visible."[15] He supports the premise, in line with R. Vischer's theory of empathy, that "physical forms possess a character only because we ourselves possess a body."[16] The configuration of the body organizes the apprehension of the surroundings—especially of architecture, "an art of corporeal masses"—since bodies and buildings are conditioned by gravity; architecture "is an expression of its time in so far as it reflects the corporeal essence of man and his particular habits of deportment and movement, it does not matter whether they are light and playful, or solemn and grave, or whether his attitude to life is agitated or calm: in a word, architecture expresses the 'Lebensgefühl' [attitude to life] of an epoch."[17]

By extension, the built environment ought to be discussed in terms of bodily involvement. Following Leon Battista Alberti's and Francesco di Giorgio's tradition of comparing buildings to bodies, Wölfflin stresses that, for example, a column is not body-like but it is a body with its own sensate response. If architecture is an animate structure, then it should incorporate breathing patterns, muscle tension, skin and temperature variations, and other physiological reactions; proportions and shapes have qualities that are related to the experience of the human condition in space—horizontal things "rest," vertical things "stand," and the square is "clumsy, ponderous, contented, boring, good natured, stupid."[18]

In "The Causes of the Change in Style," Wölfflin examines change and constancy in architecture. The argument begins by asking, "Why did the Renaissance come to an end?" and "Why was it followed, particularly, by the Baroque?"[19] Both interrogations investigate the course of deterioration of styles, accused of being insufficient, and their later disposal. Wölfflin formulates two possible causes. The first is that the sensibility of individuals becomes "blunted," producing an architectural boredom that encourages the production of the new; the second is that the change of sensibility is due to fluctuations in the spirit of the age—new conditions arise and require the creation of corresponding architecture.[20] In these hypotheses, the assumption is that the organs of perception, of creators and users, become numbed either by the excessive exposure to the same architecture or by the unfulfilling quality of certain buildings. The offerings of the environment have no potential to provoke emotional and intellectual reactions due to their inability to suggest incidents of interest.

To avoid blunting, architects ought to produce spaces of "great vital feelings or expressive moods that derive from our embodied condition"; if a building has harmonious proportions, then inhabitants will respond with agreeable sensations.[21] For Wölfflin, architecture is the only expression that can avoid stylistic tiredness because it has no representational limits and "no consummation or finality," which urges the design of atypical forms and spatial possibilities, disregarding function. However, in his view, the modern cult of "the atmospheric," "unlimited space and the elusive magic of light" is detrimental, since its tendency to produce abstraction damages "the empathic response of the human body."[22]

Göller, a professor of architecture at the Stuttgart Polytechnikum, delved into the formal aspects of buildings. In his influential lecture, "What Is the Cause of Perpetual Style Change in Architecture?"[23] and his major publication, *The Origin of Architectural Style: A History of Architecture According to the Origin and Development of Ideas of Form* (1888), he produces a systematic reflection on how perception can be accountable for the continuous evolution of architectural styles.[24] He asserts that "the appreciation of beauty in architecture [is] fundamentally a psychological act that takes place within the imagination," unlike the corporality of empathy.[25] Perception is thus an activity that extends the processes of the two-dimensional retina to the movements and feelings of the three-dimensional being, only to influence the mind through the experience of space. The sequence of body–mind–space begins with the cultivation of "memory images," *Gedächnisbild*, "the unconscious mental cause of the pleasure we take in ... form." Visual perception of any object slowly builds up in the mind after repeated exposure, taking into account previous experiences, accumulated knowledge, and sensory intelligence. It resembles an imprinting process in which "the individual's sense of form is dependent on memory content, that is to say, on images of forms seen earlier and retained in the memory."[26] These images create a personalized version of the entity encountered, guiding orientation and circulation in or around it; in the case of architecture, which cannot be perceived in its totality at once, many viewings are required.[27] The continuous contact with a building becomes an educational practice in which the clarity gained by repetition develops an aesthetical sense.

For Göller, while the appreciation of beauty produces engagement, jading is the negative counterpart, *Ermüdung*, of the capacity of architecture to occupy the attention of its users. It occurs when the form of a building stops creating images in the mind, turning experience into monotonous repetition—"pleasure in the beauty of a meaningless form diminishes when its image becomes too clear and complete in our memory. It is this far-reaching psychological law of 'jading' of the sense of form, which imposes perpetual style change on architecture." In this manner, the experience of the built environment plateaus when its designs are not capable of suggesting anything more than its physical presence; "we know that is happening, but we cannot stop it. It is only too obvious that we are following a law, the same law that once pushed the High Renaissance itself into the Baroque, the early Gothic into the late Gothic—the same law that has carried every other style from ascent to flowering and from flowering to decay."[28]

If the individual becomes tired of configurations that are too easy to remember, then the task of architects is to invent ways of arranging building masses—finding new ways to combine conventional forms or intensifying them. As indicated by the law of jading, the mediation of boredom instigates creation and critical perception. For Göller, "without jading, nothing new would ever have been sought nor anything more beautiful ever found." Since architectural innovation is a long-term sequence of events, the appropriate response to jading is not only change but also novel ways of spatial experience, although "even with the noblest forms, jading is inevitable."[29]

Constancy and Change

As prototypes of boredom, blunting and jading are conditions that move back and forth from the corporeal and experiential to the architectural and spatial. They signal how the understanding of architecture as the creation of buildings moved toward the modern concern with space as an interceding agency. Focusing on inwardness, Wölfflin and Göller interrogate the emotional and intellectual location of individuals to reveal formal exhaustion as the cause of creation and stylistic variation in architecture; both theorists discount historical particularities, such as technological or cultural development, to expose change as abstract operations that occur in abstract space. Although the Hegelian formula of thesis, antithesis, and synthesis can explain the movement from the Renaissance to the Baroque and to the Modern, the constant presence of boredom points to a cycle of repetition in which the condition surfaces as the meta-factor of transformation, similar to the modern and postmodern architectural concerns with crisis and alteration. In 1961, in the first Walter Gropius Lecture at Harvard University Graduate School of Design, entitled "Constancy, Change and Architecture," Sigfried Giedion affirmed that fatigue is the cause of the difficulties faced by modernist architecture.[30] This idea was transposed to the introduction of the fourth edition of *Space, Time and Architecture* (1961), in which boredom was paired with confusion as the forces behind the architecture of the 1960s. Comparably, in 1989, the symposium "Constancy and Change in Architecture," arranged by the Center for the Advancement of Studies in Architecture (CASA) of the University of Texas, delved into the theme. With the participation of Christian Norberg-Schultz, Kenneth Frampton, Karsten Harries, and other renowned figures, the debates were based on assumptions similar to those posed by Wölfflin and Göller a century earlier, highlighting the persistent need of the discipline to evaluate the built environment by identifying moments of insecurity. For the organizers, Malcolm Quantrill and Bruce Webb, exhaustion with the styles of form and the speculation about their future demonstrate "the immaterial existence of architecture as the embodiment of powerful impulses which flex first in the human psyche as poetic constructs of dwelling."[31]

CHAPTER 6
CONEY ISLAND, MISLEADING STRUCTURES*

> It is marvelous what you can do in the way of arousing human emotions by the use you can make architecturally, of simple lines. Luna Park is built on that theory—and the result has proven that theory's worth.
>
> Frederic Thompson (1903)

In *Delirious New York* (1978), Rem Koolhaas opens the investigation of Manhattan by referring to Coney Island, the peninsula southwest of Brooklyn, famous for its beach and amusement parks—Steeplechase (1895), Luna Park (1903), and Dreamland (1904). The neighborhood is presented as a primordial and independent unit, analogous to the center of New York, with infrastructural and architectural components of specific function and symbolism. According to Koolhaas, Coney Island incorporates vital yet unofficial principles of modernization, "a laughing mirror-image of the seriousness with which the rest of the world is obsessed with Progress." Constructed through a "technology of the fantastic," this environment takes advantage of the unfilled fissures in the blueprint of modern everyday life.[1] Coney Island is a destination of leisure and recreation that relies on a culture of distraction, consumerism, and moral license, a compensation for the solemnity of the authoritatively urban. This fundamental organization became adversely evident at the peak of its existence in the first decade of the twentieth century, when Maxim Gorky, a social realist and a politically committed writer, identified boredom as the defining and most pervasive constituent of its bright and compelling architecture.

In an article titled "Boredom," published in *The Independent Magazine* on August 8, 1907, Gorky portrays Coney Island as a realm where exterior and interior architecture—buildings, enclosed rooms, and interstitial architecture, including rides, urban furniture, and porticos—entails the same possibilities of experience and meaning. Despite his admiration for the "fantastic city of fire" by night and the "white structures" by day, the report projects boredom as a rampant ailment. The condition emerges not as the dearth of the aesthetically interesting but as the opposite of enjoyment, a neutral cloth that covers, filters or exhibits all aspects of reality in their most essential form; every object, subject, and event becomes equally unimportant. Consequently, the realization of the absence of salient moments of significance dawns unwanted, evincing the discord between the idealistic yearnings of inwardness and the tangible imperfections of the outward world: "the cold gleam of the dead fire bares the stupidity of it all. Its pompous glitter rests upon everything 'round about the people."[2]

For Gorky, boredom implies disengagement, which in turn establishes an ambiguous relationship between individuals and the built environment. On the one hand, boredom

Boredom, Architecture, and Spatial Experience

emerges through the qualities of the surrounding architecture—spaces turn boring; on the other, it acts on the body by inscribing habits and affecting perception, attention, and memory—visitors become bored. Since these two instances do not merge solely into a corporeal affliction resulting from the exposure to urban life, the condition, commonly shared, exists and lasts as long as human inhabitation prevails in Coney Island. Unlike the contemporaneous narratives that provide phenomenological descriptions of boredom, Gorky employs simple and basic relations of space—inside and outside, public and private, functional and symbolic—to expose the condition as an unpreventable symptom of modernity and capitalism, in constant state of production. Significantly, not only does he conceptualize architecture as a medium of expression with ideological and thus historical specificity, but also he stresses the capacity of the built environment to induce emotions so profound that they become imperceptible to its users.

Mistreating New York, Misleading Coney Island

The article comprises a brief foreword by the editor of the magazine, three photographs—a portrait of the author and two of Luna Park—and nine segments with impressions of Coney Island (Figures 6.1 and 6.2). In the introductory note, readers are made aware

Figure 6.1 The main promenade of Luna Park during daytime, from "Boredom," *The Independent Magazine* (August 8, 1907), 312.

Figure 6.2 Luna Park at night, from "Boredom," *The Independent Magazine* (August 8, 1907), 315.

that Gorky is an adopted last name that means "The Bitter One," and they are also advised to understand the commentary as a subjective and polemical provocation, derived from the writer's visit to New York the previous year: "when Maxim Gorky was in this country last summer he seemed to find life and its conditions everywhere as bad as in darkest Russia.... After reading it one knows better how to interpret his pictures of Russian life."[3]

Accompanied by Maria Andreeva, his second—common-law—wife, Gorky arrived in the United States on April 10, 1906. The travel was arranged by the Bolshevik faction of the Russian Social-Democratic Workers' Party with the objective of obtaining funds for the Revolution.[4] Despite the enthusiastic reception by the American public and the initial support of important members of the "A" club of writers, including Jack London and Mark Twain, the campaign proved fruitless after the press released details of the private life of the author.[5] Unable to prevent the couple's entry into the country, the Russian Embassy in New York prepared and distributed information concerning the relationship with Andreeva. The attack took advantage of the prevailing conservatism of American society, in the knowledge that Gorky would be condemned and ostracized for breaking the conventions of marriage and family. On April 14, two photographs appeared on the front page of *The New York World*; one was of the writer, his first wife and their two children, and the other was of his new companion. The caption identified the "so-called Mme Gorky who is not Mme Gorky at all, but a Russian actress Andreeva, with whom he has been living since his separation from his wife."[6] The following day, *The New York Times* added, "She is not Mme Gorky, though he calls her so. . . . He says she's his wife in his eyes."[7]

Gorky and his party were immediately evicted from three hotels and all scheduled events were cancelled.[8] According to a cable sent on May 14 to the *New York Herald* by Ekaterina Peshkova, the writer's first wife and a renowned human rights activist, the intrusion of the media into his private life astounded Gorky, revealing to him how the freedom that the United States proclaimed masked prejudices that did not exist in Russia.[9] That summer, in an attempt to distract and comfort him, his friends and supporters organized a trip by trolley through Brooklyn and Long Island to Coney Island.[10] In one of his last letters before leaving New York for Italy on October 13, he wrote about his reaction: "What they do here, how they work, how much energy, ignorance, self-satisfaction. . . . I am marvelling and cursing at the same time! I am bored, and I am happy, and the devil take it; it is very funny!"[11]

Flimsy White Structures

Almost a year later, writing from Capri and in Russian, the author reflected on his visit to Coney Island in "Boredom." Narrated in the third person, in prose and poetic language, the account is condemnatory yet evocative, essentially ambivalent. The architecture of the amusement parks, entangled in the general description, is an agent that defines actions and the possibilities of experience. Yet edifices and locations are vaguely reconstructed and rapidly grouped—"dozens of white buildings, monstrously diverse, not one with even the suggestion of beauty."[12] The discard of their particularities insinuates a generic realm in which all forms and spaces are of the same value. By implication, boredom does not arise as an accidental outcome or as the desired effect of a certain type of architecture, nor does architecture constitute the representation of a prevailing sentiment; instead, boredom is a fulcrum for the articulation of space that occurs between the buildings and the crowd.

For Gorky, the architectural parameters of Coney Island delineate a realm of commodity where consumers of mass entertainment spend their Sunday, the day of the week that embodies middle-class boredom.[13] Transpiring between the completion and the beginning of the working cycle, the seventh day is for paid sin, paid confession, and paid repentance—a sequence in which religious and moral convictions complement the production activities of capitalism, aided by alcohol consumption—"they drink in the vile poison with silent rapture. The poison contaminates their souls. Boredom whirls about in an idle dance, expiring in the agony of its inanition."[14] Suggesting that the popularity of Coney Island responds to the human dependence on the surroundings, the writer observes that visitors seek to escape from the demands of the urban and industrial life by opting to rest in an environment artificially constructed and based on mechanized repetition, whose monotony is the same as that of offices and factories but looks different. The edifices and spaces of fantasy and distraction create an "architectural other" that materialize distant and exotic as well as real and imagined geographies, imposing their presence with a vocabulary of excitement; moon landscapes, a dwarf village, hanging gardens à la Babylon, a submarine, the biggest ballroom in the world, a circus, scientific facilities to incubate newborns, Japanese gardens, the canals of Venice, and many other thematic recreations conjure an intangible world. Enhanced by the arbitrary juxtaposition of disparate themes, this architecture shortens the distance between the anticipations and the experience of visitors, with the aim to provoke either the pleasure of an impish enactment or the delusion of living with alternate values. Similar to tourism, the fictional journeys to other locations lead not to new social or cultural possibilities but toward the passive acceptance of the established routine, overriding the emergence of novel sensibilities.

Because its commercial success depended on inclusivity and the increase of permissibility, Coney Island strengthened and validated practices of leisure. Amusement parks, such as Steeplechase, Luna, and Dreamland, provided a playful but corrective solution to the rigidity of Manhattan, a mechanism for the release of social pressure, which also benefited from the reduction of class consciousness.[15] In part by design and in part inadvertently, the whimsical offerings provided meaning to urban boredom, compelling individuals to endure their own habits since recreation can only be attained after a prosperous sequence of labor.[16] For Gorky, the entertainment of Coney Island responded to the will to be distracted as well as to the need of public legitimization: "the men's faces, shaven even to the mustache, all strangely like one another, are grave and immobile. The majority bring their wives and children along, and feel that they are benefactors of their families, because they provide not only bread, but also magnificent shows."[17]

Unlike the rationality and verticality of the "blasé attitude" posed by Simmel—a physiological exhaustion resulting from the impositions of the metropolis, "violently" and "brutally" tearing the nervous system—the boredom of Gorky is emotional and horizontal.[18] It is existential and all encompassing, a root-like structure in which individuals and social values inform the creation of the environment, and in turn the environment influences inhabitants by imposing modes of spatial occupation. Derived from the succession from over- to under-stimulation, this arrangement is diffuse, unclean, and ultimately infectious; it acts like "the blue mist of the ocean vapours" that mingles with "the drab smoke of the metropolis," enveloping all spaces in "a transparent sheet, in which they quiver like a mirage."[19] The boredom of Coney Island is vital to its function and existence, but it can only be detected—and used subversively—when standing outside it, from a vantage point free of its influence.

Stifling Spaces

The temporal, geographical, and cultural separation from Coney Island allowed Gorky to discern boredom as a ubiquity that defined its entirety, blurring the differences between the interior, individual, and private and the exterior, social, and public. Becoming indistinguishable, all spheres are contaminated by the values of modernity and the predictability of economic transactions—"the melancholy wail of life driven by the power of gold, the cold, cynical whistle of the Yellow Devil." As posed in "Boredom," Coney Island constitutes not an appendage of New York but an autonomous entity, endlessly active, insatiate and hungry, burning but not consuming. From distance and at night, it appears as a fascinating capital with a luminous skyline, simultaneously rising from and reflecting onto the dark Atlantic—a lesser Manhattan of "thousands of ruddy sparks" and "shapely towers of miraculous castles, palaces and temples." But from close by and during the light of day, what seemed glistening, playful, and titillating is revealed as an environment in decay, an ugly and absurd disarray of straight lines, cheap and hastily constructed, unarticulated and incongruous: "they are built of wood, and smeared over with peeling white paint, which gives them the appearance of suffering with the same skin disease. The high turrets and low colonnades extend in two dead-even lines insipidly pressing upon each other. Everything is stripped naked by the dispassionate glare."[20]

Comparable to "a dumbfounded fool with wide-open mouth," the windows and openings of buildings subsume into thresholds incapable of separating outside from inside, impressing a continuous veneer of sameness. Every surface is a contrived and conceited façade, normative and biased, short-lived and incapable of delivering catharsis—"the soul is seized with a desire for a living, beautiful fire, a sublime fire, which should free the people from the slavery of a varied boredom. For this boredom . . . blinds their eyes." The omnipresent electric light, essential to this domain, impedes the casting of shadows, with every hour becoming both day and night, or neither—"the glare is everywhere." Allowing the endless replication of commercial rituals—eating, drinking, smoking, shopping—this twenty-four-hour glow is overpowering and uncanny. Coney Island seems to rest on an infinite space, without a center of gravity or coordinates of location. The leveling of the hierarchy of buildings and the disappearance of points of entry and exit put visitors in a condition of vulnerability, estrangement, and disembodiment, contributing to the "withering" of consciousness and "routing" of thoughts.[21]

By interfering in the flow between reason and emotion, the disoriented visitors to Coney Island turn submissive and—in passive attempts to transgress—cruel. Poignantly, Gorky describes a cage with a monkey and its baby encircled by weary sightseers who enjoy the exposure of the space of the animals in the public realm of the humans. Opiated by boredom, "white-skinned savages, men and women in straw hats and hats with feathers" find commonality in the exploitation of the animals. The crowd is mollified by inflicting terror: "sometimes one of the musicians turns the stupid, brass bellow of his instrument upon the monkey, and overwhelms the animal with a deafening noise. The little baby timidly clasps the mother's body still harder, shows its teeth and looks at the musician sharply. The people laugh and nod their heads approvingly to the musician."[22]

Reversing the condition, visitors occupy moveable enclosures and units of confinement, some of them geometric and others resembling boats and carriages, to simulate the intensity of danger. The ringing lines of the metallic and wooden assemblies, rides that take visitors up into the sky only to spin and plunge them down, allow an extreme and dynamic communion with others as well as with the environment, in between inside and outside. As temporary places of inhabitation, the structures are impersonal, permeated by repetitious, tired, and tiring music that "rends the air"—"the orchestra is poor, the musicians worn out."[23] As if coordinated with the automated movement of the architecture of commodified thrill, the cloying melodies dictate a rhythm of action that suspends attention and, like a mantra, induces a state of drowsiness, between alertness and unconsciousness. The persistent songs, the noise of the machinery, the almost silent movement of the multitudes, and the barely recognizable human speech create a thick taut chord that fills the void of silence. If immersed in the space of Coney Island, boredom subtly but decisively deafens and impairs: "even the circus horses ... turn cautiously aside, and nervously twitch their sharp ears, as it they wanted to shake off the rasping tin sounds. The music of the poor for the amusement of slaves puts strange notions into your head."[24]

After Boredom

On August 9, 1907, the day after the publication of "Boredom," *The New York Times* responded in a short column titled "Gorky on Coney." Mainly composed of quotes from the essay and echoing the opening warning of the editor, it affirmed that the diagnosis of boredom as a malady of Coney Island was a projection of the boredom of the writer of "melancholic tendency."[25] Nevertheless, the depiction of the beach and amusements parks as a complete and independent spatial entity is acknowledged as accurate.[26] According to the newspaper, the "black bile" of Gorky is "atoned" by the admiring and appreciative sight of a "whole."[27] Although the author admires the American city as a production of a "fantasy of stone, glass, and iron" with "amazing" houses and machines, the presence of boredom unveils an environment of problematized inhabitation into which is embedded the prosaic search for excitement and whatever is interesting within the metropolis.[28] On Coney Island, interior and exterior spaces are part of an architecture of sameness and repetition that offers many possibilities for distraction but none for meaningfulness; expectations must therefore be enacted in the interiority of the individual, the center of experimentation and difference.

To Koolhaas, this derogatory verdict marked the end of Coney Island as an urban laboratory, "the incubator for Manhattan's incipient themes and infant mythology." The awareness of boredom and the disqualification of the architecture of the fantastic eliminated its independence. By the end of the first decade of the twentieth century, the public sensibility no longer favored thematic practices of recreation since they were suddenly deemed trivial, frivolous, and in bad taste. Koolhaas alleges that the condemnation of "Boredom," accompanied by "a subsequent series of similar misreadings," prompted the proposal "to raze the City of Towers, to root out every trace of the infamous infrastructure as if it were a poisonous weed and to restore the surface of the earth to its 'natural' state, a thin layer of grass."[29] Aligned with Gorky's vision of an alternate political and socioeconomic order, in the new Coney Island boredom would not arise since leisure would entail significance, architecturally propounded by buildings designed to avoid identical spaces.

PART 2
CIRCULAR TRAJECTORIES

CHAPTER 7
A UNITY OF DISARRAY

In the twentieth century, the production and experience of the built environment is suffused with boredom. In architectural elaborations, its identification exposes the contradictions of the modern era; Le Corbusier quaintly noted,

> Truth to tell, the modern man is bored to tears in his home; so he goes to his club. The modern woman is bored outside her boudoir; she goes to tea-parties. The modern man and woman are bored at home; they go to night-clubs. But lesser folk who have no clubs gather together in the evening under the chandelier and hardly dare to walk through the labyrinth of their furniture which takes up the whole room and is all their fortune and their pride.[1]

New technologies supported the advancement of typologies and commodities of architecture, including facilities for industrial production, recreation, and the control of interior environments. Additionally, as cities consolidated and densified, urban living molded social and cultural processes, with attendant fragmentation and alienation. To Le Corbusier, "modern man and woman" of the privileged classes had access to conveniences that procured comfort—open-plan spaces and the mechanized control of water, light, and temperature, "machines for living in"—as well as time and economic resources for entertainment and leisure—cinemas, museums, stadia, and education. Meanwhile, the "lesser folk" were confined to the remnants of the nineteenth century, dwelling in multifunctional and congested rooms articulated by long corridors. According to Clement Greenberg, the peasants and immigrants, the recently arrived residents of the metropolis, discovered a "capacity for boredom" and thus pressured "society to provide them with a kind of culture fit for their own consumption."[2] Although the "modern man and woman" and the "lesser folk" shared the city as a common space, where the routines and habits of capitalism take place, their strategies to relieve boredom accentuated their different ways of inhabiting it.

The modern built environment outlined a mode of fundamental everyday of conflict. As Marshall Berman observes, the twentieth century witnessed the achievement of "spectacular triumphs in art and thought," but also the introduction of "incommensurable private languages" and the loss of the "vividness, resonance and depth" of those activities committed to the materialization of progress. The city promised "adventure, power, joy, growth of ourselves and the world," but at the same time questioned "everything we have, everything we know, everything we are." The incapacity to sustain interest, despite abundant stimulation, confirmed boredom as an inevitable space of waiting and unplanned action, elevating its presence as an essential component of modernity. In this manner, the inseparability of the boring from the interesting provided "a unity of disunity," "a maelstrom of perpetual disintegration and renewal, of struggle and contradiction, of ambiguity and anguish."[3]

Within this setting of circular trajectories, the second section of this book explores boredom as a pressing concern in the understanding of the modern built environment, from the early twentieth century to the 1970s. It is contextualized through the relationship between financial cycles and expressions of the condition in architecture and spatial considerations in art and critical writings, informed by psychology and psychoanalysis. The episodes explore how boredom, which remains undesired but begins to expose its role in creative acts, evolved from denoting exhaustion and confusion to being analytical and critical, gaining relevance for architecture.

Surrounded by Interests

If boredom is undesirable, then the question arises of why its triggers are tolerated and validated. Albert O. Hirschman differentiates the emotionality, heroics, and religiosity of medieval passions from the rationality, egotism, and secularity of modern interests, as a change derived from the political determination to create a uniform and easy to govern society. The implications of achieving glory and grandiosity, driven by irrepressible and irrational sentiments, entailed volatility and had to be controlled through economic measures rather than "through moralistic exhortation or the threat of damnation."[4] Accordingly, philosophers and theorists of the sixteenth and seventeenth centuries— mainly Niccolò Machiavelli, Hirschman says—encouraged the fulfillment of the totality of human aspirations by paving the way for the pursuit of the security of both person and nation. Originally not limited to financial gain, the quest for interests resembled avarice but without the aggressive measures to obtain wealth; it is an individual enterprise but shared by everyone, counteracting the passions by setting a path of minimal risk and schemed procedures with calculated outcomes. By assuring the high possibility of obtaining benefits, the efforts of the majority turn pragmatic, repetitious, foreseeable, and innocuous, with moral and social paradigms focused on self-preoccupation. Hirschman cites John Maynard Keynes, who asserts that "it is better that a man should tyrannize over his bank balance than over his fellow-citizens; and whilst the former is sometimes denounced as being but a means to the latter, sometimes at least it is an alternative."[5]

Subsequently, when the interests morphed exclusively into the will to obtain monetary surplus, further predictability and constancy appeared. These two aspects ensure the same practices in all locations and in all individuals, passing sameness from one person to another and from one generation to the next. The ensuing habits universalize and encourage financial insatiability, the consistent trait of the modern individual—ostensibly harmless, innocent, and gentle, for the same class and family.[6] To Hirschman, the "calm desire for wealth" preceded the turbulent development of capitalism as the mechanism "to repress certain human drives and proclivities and to fashion a less multifaced, less unpredictable, and more 'one dimensional' human personality." As social and personal motivations, the interests of the individual turned into forces that promoted populations willing to endure monotonous and exhausting processes of labor as long as earnings could be secured in advance. Nonetheless, what *"capitalism was supposed to accomplish . . . was soon to be denounced as its worst feature."* On the one hand, "peaceful, tranquil, and business-minded" modern Europe turned "empty, petty, and boring"; "the new world seemed to lack nobility, grandeur, mystery, and, above all, passion." On the other, "territorial ambition, the desire for colonial expansion, and the warlike spirit in general [are] not the inevitable consequence of the capitalist system, as the Marxist would have it," but rather constitute residues of pre-modern sensibilities, ritualistic and symbolic.[7]

Suffused with Boredom

Metaphorically similar to the menacing fog of Paris described by Jean-Paul Sartre in *Nausea* (1928)—"not the real fog, that had gone a long time ago . . . but the other, the one the streets were still full of, which came out of the walls and pavements"—boredom evolved as an inescapable presence in entrepreneurial and consumerist endeavors.[8] To Ernest Mandel, following the understanding of economic capitalism as the sequence of periods of prosperity and decline, since these processes "press outwards from the center—in other words, its historic birthday places—towards the periphery," nodes of capitalist and industrial importance, such as London, New York, and Paris, became referential and extended their influence to "colonial and semi-colonial countries—the so-called 'developing' countries."[9] The new markets were converted areas where simple production grew as the accelerated yet tiresome reproduction of commodities, susceptible to uniformity. The economic impulse of the interests informed and organized the possibilities of urban planning and the construction of generic architecture, propagating "the same ferro-concrete, steel and glass buildings, the same airports, the same railways with their stations and loudspeakers, the same vast cities that gradually engulf so much of the population."[10]

While in the nineteenth century, mechanized manufacturing and programmed development superseded the pre-capitalist arrangement of labor, in the twentieth century capitalism rapidly gained vigor as the economic international order, corroborated by the fluctuation of waves of economic growth. This continuous movement avoids inertia and the tendency toward stability. According to Kondratieff, capitalist economy thwarts the moment of equilibrium by constantly changing, under the fallacious excuse of delivering progress; like boredom, the propulsion of material advancement creates the illusion that a better future is being assembled. Particularly evident in the construction of architectural and infrastructural projects, *"the replacement and expansion of the fund of these goods does not take place smoothly but in spurts."*[11] These moments of creation constitute accomplishments that respond to the performance of capitalism, resembling an axis; if equilibrium changes, then the interests change and so do the conditions for the ideation and construction of the built environment.

Third Cycle

Although Kondratieff posed long cycles of economic development only until the third rising wave of 1891 to 1920, anticipating the following downward movement, these periods have been extended to the rest of the twentieth century by other theorists, who agree on their sequence until the 1970s and their coincidence in Europe and the United States. With small variations, Mandel, Nathan Mager, and Walt Rostow maintain that the third cycle of capitalism lasted until between 1937 and 1939, and the fourth until the recession of 1974.

The peak of the upward swing of the third cycle occurred when the first Model T came out of the Ford plant in Detroit in 1908, the beginning of the age of oil, automobiles, and mass production. To Mandel, the origins of this period are the consolidation of European imperialism and the expansion of capital investments in the colonies, creating new markets in Asia, Africa, and Oceania, the generalization of monopolies and the slow rise in the price of raw materials.[12] The rapid accretion of capital was supported by technological innovation and its role in the productivity of labor, which led to the increase in the rate of surplus-value that permitted continuous profit. These conditions necessitated and hence prompted the construction of factories and offices, affecting the experience of people working in these spaces and living in expanding cities. For Braudel, the urban everyday was determined by poverty because the industries that provided work to the masses "cared little about how they lived." As a reaction, socialist ideologies arose to organize labor and attain better conditions for the procurement of the interests, with the aim to achieve the same for everyone. In Great Britain, the Independent Labour Party was established in 1893, and the General Federation of Trade Union was created five years later. This contributed to a new government in 1906 that passed a series of welfare laws, which promised social transformation. In France, two socialist parties were founded in 1901, the Parti socialiste de France and the Parti socialiste français, merging into the Parti socialiste unifié in 1906. In Germany, the resignation of Otto von Bismarck in 1890 led to the institution of trade unions, which increased in popularity in the following decades. As Braudel remarks, "it could be argued that in 1914 the West was not only on the brink of war, but also on the brink of Socialism. The Socialists were close to seizing power and building a Europe as modern as it is today."[13]

During the 1910s, the United States not only confirmed its industrial character in the proliferation of modern cities but also implemented internal and external policies designed to avoid stasis, as if the maturity of the country needed to be tested. These processes were initiated and guided by Theodore Roosevelt, who at a young age was diagnosed with *neurasthenia*, the American term used to denote the boredom from "overcivilization."[14] While neurasthenic men were encouraged to explore the outdoors and be physically active in communion with other men, neurasthenic women were prescribed interior confinement and isolation from society. Responding to those therapeutic and prophylactic recommendations for male sufferers, beginning in 1906, Roosevelt created domestic programs that established national parks, forests, and monuments to nature and wildlife.[15] Outside the country, the boredom of Roosevelt became evident through the international display of political influence and military power. According to Braudel, the war waged against Spain for Cuba and the Philippines in 1898 and the creation of the Great White Fleet to tour the world as a testament of American dominance in 1907 were both decisions that related to "Theodore Roosevelt's writing at the time that 'the United States needed a war', or that it had to be given 'something to think about other than material gain.'"[16] The World War I, which interrupted governmental attempts to create progressive social programs, fortified instead the capitalist system that was based on mass consumption.

The downward swing began between 1914 and 1920, reaching its lowest point in 1929, at the onset of the American depression, and lasting until 1937. This period was defined by the effects of the war—commonly described as "moments of boredom punctuated by moments of terror"—and the Russian Revolution.[17] Together, the two events caused the disruption of world trade, the regression of industrial production, the slow valorization of capital, and the narrowing of the global market. While Britain maintained its position as the optimum center for credit, maritime insurance, and reinsurance until 1939, the crisis of the 1930s paused the thriving economy of the United States. In line with Kondratieff's affirmation that periods of recession invigorate research and the creation of conditions for the implementation of knowledge, the economic depression helped to redefine the infrastructure of urban expansion. With the planning of roads, highways, ports, and airports, from the 1920s onwards, came technologies and materials of construction based on oil and electricity. Petrochemicals and synthetic composites, transport and motorized equipment for building, analogue worldwide systems of communication—telephone, telex, cablegram—and the widespread use of electricity allowed the bulk production of generic residences with their new home appliances and interior climate control units, all designed with the aid of normalizing handbooks of architecture.[18]

Fourth Cycle

The fourth cycle begins with the recovery phase from 1937 to 1948, encompassing World War II. Socialist ideologies aimed for equality and communal wellbeing, manifested primarily in the establishment of the social security system in 1946 in France and in 1948 in Great Britain. The progress of these political beliefs paralleled the weakening of the working class, which together permitted the rise in the rate of profit, furthering the accumulation of capital and the implementation of innovative technologies conceived in the recession period. Although the world market shrank due to the extension of non-capitalist zones—Eastern Europe, China, North Korea, North Vietnam, and Cuba—it was strengthened by the intensification of the division of labor, producing capital for the urban planning and architecture of post-war reconstruction.

In this cycle, modernist architecture flourished in Western Europe and the countries under fascist governments adopted neoclassicism as the official style. Josef Frank produced functionalist public housing in Sweden that was influenced by Leon Battista

Alberti's *De re aedificatoria* (1452). He believed that a misunderstanding of *varietas*, as the rich ornamentation of surfaces with classic motifs rather than an optimistic and lively multiplicity that favored a lifestyle of democracy and eclecticism, became the expression of totalitarian systems that sought not only repetition and sameness but also servitude and predictability. Frank affirmed as early as in 1931 that the architecture produced in Germany could not be considered part of the evolutionary line of the classic spirit; in his view, true varietas rejects "closed systems," "absolute beauty," and "aesthetic uniformity."[19] In 1958, Frank complained of a similar condition in Scandinavia, manifest in residential structures that resembled the United Nations building (1952) in New York by Oscar Niemeyer, Le Corbusier, and Harrison & Abramovitz. The only difference was that the towers in Sweden had only twelve to sixteen stories, looking "disconsolate" and "purse-proud with all that metal."[20] To the architect, the lack of varietas in the built environment is symptomatic of the reigning political ideology and alters the behavior of its inhabitants by causing boredom:

> As far as Swedish boredom is concerned (Swedish sadness they call it in England) it is a quality well known also among the natives and discussed in the papers every day. There is specially the problem whether this has to do with the welfare state and the general prosperity, which, I hope, is not the case. But it is so that people are only concerned with their material well being [*sic*], that there are no problems and above all no contrasts, which has made the Swedish literature as well unbelievable dull. ... All people try for speedy success, which is not much different anywhere else. Our problematic era is evidently passed and what calls itself today Avant Garde is (to use another militaristic expression) really marauders who pillage the leftovers without opposition.[21]

In turn, the phase of prosperity between 1948 and 1966 was defined by welfare, following the economic and technological paradigms of big markets, the standardization of products, and metropolitan centralization. For Braudel, the slow attempts to create the Common Market in Europe in 1957 revealed a continent where every country wanted to experience wealth through "a moderate, pragmatic Socialism," but carefully protected national interests to avoid international homogenization.[22]

The resistance to similarity and the crisis of meaning became evident in the practices of labor and its management, psychological investigations, and art and cultural manifestations—all incorporating the built environment in the creation and nurturing of boredom. The condemnation of the monotony of factory work, epitomized by the Ford and Taylor systems, increased the concern with work satisfaction. However, instead of reconsidering the mechanisms of production, factories and industries concentrated on improving regulations and settings to increase productivity. In 1961, the Oklahoma State Department of Health and the Extension Division of the General Services of the University of Oklahoma produced a documentary titled *Boredom at Work*. Directed by Daniel L. Chichester, with the psychiatric advice from Alfred A. Hellams, the two films comprising the educational series delve into boredom as an "emotional problem in business, industry ... and life itself." They narrate the life of the fictional Hugh Marriott, father and main provider of a middle-class family living in a suburb, who unwillingly works in an office of a real estate company, surrounded by architects who only interact among themselves. The first part, titled "The Empty Life," identifies boredom as Hugh's problem; he complains of having "lost his zest," and being "bored stiff" and incapable of finding anything of "interest at home or at the office." Boredom is posed as a psychological malady—individual, with roots in his relationship with his mother, accumulative and requiring analytical therapy. Also compared to a contagious virus, the condition causes loneliness and callousness and thus a lack of social and professional success, turning Hugh into "a wet blanket."[23] The second part, titled "The Search for Zest," follows the protagonist as he acknowledges his boredom and overcomes it; with the help of regular visits to a psychiatrist, he is able to identify an affinity for the unpredictability of being in nature and for the excitement of working on construction sites. This realization leads to his success and happiness, as he faces his inner "drives with honesty" and learns to "release his tensions."[24] In the films, boredom is normalized not only as an illness to which everyone is vulnerable but also as a conflict between what the sufferer wants and what the sufferer has. The conclusion is that the modern individual can avoid any monotony of work by finding the ideal position in the system, achieving existential significance by engaging with the surroundings and evading the routine by pursuing a variety of interests.

The scientific study of boredom was pioneered in the 1950s. In an article titled "On Boredom," published in 1953 as the opening contribution in the first issue of the *Journal of the American Psychoanalytic Association*, Ralph Greenson describes the "uniqueness of the feeling of being bored" as "a passive, expectant attitude with the hope that the external world will supply the satisfactions."[25] Similarly, the effects of the exposure to uninteresting environments, "where nothing at all happens," was investigated in 1951 by a group of psychologists from McGill University, supported by a grant from the Defence Research Board of Canada. The results of the systematic study were published in 1957 in *Scientific American* as "The Pathology of Boredom" by Woodburn Heron, a member of the investigation team. To understand why aviators and other military personnel in charge of security tasks "sometimes suffer hallucinations during long, monotonous" situations, male college students were recruited and paid $20 per day to lay on a bed in a lighted cubicle twenty-four hours a day, for as long as they could endure. They wore plastic visors to prevent pattern vision, cotton gloves and cardboard cuffs extending beyond the fingertips to restrict perception by touch, and a U-shaped foam rubber pillow to limit auditory perception—constantly surrounded by a hum of air-conditioning equipment to mask all sounds.[26]

Through tests that measured the consequences in the intellectual capacity of the participants, the laboratory experiment determined that boredom not only lessened rational thinking but also caused irritability, sensorial alterations, and emotional distress. The confinement made them lose their "sense of perspective" and affected their perception of orientation and distance; after emerging from isolation, "the world seemed to be in movement."[27] In 1959, corroborating these analyses, Ernest Schachtel maintained that the existential emptiness produced by boredom, evidenced either in self-confinement or in frantic attempts to be busy, cripples all possible modes of spatial experience. For the psychologist, since sensory communication with the outside is disrupted, the bored patient becomes distrustful and demands engagement with the environment, responding to the condition with exaggerated self-awareness:

> I am excited. If I allow this excitation to continue I shall get anxious. Therefore I tell myself, I am not at all excited. I don't want to do anything. Simultaneously, however, I feel I do want to do something; but I have forgotten my original goal and do not know what I want to do. The external world must do something to relieve me of my tension without making me anxious. It must make me do something, but so that I shall not be responsible for it. It must divert me, distract me, so that what I do will be sufficiently remote from my original goal.[28]

Anticipating Schachtel's observations, as well as Heron's affirmation that "a changing sensory environment seems essential for human beings" because "variety is not the spice of life ... it is the very stuff of it," in 1953 Gordon Pask produced the Musicolour system, a mechanical and artistic instrument that emanates colors to which a musician actively responds.[29] The cybernetic project was originally "inspired by the concept of synaesthesia and the general proposition that the aesthetic value of a work can be enhanced if the work is simultaneously presented in more than one sensory modality." Yet Pask realized that the Musicolour could learn to reply, becoming equally sensitive to the lack of stimulation or repetitive input; if the system "gets bored," then it "directs its attention to the potentially novel," forcing the performer to react by procuring new arrangements.[30] This machine informed the computational programs that John and Julia Frazer engineered in 1978 for the unrealized Generator (1976–9), devised by Cedric Price. This design, for an activity center located in the White Oak Plantation, on the border between Georgia and Florida, combined cubes, catwalks, screens, and boardwalks that could be moved by a crane following the will of the visitors. In addition to including facilitators to guide the activities, Price used four computational programs to produce a mobile architecture that responded to the data provided by users. Three were related to the arrangement of the temporal configuration of the structure, and the fourth attempted to obtain reactions from the visitors by engendering unrequested plans and improvements. According to the Frazers, the capacity of the system to avoid boredom by giving flexibility and unpredictability proved that the building was "intelligent," possessing a "mind of its own."[31]

Multiple cultural and artistic expressions accompanied the prosperity of the 1960s, exposing boredom not only as a circumstance of space but also as a motivator to alter space, either positively, by infusing buildings, rooms, and events with added boredom, or negatively, by minimizing opportunities for its surfacing. In a diary entry of 1965, Susan Sontag validated boredom by declaring that "most of the interesting art of our time is boring. Jasper Johns is boring. Beckett is boring, Robbe-Grillet is boring," and declaring that "maybe art has to be boring, now. (Which obviously doesn't mean that boring art is necessarily good—obviously)."³² In her view, boredom allows the redirection of attention by questioning modes of isolated concentration and thus enforces the combination of sources and approaches to process information, such as "listening for sense rather than sound" in order to elude "being too message-oriented."³³

Existing beyond the two-dimensional realm, boredom encourages the consideration of numerous and simultaneous frames of experience, either moderate and controlled or extreme and unconstrained. In the case of scarce stimulation, the long films by Andy Warhol, such as *Sleep* (1963), *Empire* (1964), and *Four Stars* (1967), and the multi-media experimentations of Fluxus, such as John Cage's performance of *Vexations* (1963), a piece by Erik Satie in which a thirty-two-bar piece is played 840 times in twenty-five hours, create spaces to "get slow and lost," where only that which is the same is replicated, merging art and environment—figure and ground—to displace the references of location.³⁴ Through the insistence on monotony, the immediate becomes the basis for concentration, with neither foreseeable future nor pending desire; all expectations emerge only from the close encounter with the surroundings, disregarding the modern principles of productivity and the Romantic belief in existential meaning.³⁵ In the case of abundant stimuli that negate boredom derived from minimal sources, varied and multiple points of attention produce stereophonic conditions of distraction. To Sontag, the dandy cherishes Camp because its vulgarity and maximalism serve as an antidote to the modern asceticism. The eagerness for excess is architecturally typified by the Art Nouveau of Métro entrances in Paris, designed by Hector Guimard (1890s), and the hat-shaped Brown Derby Restaurant on Sunset Boulevard (1926–80); it is glorified through "texture, sensuous surface, and style at the expense of content."³⁶ In Sontag's notes, exposing the interrelation between boredom and economic circumstances, the respite offered by Camp can only be possible in prosperity, "in societies or circles capable of experiencing the psychopathology of affluence."³⁷

In architecture, beginning in 1966, Robert Venturi referred to boredom, coining the postmodernism maxim "less is a bore," to denounce the planeness of modernism, represented by Le Corbusier and Mies van der Rohe and his dictum "less is more." Ambiguously, though coherent with Venturi's discourse against clarity, the condition serves as a pejorative epithet to denote exhaustion with the strictness of functionalism, but it also conveys a set of design objectives. Partly, as in Price, adopting the criticality of boredom is intended to overthrow modernist values by unveiling its buildings as heroic representations of technology; and importantly, as in Warhol and Fluxus, the use of the creativity of boredom is the pivot by which to overcome a pretentious past. In *Complexity and Contradiction* (1966), Venturi briefly dissects the Wiley House (1953) by Philip Johnson, affirming that the explicit separation of public from private in two modular pavilions offers "an oversimplified program for living—an abstract theory of either-or." Unlike the apparent effortlessness and ease of design achieved in the Glass House (1949), the Wiley House produces "simpleness" and "bland architecture," the outcome of "blatant simplification" and lack of intelligence.³⁸ Venturi defines boredom as the lack of intricacy, advocating for conceptual and aesthetical inclusion rather than exclusion for expressive purposes. In *Learning from Las Vegas* (1972), Venturi, Denisse Scott Brown, and Steven

Izenour ask, "Is boring architecture interesting?" Comparing Crawford Manor (1966) by Paul Rudolph with the Guild House (1963) by Venturi and Rauch, Cope and Lippincott, the authors present a dialectical list of "the interesting" and "the boring," reversing their assumed positivity and negativity. The first category is connected to the modernism of Rudolph and other architects of the same trend, and it describes their work as "ugly and ordinary while looking heroic and original." "The interesting" prompts irrelevancy; the "reformist-progressive social and industrial aims" that the images of their projects suggest cannot be achieved when symbolism is disregarded and self-referentiality is staged. This "dry expressionism" is "empty and boring—and in the end irresponsible" because it rejects ornament, turning buildings into "one big ornament." The second category conveys an architecture of significance. The Guild House achieves "the boring" by using "explicit 'denotative' symbolism," "symbolic and applied ornament," "mixed media," "decoration by the attaching of superficial elements," "representational art," "evocative architecture," "societal messages," "propaganda," and "high *and* low art." This coveted boredom is "evolutionary," "old but with new meaning," "ordinary," "expedient," "pretty in form," "inconsistent," "conventional in technology," "tending toward urban sprawl," "starting from client's value system," and of "cheap" appearance.[39]

The Last Remnants of Joy

After the upward economic swing peaked in 1966, a period of economic decline lasted until 1973, followed in turn by a brief depression in 1974. According to Heilbroner, by the late 1960s "there were many signs of older forms of crisis-proneness—a tightening of labour markets, a mounting indiscipline in the labour process, a frowning satiation in important markets."[40] The origins can be identified in the increase of international competition, the slowing of the expansion of the world market, and the rise of class struggles that resulted from unemployment and the incapacity of the imperialist countries to incorporate all members of society into the production system. The overall deterioration became evident in the protests of May 1968 in Paris, when disenchantment and boredom were adopted as tropes by which to question urban modernity—as Guy Debord lamented, "once again, morning in the same streets. Once again the fatigue of so many similarly passed nights. It is a walk that has lasted a long time."[41] Grieving the loss of the city as a space of experimentation, the artists and intellectuals of the Situationism International, including Debord and Ivan Chtcheglov, censured modern architecture and urban planning as purveyors of the falsely spectacular and accomplices of inescapable determinism that repressed emotional spontaneity. The attempt to ignore the logical and geological formation of the city by substituting the original and meaningful conceptions of space with "the sophistication of the machines" had led to alienation—"the inability to invent a technique for the liberation of everyday experience."[42] According to Chtcheglov, "we are bored in the city" because of the abstraction of modernist architecture and its attempts to become mythical by disregarding history. In his view, Le Corbusier had championed the destruction of "the last remnants of joy":

We will leave Monsieur Le Corbusier's style to him, a style suitable for factories and hospitals, and no doubt eventually for prisons. (Doesn't he already build churches?) Some sort of psychological repression dominates this individual—whose face is as ugly as his conceptions of the world—such that he wants to squash people under ignoble masses of reinforced concrete, a noble material that should rather be used to enable an aerial articulation of space that could surpass the flamboyant Gothic style. His cretinizing influence is immense. A Le Corbusier model is the only image that arouses in me the idea of immediate suicide.[43]

Coinciding with the economic crisis of 1974, produced by the unexpected increase in the price of oil by the Organization of Petroleum Exporting Countries (OPEC) in response to the Israeli-Arab conflict, the incendiary politics of Punk extended the principles of Situationism and rebelled against the routine of the establishment in Britain. Opposing religion and the state, traditional home and family, and the division of work and leisure, this movement aimed to demystify modernism by manifesting inconformity, anti-authoritarianism, do-it-yourself ethics, and resistance against selling out. Punk was a discourse of sincerity and commitment, of the passions against the interests, sarcastic and disaffected, different from the nihilism of the early twentieth century.[44] Its members occupied public spaces; the stationary inhabitation of sidewalks and squares not only disrupted the rhythm of the activities of capitalist production but also challenged the calculations of architecture and planning. Instead of being the center of progress, the city became the symbol of "No Future," a slogan made popular in 1977 by the Sex Pistols in "God Save the Queen."[45] In the same year, the poster for their song "Pretty Vacant" featured two buses with different destinations, one to "Nowhere" and the other to "Boredom."[46]

In the United States, between 1973 and 1975, unemployment increased by three-quarters while the oligopolies that dominated the domestic markets consolidated. Eight percent of professional workers were left without income and ninety percent of black adolescents became job seekers; at the same time, about 200 enterprises imposed an impersonal system of corporations, controlling approximately half of the American wealth. To Braudel, monopolies, crypto-monopolies, and oligopolies and their labor unions, accompanied by the countervailing power of governments, engendered "something like neo-capitalism," "adaptable in its developed form to twentieth century conditions, and already very different from traditional capitalism." This system, supported by technological development and computational aids, mainly the Intel microprocessor created in 1971 in California, intensified the predictability and sameness of boredom. Neo-capitalism epitomizes the search for economic gain, characterized by "efficiency, including automation and its offshoots; mass production for an enormous homogeneous market with standardizes tastes, encouraged by all-pervasive, all-powerful advertising."[47]

Although the market recovered by 1978, a bearish mood persisted in the financial and business world. To Heilbroner, the enduring crisis "was not one of present realities but of expected developments, not one of economics alone but of belief." The conditions that allowed and bolstered the search for interests had created meaningless architecture that not only failed to represent the economic and social variations but also exploited the natural environment—"the complex and interconnected constraints of our energy supplies, our resource availabilities, our pollution dangers."[48] The gloom of the late 1970s was underpinned by the realization that the resources of capitalism might be endangered. Despite environmentalism could have become an agent against monotony, in the form of activism, it turned into another task of capitalism, installing boredom by being a societal responsibility and a marketing instrument.[49]

CHAPTER 8
MARTIN HEIDEGGER'S URGE TO BE AT HOME

References to boredom during the twentieth century are ubiquitous, but the philosophical account by Martin Heidegger is regarded as the most detailed and best structured, conveyed through instances of the everyday and framed by modern architecture. Extensively developed in a seminar series at the University of Freiburg in the winter of 1929–30 and published as *The Fundamental Concepts of Metaphysics: World, Finitude, Solitude*, the lectures oppose the rationalism of René Descartes and Immanuel Kant that separates subject from object and environment.[1] The philosopher argues that the temporal aspect of boredom echoes the essence of being human, which can only be understood in relation to the world, in a process of identifying what stays the same during the oscillation to other states. The dissection of boredom not only condemns the modern understanding of reality but also considers philosophy and metaphysics—"neither science nor the proclamation of world views"—as methods to regain physical, intellectual, and emotional wholeness.[2] While history records socioeconomic, cultural, and political change, philosophy and metaphysics analyze the systems that remain unaffected, moving in circles, unlike the linearity of science and progress.[3] As the repetitious consideration of the environment and its phenomena, circling drives "us" nowhere and "makes us feel dizzy and dizziness is something uncanny"—the ideal condition by which to understand the world and pursue home:

> This boredom becomes essential of its own accord, if only we are not opposed to it, if we do not always immediately react to protect ourselves, if instead we make room for it. This is what we must first learn: *not to resist straightaway* but *to let resonate*. Yet how are we to make room for this initially inessential, ungraspable boredom? Only by not being opposed to it, but letting it approach us and tell us what it wants, what is going on with it.... We must do this, however, not in the sense of dissecting some psychological experience, but in such a way that we thereby approach ourselves. Whom? Ourselves—*ourselves as a Da-sein*. (Ambiguity!)[4]

Attuning Everywhere

Since philosophy had "not yet succeeded in achieving what it has been attempting since Descartes (the beginning of modernity), namely to raise itself to the rank of science, of absolute science," *The Fundamental Concepts of Metaphysics* commences by conceiving philosophy as philosophizing.[5] This epistemological mode intends to surpass the recollection of data while reassessing the world as home. Referencing the understanding of Novalis's mysticism as "homesickness, an urge to be at home everywhere," Heidegger locates the modern individual out of home, a circumstance that needs to be acknowledged and eventually rectified.[6] The path to finding home, or returning to it, demands philosophizing, since "to be at home everywhere means to be at once and at all times within the whole"; the whole is the world and the world is home.[7] If the individual is not at home in the world, then boredom arises as a symptom of homesickness—an inadequate, ruptured, and fragmented relation to the whole.

Consequently, philosophers must include themselves in metaphysical questioning, while scientists impose distance between themselves and their objects of study. The fixation with objective truth "no longer starts from the existence of God or from proofs of God, but from consciousness, from the I"; nonetheless, the I is uncritically adopted "as the *most secure and unquestioned foundation*," excluding it from the process of philosophizing.[8] To reincorporate the questioner and connect the individual with the world, Heidegger employs attunements, or moods, conditions emerging from the I.[9] Instead of being adornments or side effects of the intellect, they provide a continuum, even when fluctuating from one to another, "like an atmosphere in which we first immerse ourselves in each case and which then attunes us through and through," or "like the utterly fleeting and ungraspable shadows of clouds flitting across the landscape."[10]

Boredom thus grounds the individual in the modern world, guiding inhabitation. It informs spatial occupation, movement, and experience as well as intellectual and emotional processes.[11] While emotions like happiness, frustration, or guilt are fleetingly specific, boredom is long lasting and consistently intense, less likely to be triggered by isolated events. As a mood, the condition articulates the psychic with the body and the environment by creating a disposition that reveals how individuals exist in the world. Resembling a fulcrum, this nexus concatenates interiority and exteriority, uncovering the unity of the individual with the surroundings; "an attunement is a way, not merely a form or a mode, but a way [*Weise*]—in the sense of a melody that does not merely hover over the so-called proper being at hand of man, but that sets the tone for such being, i.e., attunes and determines the manner and way [*Art und Wie*] of his being."[12]

Boredom is closer to a sense of self and place than to a cognitive state, and cannot be designed, imposed or disposed through concentrated effort. It is "already there" and all the individual can do is to ascertain its presence, which thus initiates a process of "awakening"—philosophizing can only occur if a fundamental mood is allowed to "become wakeful."[13] For Heidegger, this process presupposes a contradiction, since "whatever is sleeping is in a peculiar way absent yet there. . . . This is strange: attunement is something that is simultaneously there and not there."[14] The capacity of boredom for both "being-*there* [*Da-sein*]" and "being-*away* [*Weg-sein*]" discloses potentiality and latency as qualities of being human, defining the present in relation to the options of the future and giving "Dasein *subsistence and possibility* in its very foundations." Hence, boredom becomes evident because "we *do not want* to know about it"; the efforts to "pass the time" by being absorbed by busyness "attune us in such a way that it seems as though we were not attuned at all"—"we 'know'—in a strange kind of knowing—that boredom can return at any time. Thus it is already there.... This does not at all mean that we do not wish to be conscious of it, but rather that we do not wish to let it be awake—it, this boredom which, in the end, is already awake."[15]

Ultimately, boredom is fundamental for philosophizing and thus getting closer to home. Since in boredom the world manifests itself in its most basic state—indifferently, without a center of gravity—then through boredom the world can be grasped in its most essential facet. According to Heidegger, this fundamental mood not only questions the specific relations between the individual and the world, allowing the identification of a position within a location, but also serves as a reminder of mortality and the nothingness covered by the superficial everydayness and irrelevant publicness of modernity.[16]

Boredom, the Space of Modernity

Heidegger recommends paying attention to boredom because of its seemingly unimportant qualities. Its mild, timid, and silent expressions tend to escape "the subject" and "the social" but emerge in "the communal"—as an "us," historically rooted and collectively shared. To demonstrate the pervasiveness of the condition, the philosopher refers to four contemporaneous social interpretations, scholarly contributions by Oswald Spengler, Ludwig Klages, Max Scheler, and Leopold Ziegler that he portrays as reductive accounts of the reorganization of the experience of the city. Their content is dismissed as trivial, tending to generalizations and lacking in originality. Yet they are relevant as cultural manifestations that not only penetrate and influence mass media but also disclose "the spiritual space—if one may say such a thing—in which we move."[17] The insistence of these authors on asking, "Where do we stand?" instead of "How do things stand with us?" objectifies and rarefies the understanding of the world, with futility:

> What is happening here?, we ask anew. Must we first make ourselves interesting to ourselves again? Why *must* we do this? Perhaps because we ourselves have become *bored* with ourselves? Is man himself now supposed to have become bored with himself? Why so? *Do things ultimately stand in such a way with us that a profound boredom draws back and forth like a silent fog in the abysses of Dasein?*[18]

Extending the boredom diagnosed in academia to the alienation inflicted by modernity, Heidegger asserts that the sequence of daily activities—working, consuming, resting—constitutes an index of the efforts of progress as well as a point of departure to gain insight into the inner processes of the individual. The boredom of the everyday enables philosophizing as long as it exceeds everydayness and establishes a reflective dialogue that challenges the individualism propelled by Romanticism and the rhythm dictated by the mechanical control of time. Therefore, moments in between the activities of production organized by capitalism—temporal residues dedicated to waiting—must pass, since "living by the clock brings forth boredom by turning time into a series of present moments which must be filled up."[19]

Boredom, Architecture, and Spatial Experience

In boredom, time implodes into an "eternal now" and space expands into an "infinite here," merging interiority and exteriority and problematizing their interrelation—the "situatedness" of the individual.[20] The specificity of the physical environment is contested since every possible spatial configuration susceptible of inhabitation assumes irrelevance—"the architecture of this space" encounters the possibilities of "the architecture of another space," demanding critical evaluation and the profiling of a desired environment. During boredom, the corporeal agitation that attempts to find the most genuine space of dwelling does not reduce the continuous fantasies about the ideal space of belonging; unlike displacement, the condition arises because the individual wants to be in a different but unidentified physical, intellectual, or emotional location.

Bored by Something, Bored with Something, and Being Bored

Before identifying three typologies, Heidegger differentiates boredom from boringness—"what makes something *boring* what it is whenever it is *boring* us." Boringness is not a relationship but a property that can predispose to boredom, without constituting the tangible counterpart of the fundamental mood. To clarify, he describes an old book. The entirety of the object, its content and physical construction, constitutes boringness; it is "badly written, tastelessly printed and presented." The volume is wearisome, tedious, arid, irrelevant, and meaningless, failing to provide the possibility of engagement. This linear condition of cause and effect entails the individual's concern and appraisal, since wearisomeness, tediousness, aridness, irrelevancy, and meaninglessness are characteristics defined personally, by "the way in which we are *affected* or not affected." As such, boringness "*belongs to the object*" and it is "*taken from the subject.*"[21]

If boringness leads to boredom, then the individual is "held in limbo" and "left empty"—the two structural moments of the condition. Similar to an interrupted process of sublimation, boredom elevates the individual to a space above the physical world, a threshold dependent on the environment but detached from it. The experience of being bored occurs not only because "each thing has its time" but also because the individual is susceptible to the surroundings; as "a hybrid," boredom is "partly objective, partly subjective."[22]

The first typology arises when the subject "becomes bored *by* something"; that is, through the exposure to boringness. It supposes a gradual encounter with "that which is boring," in the present and within the boundaries of the immediate environment. Heidegger gives the example of waiting in a train station. Like the boring book, the building is depicted as a "tasteless station of some lonely minor railway." The situation is dramatized by imagining that "we," by mistake, have arrived four hours earlier than the scheduled time of departure. Due to its architectural and symbolic features—canopies and light structures that protect from the weather, with undefined limits, archetypical of the Industrial Revolution—the train station constitutes a moment of dual directions, in between interior and exterior spaces, movement and stasis, departing and returning, the natural and the technological, the urban and the rural. Heidegger portrays the station as confusing and uninspiring:

> We read the timetables or study the table giving the various distances from this station to other places we are not otherwise acquainted with at all. We look at the clock—only a quarter of an hour has gone by. Then we go out onto the local road. We walk up and down, just to have something to do. But it is no use. Then we count the trees along the road, look at our watch again—exactly five minutes since we last looked at it. Fed up with walking back and forth, we sit down on a stone, draw all kinds of figures in the sand, and in so doing catch ourselves looking at our watch again—half an hour—and so on.[23]

While waiting, in the space between where the individual is and where the individual wants to be, the qualities of the environment become ancillary. Instead of contributing to diversion, the encircling architecture corroborates the presence of boredom, inducing impatience, irritation, and displeasure. The dragging of time persecutes and the immediate spatial forces impede movement and progression. Although there is an apparent freedom to mentally move and wonder while waiting, boredom immobilizes; since the individual is one with the world, then the world cannot constitute the realm of movement, refusing itself to the individual—"to where are we held, then? ... We find the answer to this question if we pay attention to where we wish to arrive through passing the time. For passing the time betrays to us *where* we want to get away from and this is precisely that place to which time in its slowness holds us."[24]

The second typology of boredom entails a subsequent moment of analysis, since "being bored *with* something" requires the retrospective examination of a situation that might have not been acknowledged as boring while it was occurring. Boredom stays and propagates, "without needing to be caused by or bound to what is boring any more." Heidegger narrates attending a dinner party. Similar to waiting in a tasteless train station, the event has a beginning and a culmination; however, it takes place in a tasteful interior, away from home yet similar to it, surrounded by people and therefore delineated by social conventions. The setting is pleasant and comfortable—light, sound, and temperature carefully controlled:

> There we find the usual food and the usual table conversation, everything is not only very tasty, but tasteful as well. Afterward people sit together having a lively discussion, as they say, perhaps listening to music, having a chat, and things are witty and amusing. And already it is time to leave.... There is nothing at all to be found that might have been boring about this evening, neither the conversation, nor the people, nor the rooms. Thus we come home quite satisfied. We cast a quick glance at the work we interrupted that evening, make a rough assessment of things and look ahead to the next day—and then it comes: I was bored after all this evening, on the occasion of this invitation.[25]

Although the environment delivers its offerings with precision and the passing of time is not slowed, "a free-floating, unimpeded boredom" emerges and becomes "more and more concentrated on us." When the event finishes, "we" realize that we were not bored "by" the dinner party but we were bored "with ourselves" in the dinner party. Responding to the essence of boredom as being there and being away, "it is not that there is nothing boring *at all*, rather what is boring us has this character of '*I know not what*.'"[26]

Although time does not press in this typology, the sequence of "nows" do not unfold but turn into a "*single stretched 'now'* which itself does not flow, but stands." Because time passes and does not accumulate, "being bored *with* something" leaves us behind, dissolving the past and the future into an extended present. Accordingly, the spaces of "where we have been" and "where we will be" take the incongruous figure of an inaccessible horizon; "without the possibility of transition, only persisting remains for it." The environment turns static and the disposition of the individual becomes still, impeding the actualization of exteriority and interiority, giving rise to the uncanny. The unfamiliarity of the standing of time and the congealment of space pause the search for home; "we are held *more towards ourselves*, somehow enticed back into the specific gravity of Dasein."[27]

The third type of boredom is the most profound one, since it is "the more silent, the less public, the quieter, the more inconspicuous and wide-ranging."[28] To Heidegger, "*it* is boring for one" defines modernity by establishing the temperament and regulating the situatedness of being-in-the-world.[29] The extensiveness and commonality of profound boredom is compared, almost esoterically, to the repetitive and irrepressible processes of the cosmos and nature; the "it" of "*it* is boring for one" is the same "it" of "it is thundering" or "it is raining," designating an unrecognizable agent but a determinate effect. Therefore, "it" does not entail the abstraction of the individual but constitutes "an undifferentiated no one"—in boredom, "name, standing, vocation, role, age and fate as mine and yours disappear." The philosopher exemplifies this typology by affirming that "'it is boring for one' to walk through the streets of a large city on a Sunday afternoon." This non-binding case differs from waiting in a train station or attending a dinner party; it entails an exterior and continuous urban space, framed by buildings and infrastructure. Moreover, on this day of the week commercial and institutional architecture is unused because it responds to the capitalist cycle of production and consumption. The city appears abandoned and calm—far from being "annoying," it simply "is."[30]

For Heidegger, profound boredom resembles an entropic fog at the edge of a groundless abyss, with the capacity to invade and transform every space, inducing dizziness and uncertainty. To escape an impending fall, by blurring the boundaries between exteriority and interiority, "it is boring for one" allows the individual to become genuine, capable of identifying "*how things stand concerning us*," authentically and in complete freedom. Since everything turns existentially equidistant—"*equally great and equally little worth*"—the individual is relieved from the conventions of the quotidian, "*bringing* the *self* in all its nakedness *to itself*." Throughout this process, the world is not a scenography that "forms space in which beings can play their roles," a vessel "whose walls have nothing to do with the contents," or a "shell that has been placed over."³¹ Instead, profound boredom reveals the world as unique for each individual, with a sole core that situates everyone in a singular time and space—being aware of this location, "this resolute self-disclosure," is the "*moment of vision* [Augenblick]."³²

As a symptom of shallowness, superficiality, and meaningless busyness, boredom is modern, but as a resonance of the temporal horizon of existence, boredom is essential. The displeasure associated with boredom is a manifestation of the refusal of the individual, obfuscated by the prevailing distractions of modernity, to acknowledge the finitude of time. Paradoxically, the circumstances that contextualize and perpetuate boredom—including "social misery, political confusion, the powerlessness of science, the erosion of art, the groundlessness of philosophy, the impotence of religion"—obstruct the possibility of being-in-the-world. Boredom oppresses but its oppression constitutes "the very *absence of any essential oppressiveness* [Bedrängnis] *in our Dasein as a whole.*" For Heidegger, boredom results from the lack of ideologies or beliefs capable of directing existence; in modernity, "each and every one of us are servants of slogans, adherents to a program, but none is the custodian of the inner greatness of Dasein and its necessities. ... The *mystery* [Geheimnis] is lacking in our Dasein."³³ Eventually, the solution is to reinstall "mystery" in order to regain "inner terror" and establish a mutual belonging that demands collective action in the quest to liberate the individual from the neutral materialism of modernity and to procure an everyday life in unity with the world, thereby closer to home.³⁴

World-forming

This examination of boredom exposes humanity in enduring unity with the environment, since the concern with "how to exist" necessarily incorporates the question, "What is world?"³⁵ Problematizing this relation, boredom unfolds as a condition of space; time and temporality can only occur in the historical and architectural specificity of the surroundings, departing from ordinary everydayness so far as to bring being into question. This expansive capacity discloses the dependence of the condition on multiple dimensions—socioeconomic, cultural, and political as well as emotional and intellectual—as a cycle of cause and effect.

Opposed to the objectivity of mundus, the world emerges as "the totality of beings outside of and other than God."³⁶ By implication, the structures and organization of the built environment constitute a prolongation of being-in-the-world, constructed by human efforts and not derived from any divine force. Heidegger contends, "man also stands over against the world. This standing-over-against is a '*having*' of world as that in which man moves, with which he engages, which he both masters and serves, and to which he is exposed"; dissimilar to "the stone (material object) [that] is *worldless*" and "the animal [that] is *poor in world*," "man is *world-forming*."³⁷ The humanity of individuals allows the conscious design, production, and inhabitation of the built environment, instituting bonds with the surroundings and raising a concern with intentionality—the purpose of the creation of architecture and spatial circumstances. When the built environment responds to the need of finding home through processes that unify and free up the individual, then its existence is justified as an essential and genuine manifestation of being-in-the-world. However, when the production of architecture is speculative and aligned with aims different to those of overcoming the uncanniness of modernity, then its existence becomes redundant—profoundly boring.

CHAPTER 9
ORAN, THE CAPITAL OF BOREDOM*

In the writings by Albert Camus, boredom and modern architecture are encountered together. The built environment exudes boredom, contaminating everyday life; in a circular and self-referential manner, the condition is symptom and ailment. In *The Plague* (1947), Oran is portrayed as a restful city on the coast of Algeria, somnolent after failed attempts to install the accelerated rhythm of capitalist production and its modernity.[1] The buildings are orthogonal and unattractive, with "no vegetation" and "no soul," composing "a town without inklings, that is to say, an entirely modern town."[2] The same lethargy generated by the surroundings is imperative in *The Stranger* (1942). In a space imbued with monotony, Sunday afternoons offer respite when everyone goes to the cinema, and the streets become deserted. With the exception of "the shopkeepers and the cats," who invariably remain in their customary places, everyone looks for distraction in settings different from those inhabited during the rest of the week. The regular pace of work and rest allies with the repetitive cycles of nature to perpetuate boredom—the sky "alone is king," always clear and blue, intolerably dull.[3] In nature and the city, prosaic tedium institutes a terrain of apparent stasis that challenges mental stability; if every reality has multiple equivalents, then referential coordinates of existence disappear, to the point of rupturing protocols of social, moral, and ethical engagement. In *The Stranger*, a man is inexplicably killed by someone who is not only remorseless but also insanely bored. The criminal, deranged and dislocated, unemployed and without urgent preoccupations, escapes an empty house and becomes feverish under the implacable sun of North Africa.

Boredom is also effect and cause of modern architecture in "The Minotaur, or the Stop in Oran" (1939). Enthused by his trips from Algiers to Oran during his university days,[4] Camus describes the city as "the capital of boredom," "besieged by innocence and beauty," surrounded by nature that architects decidedly ignore; its constructions, flat and taut in both form and expression, protectively turn their backs to the ocean.[5] Rather than being a realm of latency, Oran is a realm of endless waiting where nothing happens and nothing is expected to occur. As a result, its inhabitants are simultaneously idle and restless: passive in their efforts to explore where they live yet vigorous in adopting imported models of behavior, acting as if they were in the United States of America. In between the built environment and the practices of its occupants, the Minotaur reigns in a labyrinth of boredom—a state of ambiguity and ambivalence that exposes absurdity. For Camus, Oran is a space of pause and delay, which corroborates the suspicion that, surpassing all efforts of rationalization, the world is unfathomable.[6]

Boredom, Architecture, and Spatial Experience

Figure 9.1 Oran from the fort of Santa Cruz (1930). Photograph by M. Lavina.

Labyrinthine Boredom

The alternate title of "The Minotaur" is "The Stop in Oran," denoting an omnipresent narrator who is forcibly or accidentally caught in the city, in a moment of rest in the journey to another destination. The foreign voice imposes critical distance, not only separating itself from the conditions of Oran and dissociating Oran from the rest of the world, but also creating a parenthetical space for reflection (Figure 9.1).[7] Within this enclosure, five sections tell an incomplete and anticlimactic story; "The Street," "The Desert of Oran," "Sports," "Monuments," and "Ariadne's Stone" diagnose and elliptically confirm boredom as the essence of the city. The condition is abundant and porous, permitting the infiltration of parallel dimensions and temporalities through the many fissures of modernity. Among the people of Oran, the twelve Apostles, protagonists from the novels by Nikolai Gogol and Gustave Flaubert and his friends, as well as temples from antiquity, the edifices of Florence and Athens, and many others, all meander like ghosts, luxuriant and eccentric figures that contrast with the scarcity and simplicity of the city:

> Atlas's task is easy; it is sufficient to choose one's hour. Then one realizes that for an hour, a month, a year, these shores can indulge in freedom. They welcome pell-mell, without even looking at them, the monk, the civil servant, or the conqueror. There are days when I expected to meet, in the streets of Oran, Descartes or Cesare Borgia.[8]

In "The Minotaur," boredom is a system of organization rather than a form, unceasingly informing the production of architecture and therefore characterizing Oran. Far from

Oran, the Capital of Boredom

being subjective, the condition is the result of a process of historical layering that, despite having been shaped by Spanish, Ottoman, and French invasions, has been unsuccessful in creating identity. It holds Oran in limbo, a dimension devoid not only of past and future but also of permanent materiality. Similar to being between one location and another, the city neither provides a stable "here" nor constitutes a significant "there"; instead, it establishes a field of suspension that paradoxically depends on the particularities of its architecture but is detached from its physical attributes.[9] Although unwanted at first, boredom turns incantatory and captivating, magnetically seducing the sensitive narrator, who becomes intrigued and perplexed with the possibilities of exploration, even rejoicing in them: "she bursts the unfortunate stage setting with which she is covered; she shrieks forth between all the houses and over all the roofs." Nonetheless, Oran defers engagement and immersion by deceivingly and reductively appearing as an amalgam of solid fences. In this space—challenging the immaterial, inspirational, and vertical connotations of ennui—boredom signals to the material, ordinary, and horizontal, without possibility of sublimation; "in the beginning you wander in the labyrinth, seeking the sea like the sign of Ariadne. But you turn round and round in pale and oppressive streets, and eventually the Minotaur devours the people of Oran: the Minotaur is boredom."[10]

Resonating with "The Labyrinth" (1936) by Georges Bataille, the boredom in Oran resembles a complex maze, "where what had suddenly come forward strangely loses its way."[11] The periphery attracts, acting centripetally, but while the border is initially simple and clear, it becomes convoluted and confusing as the center—a purely urban core of high-density avenues, streets, and blocks—approaches. To Bataille, if one city is annexed to another as a part of an empire, together they constitute a larger labyrinth, organized around the most modern—or boring—configuration. Ultimately, all settlements in the world are susceptible to unification under the same structure, installing the generic.

The Dustiest City

Oran is the opposite of Paris or London, capitals of fabricated excitement, full of the revolutions of the past that have produced many expressions and left many residues. For Camus, the boisterous exhibition of historical data constitutes a source of distraction and stimuli but not of significance. Regardless of their elaborate architecture, the cities of Europe are no more than silent wastelands that promote introspection and aloofness— "the great value of such overpopulated islands is that in them the heart strips bare. Silence is no longer possible except in noisy cities."[12] In this respect, Oran is simultaneously similar and different. The Algerian city is also made of stone, but its architecture exposes its mineral tincture by being formally simple and devoid of memory, lacking reverberations from previous eras. The buildings, haphazardly scattered over a rocky landscape, like a matrix of alien appearance, are incapable of suggesting more than their "heavy beauty." This "magnificent anarchy" is candidly arid, impossible to understand or redeem. Santa Cruz, for example, one of the three interconnected forts constructed in the sixteenth century, located in one of the highest geographical points, facing the bay, is "cut out of the rock, the mountains, the flat sea, the violent wind and the sun, the great cranes of the harbor, the trains, the hangars, the quays, and the huge ramps climbing up the city's rock, and in the city itself these diversions and this boredom, this hubbub and this solitude."[13]

The "very ugly constructions" configure a "walled town that turns its back, that has been built up by turning back on itself like a snail."[14] Reminiscent of the mollusk, Oran carries its architecture as an unchanging shelter. A contorted yellow wall protects the inhabitants from the persistence of nature, creating an "indifferent dialogue" between land and sea that produces too much despair as well as too much exhilaration. Because the people of Oran have forgotten how to live among the stones of nature, they have taken refuge among the stones created by themselves, with a sensibility closer to the coarse ground than to the smooth sky but with neither poetry nor spirituality; human development is outlawed and thus impossible to historicize. Camus observes that the opposition of the built environment to the natural surroundings constitutes the merit of Oran, demarcating a sanctuary of boredom, protected "by an army in which every stone is a soldier."[15]

In the "dustiest of cities" where "the pebble is king," the slowness of pre-modern time becomes evident in the obstinate presence of dust. The fine material covers and homogenizes the city and its contents, flying and resettling to subtly configure new surfaces. It moves if there is wind and its concentration changes if the weather varies; the streets become sandy in high temperatures and muddy when it rains. Furthermore, dust thickens the air—the few trees in the city have turned into "petrified plants whose branches give off an acrid, dusty smell." Unlike the gray pollution of the metropolis, the dust in Oran extends the ochre desert into the urban and architectural, instating untidiness, blurring the relation between standing figures, ground, and sky, mattifying and texturizing. The mineral coating "contributes to the dense and impassible universe in which the heart and mind are never distracted from themselves, nor from their sole object, which is man."[16]

Stone Monuments

Notwithstanding the dryness, the architecture of Oran is consistently extravagant, always with an "absurd look." The entirety of the fabricated environment—from buildings to furniture and even products for sale in shops—is vulgar and kitschy:

> All the bad taste of Europe and the Orient has managed to converge in them. One finds, helter-skelter, marble greyhounds, ballerinas with swans, versions of Diana the huntress in green galalith, discus-throwers and reapers, everything that is used for birthday and wedding gifts, the whole race of painful figurines constantly called forth by a commercial and playful genie on our mantelpieces.

Oran, the Capital of Boredom

Moreover, replicas and antiques abound, such as "plaster models of deformed feet," "a group of Rembrandt drawings 'sacrificed at 150 francs each,'" "an eighteenth-century pastel," "a mechanical donkey made of plush, bottles of Provence water for preserving green olives, and a wretched wooden virgin with an indecent smile." As material culture, this merchandise is neither more attractive nor more repellent than any other found in other cities. But in Oran, these objects do not serve as capital since commercial transactions scarcely occur, becoming instead static adornments, incapable of initiating any ritual of exchange. Analogously, cafés, restaurants, stores, and even funeral establishments constitute centers of waiting, as locations where space has conquered time and thus eliminated its passing. Even though their architectural arrangements have integrated international canons, they lack activity, abandoned to impassive dwellers whose lassitude prompts the question, "Can one be moved by a city where nothing attracts the mind, where the very ugliness is anonymous, where the past is reduced to nothing? Emptiness, boredom, an indifferent sky, what are the charms of such places?"[17]

Drawing from the existing architecture of the Algerian city, Camus identifies three types of monuments: civic buildings, busts and sculptures in public spaces, and modern infrastructure. The first category is exemplified by the Maison du Colon, built in 1902 on the former Karguentah farm that pioneered the plantation of tobacco (Figure 9.2). Designed by the architect Wolf to accommodate all agricultural institutions, the triangular plan responds to the shape of the site, defined in the late nineteenth century by the rails of two intersecting car-trams.[18] In the top, a prominent frieze ties the volume,

Figure 9.2 Maison du Colon (c. 1940). Unknown photographer. Courtesy of the Musée de l'Histoire vivante—Montreuil.

with an intermittent ribbon of colorful mosaics that depict not only the benefits of nature organized by human activity but also a fictional relationship of conviviality between local inhabitants and colonizers.[19] An inscription in the front reads, "To the glory of the colonization work of France," updated in 1930 with the addition, "Commemorating the centenary of Algeria." In its narrowest side, two tall columns create the main entrance, crowned by a pyramidal pinnacle that resembles an extruded labyrinth, redolent of the Minotaur. To the ironic narrator, the "delicate building" exhibits the three main virtues of the people of Oran—"boldness in taste, love of violence, and a feeling for historical syntheses." The syncretic style combines Egypt, Byzantium, and Munich to configure "a piece of pastry in the shape of a bowl upside down," historically insipid and, deceivingly, of neutral ideology.[20]

The second type of monument is the sculpted figures in squares. Contrasting with the Maison, the numerous "imperial marshals, ministers, and local benefactors" are faithful to their historical specificity. Their static temporality quarantines them, materializing the boring rather than the heroic. As irrelevant headstones, the solid tributes to the past do not succeed in establishing relations with the present, being instead territorial markers imposed by foreign civilizations. The exception to these unconvincing objects are two lions flanking the main door of the Place d'Armes. Crafted by the artist Cain in 1888, they are of low artistic value; their faces are "hilarious snouts in the square of a mercantile province overseas."[21] However, they are cherished by the people of Oran, and their representative force exceeds their material insignificance. The lions are repositories of legend and memory, echoing the Arabic term *Wahran*, which means "two lions"; like the stony dignitaries, the sculpted animals embody the will of the ephemeral to last, but unlike the human models, they are majestic and alive.[22] The residents believe they become animated at midnight to parade around the building and mark their domain. In case of catastrophe, the lions would be saved and preserved—"they have the same chances as the ruins of Angkor."[23]

The third kind of monument is that of modern public works that structure the coast for ten kilometers. More than edifices and statues, such assembly contribute to "transforming the most luminous of bays into a gigantic harbour." This enterprise is not concerned with planning or progress. For the observer in "The Minotaur," the construction of infrastructure is an excuse for the locals to be in contact with stone and produce dust, the most genuine testament of the city. The exploitation and transformation of the nearby mines satisfy their disquiet and their need to act—"one must choose doing that or nothing."[24]

Despite its publicness, this architectural triad is timid and introverted. The collision of idiosyncratic temporalities causes rhythmical incompatibility; the structures are self-indulgent, uninteresting, and too familiar, with components unable to resonate with each other or to extend their influence to spaces beyond their immediacy. In Oran, municipal buildings, open areas, and roads are variations of the same condition of fracture, seclusion, and delay. Contrary to the suspense of the future, they operate within the limits of the present, inept in the task of evoking an alternate reality.

Oran, the Capital of Boredom

Without Ariadne or Theseus

In the myth of the Minotaur, Ariadne falls in love with Theseus, the slayer of the half-bull creature who escapes the labyrinth with the help of a thread provided by the infatuated woman. If the Minotaur is boredom and the labyrinth is Oran, as explored by Camus, then evading the first requires staying within and then navigating out of the space of the second. Nevertheless, the inhabitants of the Algerian city are not willing to leave. They dwell in the labyrinth, immersed in the boredom inflicted by the Minotaur but unaware of their circumstance. Since Ariadne and Theseus are not present to strategize the rescue, apathy surfaces to instigate social anonymity; "the result is such that the only instructive circles remain those of poker-players, boxing enthusiasts, bowlers, and the local associations."[25]

In Oran, boredom is contagious, inhibiting thinking and feeling, evident in the public sphere. Interpersonal relations, saturated with the condition, promote a mode of alertness that lingers in the outside world. The fixation with exteriority oppresses, paralyzing ontological movement and thus pausing the processes of interiority.[26] Stagnation favors boredom, and the boredom of Oran defies not only the Cartesian proposition of "I think, therefore I am" but also its equivalent, "I feel, therefore I am."[27] To avoid internal confrontation, the residents turn their attention to other residents.

The interest in the other compels occupation, simply to pass the time. For Camus, the adopted practices of the inhabitants of Oran are superfluous and directed to avoid monotony, framed by encouraging façades painted with devious advertisements that proclaim non-boringness—"sumptuous," "splendid," "extraordinary," "amazing," "staggering," and "tremendous" are common adjectives in billboards and signs. Embodying these epithets, a parade of male youngsters get their shoes shined to display them to their female counterparts on the boulevard. With approximations to the aesthetics of American films, the "softhearted gangsters" find solace from boredom in the acting of an imported reality, dressing up and strutting:

> With wavy, oiled hair protruding from under a felt hat slanted over the left ear and peaked over the right eye, the neck encircled by a collar big enough to accommodate the straggling hair, the microscopic knot of the necktie kept in place by a regulation pin, with thigh-length coat and waist close to the hips, with light-colored and noticeably short trousers, with dazzlingly shiny triple-soled shoes, every evening those youths make the sidewalks ring with their metal-tipped shoes.

Known as the "Clarques" for their imitation of "the bearing, forthrightness, and superiority of Mr Clark Gable," they are accompanied by "Marlenes."[28] Although the young women flaunt their make-up, also movie inspired, their faces are emotionless, always staring to the horizon. The facial ornamentation is consonant with the bright patina of the shoes of the male adolescents and the enticing colors of the posters that offer adventure. In all cases, by being flamboyant and thin, the pictorial surfaces constitute excuses for facile sociability, distracting rather than engaging.

While the young circles of Oran extend their leisure activities from the city to the ocean—"at eleven a.m., coming down from the plateau, all that young flesh, lightly clothed in motley materials, breaks on the sand like a multicolored wave"—the working men gather around a boxing ring.[29] The closeness to the quadrangular stage unveils relations of social power, yet the surrounding space serves as a container of fraternity and naïve morality. Having to decide which boxer to support demands involvement with others, contracting the distance of the purely spectacular between actors and public and therefore providing a sense of shared purpose, with the possibility of emotional release.[30] Boxing attunes the spectators, mostly men of European descent, to a self-induced state of fascination that does not expose private vulnerabilities.[31] During the fight, the attendees compose an unfolding narrative that requires collaboration and concentration, anticipating bodily movements and speculating about strategies of attack, as if the result could be logically predicted.[32]

The event takes place in the Central Sporting Club, on the rue du Fondouk. The building appears improvised, "in the back of a sort of whitewashed garage, covered with corrugated iron and violently lighted."[33] In line with the Arabic *fondouk*, meaning "inn," the space provides a temporary shelter that induces expression.[34] The hermetic walls permit loudness, fusing songs by Tino Rossi with the chants of the crowd to produce a deafening and inchoate sound. Simultaneously, the enclosure creates an ambiance of sentimentality that transforms the event into an act of social memory; one of the "young hopefuls" is from Oran and the other from Algiers. Likened by the narrator to the rivalry between Pisa and Florence, the contestants become civic representatives of historical and political tension, re-enacting a hundred-year-old conflict. In addition, since witnessing the combat from the periphery of the arena does not provide sufficient catharsis, spontaneous fights ensue between members of the public—"chairs are brandished, the police clear a path, excitement is at its height." Nonetheless, gradually, after the climax of the first match, the second reinstates sobriety, resynchronizing the audience with the ordinary tempo:

> The band of faithfuls is now no more than a group of black-and-white shadows disappearing into the night. For force and violence are solitary gods. They contribute nothing to memory. On the contrary, they distribute their miracles by the handful in the present. They are made for this race without past which celebrates its communions around the prize ring. These are rather difficult rites but ones that simplify everything. Good and evil, winner and loser. At Corinth two temples stood side by side, the temple of Violence and the temple of Necessity.[35]

In Oran, not being bored is an unusual condition, only achieved by those in the labyrinth who know how to find a space of exception. In between sparse moments of distraction, waiting becomes the dominant disposition, perpetuating sameness by refusing creation and destruction as well as transcendence and transgression. The inhabitants coherently defend boredom, suggesting that their identity depends on absence rather than presence, by remaining within the boundaries of the city, unwilling to realize that nothingness is as unfeasible as fullness: "like that friend of Flaubert who, on the point of death … exclaimed: 'Close the window; it's too beautiful.' They have closed the window, they have walled themselves in, they have cast out the landscape."[36]

Awaiting Oran

Although "The Minotaur" was written in 1939, it was not published until 1954. In an introductory note, Camus dedicates the essay to Pierre Galindo, the alleged informant of the assassination narrated in *The Stranger*, and briefly reconsiders the portrayal of Oran.[37] He pledges that the city has changed, since "all the imperfections have been (or will be) remedied."[38] At the onset of the Algerian war, the built environment remained intact—"jealously respected"—steeping the space with boredom and therefore propelling radical change, ending the period of waiting and entering a new reality independent from France.[39] Camus does not support the separation but rather is in favor of an increased political autonomy that envisioned communal wellbeing and cohabitation with the past, and so he liberates Oran from its distinctive lethargy. The transformed city is a site of possibility—beautiful, happy, and truthful—no longer in need of taciturn writers but instead expecting tourists who will lionize its architecture.

CHAPTER 10
INTERNATIONAL STYLE CONFUSIONS: SIGFRIED GIEDION

The concern with how emotions relate to architecture, before and after its materialization, frames the architectural historiography by Sigfried Giedion. He employs instances of art and processes of mechanization to support an account of the modern built environment characterized by the lack of synchronization between interiority and exteriority. In the foreword to the fourth edition of *Space, Time and Architecture* (1941), Giedion affirms himself preoccupied with "contemporary man's separation between thinking and feeling—with his split personality—and with the unconscious parallelism of methods employed in art and science." Recapitulating the argument developed in *Mechanization Takes Command* (1948), the dichotomies between "thinking and feeling" and "inner and outer reality" are posed as problems produced by modernization, namely the effects of industrial production, which might be solved "by re-establishing the dynamic equilibrium that governs their relationships."[1]

Despite stressing that architecture has emotional origins and sequels, Giedion does not elaborate on any specific sentiment. Instead, as an overarching approach rather than as a resolute observation, he either points towards positive and enjoyable conditions of inhabitation as the goal of architectural design, or exposes undesired moments of confusion and exhaustion as negative expressions of the modern era. In "The Need for a New Monumentality" (1944), celebratory architecture typifies the emotionality of the built environment. Opening the article with the epigraph "Motto: Emotional training is necessary today. For whom? First of all for those who govern and administer the people," the essay looks back to the nineteenth century as a period of crisis and "pseudo-monumentality" that failed to produce radical meaning. In Giedion's view, architects were undirected, repeating "shapes from bygone periods . . . for any kind of building." The configurations of the past turned into "mere clichés without emotional justification" or symbolism; secularization endangered and slowed the design of cathedrals and churches, and the emerging nation-states ended the construction of palaces. Analogous to the disconnection between inner and outer life, interior spaces became separated from their exterior expression, confusing public taste due to the promotion of eclecticism and the banalization of architecture. For the historian, the modern condition originated in the indiscriminate proliferation of all monumental motifs of the past—"in ancient Greece monumentality was used rarely and then only to serve the gods and, to a certain extent, the life of the community."[2]

Accordingly, the lack of creativity in the nineteenth century led to the loss of referential coordinates in the early twentieth century. The new sentiments of anomie, anxiety, and boredom, intensified by the developments of urbanization, forced the reconsideration of "monumental edifices."[3] Rather than trying to renovate them, architects turned their attention to the everyday with "joy and excitement," designing market halls, factories, and exhibition buildings; "there was no denying that they lacked the splendour of buildings of bygone periods, which had been nourished by handicraft and a long tradition. They were naked and rough, but they were true. Nothing else could have served as the point of departure for a language of our own."[4]

Those experiments that insisted on the monumental only provided redundancy since the feelings and attitudes they represented belonged to the past. To Giedion, this architecture became irrelevant, desynchronized with the spirit of the epoch, and therefore incapable of projecting an accurate image of society. Comparable to Napoleon Bonaparte's reputation of a "self-made man," "imitating the manner of a former ruling class" and "inwardly uncertain," the outdated model of repetition was the scheme for a civic building proposed by J. N. L. Durand. In his series of lectures *Précis de leçons d'architecture* (1801–5), which were translated, reprinted, and used internationally, a diagrammatic drawing presents a colonnade in the front, with a higher section in the back, crowned by a dome in the middle. The symmetrical composition was intended for any program, whether cultural or political, and for any European capital, to "whatever consequences it may lead."[5] In "The Need for a New Monumentality," this typology is epitomized by the Haus der Deutschen Kunst (1937) in Munich by Paul Ludwig Troost, the Mellon Institute (1937) in Pittsburgh by Benno Janssen, and the League of Nations (1935) in Geneva, a collaboration of Carlo Broggi, Julien Flegenheimer, Camille Lefèvre, Henri Paul Nénot, and Joseph Vago, the five architects shortlisted in the international competition of 1920. Giedion disregards the agency of the creators by omitting their names and crediting only Adolf Hitler in the caption for the photograph of the Haus der Deutschen Kunst, blaming "*those who govern and administer*" for the existence of architecture that followed a 140-year-old canon.[6]

In *Architecture, You and Me* (1958), Giedion included a revised version of the essay, highlighting not only the capacity of architecture to represent common values but also the vulnerability of those who experience it. To contribute to the "emotional training" of everyone and avoid the construction of anachronistic structures that perpetuate the disconnection between institutions and citizens, buildings should be long-lasting constructions capable of fostering communality, particularly civic centers.[7] Surrounded by greenery, separated from slums, and financed by collective efforts, these buildings are free from capitalism and any understanding of cities "as mere agglomerations of jobs and traffic lights."[8] Through dedicated design, the connection between thinking and feeling could be re-established, becoming an organizational system capable of providing continuity and constancy rather than superficiality, ephemerality, and unstable change; "in other words—as a result of bitter experiences—we are concerned to know what can be changed and what can not be changed in human nature without disturbing its equipoise." Comparing architects to psychologists, Giedion poses the production of the built environment as the means to reach the emotional apparatus of the average individual. By avoiding repetitious configurations that lead to a deficit of meaning—boredom—"the inherent, though unconscious, feeling may slowly be awakened by the original expression of a new community life."[9]

Superficialities of All Kinds

The separation between methods of thinking and methods of feeling turned specific in the introduction of *Space, Time and Architecture*, added in December 1961. Titled "Architecture of the 1960's: Hopes and Fears," it begins with "Confusion and Boredom," a subsection of six paragraphs dedicated to showing how the two sentiments prevail as the outlining qualities of mid-twentieth century architecture. Giedion defines confusion, manifested in the focus on the present and on escapist "superficialities of all kinds," as "uncertainty, what to do and where to go." Unlike this precise explanation, the definition of boredom is diffuse, attendant rather than independent, as an umbrella condition that covers the many effects of the loss of direction and orientation—the fatigue that indicates depletion of creativity, the total expenditure of intellectual and emotional resources. Confusion and boredom act together as a unit, demanding the revaluation of the practice of architecture as well as its interpretation by critics and theorists; the crisis is disciplinary and "everyone is aware of it."[10]

To investigate "if and how modern architecture should evolve," Giedion refers to the symposium "The International Style—Death or Metamorphosis?," held in New York in the spring of 1961. Without discussing the event in detail, the historian challenges the premise that the architecture of the International Style is a fashion that has "grown thin," as indicated by the title. To him, this misapprehension has a valid origin but an erroneous implication. It suggests that the exhaustion with this kind of architecture has occurred not only because it is "everywhere"—"in smallbreasted, gothic-styled colleges, in a lacework of glittering details inside and outside, in the toothpick stilts and assembly of isolated buildings of the largest cultural center"—but also because its careless iteration has favored "a romantic orgy" of "playboy architecture," demarcated by the "random" combination of fragments of the past, "jumping from one sensation to another and quickly bored with everything."[11] These historicist examinations are posed as transient but dangerous due to their capacity to extend from the United States to the world, becoming canonical. Although the name of the symposium exposes the International Style as a school of design that has reached its highest point—vulnerable to decay and extinction—Giedion asserts that this architecture is in a formative period, neither constituting a "style" nor being "international," since it is "hovering in mid-air, with no roots anywhere."[12] Alternatively, the International Style has to be undertaken as an "approach," unrelated to particular configurations and formal expressions but concerned with the "interpretation of a way of life valid for our period." Since "there can only be the question of evolving a new tradition," the concern with "death or metamorphosis" is untenable.[13]

The Symposium

The symposium "The International Style—Death or Metamorphosis?" was organized by the Architectural League of New York and sponsored by *Architectural Forum*, a monthly magazine. It was part of a series of five public and non-profit events called "The New

THE ARCHITECTURAL LEAGUE OF NEW YORK
115 East 40th Street
New York 16, New York

"The New Forces in Architecture"

A Series of Forums arranged by the Architectural League of New York

<u>THE INTERNATIONAL STYLE - Death or Metamorphosis</u>
Thursday, March 30th, 8:30 P.M.

Panelists:
<u>Reyner Banham</u>
    England's brilliant and outspoken "Shaw of Architecture", Assistant Executive Editor of the Architectural Review of London, is flying over especially for this epic discourse. Having referred to much of U.S. architecture as "Ballet Dancing" he will no doubt subject the recent past and the present to a witty scourge for its sins and aberrations.
<u>Philip C. Johnson</u>
    One of modern architecture's great architects as well as one of its most important interpreters and spokesmen, will no doubt see the past and the future in a very different light from Banham's emphasis on the technological age and its responsibilities.

<u>INDIVIDUAL EXPRESSION versus ORDER - The Issue in Architecture Today</u>
Thursday, April 20th, 8:30 P.M.

Panelists:
<u>Aline B. Saarinen</u>
    Author and influential critic of architecture, is in a unique position to discuss the dilemma of architecture today.
<u>Marcel Breuer</u>
    Brilliant designer, distinguished architect and formgiver of modern architecture. Breuer's work encompasses the period from the late twenties to the present and therefore brings perspective to any endeavor.
<u>Paul M. Rudolph</u>
    One of the most important young men in architecture today. Head of the School of Architecture at Yale.

August Heckscher - Executive Director of the Twentieth Century Fund, will be moderator for both meetings.

Both forums will be in the handsome and comfortable Grace Rainey Rogers Auditorium of the Metropolitan Museum of Art, Fifth Avenue at 82nd Street, whose policy strictly limits the number of tickets sold. Reservations ($2.00 each) are now available at the Architectural League, 115 East 40th Street, N.Y.C. 16. The programs will <u>not</u> be broadcast on the dates presented, though they will be taped for later use on <u>East</u> and West Coast radio stations.

We are confident you will find these forums even more stimulating than the three lively discussions which have preceded them in this widely acclaimed series. Won't you send your check or drop by the League for your tickets today?

For The Architectural League

Figure 10.1 Press release for the symposium 'The International Style—Death or Metamorphosis?' (1961). Archives of American Art, Smithsonian Institution. Architectural League of New York records, 1880s–1974; 1960 League-Sponsored Functions and Events. Box 88. Folder 39, "New Forces in Architecture," 1960–1.

International Style Confusions: Sigfried Giedion

```
T H E   A R C H I T E C T U R A L   L E A G U E   O F   N E W   Y O R K

                    invites you to attend

                  a reception and Buffet Supper


                  AUGUST HECKSCHER - Moderator

                         Guest Speakers

                Reyner Banham, Executive Editor of the
                      Architectural Review in England

                Philip Johnson, Architect , A.I.A.

                 on the fourth of a series of Forums

                          presented by

                The Architectural League of New York

                              and

                      Architectural Forum

              SUBJECT - "THE INTERNATIONAL STYLE - DEATH OR
                              METAMORPHOSIS"


      Thursday         March 30, 1961          Jose A. Fernandez, Chairman
      Cocktails        6:00 P.M.               Ulric Franzen, Co-Chairman
      Buffet Supper    7:00 P.M.
      Price            5.25                    Current Work Committee

      Reservations not cancelled three (3) days in advance will be charged.

      Buses depart at 8:00 P.M. for the Forum session.
```

```
      THE ARCHITECTURAL LEAGUE OF NEW YORK, 115 East 40 Street, New York 16, New York

      "INTERNATIONAL STYLE - DEATH OR METAMORPHOSIS"   THURSDAY, MARCH 30, 1961

           I shall_____ shall not_____ attend the Buffet

           Please reserve_____ place(s).


                            _____
                            Please Print Name

           Check to accompany reservations
```

Figure 10.2 Invitation to the cocktail reception and dinner for the symposium "The International Style—Death or Metamorphosis?" (1961). Archives of American Art, Smithsonian Institution. Architectural League of New York records, 1880s–1974; 1960 League-Sponsored Functions and Events. Box 88. Folder 39, "New Forces in Architecture," 1960–1.

Forces of Architecture," which took place from October 1960 to April 1961.[14] According to Douglas P. Haskell, editor of the publication, the dominating question in the debates was "How does today's architecture best fit in nature, in the city, in time, in style, in character?"[15] Scheduled at 8.30 pm and with a cost of $2 (US) per session or $8 for the series if bought in advance,[16] each evening featured a discussion among high-profile guest speakers, moderated by August Heckscher, a political activist and then executive director of the Twentieth Century Fund.[17] Before the main event, with an additional cost of $5.25 and by invitation only, the Architectural League hosted a cocktail reception from 6 to 7 pm, followed by a "buffet supper" from 7 to 8 pm, and then a bus ride to the venue (Figures 10.1 and 10.2). In the letters of invitation, the pre-symposium gatherings were described as an opportunity to "contribute to a wider feeling of participation in League affairs among our members."[18]

To deliver these objectives—the mapping of the situation of architecture, the promotion of the League, professional interaction—each night had a different theme, probably proposed by the chairman, José A. Fernández, and the co-chairman, Ulrich Franzen, and approved by the president of the League, Robert W. Cutler.[19] The first meeting was titled "Critique: Environment and Act," held on October 27 with the participation of Vincent Scully Jr. The second, on December 8, was "The New Art of Urban Design—Are We Equipped?," with Catherine Baner Wurster, Josep L. Sert, Louis I. Kahn, and Ernest Van den Haag. The third evening, on February 16, was a conversation, "Art in Our Society," between Peter Blake, Leslie Hyams, Samuel M. Kootz, and Jack Levine; unlike the others, it was moderated by Ralph E. Colin, an attorney active in the cultural life of New York.[20] On March 30, the fourth meeting presented Philip Johnson and Reyner Banham, who pondered modern architecture in a duel called "The International Style—Death or Metamorphosis?" The final session featured Marcel Breuer, Aline Saarinen, and Paul Rudolph in "Individual Expression Versus Order—The Issue in Architecture," on April 20. While the third and fifth gatherings were held at the "handsome and comfortable" Grace Rainey Rogers Auditorium at the Metropolitan Museum of Art, the other three took place in different venues; "the locales of the evenings varied architecturally from the steep capaciousness of Harrison & Abramovitz' Caspary Auditorium at the Rockefeller Institute to the Italianate uncalm of Gio Ponti's auditorium in the Time and Life Building (with two of the evenings at the Metropolitan Museum's larger, more neutral auditorium)."[21]

The *Architectural Forum* described the series as successful, attracting "crowds of eager listeners, sometimes overflowing the appointed spaces."[22] The audience was varied, tending towards the elite but mixing academics, members of the press, practitioners, delegates of the construction industry, and even union authorities. The discussions were "hot at times," with "definite" opinions.[23] Among the attendants who purchased tickets for the series were George S. Barrows and Mary Jane Lightbown of the Department of Architecture and Design of MoMA; Dora Brahms, architect of interiors; Peter W. Eller, chairman of the Board of Governors of the Building Trades Employers Association; Peter Flack, founder of Skyscraper Outfitting; Edward L. Friedman, architect at I. M. Pei & Associates; Geoffrey Hellman, reporter at *The New Yorker*; Jean Koefoed, publisher; Ben H. Krey, electrical engineer; Sibyl Moholy-Nagy, art and architectural historian;

International Style Confusions: Sigfried Giedion

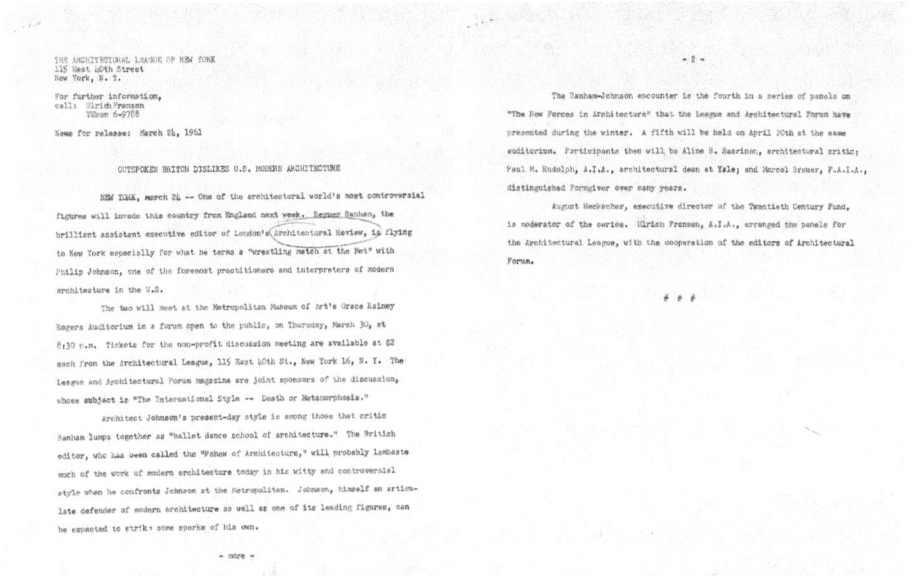

Figure 10.3 Press release titled "Outspoken Briton Dislikes U.S. Architecture" (March 24, 1961). Douglas Putnam Haskell papers, 1866–1979 (bulk 1949–64), Avery Architectural & Fine Arts Library, Columbia University.

Benjamin Moscowitz, co-founder of de Young, Moscowitz & Rosenberg; Ralph A. Partan, independent architect; Walther Prokosch, partner of Tippets, Abbott, McCarthy, Strattony; Wallace H. Randolph, architectural writer; William C. Shopsin, author and preservationist; and Richard W. Snibbe, cofounder of Ballard, Todd & Snibbe.[24]

Under the responsibility of the co-chairman, a press release for "The International Style—Death or Metamorphosis?" was distributed on March 24, six days before the event (Figure 10.3). Focusing on Banham's visit, the heading reads "Modern Briton Dislikes U.S. Modern Architecture." The historian is introduced as "one of the architectural world's most controversial figures" and is nicknamed the "Pshaw of Architecture," denoting an impatient and contemptuous character of "witty and controversial style."[25] In a more composed manner, his counterpart is characterized as "one of the foremost practitioners and interpreters of modern architecture in the U.S." and as "an articulate defender of modern architecture." Banham is quoted as having referred to "Johnson's present-day style" as a "ballet dance school of architecture," not only victimizing the architect but also suggesting that American architecture was amateur, superficial, and aspirational. In the same sensationalist tone and as if the event would be a popular spectacle, the encounter is posed as a "wrestling match at the Met"; the press release promised that Banham "will probably lambaste much of the work of modern architecture," but Johnson "can be expected to strike some sparks of his own."[26] In an earlier description of the "epic discourse" prepared by the League as part of their dissemination campaign, Banham is depicted as a "brilliant and outspoken" critic who

93

"will no doubt subject the recent past and the present to a witty scourge for its sins and aberrations," with emphasis on "the technological age and its responsibilities."[27]

The magazine covered the series in two sections of the June 1961 issue. The first was in the introductory note "In the Forum," written by the editor. Contrasting with the confusion and boredom diagnosed by Giedion, Haskell denounces "the current nonsense about there being a formless 'chaoticism' (what a horrible word formation!)." Instead of tiredness, the editor identifies diversity and richness of expression, since "barriers have broken down and ideas are blossoming in profusion," defying "the one-liners, the single-thoughters, panacea-mongers, and art puritans." As such, the predicament was one not of creativity but of categorization. Haskell declares that critics and academics ought to understand that modern architecture is "what modern architects made" rather than "a single dogma"; the quality of the built environment does not depend on aesthetical uniformity but on the capacity of "formgivers"—"not just one"—to create architecture that "fits."[28] Suitably, the second article is titled "Architecture—Fitting and Befitting" (Figure 10.4). Composed of excerpts from selected interventions of four of the five symposia, it portrays them as occasions where "the pundits are pondering both the physical problems and appropriateness of current design trends."[29] In the space dedicated to "The International Style—Death or Metamorphosis?," the transcribed passages from the speeches by Johnson and Banham appear below their photographs.[30] The former, in photojournalist style, has an expression of attention, as if he would be listening to someone, in an eventful environment; the latter, in a traditional portrait, poses authoritatively, with a black background (Figure 10.4).[31]

Always Bored Johnson

Recognizing his influence in the naming and consolidation of the International Style, the summary of the talk by Philip Johnson focuses on the continuity of the trend and on the design of buildings. The architect, always questioned for his varied style affiliations and who in 1996 declared that the force behind all his efforts in architecture was "a desire to be famous, and a hatred of boredom," distinguishes "three quite interesting ways of doing architectural design right now, intertwined, none of them a style."[32] The first and "strongest" is the "grand, modern, 40-year tradition" of the International Style—a label "reviled by Giedion"—left unexplained by Johnson so as to avoid defining "style" while justifying its inclusion in the label of the revered movement.[33] The second and third emerging "ways" of architecture constitute Johnson's attempt to establish connections with Britain and, by inference, with Banham. Brutalism—"not a good name, but a name"—and Neohistoricism—"the other popular direction"—are rendered as "attitudes" and not as "ways of forming." Yet, focusing on the creation of form, Brutalism is described as "apt to bring us great concrete beams—muscle-flexing, one English critic calls it—and tiny windows, funny shaped, scattered in great brick walls. Much inside and outside movement, and a great many pieces of concrete exposed." Without detailing its aesthetic qualities, Neohistoricism is defended against those who claim that "this idea of a return

International Style Confusions: Sigfried Giedion

Figure 10.4 "Architecture—Fitting and Befitting," excerpts of the speeches delivered by Philip Johnson and Reyner Banham at the symposium "The International Style—Death or Metamorphosis?" *Architectural Forum* (June 1961), 86–7.

to an interest in history is a slap at the whole Modern Movement, capital M capital M."[34] Probably by then already "bored with Mies" and foreseeing his venture into postmodernism, Johnson applauds the return of history as "a proper study"—"we cannot today *not* know history.... It's a stimulating and new feeling of freedom."[35] For the architect, the inclusion of the past in the present and future of the discipline opens possibilities of diversity, avoiding homogeneity:

> We no longer have to judge buildings by how little or how much history they have in them.... It is not new-Baroque, it is not anti-international, it's not anti-modern, it's only faintly anti-functionalist. It is also slightly anti-rational ... but in being anti-rational, aren't we following merely in the philosophical trend of our day? ... We have no wish to revolt against the past; we can acknowledge the leadership of our great elders. But we can be freer.[36]

Never Bored Banham

Sixteen years Johnson's junior, Banham traveled to the United States for the first time to participate in the symposium.[37] Since the League did not have information on the critic—"in the FORUM files, Time bio files, and he's not listed in Who's Who and other directories"—his publicist provided facts about his life over the phone.[38] In addition to his date and place of birth, education, and publications, private details were divulged about Banham's professional interest in technology and science—"he is married; has two children. His hobbies are watching car races; cleaning his wife's bubble car, and reading scientific magazines. His father created a family motto: 'If it has wheels we are interested.'"[39]

Unlike Johnson's stress on forming, the transcribed selection of Banham's speech reveals his concern with what happens once buildings are constructed, arguing that "behind the diversification of architecture" there is "a diversification of sociological and other human impulses." To him, the role of architects is thus less connected with developing and assembling aesthetical theories and more with posing fundamental questions of inhabitation: "How do people live? How are these ways of living viable? How can we create buildings which will enable them to develop the potentialities of that matter of living?" These questions are far from the understanding of architecture as the creation of "a single style or even a graded series of styles," and are instead closer to the conceptualization of the discipline as the design of conditions of space. Banham recalls the first "Congrés international d'architecture moderne" (CIAM), held in 1928 in La Sarraz, in which Le Corbusier and Giedion participated, and its prescription of standards for architecture and town planning—"what people should expect: you know, sun, space, trees, reinforced concrete, things like that." These "basics of the good life," of the "good old days," differed from the explorations of the last CIAM, held in 1959 in Otterlo. With a tone antagonistic to normative formulations, "people brought actual projects they were working on" to this event: "this is what people in Italy were doing for the peasants in the south; this is what people in England were proposing for the traffic planning of London, and so on."[40]

Although seemingly following Johnson's affirmation that "style" was metamorphosing into "attitude," Banham's speech is informed by the forces that produce architecture rather than by the specific mannerisms of its formal expressions. Encouraging the collaboration with other specialties—"not only of sociologists but of biological studies and things like that"—the British critic appeals for a "scientifically humane attitude," capable of constructing architecture "for men and by men."[41]

The Very Backbone of Human Society

On April 15, six weeks before "The International Style—Death or Metamorphosis?," Giedion delivered the first Walter Gropius Lecture at Harvard University Graduate School of Design. Titled "Constancy, Change and Architecture," it not only contained the same argument posed in "Confusion and Boredom," using almost the same text, but also followed the twofold division of the volumes of *The Eternal Present* (1964)—"The Beginnings of Art" and "The Beginnings of Architecture."[42] In the former, architecture is compared to entertainment and mass media, condemning frivolous change:

At the present time the problem of constancy is of special consequence, since the threads of the past and of tomorrow have been brought into disorder by an incessant demand for change for change's sake. We have become worshipers of the day-to-day. Life runs along like a television program: one show following relentlessly upon another, barely glancing at problems with never a notion of taking hold of them organically. This has led to an inner uncertainty, to extreme shortcomings in all essential phases of life: to what Heidegger calls "a forgetfulness of being."[43]

Hence, to activate the meaningful in architecture, history is reinstalled, surpassing the purely descriptive. The study of antiquity is actualized by being contrasted to the present and the present is contextualized by establishing connections with the past. For instance, the experimental phase of the Egyptian pyramids is likened to the period "from the beginning of iron construction to the Eiffel Tower." Similarly, the size of the hypostyle in Karnak is portrayed as "large enough to accommodate the entire cathedral of Notre Dame in Paris," and the weight of the Ptolemaic Pylon I of the great temple of Amon as equal to "an early Chicago skyscraper."[44] Giedion overlays different temporalities of architecture to separate the constant from the temporary; what does not change is the fundamental capacity of buildings to symbolize and represent, and what varies is the fashionable and forgettable.

In the lecture, after identifying the confusion and exhaustion in the discipline—without explicitly referring to boredom—Giedion illustrates redundant architecture with regional movements, which are different from the universalizing International Style. The interest in "coziness" of balconies and porches of the "New Empiricism" in Sweden, the "Bay Region Style" in the United States, and the "golden nineties" of "the second-hand beauties of New York Public Library's cast-iron candelabras and the sculptures on the pediments of Grand Central Terminal" are symptomatic of gratuitous variation. They appear impure and inessential, "parallel with the present tendency to enliven a façade by the use of fragments of historical styles thus often messing up a perfectly good plan as well as publicising a lack of creative imagination." These experimentations are the result of doubt and the understanding of history as a pattern book rather than as the change of space in time, "contradictory to the real meaning of contemporary architecture." Without speculating on what could be the appropriate new order, Giedion recognizes a deficit of significance in the built environment and implies that architecture should be assertive. Comparable to Heidegger's diagnosis of boredom as a malady so deeply rooted in modernity that it has become imperceptible, "confusion and exhaustion" derive from "the approach of man today" and thus govern and reinforce every production of the built environment. They are not properties of architecture but rather are embedded in architecture, as a cultural expression that has turned into a complicit enabler of the processes of modernization—"architecture ... provides the corporal and the psychic shelter for this formation."[45]

To Giedion, constancy and change are evident in the variety of architecture throughout history; "the very different creations of the Romans, of Mediaeval man, and of the

Baroque period reflect the constantly changing relations between man and the outer world." Although human existence is outlined by change—aging, weather, systems of government, and interpersonal ties—what remains invariable are the attempts to reach "equilibrium between man and his environment, between inner and outer reality." These efforts are "never static," always "involved in continuous change ... like a tight-rope dancer who, by small adjustments, maintains a precarious balance between his being and the empty void."[46] Constancy entails continuation, persistence, and "the ability of the human mind suddenly to bring to life things that have been left slumbering through long ages"; "for us to establish our position at the present time—which has closer ties with the whole of the human past than any other period before it—it is essential to understand the continuity through the past, present, and future."[47]

In this manner, while space constitutes the invariable component of architecture—infinite and neutral, the most fundamental condition capable of being manipulated and populated—architecture fluctuates and exposes different attitudes toward space. The built environment is therefore expressive, defined by objects vulnerable to being perceived as boring. They can be of different styles, repeating the past or constructing what has not been imagined yet, producing clarity or confusion—both experiential and in the discipline—as well as perpetuating their presence or promoting their own replacement. Giedion remarks, "the effect of this transfiguration which lifts space into the realm of the emotions is termed space conception." Acting as archives of history, space conceptions expose how the relationships with the built environment have morphed; they are "instinctive," "unconscious to [their] authors," and "compulsive," providing "an insight into the attitude of a period to the cosmos, to man and to eternal values."[48] The advent of verticality in ancient Egypt, the most important space conception in history, not only responded to its symbolic directionality that points towards the sky but also to the emergence of a social hierarchy.[49] Through the development of spatial relations between ascending terraces, the progression from the horizontal—"the line of repose"—to the vertical—"the line of movement"—reflects a new political order susceptible to and responsible for numerous architectural stylistic expressions.[50]

While Göller and Wölfflin suggested that an interest in space, light, and atmosphere is a property of modern architecture, Giedion poses those conditions as the essential components of all architecture throughout history: "light and space are inseparable. If light is eliminated, the emotional content of space disappears. In the dark there is no difference between the emotional evaluation of a chasm and that of a highly modelled interior." Conditions of space are not limited to the creation of enclosures or verticality and horizontality, since volumes emanate "a certain radiation," which "even though this cannot be directly measured, it exists, like the area of an electromagnetic field. Our eyes record it and it is apparent in our psychic reaction." Corroborated by Le Corbusier's assertion that the task of architects is to vitalize the planes of volumes—"to find in the surfaces the accentuation and generation of form"—Giedion finds that the binding of thinking and feeling through architecture is typified in the ascending planes of the Rockefeller Centre (1939) in New York, designed by Raymond Hood. In his view, the demand for spatial and historical continuity constitutes "the very backbone of human society," with the task to assemble "a new tradition." By combining and extending different eras, architecture ought to facilitate the reconnection between interiority and exteriority; "in the long run, explorations of the inner space of our emotive spheres will prove more important than Icarus dreams of chasing after the moon."[51]

Enlivening the Discipline

If confusion and boredom are the result of "the approach of man today," which forcefully leads to the consideration of "constancy and change" in architecture, then the question of the death or metamorphosis of the International Style is indicative of the modern demand for innovation. It appears as a fashionable rather than fundamental enquiry, concerned with the periodization of architectural trends and consonant with the economic bonanza of the 1950s. As presented in the introduction to *Space, Time and Architecture*, the symposium organized by the Architectural League established a connection to confusion and boredom that denounced and had the potential to enlighten those who interpret the built environment as well as those who produce unessential architecture. In the first case, the crisis of the International Style belongs to bored and boring academics, critics, and institutions—including Johnson, Banham, and the League—incapable of identifying the meaning and continuity of modern architecture. In the second, the condition is the outcome of playboy architecture that interrupts the development of the space conception of the era, opposed to architecture capable of expressing and symbolizing the forces of the period—socioeconomic, political, and cultural. In this manner, "The International Style—Death or Metamorphosis?" was an attempt to enliven the architectural milieu by promoting the discussion of circumstances of change, of those features that oscillate over time and become exhausting and exhausted, needing reconfiguration while commanding technological progress. According to Giedion, modern architecture—and by then the International Style—can endure and avoid stagnation as long as space is acknowledged as constant. To achieve both, the methods of thinking ought to cooperate with the methods of feeling to produce significance—the opposite of boredom.

CHAPTER 11
LOS ANGELES, FLAT ENOUGH

Boredom is particularly evident in the vastness of Los Angeles. Aldous Huxley dubs it the "City of Dreadful Joy," where Pantagruel, the scholarly and adventurous giant of François Rabelais, would have died of "fatigue and boredom."[1] With the same wit, Simone de Beauvoir refers to it as a "fairground of wonders" that exudes weariness, and James M. Cain writes that the abundance of "nutty religions" in the "urban paradise" relieves its inhabitants from the invariability of their surroundings.[2] More extremely, Charles Bukowski poses the city as a blank grid through which people meander, disoriented, barely surviving on cynical humor.[3] For Reyner Banham, Los Angeles is an extraordinary object of study, equally ugly and beautiful, capable of exposing the formation of a modern settlement characterized by the excitement for the new and the inevitability of boredom, its counterpart—both climatically nurtured.[4] As the world's most spacious city, Los Angeles acts as an industrial container demarcated by its surroundings, with a tight porosity that retains unity and protects it from exterior influences, like a plastic form inflated by its own machinery.[5]

In *Los Angeles: The Architecture of Four Ecologies* (1971)—published a year before *Learning from Las Vegas* by Venturi, Scott Brown, and Izenour, and after Archigram had declared that "transient situations [are] more important for the definition of space than buildings"[6]—Banham combines natural processes, historical incidents, and technological progress to explain the city as "an unrepeatable circumstance." In his view, "the combination of landscape, sea, Spaniards, Anglo-Saxons, the Pacific Electric Railroad, freeways and Hollywood … gave the place an instant culture."[7] Despite this rareness, "most observers report monotony" and "confusion rather than variety" due to their incapacity to appreciate the fruition of Los Angeles: "it has escaped them because it is unique (like all the best unities) and without any handy terms of comparison."[8] Unlike the conception of the urban as the realm of openness, the Californian city welds the domestic interior with the public exterior. Historically, this hyperspace not only contains the fire residues, seen from kilometers away, of the Valley of Smokes, the name given it by pre-Hispanic dwellers,[9] but also the domiciliary sky of the colonizing virgin and angels of The Town of Our Lady the Queen of the Angels of the Porciúncula River, as it was known by the Spanish conquerors.[10] Scientifically, this enclosure defies the Darwinian category of environment and the positivist discourse of ecology that distances organisms from their milieu. Human presence is inseparable from the urban formation; both act in unison and in perennial exchange. Acknowledging this connection, and in order to trace its fundamental qualities, Banham identifies "four ecologies" as a multi-layered system of topological relations.[11]

In the narrative of the book, boredom appears scattered throughout and across the organizing strata—"Surfurbia," "Foothills," "The Plains of Id," "Autopia"—and their subsequent architecture—"Exotic Pioneers," "Fantastic," "The Exiles," "The Style that Nearly. . . ." However, the condition remains in the background, an experiential result of the metropolitan configurations. In Los Angeles, buildings are dispersed, without correspondence between each other, and are of big proportions, even when compared to the air above and the nearby ocean. Freeways, highways, and boulevards impose order and organize vistas that do not converge and do not emanate from a center; instead, what is considered downtown functions as a void that arranges through absence. In this ambit, boredom is a non-gravitational force, neither centrifugal nor centripetal, which consolidates a homogeneous field of suspension, because its effects not only challenge the traditional relationships of urban and architectural hierarchy but also suggest new orders of spatial organization.[12]

Boredom in the Ecologies of Los Angeles

A silent character in *Los Angeles*, boredom is part of an architectural historiography concerned with environmental regulation and the endeavors of technology. On the one hand, the condition resonates with the use of standardized materials that contribute to the serial design and construction of edifices, particularly of housing projects; on the other, it is similar to comfort, the zone of pure rest and security, where external disturbance is eradicated.[13] Boredom links experience to the mechanisms that control the measurable qualities of interior architecture, such as light, air, and temperature, and thus allows the probing of the physical offerings and the intangible suggestions of architecture. If the inhabitation of the modern built environment is outlined by homelessness, as Heidegger avows, then the consequent search for home constitutes the motor of innovation that relentlessly powers the industry of architecture.

Banham distinguishes "Surfurbia" as the first ecology of Los Angeles. It comprises the culture of the beach and warm weather, "a place where a man needs to own only what he stands up in," since the requirements for sustenance are minimal—"something to eat," "a couple of boards," "a pair of frayed shorts and sun-glasses." Wellbeing emerges not from material prosperity but rather from the repetitious oscillation from elation to relaxation. The lifestyle and practices of surfers—lying by the ocean, waiting for optimal conditions to slide into the waves, and exercising frequently—are a rejection of the boredom caused by the sequence of the activities of production required by the modern consumer society, fetishized by the media. "Doing nothing" produces time and space for reflection. This state of repose, accompanied by the always shining sun of California, kindles tolerance against the indifference that persists in "moral postures, political attitudes, ethnic groupings, and individual psychologies."[14]

In turn, Banham finds the simplicity of this way of life in its architectural counterpart in the work of "Exotic Pioneers," represented by the rectilinear Hunt House (1957) by Craig Ellwood. This type of design procures enjoyment by establishing visual and spatial connections with the encircling nature; its H-shaped plan that alternates open spaces with covered areas allows day-to-day climate to infiltrate the routine of the house. The orthogonality of its configuration, manifested by a conventional wooden structure, projects a homogeneous and continuous interior space, articulated by furniture and program rather than by solid walls. Although the purpose of this architecture is to battle everyday boredom, it exposes an underlying sameness. In Banham's view, much of the modern architecture in Los Angeles derives from "ever-present" conditions that "can be taken for granted." The cycles of weather, by which nature is brought into the same realm as culture, but lacking historical nuance, are juxtaposed to the Spanish Colonial Revival style as primordial forces behind the buildings of the city—both worth commenting on when they are "outstandingly beautiful or conspicuously horrible."[15]

Along the intuitive layering of meteorological conditions and history, the geology of the city and its manipulation establish "Foothills" as the second ecology. The alteration of hills and slopes to accommodate architectural structures are part of a topographical evolution; the cropping and shaping of natural formations respond to the need for creating space for residences, administrative services, cultural venues, and other typologies required by modernity. They last as long as they are profitable, as in the case of the Hollywood Bowl amphitheater, home of the eponymous orchestra and Los Angeles Philharmonic. Owned by the County of Los Angeles, this space of entertainment has been submitted to multiple architectural changes, not only to augment its capacity but also to maintain the interest of the public.[16] This kind of architecture, which Banham calls "Fantastic," extends progressively to the surrounding plains, with numerous components ordered by strict geometry and carefully adorned, like an American hamburger:

> Assembled with proper care it can be a work of visual art as well; indeed, it must be considered as visual art first and foremost, since some components are present in too small a quantity generally to make a significant gustatory as opposed to visual contribution—for instance, the seemingly mandatory ring of red-dyed apple, which does a lot for the eye as a foil to the general greenery of the salads, but precious little for the palate.[17]

Resembling culinary garnish, the particles and additions that give form to buildings are not functionally essential. Yet they generate emblematic images and settings, most of them without explicit messages but others with the aim to attract customers to commercial facilities. In these cases, the built environment demands responsiveness, desperately extending its appendages to denote presence and the capacity for being consumed. Contrary to the integrated design pioneered by Buckminster Fuller in the 1950s and 1960s, the architecture of Los Angeles is concerned with individuality. To compete against each other, buildings are conceived in isolation and with memorable shapes that disregard context and that promote clichés, such as the Brown Derby restaurant in the shape of a hat, the Cream Cans painted as cream cans, the Hoot Hoot I Scream outlet designed as an owl, and the Bonzo dogs that sold hot dogs. During their heyday in the first half of the twentieth century, these envelopes packaged simple ideas taken from the quotidian, transforming ordinary objects into objects of desire through architecture and anticipating the art of Andy Warhol.

Boredom, Architecture, and Spatial Experience

In the second ecology of Los Angeles, architectural structures and symbols "are one and the same thing."[18] For Banham, the Spadena House (1925) by Henry Oliver, designed as the Witch House from the Hansel and Gretel tale,[19] and the Wayfarers "Glass" Chapel (1949) by Lloyd Wright are examples of designs that purposely differ from traditional images of the built environment. Their novelty secures initial notice, but the clarity of their single concept risks the possibility of boredom becoming an outcome of their simplicity, incapable of suggesting more than their thematic reality. These experiments are not the result of low-quality design or defective construction; to the critic, while Oliver's creation is an easy transposition of a movie set that nevertheless demanded advanced building skills, Wright's chapel is a serious and respectable piece of architecture with an elaborate geometry and an intelligent use of technology. What connects them is their "Pop fantasy," "comparable to the wilder kind of gourmet-style restaurants."[20]

Unlike the implementation of the iconic in Las Vegas—"unashamedly middle-aged," with "boring buildings" such as the Beaux-Arts Caesars Palace—Los Angeles constantly creates new architectural motifs. To Banham, although both cities provide entertainment, permissiveness, and inclusion, only the Californian city is capable of projecting the future. Las Vegas re-enacts the past for immediate consumption, with architecture that appears as "an extreme suburban variant of Los Angeles," "as much a marginal gloss on Los Angeles as was Brighton Pavilion in Regency London." There is no boredom in Las Vegas, but neither is there creativity, since its architecture is dedicated to a transient population, concerned with the present and devoid of memory. Dissimilarly, the boredom of Los Angeles offers moments of rest and reflection that propel movement, incorporating the past into the future and nurturing a field of possibilities and experimentation. The condition is therefore essential to "the greatest concentration of fantasy-production, as an industry and as an institution, in the history of Western man."[21]

Nonetheless, the architectural apparatus dedicated to the ideation, production, and administration of the fantastic and spectacular is not appealing. The making of films, television, the arts, and technology requires vast and plain structures that function as neutral containers; sometimes covered with fake façades or posters with movie scenes, their exterior does not follow the complexity of their inventions. Like boredom, they are austere and introverted, promising something they cannot embody. Banham notes that the only exception to the uniformity of factories and public architecture is the Water and Power Building (1964) by Albert C. Martin, located amongst "the boredoms of the Civic Center area." The volume "graces the scene and lifts the spirit," and "sits in firm control of the whole basis of human existence in Los Angeles." Along with signs and billboards—endemic of Los Angeles, in persistent transformation from the novel to the obsolete, necessitating constant replacement—it is the only gesture "that matches the style and scale of the city." During the day, the Water and Power Building "is a conventional rectangular office block closing the end of an uninspired civic vista," but at night, the gray context is lit by "this brilliant cube of diamond-cool light riding above the lesser lights of downtown."[22] It is ambiguous, with the capacity to be of both low and high resolution and both restful and stimulating, boring and interesting.

The majority of Los Angeles rests on a large, flat surface. The unchanging topography constitutes the third ecology, which Banham terms "The Plains of Id," with a psychoanalytical tone. This horizontality defines "an endless plain endlessly gridded with endless streets." But the city is marked by the seemingly interminable land as well as by repetitive residential architecture, "ticky-tacky houses clustered in indistinguishable neighborhoods, slashed across by endless freeways ... and so on ... endlessly."[23] Standing in Griffith Park Observatory, 346 meters above sea level, Banham describes the "plain, endless, boring" city to the south:[24]

> [T]he interminable parallels of Vermont, Normandie and Western Avenues stretching south as far as the eye can penetrate the urban haze, intersecting at absolutely precise right angles the east-west parallels of Hollywood, Sunset and Santa Monica Boulevards, Melrose Avenue, Beverly Boulevard, Third Street, Wilshire Boulevard, under the San Mo freeway, past Exposition Park and the campus of the University of Southern California and ever south, across Slauson, Florence, Manchester, Century, Imperial ... on a clear day—a very clear day—the visible geometry extends twenty-odd miles to San Pedro.[25]

If the thickness of the air permits, the panorama is one of the greatest in the world and "one of the most daunting." The "sheer size" and "sheer lack of quality" create difficulties "that have destroyed any community spirit that may once have existed," as in Watts, a neighborhood of more than 3000 square meters inhabited by a young population prone to social conflict, isolated despite its closeness to Normandie Avenue, one of the longest north–south streets in the city.[26] The buildings of Watts are indistinguishable from each other, creating "a totally nowhere place," with the exception of the sculptural towers of Simon Rodia, "testimony to a genuinely original creative spirit."[27] Serially designed condominiums and tenement buildings as well as semi-detached and detached houses ordered by catalogue comprise vast areas of agglomeration of the identical. Constructed as empty modular shells, they serve as storage for personal possessions rather than as the means for individuation or for a sense of belonging.

As elaborated by Banham, this monotony of Los Angeles echoes *The Ego and the Id* (1933) by Sigmund Freud, whose work was popular in the Californian culture of the mid-twentieth century. The flatness of the plains acts as the Id, for it constitutes the most basic material condition of the city, partly hereditary and innate, partly repressed and acquired. The terrain is a mediating agent, a reservoir of energy that passes its essential evenness to the built environment and to those who occupy it, promoting the instinctual adoption of spatial arrangements. In addition, aligned with Freud's diagnoses of deviations, defects, and malfunctions of behavior as alternative economies, explored in *The Psychopathology of the Everyday Life* (1901), characterlessness does not result from forgetting how to create character.[28] Instead, following the psychoanalyst, Banham suggests that the absence of features is a mechanism by which either to avoid confronting a difficult or painful situation—the flatness—or to offset the pleasure obtained from another source—the weather. Like a neurasthenic patient who mistrusts memory and thus writes a memorandum before visiting the therapist, characterlessness is an expression of a condition rather than the condition itself.[29] The critic succinctly and decisively concedes that what is daunting about Los Angeles is that it "is most like other cities: Anywhereswille/Nowheresville"—"here, indeed, are the only commercial streets in the US that can compare with the immense length of East Colfax in Denver; the only parts of Los Angeles flat enough and boring enough to compare with the cities of the Middle West."[30]

By being equivalent to other topographies and architectures, the flat and boring parts of Los Angeles become replaceable. Banham reflects that if "most of what is contained within the rough central parallelogram of the Santa Monica, Harbor, Santa Ana, and San Bernardino freeways could disappear overnight . . . the bulk of the citizenry would never even notice." Nonetheless, what appears insignificant is what determines the relevant, by establishing a measure of comparison; since industrial, commercial, and civic buildings are "a gutless-looking collection," "neither tough-minded nor sensitive, nor architectural monuments, nor Pop extravaganzas," the architecture of "The Exiles" ought to proliferate in the "The Plains of the Id." Residences and small-scale buildings designed by European immigrants have the ability to convey the flamboyance and natural qualities of Los Angeles, giving "Southern California an independent body of modern architecture contemporary with the rise of the International Style in Europe."[31] Banham describes and illustrates with photographs of the Schindler/Chase (1921), Lovell (1926), Oliver (1933), and Tischler (1950) houses by Rudolf M. Schindler; the CBS Headquarters (1936) by William Lescaze; the Health (1929) and Hammerman (1949) houses, Strathmore apartments (1938), Northwestern Mutual Insurance Offices (1950), and Garden Grove drive-in Church (1962) by Richard Neutra; the Abell house (1937) by Thornton Abell; and the Ships Restaurant (1963) by Armet and Davies—all frequently framed by the artificial landscape created in the interstitial spaces of the freeways.

As extensions of streets, avenues, and boulevards, the sculptural structures of the highways compose "Autopia," the fourth ecology. In *Los Angeles*, these transportation surfaces are naturalized, posed as organic growths rather than merely practical constructions, impossible to eliminate. Typified by the intersection of the Santa Monica and San Diego freeways, this architecture is "one of the greater works of man," "a pattern on the map," "a monument against the sky," and "a kinetic experience as one sweeps through it." Banham affirms that the adverse effects of automobiles are minimal; when the traffic is compared to the traffic in London, the objections of the residents of Los Angeles—"being stuck in a jam in the October heat with the kids in the back puking with the smog"—are "little more than rhetorical tropes, like the English complaints about the weather."[32] As if Heidegger's metaphor of "boredom as fog in the abyss of the world" had been materialized as "boredom as smog in the basin of Los Angeles," pollution and vehicular congestion serve as indicators of an enclosed environment, unhealthy due to overpopulation.[33] The danger is psychological rather than physical; for instance, in the crisis of Black Wednesday, September 8, 1943, temperature inversions trapped smog over the plains and created a noxious brew, 150 meters thick, bringing the city to a standstill and breaking "the legend of the land of eternal sunshine."[34]

Los Angeles, Flat Enough

Although sometimes victims of the conflicting interrelation between topography, climate, and the need for commuting, Los Angeles is ideal for drivers, with "their white-wall tyres ... singing over the diamond-cut anti-skid grooves in the concrete road surface, the selector-levers of their automatic gearboxes ... firmly in *Drive*, and the radio ... on."[35] The maneuvering of the wheel along freeways and highways opens possibilities of introspection between mindlessness and mindfulness. The long drives in Los Angeles require alertness to the outside world, but they also permit aloofness and reflection, experienced within the personal microcosms and alter egos of vehicles that move from real time and physical space to the endless time and personal space of thought and memory—from the superficiality of the everyday to the profoundly existential.[36] Disagreeing with Brock Yates, a journalist and editor of *Car and Driver*, who regarded freeways as an "existential limbo where man sets out each day in search of western-style individualism," Banham observes that those behind the wheel tend to be "relaxed and well-adjusted characters without an identity problem in the world."[37]

Similar to a repetitive intonation, the habitual operations and gestures of driving promote automatism. Checking mirrors and the texture of the asphalt, following the curves of the road while reading signs and controlling velocity, signaling when turning, and listening to the roar of the machine all impose codes of communication among individuals performing similar actions. The boredom of driving connects the individual with the social and the communal, since the basic conditions for every automobile are the same, under identical regulations, surpassing differences of machinery, wealth, and levels of comfort. Importantly, the codes of behavior across all automobiles require not speech but attitudes of movement, directionality, and proximity. As a mechanical extension of the body, the car expresses personality and resists urban anonymity; every private capsule is a living organism that dwells amidst infrastructure, registering the driver's capacity to navigate the city. The multiple journeys to the same destinations generate a sense of familiarity with the surroundings. After driving, when a destination has been reached, locations change, forcing the individual not only to self-transform according to the new setting but also to evaluate inner alterations; what remains unchanged is the genuine, and what can be disregarded is the contrived.[38]

A Different World

When compared to European models of urbanism, Los Angeles appears different and uncanny, inquisitive and transgressive. Banham acknowledges this strangeness, which is subject to "the attention that Sodom and Gomorrah have received, primarily a reflection of other peoples' bad consciences." In line with the criticality of boredom, the city is a provocation that questions "the intellectual repose and professional livelihood of many architects, artists, planners, and environmentalists," including the modern visions of the Futurists and Le Corbusier as well as the anti-modern prescriptions of Jane Jacobs and Sibyl Moholy-Nagy. As a successful case of alterity and radical otherness—"*une architecture autre*"—it provides not only a particular sense of place but also the functions of any capital, "in terms of size, cosmopolitan style, creative energy, international influence, distinctive way of life and corporate personality."[39]

Even though the vastness of Los Angeles requires strategies to cope with the relationship between space and time, it does not entail increased anomie or alienation. Its residents, who often comprise social arrangements alternative to the traditional family unit, and whose homes avoid the forced closeness arising from the high density typical of New York or London, have created mechanisms of interaction and involvement unique to their circumstances, which proves that "there are as many possible cities as there are possible forms of human society" and suggests "that there is no simple correlation between urban form and social form." As such, the city is not a built environment that is a symbolic expression of ideas or sentiments; architecture is rather a tool for experimentation and the creation of interpersonal relations, shaping experience and cultural values, without endangering tradition since it never departed from it. For Banham, Los Angeles reveals that "town planning inherited from Renaissance humanism … is … simple-mindedly mechanistic," inherent "to the mechanical fallacy that there is a necessary causal connexion between built form and human life, between the mechanisms of the city and the styles of architecture practised there." The architecture of the fantastic, the houses by exiles, the freeways, and the automobiles are all components of a unique world, lying on an extensive plane, protected by mountains, ocean, and air. They constitute "equal fragments of a great dream of the urban homestead, the dream of a good life outside the squalors of the European type of city."[40]

Another Boredom, the Ecologies of Evil

Soon after the release of *Los Angeles*, Peter Plagens condemned Banham's efforts to portray the city as a realm of symbiotic interaction. In a review for *Artforum*, titled "Los Angeles: The Ecologies of Evil" (1972), he calls the publication "a fattened hifalutin tourist brochure" of "nearly comic ineptness," incapable of providing a profound analysis of the everyday life of the Angelenos (Figure 11.1). Banham is portrayed as a "hipster" who not only lacks sensibility and critical observation skills but also studies Los Angeles from a distance, "through a telescope from Santa Barbara," since "the fashionable sonofabitch doesn't have to live here." The system of ecologies and corresponding architectures is a marketing strategy to create slogans, comparable to "gilded versions of the chapters of a Chamber of Commerce guidebook." Although Plagens acknowledges that the tendency to reduce the banal to highlight the spectacular is not exclusive to Banham, he finds *Los Angeles* to be contradictory and insincere. The narrative "purports to liberate us from the tyranny of big time architectural monuments in favor of everyday pop," but it "ends up in Beverly Hills and the beaches and all is lost." The resulting distortion "ignores the daily grind, the millionfold smalltime commercial transactions, the lives of the workers and shopkeepers, police and criminals, housewives and teachers, and unemployed and elderly."[41]

Figure 11.1 First page of "Los Angeles: The Ecologies of Evil." *Artforum* (December 1972), 67. © *Artforum*.

Framed by the Californian bonanza of the 1960s, boredom appears for Banham as a creative act, in the Warhol sense of "it's so bad, it's good." For Plagens, however, the condition emerges as the vacuity of a realm fixated with appearances, "all flesh and no soul, all buildings and no architecture, all property and no land, all electricity and no light, all billboards and nothing to say, all ideas and no principles." The staleness of Los Angeles is a component of the land as an object of commercial transaction, with corresponding activities distributed along "the wide, flat, smoggy streets." Von's markets, Ralph's markets, Lucky markets, Alpha Beta markets, and Boy's markets constitute many iterations of shops and bazaars, though their appeal dissolves, since all of them offer commodification rather than opportunities for sociability. Their effects are both tangible and intangible. The fixation with wealth engenders "a spiritual disease, a thinly disguised sense of hopelessness and frenetic ennui"; and the aspiration for social standards promotes the adoption of practices of "instant gratification in sparklefront apartments, food photographs on Denny's menus, aggressively customized cars, unmanageable choppers." Consequently, the validation offered by Banham is "quite dangerous" because it can produce a "trickle-down effect," encouraging the "color coordinated" upper middle classes—"the hacks who do shopping centers, Hawaiian restaurants, and savings-and-loans, the dried-up civil servants in the division of highways, and the legions of show-biz fringies"—to perpetuate the status quo.[42]

To Plagens, the everyday boredom of Los Angeles is manifested in the patterns of transportation. In a city dominated by automobile infrastructure—"two thirds of downtown Los Angeles is occupied by parking lots and structures, streets, and freeways"—cycling and walking expose the arrogance of the motorized city: "you contemplate suicide (depression, not fatigue), every five miles."[43] Unlike J. G. Ballard's exaltation of transgressive driving but similar to his depiction of it as the awareness of the other—"their bodies ..., their assignations, escapes, boredom"—Plagens portrays driving as slaving, isolating, and distressing, mediated by impersonal machinery.[44] The traffic congestion promotes social fragmentation and pollutes the air, a "horizontal, open air prison" that inflicts vulnerability.[45] In an extreme manner, the experience of riding public buses exposes the uncomfortable need for mobility, filled with waiting, poor surroundings, and stigma:

> [T]here must be people on those buses who never, or hardly ever, ride in cars. People to whom distance is always measured by waiting time, and crowded push and shove, and little pink pieces of paper for transfers, and then the walk to the final destination. ... [T]he old and poor and tired people huddled on buses or benches, windy corners, cold walls, dirty windows, thick perspiration, air, jouncing and sliding along the streets, lurching and bumping between corners, surrounded by strangers, late, hurried, and uncomfortable.[46]

With the exception of certain type of residences—"creaking Victorian houses, the small buildings of European expatriates like Neutra"—and the architecture of freeways, most of the built environment is worthless. It constitutes a "multimillion-dollar garbage" product of capitalist interests, particularly on Wilshire Boulevard and the scattered "monstrous" public buildings, including "the Pauley Pavilion, the Sports Arena, the 'fabulous' Forum, the County Art Museum, the new courthouses, the LAX restaurant, a dozen new glass towers downtown, the gateway to Westwood, Sunset and Vine, glamorous 'entire city' shopping centers." To Plagens, "L.A.'s architecture generally stinks," although it carries "a jasminelike scent of possibility" that necessitates a "revolution of hardcore planning," with policies and measures to "get the cars off the freeways and replace them with thousands of free propane buses," "discourage the business of every single-unit dwelling facing a spacious street," "quit building shopping centers," and "quit selling dune buggies and electric combs so SoCal Edison and Union Oil won't have their excuses to duplicate Carthage in Redondo Beach."[47] Opposed to the organic growth endorsed by Banham, the aim is to reduce the immensity of Los Angeles, following Neutra, the architect of health and wellbeing: "if everybody householded land in such patio or atrium houses, Los Angeles would have 40% of its size, of its pole lines, and endless expensive roads. It might have half its traffic to wreck nerves and half the exhaust gases to pollute the blue sky and breathing lungs."[48]

The Hyperspace of Los Angeles, the Hyperspace of Boredom

Banham and Plagens both portray Los Angeles as a space of suspension, without gravitational force but pressed from above by its atmosphere and resisted from below by its architecture. The city is a world of its own, wrapped in an invisible membrane that exerts influence on its inhabitants and percolates exterior elements. Anticipating Fredric Jameson's theorizations on the postmodern waning of emotional intensity and spatial neutrality, *Los Angeles: The Architecture of Four Ecologies* and "Los Angeles: The Ecologies of Evil" incorporate boredom as a condition that emerges from the architectural and modifies the environmental. In Banham, boredom is inconspicuous, related to the repetition of urban configurations, forms, and materials in buildings, circumscribing the possibilities of the new. In Plagens, the condition is troubling, since it is an undesirable circumstance that derives from inefficient planning and demands urban reorganization. In both, the idea of boredom as a confined space resonates with their depiction of Los Angeles as a realm of introversion, independent from tradition and in continuous adjustment. Free from deterministic relationships of style, function, and power, this built environment cannot be interpreted and experienced in the same manner as the hegemonic constructions of modernist architecture, not only because the configurations are different but also because perception is altered. Additionally, the British and American critics agree that boredom is a symptom of the interaction between the many layers, or ecologies, of the city. For example, the signs and billboards of Los Angeles promote commodification and the transfiguration of every object and subject into a two-dimensional image, boosting the appetite for photography and predisposing the viewer to the flatness of the banal. The building industry also determines sensibility by not offering choice but a selection of possibilities—the colors, shapes, and textures of construction materials—allied with fabricated notions of prosperity, which in turn increases uniformity; rather than mediating between individuals and environment, boredom is one with the environment.

The boredom of Los Angeles problematizes not only space but also time. In the capitalist system, the long moments of commuting remind individuals that time is money, and boredom thus becomes an indicator of lack of financial gain, marking social differences. The bored individual is either wealthy or poor; the first dwells in spaces of luxury and consumption, whereas the second struggles to access the spaces of production. In between, the middle class, aware of the contradictions and utopias of capitalism, occupies the spaces of habit and routine, alternating prearranged days of work with days of rest. In the accounts by Banham and Plagens, the residents of Los Angeles are portrayed as passive creatures or actors following a script, subjected to the impositions of their surroundings.[49] Even in the case of celebrated architects, such as Neutra and Schindler, their creativity and agency are reduced by the overwhelming qualities of the city. Their production is not lethargic but submissive to the Californian weather and topography, in a way that is similar to each other and easy to group, anonymous rather than singular, confirming Banham's assertion that "Americans do not monumentalize or make architecture ... America's monumental space is ... the great outdoors."[50]

The imposing basin of Los Angeles configures a hyperurban space in which the architecture of interiors—domestic and private—is not qualitatively different from the architecture of exteriors—public and shared. Analogous to the ubiquity of boredom, the space of the city penetrates the space of architecture. Partitions, doors, and windows articulate function but not character, permitting and inviting the inhabitation of all spaces, including roads and freeways. As the most basic module of dwelling, the automobile transforms the notion of individual space since it liberates the notion of home from the need for a fixed location, with an immobile architecture. The body becomes the locus of reference, itinerant and in motion, attentive to distances and with a surrounding area of influence that interacts with other bodies in incessant displacement. By implication, the change of settings of the corporeal prioritizes interiority. If the body moves but emotions and thoughts remain unaffected, then boredom sets in; the same occurs if emotions and thoughts are in constant realignment but the body is not.

Jameson suggests that the difference of speed in movement between interiority and exteriority is a trait that exposes detachment from the modern, as in the experience of visiting the lobby of the Westin Bonaventure Hotel (1976) in Los Angeles, designed and developed by John Portman. Unlike the focus on sentiments and intellectual elaborations that favor the temporal, the postmodern experience turns to the spatial to expose "a mutation in the object unaccompanied as yet by any equivalent mutation in the subject." The lack of "perceptual equipment to match this new hyperspace" responds to the inheritance and persistence of previous manners of inhabitation. In the escalators of the imposing atrium of the Bonaventure, where the commerce of the city infiltrates the interior of the building and the language of volumes and depth proves futile, walking and strolling are "underscored, symbolized, reified, and replaced by a transportation machine which becomes the allegorical signifier of that older promenade we are no longer allowed to conduct on our own." Thus boredom that arises from the disorientation imposed by architecture demands new sensorial capacities for expanding "our body to some new, yet unimaginable, perhaps ultimately impossible, dimensions."[51] In the meantime, standardized informative signs and diagrams facilitate circulation and avoid confusion, restoring modernist coordinates of space and therefore helping everyone find their place.

PART 3
EXTENDED THRESHOLDS

CHAPTER 12
POTENTIAL ARCHITECTURES

In the late 1970s, the character of boredom changed from being an experiential outcome of the modern built environment, related to monotony and uniformity, to being the adversary of multiplicity. Although still negative, the condition advanced its criticality to propose the creation of alternate architectures, as a force of transgression with possibilities for relief through the design of innovative spaces. To Niels Prak, who was influenced by Gestalt theories and the psychology of arousal and curiosity, and who in 1977 elaborated on the visual perception of buildings, redundancy in architecture facilitates adjustment, novelty, and the picking up of information. Although repetition is uncongenial and leads to boredom and confusion, "the advantages are beneficial on the whole," since "we can react adequately to the unexpected. Our orientation on information and the future course of events has led to our exploration of the world, the construction of tools and finally our technological dominance over parts of nature." Hence, the need to create difference in the built environment is fundamental to evolutionary subsistence. "The aboriginal man," he states, who lacked "the advantages of overpowering strength, great speed, claws or a hard shell, had to survive by wits.... Some authors believe that the need to stimulate the organism by a variety of experiences and exposure to information is just as much a primary drive as hunger or thirst."[1]

Coinciding with the rise of the study of boredom in psychology, the concern with the effects of architecture marked the growing awareness of circumstances of space.[2] Writing in 1991, Fredric Jameson concludes that postmodernism depends on "a certain spatial turn"—space becomes "the *novum* ... the breakthrough into new forms of life itself, the radically emergent." It is also characterized by reactions to a waning sensibility that increases and leads to the search for diversity and multiplicity. To Jameson, who extends the materialism of the Marxist and Freudian traditions, boredom is "not so much an objective property of things and works" but rather "a response to the blockage of energies (whether those be grasped in terms of desire or praxis)"—"interesting as a reaction to situations of paralysis and also, no doubt, as defense mechanism or avoidance behaviour." In postmodernity, the condition increases the distance between environments and temporalities, acting as a historical "symptom of our own existential, ideological, and cultural limits, an index of what has to be refused in the way of other people's cultural practices and their threat to our own rationalizations about the nature and value of art." Boredom is productive as long as it is grasped as relational and spatial rather than as an aesthetic assessment of boringness, for what may appear as such to some may be interesting to others. This paradox is familiar; "if a boring text can also be good (or interesting, as we now put it), exciting texts, which incorporate diversion, distraction, temporal commodification, can also perhaps sometimes be 'bad.'"[3]

However, Prak asserts that the complaints about the lack of variety in the modern built environment came from architects rather than from users or planning authorities. As if not enough time had passed to enable the assessment of modernism, he noted that boredom rarely appeared in research reports or consumer opinions about the quality of architecture—"apparently the supposed visual simplicity of modern buildings is not bothering lay people as it does architects, or it is not perceived at all." To remedy boredom and balance excess and intricacy, the principles of the theory against visual sameness ought to be adopted by designers. They could manipulate "distances (proximity)," "alignment (continuity)," "slope of roofs (continuity and similarity)," and use "the same bricks or paint in the same color (similarity of surface treatment)"; for instance,

> Dutch architects and town planners often try to increase the visual coherence between a group of custom-built houses, because they think pronounced individualism to be anti-social, and because the character and visual coherence of the suburb is valued above the possibilities of the individual designer. Needless to say, the client often aims at the opposite effect: his custom-built house is to him a form which expresses his identity and status.

And meanwhile,

> American developers build sets of houses which, for economy of construction, are often the same in a single development. To cater for the individualistic wishes of their prospective clients, they disguise these houses as individual, custom-built units, by adding dormer windows to one, a porch to another, and by painting them in different colours.[4]

To generate favorable conditions for perception and creation, which are attributes of the mind—iterating the nineteenth-century accounts on empathy by Göller and Wölfflin—a process of training has to be followed with the aim to strengthen cognition and sensibility, and exercise the mental muscle capable of improving the decoding of the built environment. Analogous to "difficult music," complex architecture, with more information, provides possibilities for enjoyment and interpretation that increase with previous knowledge and repeated exposure. This long-term educational process would satisfy the demand for difference and improve the standards of intelligence of creators, producers, and consumers while providing cultural development. For Prak, the avoidance of boredom concerns not only the design of architecture but also "social contacts, physical and psychological events." Eventually, the role of the built environment "in the overall pattern of interactions between man and his surroundings" is unexceptional, because "in a perceptually 'rich' environment we hardly notice the architecture."[5]

Focusing on the capacity of boredom to induce creativity, this final section of the book investigates how the condition gained importance in extended thresholds—the production of postmodern architecture. The concern with variety and its social and political effects, explored through the contention of Francis Fukuyama that "history has ended" and only boredom remains, emerges during the fifth cycle of economic prosperity and decline. If the condition is a force in the creation of the built environment, then it must traverse aspects of design, planning, and the assessment of the discipline, with several episodes and actors—architects, authorities, professors and academics, the media—heralding the production of the interesting.

Creation and Destruction

In line with Prak's advocacy for variation to elude sameness, boredom has been acknowledged as a necessary moment before creation, particularly by those involved in activities of design and intellectual processing. In art, Brian O'Doherty affirms that "far from having no content, boredom is a state of potential richness"; similarly, Grayson Perry maintains that "boredom is a very creative state."[6] In philosophy, Bertrand Russell recommends not avoiding "the fructifying kind of boredom" because "a happy life must be to a great extent a quiet life, for it is only in an atmosphere of quiet that true joy can live."[7] In history, Robert Pirsig remarks that "boredom always precedes a great period of creativity"; and for William Inge, "boredom often generates wars, the supreme exhibition of human folly and wickedness."[8] In psychology, recent analyses conclude that the understanding of boredom, which is usually negative, ought to be readdressed to emphasize its positive effects, since its inherent criticality promotes associative thought.[9] According to Teresa Belton, spaces to experience the slowness of boredom should be facilitated "for the sake of creativity"; and Sandi Mann avers that boredom "is good for us and we need more of it. . . . [I]f we want to stop being so bored, we need to be a little bit *more* bored."[10] For Andreas Elpidorou, the condition "tells us something both about the world and about ourselves," which in turn enables "the pursuit of alternative goals: it 'pushes' us *out* of this non-stimulating, uninteresting, or unchallenging situation and *into* another. . . . Neither apathy, nor dislike, nor frustration can fulfill boredom's function."[11]

Nonetheless, when the environment does not provide opportunities for creation or distraction, boredom becomes an impairment that fuels the quest for the excessive and the extreme. It can surface as depression and anxiety, aggressive behavior, emotional and intellectual instability, lack of concentration, poor social relationships, lower life satisfaction, drug and alcohol abuse, eating and sexual disorders, gambling, and proneness to crime.[12] To Jeff Ferrell, these responses, which all carry stigma, constitute tests to the offerings of the surroundings, indicating that some misconduct is not committed against property or society but remonstrates against boredom. With sensibilities and values similar to those of Situationism International, public protests have fused the need for excitement with ideologies of rebellion that oppose the monotony of modernity and the vertical hierarchy of economic and political relations. Occupy demonstrations, Critical Mass rides, UrbEx excursions, skateboarding, graffiti, and other peaceable but prohibited practices within the space of the city all employ the edges of the built environment to challenge the regulations of the establishment, enacting pre-modern rituals to question the limits of what is considered public. In July 1996, when the collective Reclaim the Streets shut down the M41 motorway in London, the ensuing "festival of resistance" featured music, dancing, and theatre performances, framed by a banner that warned: "The Society that Abolishes Every Adventure Makes Its Own Abolition the Only Possible Adventure."[13]

More extremely, boredom has been identified as the motor behind the incursion of terrorism, war, and suicide, justified with similar narratives of a disenchantment with the determinism of Western modernity.[14] When the condition persists in exteriority, these destructive acts attempt meaningful appropriation and inhabitation, turning space and architecture into the desired but disputed means to express domination. In terrorism, boredom figures prominently in the explanations of those who join extremist forces as well as those who desert them. Through campaigns based on popular culture, disseminated through the internet, the offerings of adventure and the sense of communal purpose of radical groups, such as the Islamic State of Iraq and the Levant (ISIL), encourage traveling and the illegal crossing of frontiers.[15] With less ideological disillusionment, in cases of defection, boredom operates as the frustration with poor living conditions, repetitive duties, exploitation, and lack of opportunities for celebrated heroism, forcing further displacement in the pursuit of finding or regaining significant occupation.[16] In modern war, boredom not only drives the search for territorial control, with the accompanying destruction of the built environment of the past only to drive the construction of new symbolisms, but it also contributes to the pursuit of peace—the space of desire, without disruption, similar to comfort and derived from the progressive view of history that emerged in the Enlightenment. Armed combat creates practices and conditions opposed to boredom in the name of stability and prosperity, which in turn procure stasis and potentially further boredom. This cycle of conflict and amity is based on violence and the glorification of the human capacity to perform and renew systems of values and beliefs. Since modernity is predisposed to the experience of society as a space of alienation without relevant norms—"the estrangement of oneself from one's sense of self"—war is supported as an action that combines collective dogmas with individual convictions.[17] Its task is to prescribe active responses and specific obligations in order to awaken and affirm agency.

When boredom moves from the obliteration of the environment to the negation of individuality, suicide surfaces as the definitive effort to surpass the horizontality of transgression and leap into transcendence, fulfilling the yearn to dwell in a fundamentally different dimension. The intentional taking of one's own life constitutes the final disregard of the self and the perception of the world as a realm of inescapable sameness, echoing the admonitions of Thomas Aquinas about the power of acedia to induce despair. In a case of architecture and urban culture tied to the postmodern concern of morphing the temporal into the spatial, No 1 Poultry Street (1997) by James Stirling in London has turned into a poignant referent of existential boredom and suicide. Throwing themselves off the public terrace on the eighth floor, six people, all successful mid-career professionals, have died since the economic downturn of 2007.[18] In 2015, despite the erection of

1.80-meter-high barriers two years earlier and the employment of security guards to monitor anybody seen alone, the restaurant critic and blogger Wilkes McDermid jumped to his death. He wrote in his last post, "When a man is tired of London, he is tired of life; for there is in London all that life can afford ... [Samuel] Johnson was right, I am not tired of London and never have been ... however I am tired of life." In 2016, salesman Michael Halligan traveled from Dublin to follow the same steps. In his phone, several unsent messages were found. The first read, "I am bored of life and the future possibilities disinterest me. It's nobody's fault. Nothing could have been done to change it." The second, "I no longer try to adapt myself to others." The third, "I am not made for this world." And the last, "I have cracked."[19] Yet in the succeeding inquests, the architecture of the building—with its triangular plan responding to the site, open atrium, rounded clock tower, projecting balconies, and stripy façade, recognized as an epitome of postmodernism in need of preservation—was declared a non-participatory factor.

Boredom at the End of History

To Francis Fukuyama, "history has ended," and thus liberalism and attendant processes of homogenization have become the historical causes of continuous acts of transgression. In "Have We Reached the End of History?" (1989), he argues that the ideological maxims of the Western world have remained unchanged since the defeat, in 1806, of the Prussian monarchy by Napoleon Bonaparte in the Battle of Jena. Based on Alexandre Kojève's interpretation of the philosophy of Georg W. F. Hegel that confirms the absolute truth of the principles of liberty, fraternity, and equality of the French Revolution, and resurrects the belief that history culminates in a moment of rationality, the twentieth century is posed as a circular and pugnacious period. It departed from Western liberal democracy, contended with "the remnants of absolutism, then bolshevism and fascism, and finally an updated Marxism," only to return to liberalism, neither as its completion nor as the convergence between capitalism and socialism but as an undisputed and pervasive system of governance.[20] This final form of state resolves contradictions and satisfies all human needs, leaving the pursuit of financial interests as the only common goal.

With global influence, the efforts after the end of history to expand and materialize liberalism, spatial manifestations heralded by the "flabby, prosperous, self-satisfied, inward-looking, weak-willed" societies of Europe and North America, have fostered a monoculture of information and consumerism. As Fukuyama notes, the omnipresence of televisions in China, the proliferation of chain restaurants and clothing stores in Moscow, the Japanese department stores playing Beethoven, and the same rock music enjoyed across the world—"in Prague, Rangoon and Teheran"—are not consequences of the culmination of the Cold War but "the end point of mankind's ideological evolution."[21] Derived from the realm of ideas and emotional consciousness, the extensive search for sameness guides the course of the future, as the expression of a theoretical maxim in the process of being realized. The opening of the markets during the 1980s in China and the

Soviet Union did not mark the triumph of "the material over the ideal" but exposed the internalization of a different sentiment; in both countries, Marxism-Leninism had been perceived as absurd and devoid of meaning since the early 1970s.[22] The quest for the execution of liberalism creates a systematic thread of imperfect uniformity with "ideological pretensions of representing different and higher forms of human society." If history ended in 1806, and with it all ideological creation, the task of the homogenous state is to impose universality through a free market economy, in the form of "a liberal democracy in the political sphere combined with easy access to VCRs and stereos in the economic."[23]

The undertaking to achieve identical and widespread factors of regulation, which in the late 1980s seemed confirmed by the ubiquitous presence of liberalism and its advocacy for peace, barely threatened by religious fundamentalism and nationalism, entails the continuation of international and ethnic armed conflicts due to its incompletion.[24] The difference in development between almost equal states creates historical and post-historical conditions, with belligerence as validation. To Fukuyama, "Palestinians and Kurds, Sikhs and Tamils, Irish Catholics and Walloons, Armenians and Azeris, will continue to have their unresolved grievances. This implies that terrorism and wars of national liberation will continue to be an important item on the international agenda."[25] In addition to these forceful attempts of transcendence, the end of history will be "a very sad time" because the values and beliefs that propel imagination and idealism—as cultural development—"will be replaced by economic calculation, the endless solving of technical problems, environmental concerns, and the satisfaction of sophisticated consumer demands."[26] In this prediction, the production of architecture turns into a problem of boredom with the present, an exaggerated preservation rather than creation with a focus on the museum as the recipient of the nostalgia for history:

> Such nostalgia, in fact, will continue to fuel competition and conflict even in the post historical world for some time to come. Even though I recognize its inevitability, I have the most ambivalent feelings for the civilization that has been created in Europe since 1945, with its north Atlantic and Asian offshoots. Perhaps this very prospect of centuries of boredom at the end of history will serve to get history started once again.[27]

Fifth Cycle

According to Robert Heilbroner, the economic cycles of boom and crash will continue to exist as long as capitalism prevails, but their pace might increase. In 1978, wondering how long planned capitalism would last, he observed that "the era of competitive capitalism lasted 175 years, from roughly 1700 to 1875; the era of monopoly capitalism, 55 years, from 1875 to 1930; and welfare capitalism, 43 years, from 1930 to 1973." Despite their different length, these processes are primarily defined by boredom with the immediate past and the consequent emergence of the novel. With instances of disruption,

Potential Architectures

"for crisis can, and usually does, play a constructive role, even though it brings blockage," the succession from stagnation to creativity turns into a recurrent meta-structure rather than the upshot of unexpected spurs of genius.[28]

The transformations caused by economic sequences are systemic, imposing new references and sensibilities, like the older monopoly capitalism supporting the consolidation of metropolises, or the multinational and high-tech mutation creating virtual dimensions. To Carlota Pérez, this macro phenomenon is rooted in the micro foundations of technical change. Distinguishing innovation, the "commercial introduction of a new product," from invention, which "belongs to the realm of science and technology," she affirms that "the meaningful space" that drives change is located "at the convergence of technology, the economy—and the socio-institutional context." Far from being introduced in isolation, the changes of innovation occur as the collective effort of producers, designers, distributors, and consumers, who, in their aim to avert boredom, identify and boost a dominant design that becomes paradigmatic, with a collectively shared logic and a reasonable cost that guarantees commercial success. Once maturity is reached, when the variations of the chosen model are minimal and the market becomes saturated, financial investment derived from the profit of the previous phase propels further innovation, in an incremental manner, informing the direction of research, educational endeavors, and cultural expressions—the parameters that inform what is regarded as boring, interesting, and ultimately canonical.[29]

Extending the long waves of Kondratieff but stressing the transformative consequences of the economy in every aspect of everyday life, Pérez locates the fifth cycle of capitalism in the technological revolution of digital information and telecommunications, developed in the United States in the early 1970s before spreading rapidly to Europe and Asia. Centered on the microprocessor, it assembled "calculators, games, civil and military miniaturising and digitalising of control instruments," only to create "an overlapping sequence of minicomputers and personal computers, software, telecoms and Internet that have each opened new system trajectories, while being strongly inter-related and inter-dependent ... expanding together with intense feedback loops in both technologies and markets."[30] This revolution fostered industries, including software engineering, biotechnology, and building materials, that provided new infrastructures, such as high-speed transportation and radio and satellite transmission. As a result, these innovations spawned virtual spaces that rely on instant information, connectivity, decentralized integration, and network structures, highlighting knowledge as capital, heterogeneity, adaptability, the segmentation of markets, and ultimately the interaction between the global and the local.

This cycle projects an upward swing from between 1973 and 1975 to between 1998 and 2000. As Pérez claims, this prosperous phase is defined by the abundance of regularized stimuli as digitalization propels a higher form of worldwide standardization with associated codes of interrelation and experience. Confirming the contradictory essence of the modern era, the rampant expansion of technology required strict mechanisms of production and monotonous processes of control and consumption. According to Heilbroner, the consequent "ever-greater socialization of the economic structure" of technological expansion surfaced next to "what seems to be a concomitant disaffection, indifference, and antipathy of a population unable to find satisfaction in the plastic wealth or the impersonal employments that industrialism generates."[31] In this period, technology and boredom fortified their complementary relationship; the temporality without purpose of boredom is validated, supported, and lengthened by the efficiency of technology, which provides random information with the aim to excite and entertain.[32] Despite its efforts, the surfeit of technology does not entail the meaningful, tending to produce instead insufficiency while bolstering the creation of more and new devices for all functions—vast in reach and high in velocity, small and prosthetic, efficient in allowing the individual to endure boredom in comfort or to prevent its emergence prophylactically. Nonetheless, in the same manner, boredom emerges as an effective neutralizer of the overwhelming offerings of technology; just as technology can alleviate boredom, so can boredom deaden the incessant variations of technology, making it appear banal.

Since the 1980s, this mutual relationship sustained the regulatory principles of progress, affirming the laws of capitalism and giving rise to the information society. For Orrin Klapp, the boredom of this culture is the result of redundancy and noise, which "outstrips the 'slow horse' of meaning"; "it is a major paradox that growing leisure and affluence and mounting information and stimulation we call progress lead to boredom—a deficit in the quality of life." Arranged around mass media and the belief that new stimuli and constant communication equals progress and shortens the distance to fulfillment, the information society encourages industries to increase the production of the processed and packaged. This high-input system clutters—"we suffer a lag in which the slow horse of meaning is unable to keep up with the fast horse of mere information."[33] As Alvin Toffler predicted, the "future shock" of information establishes a sensibility of boredom and permanent distraction, defined by having to choose what to incorporate and what to disregard. The unified informatization mediates the inhabitation of the environment, blurring its material particularities and so favoring the possibilities of the computer-generated. Through screens, which are necessary to operate in space and which present the same intelligence regardless of location, experience morphs into the functional repetition of codes and input of data, weakening the corporeal and dividing attention.[34] To David Foster Wallace, who summarizes the last quarter of the twentieth century, technology, boredom, and entertainment are co-dependent proxies:

> Admittedly, the whole thing's pretty confusing, and hard to talk about abstractly... but surely something must lie behind not just Muzak in dull or tedious places anymore but now also actual TV in waiting rooms, supermarkets' checkouts, airports' gates, SUVs' backseats. Walkmen, iPods, BlackBerries, cell phones that attach to your head. This terror of silence with nothing diverting to do. I can't think anyone really believes that today's so-called "information society" is just about information.[35]

As part of this increasing speed in technology, with attendant boredom due to overexcitement, the production of architecture along with its related industries became more sophisticated, with rapid means to organize information and render representations. Although the digital conceptualization of space remains predominantly Euclidean and Cartesian—isotropic, based on the X, Y, Z, and U factors, the fourth enabling the addition of points ad infinitum—the creation of complexity became precise and repeatable, empowering and compelling innovation in the discipline. Bernard Cache remarks that the feeling of omnipotence of computer-aided design is the result of the capacity to create surfaces that defy spatial coherence, with the challenge of turning the non-standard into the standard to enable fabrication and secure profitability. Consequently, echoing Fukuyama's elaboration on the consolidation of liberalism in the pursuit of homogeneity, the dependence of the new on technological advancement appears as a condition of post-industrialism and the productivity of services rather than as the concern with conceptual breakthrough.[36] The capacity to create technology for architecture depends on the vigor of the economy—the more resources, the more rapidly the cycle is completed, impelling obsolescence to secure the survival of the system and thus dictating the pace of the creation and discard of architecture.

Boredom, an Architectural Ideology

In postmodernity, this accelerated rhythm of creation and destruction was additionally influenced by political conditions. To Tony Judt, communism and liberalism in Europe enforced the construction of two types of environment, both infused by boredom. Under communism, the built environment echoed not only the reigning economic stagnation but also the ideological principles of totalitarianism. Everyday life in the Brezhnev era was shaped not by terror or repression but by boredom and grayness, producing disaffection with the aim to diminish political opposition. In the Soviet bloc, apartments and living facilities were inexpensive due to a scarcity of work rather than any excess of supply, with the authorities seeking to maintain the loyalty of the majority by distributing the limited resources. As a direct consequence, alcoholism and mortality increased, as did a state of distraction due to distress:

> Public architecture in Communists societies was not only aesthetically unappealing, it was shoddy and uncomfortable, a faithful mirror of the shabby authoritarianism of the system itself. As a Budapest taxi-driver once remarked to the present author, pointing to the serried ranks of dank, grimy apartment blocks that disfigure the city's outer suburbs: "We live in those. Typical Communist building—summer is hot, winter very cold."[37]

Furthermore, the few creative efforts of architecture were controlled and dedicated only to the fortification of the political hegemony. In Romania, the dictatorship of Nicolae Ceausescu, whom Judt nicknames "The Architect," imposed centralization through homogeneous monumentality in the buildings and spaces that represented his power.[38] To confirm Bucharest as the capital of the empire, he devised a project of renovation in

1978 that entailed the demolition of a historic district the size of Venice, with more than 40,000 buildings and many churches, to create space for the House of the People and the five-kilometer-long, 150-meter-wide Victory of Socialism Boulevard. For Judt, this personal imprinting in the fabric of the city was a façade: "behind the gleaming white frontages of the boulevard were run up the familiar dirty, grim, pre-cast concrete blocks. But the façade itself was aggressively, humiliatingly, unrelentingly uniform, a visual encapsulation of totalitarian rule." Fronted by a hemicycle that can accommodate half a million people, the neoclassical design by Anca Petrescu, the then twenty-five-year-old architect in charge, "was indescribably and uniquely ugly even by the standards of its genre. Grotesque, cruel and tasteless it was above all *big*."[39] As the heaviest building in the world, the House of People constitutes an architectural metaphor of absolutism, with a direct and unquestionable message of political domination.

Under liberalism, variety in the built environment and better living conditions materialized due to the economic investment required by the free market, the privatization of industries, and the support of technological development, but with a monotony by which a sentiment of discontent and despair prevailed. Constant unemployment, the loss of manufacturing activities, and the culture of individualism nurtured by conservative politicians—as Margaret Thatcher declared, "there is no such thing as Society ... there are individual men and women, and there are families"—created a crisis of meaning that forced the re-evaluation of what it means to live in modern Europe.[40] Judt mentions that the majority of the population sought material security, leaving aside ideological principles and the euphoria of the economic bonanza of the 1960s. Finding economic means was more important to young people than "changing the world," and "the fascination with collective ambitions gave way to an obsession with personal needs." In a Britain plagued by political movements founded on single issues—usually anti- rather than pro-, including environmentalism and pacifism—the sense of community and the authentic eroded; the dismantling of "all collectively-held resources" and the disdain for "any unquantifiable assets" fostered "a new realism" of anomie.[41] As happened in the City of London after 1986, when the financial market was deregulated and opened to international competition, public life was reduced to monetary transactions, without social responsibilities, framed by public spaces that fell into neglect and resembled commercial fairs. The affluence of the privileged few was accompanied by the poverty of the majority, with attendant squalor and delinquency; boredom then appeared to be a condition of wealth, busyness, and involvement as well as of scarcity, servitude, and lack of participation.

With the fall of the Berlin Wall and the rise of the European Union, inequality became regional rather than national, divided between the prosperous north, the upcoming south, and the poor east, marked by territorial fission and the disappearance of Russia as the last European empire. Consequently, the sense of home and belonging—the opposite of boredom—became layered, with concomitant spheres of different character that offered diverse but conflicting opportunities of significance. The spatial sphere was defined by the project of a shared economy in the name of stability, contrasting with local sensibilities expressed through nationalist separatism. Despite the homogenization caused by the euro and the neutrality of the officers in Brussels, the coalition entailed the sentiment of being part of a new collective identity. The member states were no longer independent units but rather a tightly connected landscape of high mobility due to the revamped infrastructure of transportation—bridges, tunnels, roads, trains, and ferries that extended similar projects of the late nineteenth century. And in the temporal sphere, an old Europe transitioned into a new one, challenging the design of the future. Judt remarks that the popular fascination with historical nostalgia responded to the need to be distracted, rather than any prompted by a desire to enlighten the present, illustrating "the way things weren't" in the case of Britain, or "how very different things had once been" in the case of France—particularly evident in acts of architectural preservation and iconic creation:

> [François] Mitterrand's own distinctive contribution to the national *patrimoine* was not so much to preserve or classify it as to manufacture it in real time. No French ruler since Louis XIV has marked his reign with such profusion of buildings and ceremonials. The fourteen years of Mitterrand's presidency [1981–95] were marked not only by a steady accumulation of museums, memorials, solemn inaugurations, burials and reburials; but also by herculean efforts to secure the President's *own* place in the nation's heritage: from the appalling Grande Arche at La Défense in western Paris, through the graceful Pyramid at the Louvre and the aggressively modernist Opera House by the Bastille, to the controversial new National Library on the south bank of the Seine.[42]

In 1978 and 1987, respectively, Heilbroner and Mager predicted that the upward phase of the fifth economic period of capitalism would end in the early 2000s, bringing an inevitable recession so drastic that it would challenge capitalism.[43] Anticipating the economic crisis of 2007, both economists envisaged that the unjust distribution of wealth would create extreme differences between social groups, from which would ensue violence, despair, radicalism, and the erosion of the order and predictability of the interests. For Heilbroner, "any of these may become the entering wedge of a new crisis, pushing for further adaptations that may ultimately exceed the capabilities of the system."[44] If the principles of the long wave cycles are seen as cycles of boredom and excitement, then the post-capitalist era will be defined by a universal technological system that will permit further global connectivity and a more intersected economy, nurturing standardization.[45] This homogeneous space will act as the basis of the search for meaning and difference, not as a teleology reminiscent of the preoccupations of the early twentieth century but as the conscious inhabitation of parallel realms—emotional and intellectual, interior and exterior, physical and virtual. The simultaneity of these territories emphasizes their nodes of correlation rather than the specificity of their configurations, encouraging design and creation, repetitive or not.

CHAPTER 13
ANDREW BENJAMIN'S ANTITHESIS TO BOREDOM

Expanding the postmodern concern with creation, Andrew Benjamin elaborates on how boredom incites and organizes experimentation, before the new has been generated. In "Boredom and Distraction: The Moods of Modernity" (2005), the philosopher notes that innovation as a reaction to the boring entails a threshold of potentiality—in between architectures and temporalities—without the determinism of utopias. The interpretation derives from convolute D, titled "Boredom, Eternal Return," of *The Arcades Project* (1927–40) by Walter Benjamin, where the condition appears as a malady attendant to the modern disintegration of traditional forms of experience.[1] Rather than presenting a conceptual or historical synthesis of the many original and quoted fragments, A. Benjamin poses the project of boredom as a modern meta-structure, or mega-force, with the capacity to promote the ideation of what has not been conceived yet.

Though W. Benjamin provides seductive images to describe the condition, including the cycles of cosmos and weather that blanket all, colonnades and arcades redefined by dust, and the grayness of Paris, "Boredom and Distraction" surpasses the representational. Advancing the elaborations by Søren Kierkegaard and Martin Heidegger, boredom is posed not as a symptom of any other state but rather as a consequential component of modernity. Its importance lies in the capacity to extend its effects to the interstices between interiority and exteriority, articulating both dimensions—similar to the hiatuses that simultaneously connect and divide the aphorisms that compose *The Arcades Project*. Like in Kierkegaard, the experience is undesired and demonic; yet boredom is not contained and does not entail confinement since it morphs into many configurations, invading all spaces. Corresponding with Heidegger, boredom emerges as a mood not historically random, which exists on its own as "there is" as well as in the "I" of the individual, a nexus that is lived out and thus consolidates and informs subjectivity.[2] In addition, as A. Benjamin insinuates, boredom can linger in the material, persisting in the sensible, the sensuous, and the architectural, and resonating with one of the many figures imagined in W. Benjamin's convolute D—with color, texture, temperature, and capacity to perform:

> Boredom is a warm gray fabric lined on the inside with the most lustrous and colourful of silks. In this fabric we wrap ourselves when we dream. We are at home in the arabesques of its lining. But the sleeper looks bored and gray within his sheath. And when he later wakes and wants to tell of what he dreamed, he communicates by and large only this boredom. For who would be able at one stroke to turn the lining of time to the outside? Yet to narrate dreams signifies

nothing else. And in no other way can one deal with the arcades—structures in which we relive, as in a dream, the life of our parents and grandparents, as the embryo in the womb relives the life of animals. Existence in these spaces flows then without accent, like the events in dreams.³

The Bored Mass Individual, the Boring World, and the Repetition of Boredom

A. Benjamin separates "the factual boredom of a given individual" from "the world that continues to present itself as boring." In the boredom of the individual, the condition is subjective, emerging as so imperious as to immobilize and deplete interest. Since everyone is vulnerable to it, boredom establishes a "mass individual," akin to the "us" of the profound boredom diagnosed by Heidegger but conforming to a network of interrelation rather than being an association of isolated nodes of sameness. The mass individual is simultaneously "dispersed across, though also articulated within, this matrix," responding in affirmative unison to the question of "Who is bored?" Unlike the dandy or the flâneur, it is not part of an inchoate society nor the backdrop of action of the individual; instead, the mass individual provides a political stance between personal interests and collective action, without mobilizing one into the other but involving the possibility of solidarity. Accordingly, when the world continues to present itself as boring, the individual loses importance and the "there is" of boredom becomes dominant; it affects singularity through the exterior matrix, with "a greater scope precisely because it is not subject-dependent. (This form of boredom is not more authentic. Rather it identifies a different locus of intervention and thus enjoins a different politics.)."⁴ Following W. Benjamin, the experience of architecture discloses this dual structure of boredom as "the prototype of an art work that is received in a state of distraction and through the collective [*das Kollektivum*]."⁵ Since the modern built environment systematizes the repetitive patterns of habit, then its encounter—"neither in simple contemplation nor complete absorption"—is defined by the emotional and intellectual dispositions that result from its inescapable rhythm.⁶

The "I" and the "there is" establish an ambiguous succession that departs from the consumption of the new only to witness its decay. Because the moment of boredom escapes historicizing, the act of boredom—its experience and the circumstances that trigger its rise—arranges a series of voids fixated in the present, as coordinates of an axis independent of the content of the deteriorated new.⁷ With neither future nor past, these moments derive from the anti-climactic consumption of purposeless material, which is incapable of suggesting a narrative unless the circle of reproduction is the object of desire, as W. Benjamin asserts by quoting Nietzsche: "let us think this thought in its most terrible form: existence as it is, without meaning or aim, yet recurring inevitably without any finale of nothingness: *the eternal return* ... We deny end goals: if existence had one, it would have to have been reached."⁸

Although the boring intimates further boredom and the new supports the emergence of more newness, the irruption of the boring and the distraction of the new can potentially produce more than alternative images. For A. Benjamin, both instances permit transformation by acknowledging the existing limits. When the boring and the new have been surpassed, the progression becomes evident in innovative forms and methods that procure original effects, such as, in the case of architecture, the introduction of previously unused materials and experimental technologies of construction. The new surfaces not as the action or disposition that thwarts the lethargy of boredom but as a counter-mood that balances by creating dynamism. Significantly, the resulting ambivalence turns into "the site of intervention" and "the cause of politics," since it permits variation and "the fray of edges," presaging other possibilities without being absolute.[9]

Experimentation, or the Dialectical Antithesis to Boredom

According to A. Benjamin, the move from the thematic to the philosophical in W. Benjamin's convolute D—from Charles Baudelaire to Nietzsche, intermediated mainly by Louis A. Blanqui—confirms boredom as a prevalent mood in the modern era. Rather than focusing on the provocative content of the selected quotes, W. Benjamin utilizes the subjectivity of each author by directing attention to the similarity of their concerns, indicating that repetition and sameness have implications for the understanding of history. The eternal return of the cycle defined by boredom and the new is an indispensable constituent of progress, "in an infinite perfectibility understood as an ethical task," turning into "indissoluble antinomies in the face of which the dialectical conception of historical time must be developed." If boredom arises when the future is indeterminate—the new has not yet been imagined or symbolized and thus cannot be expended—then it also constitutes the "threshold of great deeds," raising the question, "What is the dialectical antithesis?"[10]

To answer, A. Benjamin returns to the image of the gray fabric with colorful lining that covers the sleeper. From the outside, the sheath is unappealing; from the inside, not only is it beautiful, vivid, and refined, but also it provides a reality of full immersion—both sides compose an inseparable unity. W. Benjamin muses that "if sleep is the apogee of physical relaxation, boredom is the apogee of mental relaxation. Boredom is the dream bird that hatches the egg of experience."[11] The discoloration of boredom necessitates the brightness of the new to exist and become manifest, wanting one is needing the other, and thus the antithesis of boredom is the act of waking up and lifting the fabric, exposing and articulating the interior to the exterior. This movement outlines a space in between spaces, unstable and fragile but recuperating, unplanned and speculative but necessary, whereby the specificity of the dream is repositioned as the potentiality of reality. In the hypnopompic process of rousing, the future escapes predictability and calculability and thus forces the inhabitation of the front edge of the present, amidst awaiting and expectation. For A. Benjamin, due to the lack of determination or the loss of the memory of the dream, "what must be taken up is boredom as a threshold."[12] Of variable dimensions—thin or thick, wide or narrow, high or low, as circumstances allow—this spatial formation does not have to be constructed since it is already present, expecting to be traversed.[13] Passing through this threshold—"a crossing in which futurity is introduced as made possible by the present's potentiality"—requires overlooking the existing visions and depictions of the future. Without being the new, it creates space and time for becoming and forming as well as for equivocation, increasing the possibility of instances of surprise that tend to be abolished in the strict planning of modernity:

> The coat turning with a rapidity within which both the grey and the colour in an instance—the instance as "standstill"—become the opening where "great deeds" will occur. The grey and the lustrous are brought into play. Their juxtaposition will have become an opening. An opening that appears within the repetition of habit, though equally it appears within repetition as habit.[14]

As the moment after stimulation but before the consideration of design, boredom thus involves latency and possibility—interruption as well as continuation—infused with the political since it promotes "the winning of the future." Responding to convolute D, A. Benjamin concludes that "the dialectical antithesis to boredom is experimentation; experimentation both as mood and as act." However, aligned with Schopenhauer's and Sontag's views on boredom as only possible in material affluence, "there cannot be any naivety concerning experimentation," for "it occurs at the time of the commodity."[15]

CHAPTER 14
BOREDOM IN *DOMUS*

In April 1980, *Domus*, number 605, delved into boredom. Under the direction of Alessandro Mendini, the "Forum" section of the Italian magazine presented short entries by artists and intellectuals. The voices of Hermann Grosser, Fulvio Irace, Allan Kaprow, Nam June Paik, Pierre Restany, and the editorial team composed a dialogue that favored the literary and polyphonic rather than the visual and cacophonous, in a conspicuous effort to surpass the visually representational. Coherent with the postmodern critique of the architect as the autocratic figure of genius, the multiple authors contributed to a narrative that accentuated the possibilities of interrelation, the concurrence of dissimilar personalities, and the latency of open endings. The content, editorial strategy, and layout of the "Forum" not only employed boredom as a stance against modernist sensibilities but also exposed it as an inevitable component of the creative process, in need of recognition and appropriation.

The "Forum" was part of the editorial structure designed by Mendini when he assumed the role of editor-in-chief in January 1980. Conceived in collaboration with Restany, a devoted member of *Domus* since 1963, the segment helped to set the tone of each issue.[1] It appeared after the opening letter addressed to a design celebrity featured on the cover—all people from the contemporaneous present, such as Andy Warhol, in number 603, and Méret Oppenheim, in number 605 (with the exception of Andrea Palladio, in number 609). In 1980 and 1981, the "Forum" explored many conceptual themes not exclusive to architecture, closer to the philosophical and mystic than to the scientific and pragmatic; the objective was to understand their role in the production and perception of the built environment. Similar to a newspaper, it comprised multiple entries, in both Italian and English, with fixed subsections, including an interview with a relevant artist, the explanation of the origins of the subject, non-illustrational images, and a closing photo-essay of Restany in conversation either with himself and art works or with artists and architects. Over these two years, the "Forum" discussed, in chronological order: information and society, joy, the body, boredom, fashion, food, leisure-time, air, earth, water, fire, galaxy, habitat, survival, violence, Italy, the East, North, South, West, El Dorado, and the apocalypse. Exhibiting the interesting, colorful, and dynamic—the non-boring—the "Forum" was eclectic, anthropological, sensitive, and concerned with global phenomena. Part of Mendini's intention with *Domus* to provide "reports, news, doubts, truths and even paradoxical falsehoods" so that the reader "can formulate his own personal diagnosis of the constructed world, and react ... by concrete design and by imagining Utopias," the "Forum" paired architecture with the sensuous and symbolic.[2]

By the end of 1981, the "Forum" and its suggestive layout, supervised by Restany, had moved to the end of the magazine, altering its introductory character. The investigation of conceptual themes was replaced by that of the architectural production in different urban centers, such as Barcelona, Los Angeles, and London, with the promotional tone and graphic design of touristic brochures. In 1984, once the elaboration on cities as capitals of architecture was exhausted, the section turned its attention to the review of art and architectural exhibitions, and included information on books, competitions, and conferences. The following year, the "Forum" remained in the closing part, but it was reduced to two or three contributions, without the fragmented arrangement. With the departure of Mendini in 1986, the section ceased to exist.[3]

Heterogeneous Fragments

The concurrence of several perspectives in the "Forum" questioned universalization and uniformity, revealing fragmentation and heterogeneity as characteristics of the postmodern environment. In the first number of the magazine directed by Mendini, the opening letter affirms that architectural culture was experiencing "a difficult moment—of transfer and frontier—because theoretic awareness is falling apart and too many vague ghosts of cultures differing from the norm can be glimpsed." For the editor-in-chief, influenced by the rebellious attitudes of the late 1960s and the pessimistic mood resulting from the economic crisis of 1974, the failure of the Modern Movement to create and foster "a popular architecture" had led to "widespread mannerist, experimental, and fragmentary activity"; additionally, the lack of inclusiveness and pluralism was "typical of a world and of an epoch characterized by the most violent environmental degradation ever to have occurred in history."[4]

Critical of the reductive clarity of abstraction, Mendini explored the combination of diverse elements as a technique of design. For instance, the Proust Armchair (1978), one of his most acclaimed creations, amalgamates historical references of diverse origins, reassessing canons of good taste and functionality. Commissioned by Cassina in 1976 to develop a fabric motif, Mendini embarked on a two-year research that took him to the places where Marcel Proust lived and frequented. The project was inspired by the superposition of temporalities, as experienced in the "mémoire involuntaire" of the writer, beginning with a ready-made replica of an eighteenth-century armchair.[5] In addition, it maximizes the visual interaction of parts by covering the chair with a pattern derived from an enlarged section of a painting by Paul Signac and then extending its pointillism to the wooden structure. Rather than the natural, matte, and suburban tones of the original inspiration, the novel textile employs artificial, bright, and urban colors, simulating pixels of television and computer screens. This arrangement offers "a sort of kaleidoscopic-atmospheric attempt: to look at the object not as a concluded volumetric fact, but as an element among other elements."[6] Instinctual rather than rational, the Proust Armchair caters to the postmodern individual—"the sentimental robot"—with the aim to recover the memory expelled by the rhetoric of modernism.[7]

Reconsidering the origins of experience, and grounded in the aesthetics and information theory of Abraham Moles, Mendini examined the monotony of the vulgar, the neutrality of the banal, and the excesses of kitsch. These derivatives of modernity were elevated as social phenomena responsible for a common sensibility concerned with the consumption of the "multipliable and perishable," manifested in the realm of retail where the "authentically fake" is available to anyone. Due to their immediacy, these goods do not threaten the establishment; if anything, they distract the individual from becoming aware of the possibilities of transgression and potential transcendence. According to Mendini, the propositions of the tasteless are akin to the intimacy of residential interiors where the arbitrary collection of objects cannot be critiqued, but instead permit free associations that fill the emptiness of the bedroom, "a microcosm of objects that resemble as much as possible the macrocosm of the supermarket."[8]

In 1980, as if to furnish this space, Mendini exhibited a series of "banal objects" in the Forum Design in Linz. Displayed as constituents of the postmodern consumer society, the selection of ordinary home instruments—"objects with which we have grown jaded," including a coffee pot, a lamp, and a vacuum cleaner—were painted in bright colors and ornamented with delicate additions that resembled sartorial fascinators.[9] Without varying their function, the pieces turned into signs of temptation that recycled and reactivated what had become worn out, insipid, and lackluster. Their new task seemed to be the pleasurable incentive of imagination, reinstating decoration and humor to the asceticism of the modern everyday. Yet despite their sprightly appearance, the objects projected nihilism.[10] They disclosed the ephemerality of desire and the inevitability of boredom by admitting that the ideal object cannot be materialized and therefore can only be imitated and endlessly reinvented; the new, once it has been ideated, produced, and consumed, is destined to become fatiguing. For Mendini, "each new design is always just a 'redesign' of the cosmos that all forms belong to, an endless stream of 'universal cosmetics', glittering dust, illusion on bodies, clothes, objects, buildings, in the world."[11] By implication, architects and designers can only reproduce historical and ornamental patterns, since they are unable to provide definitive answers—their basic urge is to decorate in order to secure individuation. Echoing Warhol, the editor observes, "these days no one wants to be lost in the crowd; personality is everything. Everyone is different, so why not make every object different and challenging?"[12]

Procuring the architecturally unorthodox, Mendini designed the Groninger Museum in 1987. The building assembled volumes in contrasting shapes, materials, and colors, harmoniously competing for prominence, interconnected though a central node of circulation.[13] For Charles Jencks, this formal strategy was neither functional nor spectacular but instead historically emblematic—the pavilion in brick resonated with the medieval past of the city while the aluminum cylinder represented the decorative arts period. In the critic's interpretation, the architecture "is delightfully legible and as heterogeneous as the artefacts inside. No museum fatigue here, no row of endless cases as in a 19th century mausoleum-museum, no monotone of a Miesian voice droning on and putting one to sleep." Marking the success of Mendini's intentions, the collage-like arrangement reminded Jencks of two allusions of the past and the then present. The first was the Exquisite Corpse method of creation, popularized by Surrealism and Dada, in which a sequence of design is initiated by one artist and followed by the interventions of several others, without a definite end. This co-authorship referred to the designers who participated in the creation of the museum; the contributions by Philippe Starck, Michele de Lucchi, and Coop Himmelb(l)au suggested anti-elitism, democracy, and acceptance, setting a benchmark of diversity for other postmodernists. The second was the resemblance of the composition of the Museum to a main street and its "agglomeration of varying materials, functions and styles." To Jencks, the architecture of the building copies the organization of urban spaces, breaking down the scale of "the dismal megastructions of the 1960's, or even the complex villages of Hertzberger and Van Eyck, brilliant in mimicking difference through structural variation, but still singular statements of a single sensibility."[14]

"Forum" Boredom

Following the connotations of the architecture of the Roman forum, the section in *Domus* is presented as a space of public opinion, for gathering and discussion, delimited by political and ideological convictions. In the printed realm of the magazine, the gaps resulting from the conglomeration of blocks of text and images are as expressive as their content; the interstices insinuate not only the inconclusiveness of each entry but also the possibility of establishing conceptual and historical interrelations, with diagonal crossings. As an aleatory hypertext, the "Forum" liberates the reader from the constrictions of any linear and precise organization of information; like a semi-regular patchwork that lacks hierarchy and a centralized structure, the layout is dynamic at the risk of capturing partial attention.[15] The graphic design does not include special fonts or dominant photographs—only a purple background emphasizing the title of each contribution.

Similar to Mendini's idea of the perfect space—"the ground for a thousand surprises, a perfect mechanism for creativity"—the section unveils boredom as in constant fruition and historical transformation.[16] Staying away from the solely architectural, the participating authors preferred philosophical and literary references of previous centuries, quoting Søren Kierkegaard, Gustave Flaubert, and Giacomo Leopardi, among others, rather than the theoretical and critical elaborations of their own century. The excerpts are both warnings from elapsed eras as well as nodes of a non-sequential trajectory of memory. Furthermore, stressing the variety of spaces and temporalities, the featured images combine genres—credited and uncredited photographs of places, people, and art, a cartoon and a photo-novel—and are independent of the text, not illustrations but rather visual cues establishing thematic connections. In black and white, they portray instances of boredom through relationships with the environment, multicultural actions, and reactions rather than as aesthetic qualities of any specific geography.

Uniformity According to Eve and Adam

In the opening entry, the title "One Day Boredom Was Born from Uniformity" is the last line of the poem "Friends Who Agree" (1715) by Antoine Houdar de La Motte.[17] Restany discloses boredom as a state of mental restlessness that surfaces from the exposure to formal monotony and repetition, a characterization that resonates with the etymological origin of the French *ennui* and the Italian *noia*, which is the Latin *inodiare*, denoting annoyance but also stimulation. This duality is a virtue that propels creation, since "variety stops boredom." The optimistic corollary empowers the capacity for environments to promote imagination and wonder, redefining function not as a commodity to be traded but as an opportunity for engagement derived from inspiration. Quoting Jean Cocteau—"there is no useful form except changes that arouse surprise"—Restany asserts that the indulgence "in the pleasures of imaginative deviation" of the end of the millennium is a reaction to the aridity of pure functionalism and its "whole system of archetypes, examples and references." This rejection thus produces techniques of design similar to décollage—protest-design, de-architecture, anti-art, form-non-form—which rely on "the principle of dematerialization," challenging static permanency to strengthen the "passing from the object to the concept and from the real to the symbol."[18] Consequently, boredom derives from the failure to hint at any emotional or intellectual immateriality, becoming a threat to the survival of imagination. For Restany, "the great fear that hangs over the year 2000 is not of the atom, but the fear of boredom"; to confront it, he prescribes the ritual and the spiritual as the means to overcome the repetitiousness of any model. Innovation is capable of battling "the great ill of the West" as long as it is not limited to the hermetic and self-referential; it can attain wisdom through incorporating the other, as in the initiation into the liturgy of the Orient. The conclusion is that the task of new art and architecture, exemplified in the immersive spaces assembled by Nam June Paik, John Cage, Allan Kaprow, and Yves Klein, is to transform boredom from being "the great terror of life" into "the foundation for an aesthetic of action."[19]

Set between the Italian and English versions of Restany's entry is a cartoon from *The Frustrated* (1980) by Claire Bretecher that highlights "the frantic agitation of our western cities and the anguish of our hours of freedom, and the years of our old age" (Figure 14.1). The drawing portrays a woman reclining on a sofa, barefoot in a domestic interior, surrounded by an open book, an ashtray, cigarettes, and a drink, as if she were in front of a television. Despite her explicit attempts to keep herself distracted, she moans, "Questa volta sono veramente stufa" (this time I am really fed up). She has exhausted her capacity to sustain attention, which leaves her in a state of weariness and unrest, abandoned to daydreaming and other mental meanderings considered unproductive and aimless by the progressive efforts of modernism.[20]

Along the lower half of the "Forum" runs an "Eve & Adam" component, a continuous strip that evokes a podium for discussion and whose title alters the conventional order of Adam and Eve. Written anonymously, the subsection is a transcription of a consultation, an "organic, psychological, social and cosmic dialogue," among the members of the editorial team. It begins by confessing that the decision to investigate boredom was the result of attendance at a conference on art, which "set our minds working on the relation between temporal perception, sensorial perception, emotive structures and boredom arising from the duration of artistic expression in time, be it a performance, a video-installation or an audio-visual."[21]

The dialogue entry extends the discussion from boredom in the spaces of art to the origins of being bored. It is a physiological and psychological mechanism, "an alarm signal" of "the refusal to let oneself be involved." Similar to the protective function of disgust, boredom evades unsafe confinement and predictability, acting on the body—the bios—to inscribe habits and practices that achieve the interesting: "boredom is inside of us … It's a bit like some cancers: they may explode or stay silent, but we carry them within us from birth."[22] As an affection of the mind—the nous—it exerts power over irrational sentiments and logical thoughts, altering perception, attention, and memory, crucial forces behind consumerism.[23] In modern Western societies, boredom is essential in the recovery of expended energy, allowing rest and introspection as well as concentration and de-concentration. The origin of boredom also has social and ideological affiliations. As a political circumstance, the dread of being portrayed as boring modifies behavior, encouraging the adoption of alter egos to mask servitude and cultural dominations; however, being boring can turn into a strategy of power—"in human relations, boredom does indeed assume both these antithetic aspects: boredom as a closure, as impotence, and boredom as an instrument of oppression."[24] To illustrate, in the long speeches of fascist politicians, suffering boredom denotes impairment of understanding, and imposing boredom unveils access to knowledge. In the case of the built environment, complicit with mechanisms of control, the voices of the dialogue wonder if the realm of the city enforces the condition or if the condition propels the construction of settings that perpetuate its existence. Yet regardless of its cause, they agreed that boredom shapes experience and sensibility, which are reflected back into architecture, forcing the individual to adapt perceptual faculties and devise new strategies of spatial occupation; as the polis changes, so do the bios and nous of the citizen.

Two photographs in "Eve & Adam" contribute to the question of whether boredom is an essential component of being human or a modern condition nurtured by culture and society. The first shows a man squatting on top of a metal cylinder, covered by an umbrella, during a flood in a road between Delhi and Agra. To his right and left, other umbrellas suggest that other individuals are in the same situation, waiting for the rain to stop.[25] Recalling W. Benjamin's affirmation that weather and boredom are deeply related—"nothing bores the ordinary man more than the cosmos"—the non-Western scene portrays the condition as trans-cultural, inescapable, an attribute of being in the world, melding nature and architecture; the umbrellas turn into units of space that provide protection from everyday weathering, in between production and disruption.[26] The second image guides the viewer to see the scene that a guard at the Royal Palace in Rabat sees. In traditional costume, he is on duty but at rest, filling the foreground but in the shadows of the threshold of an unseen building. In front of him, in bright light, stretches the parade ground, with its ruins of the former fortress and the towering mosque; sightseers move into the distance, leaving the compound. The architecture of the past encounters the present through tourism. The visit of foreigners requires the allocation of sentinels who also become cultural indicators, as emblems of authority in the historical architecture of power. Like signposts, they guide movement, limit exploration, and—like boredom—imply that a precious core exists yet cannot be revealed, perpetuating further visitation.

The "Eve & Adam" subsection concludes by realizing that the experience of boredom is not absolute, that it comprises gradations, from being bored mildly and occasionally to severely and chronically, thus necessitating varied descriptions. The many types of boredom, "which refer to contents far removed from each other, ought to be specified with different terms." To help the dissection and verbalization of the extreme flexibility of boredom, two lists of confronting but non-corresponding near synonyms are provided, in Italian—*accidia, contrattempo, cruccio, disgusto, disturbo, fastidio, fatica, imbarazzo, impaccio, incomodo, inedia, mattana, molestia, monotonia, nausea, sazieta, seccatura, stanchezza, tedio, uggia, zuppa*—and in English—weariness, tedium, melancholy, uninterest, indifference, fatigue, tediousness, heaviness, satiation, satiety, disgust, nausea, dislike, flatness, insipidity, stuffiness, dullness, prolixity, uniformity, monotony, inactivity.[27]

Alternatives to Boredom

The second spread of the "Forum," subtitled "On the Various Possibilities to Interpret and Utilize Boredom in Art and Life," is an interview with the American artist Allan Kaprow, who compared the condition to the Zen Buddhist principle of "being in the present." For Kaprow, who was celebrated for pioneering the progression from painting to assemblages, environments, and happenings, boredom was a state of consciousness between the interior reality of the individual and the outer world. Beneath the subtitle and a photograph of the artist licking his own hand, the artist proposes that the questioner, probably Restany, "remain silent for the whole of the interview" in order to be "thoroughly bored and boring." Provocation aside, Kaprow contextualizes the implementation of boredom as a modern force of creation by mentioning the elaborations on repetition, banality, and monotony by Stéphane Mallarmé, Marcel Duchamp, and John Cage. Although Kaprow denounces their work as elitist signs better understood by educated audiences, it nevertheless constitutes "dissacratory acts" that procured the "interesting."[28] Hence, he compares the relationship between boredom and tedium to the advancement from interest to passion. Forming an allegiance, boredom and interest permit the coexistence of other phenomena, constantly creating space for more material and more information, and so evading the overpowering totality of the deficit of tedium and the surplus of passion.

Moreover, Kaprow distinguishes the facileness of "everyday boredom" from the importance of "philosophical boredom," which is "a discipline of attention known to all meditative techniques in history."[29] The philosophical boredom resembles Zen since it constitutes an "anti-intellectual" condition in which the mind is "a part of consciousness, not its determinant." Unlike the everyday kind, this boredom does not allow "getting lost in the myriad of thoughts, desires, and judgements that continuously make claims upon awareness." In principle, it ought to evolve into acceptance rather than regressing into despair or dismay; its function is to induce a militancy that forces the individual to realize "I am bored" only to ponder "Why should I be bored?" and "Why are they doing this to me?"[30] The resulting outrage devolves into self-awareness, implanting the possibility of difference and transgression as means to achieve a particular goal. For instance, extending habitual actions, such as walking or eating, by slowing their pace transforms boredom into a new state of attentiveness, inventiveness, and fascination, enabling the absorption into a previously unknown dimension and potentially providing access to the profound:

> [I]f one feels powerless or afraid to be alive, or that there is nothing inside, then boredom becomes the justification for it. You say: "I am really bored, I'm not frightened. I am just bored." And it becomes an interior game, of which one may not even be aware. But I want to learn to recognize these little tricks of my own mind in order to be ever more conscious. It's a way to learn how to live and also to prepare yourself for death.[31]

The interview with Kaprow frames two images of diverging architectures. The first is a photograph, by Robert A. Isaacs, of Daly City, a suburb of San Francisco, California (Figure 14.2). The neighborhood was planned and built in the post-war era by Henry Doelger, a prominent developer during the 1930s and 1940s who intended to create a city within a city; in addition to residential units, the project included schools, shopping centers, offices, medical facilities, churches, and parks. The photograph is titled "The Ticky Tacky Houses of Daly City," after the song, written in 1962 by Malvina Reynolds, that is a satire of suburbia and the American middle-class dreams of the 1950s.[32] The lyrics describe the architecture of the single-unit detached houses as "little boxes on the hillside," perceived as identical, "all made out of ticky-tacky," and inhabited by people of the same appearance and occupation. The endless rows of equal houses define a landscape of likeness and stability, suggesting a conformity that is enhanced by the resemblance of the units to the pixels of a low-resolution print. Of the same size and in mirrored position, the second photograph captures a man lying down at the threshold of an interior patio in a mosque in Fez, sleeping as if in the privacy of his own home. Unlike the image of Daly City, it is undated and uncredited, pairing Eastern architecture with tradition and religious beliefs, filled with detail, captured in high resolution. Similar to sleeping and dreaming, boredom emerges as the liminal space between unconsciousness and consciousness, in suspended time. As an architectural metaphor, the condition resembles the arrangement of arcades and colonnades in the second photograph, which connect and protect as well as divide and expose the possibilities of an alternate reality defined by the encounter of exteriority and interiority.

In the next spread, with the title "Instead of Boredom," Hermann Grosser describes boredom as a fracture in classical otium, the joyful and sacred space of contemplation of the harmony of the world. With the advent of the contradictions of modernity, the continuum of the perfect cosmos—"the product of victory over Chaos"—is ruptured, leaving everyone in a state of uncertainty and ambiguity and therefore evincing the awareness of dissonance with the surroundings. As a case of spatial de-synchronization,

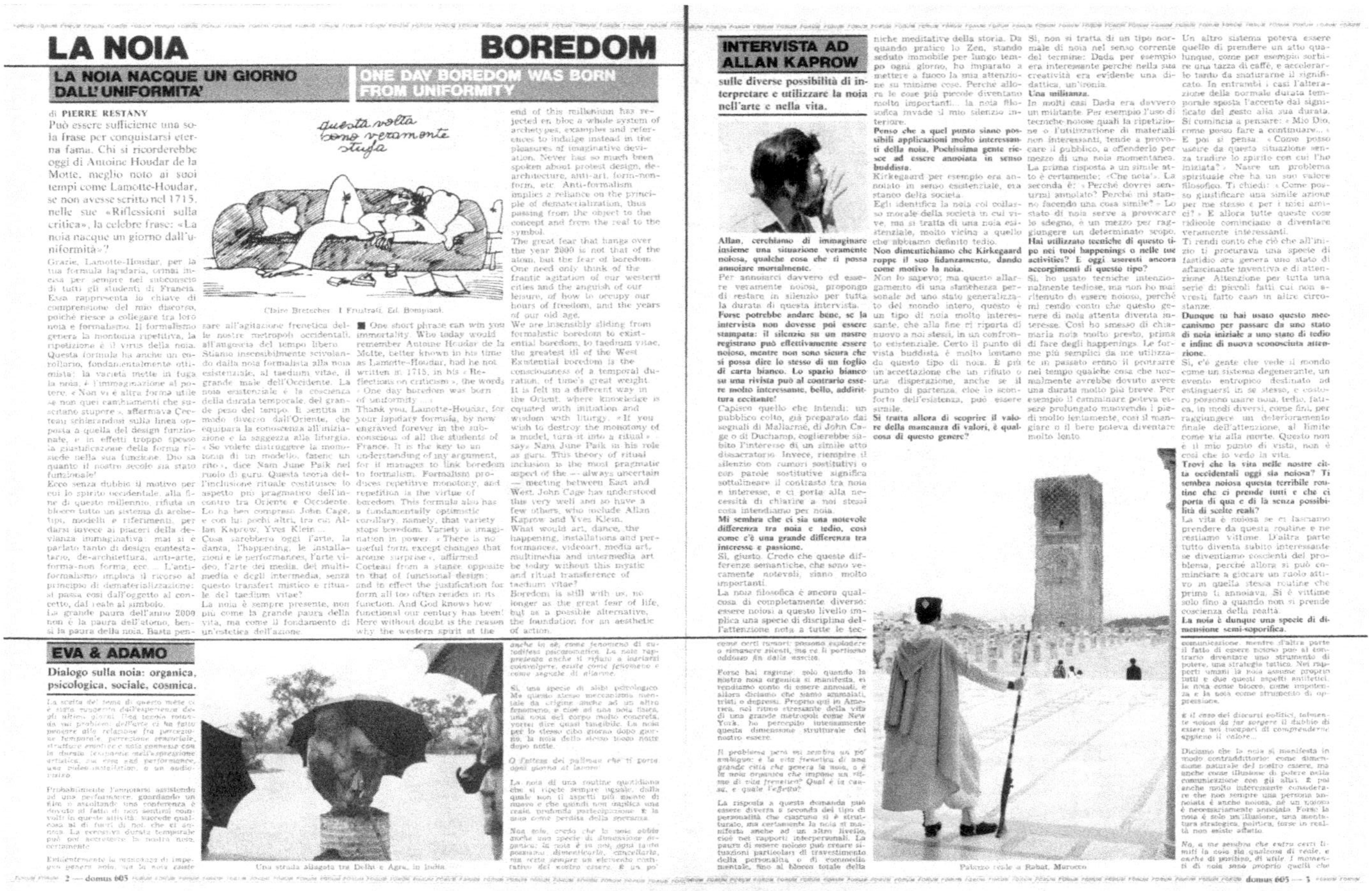
LA NOIA

BOREDOM

LA NOIA NACQUE UN GIORNO DALL'UNIFORMITA'

ONE DAY BOREDOM WAS BORN FROM UNIFORMITY

di PIERRE RESTANY

Può essere sufficiente una sola frase per conquistarsi eterna fama. Chi si ricorderebbe oggi di Antoine Houdar de la Motte, meglio noto ai suoi tempi come Lamotte-Houdar, se non avesse scritto nel 1715, nelle sue «Riflessioni sulla critica», la celebre frase: «La noia nacque un giorno dall'uniformità»?

Claire Bretecher, I Frustrati, Ed. Bompiani.

INTERVISTA AD ALLAN KAPROW

sulle diverse possibilità di interpretare e utilizzare la noia nell'arte e nella vita.

EVA & ADAMO

Dialogo sulla noia: organica, psicologica, sociale, cosmica.

Una strada allagata tra Delhi e Agra, in India.

Palazzo reale a Rabat, Marocco

2 — domus 605

domus 605 — 3

Figure 14.1 First spread of "Boredom," *Domus* 605 (April 1980).

"it is the opposite of nirvana interpreted as neglect of corporality in the satisfaction of need." Alternatively, as explained by referring to Baudelaire, boredom is dwelling in hell—"saison en enfer"—while waiting for the construction of paradise—"les paradis artificiels." In the state of anticipation for the ideal space, always in the making and always artificial, absurdity and anguish disclose the imperfection and vacuity of physical inhabitation; both veil boredom instead of unmasking its capacity to reveal "what the human condition really is."[33] For Grosser, these symptoms have created descriptions of emptiness, not actual emptiness, turning representation into an obstinate concern that has evaded the confrontation with boredom, as endlessly manifested in Franz Kafka, Jean-Paul Sartre, Alberto Moravia, Jorge Luis Borges, Samuel Beckett, and Eugène Ionesco. Their literary depictions elude the alienated position of boredom, rejecting the condition by constructing symbols and casting clichés.

Inserted between the columns of "Instead of Boredom," a photograph of "Five Panel Vertical" (1973) by Judith Bernstein cryptically points to the boredom of signs. The piece of art is composed of charcoal drawings that in the context of the "Forum" resemble the negative spaces of a colonnade, similar to the threshold of the mosque and the silhouette of the umbrellas of the previous pages. Despite this impression, the shapes created by the artist constitute a fusion of phallic imagery and carpentry screws. Their seriality and large scale, a mixture of human and machine, not only denote the oppressiveness of male hegemony but also insinuate that architecture is an accomplice in dominant systems of power. Through the interpretative appropriation of familiar symbols, "Five Panel Vertical" denounces the status quo as exhausted and irrelevant, implying that the representation of the boring and the bored might be more instrumental in the construction of a new order than the deterministic projection of utopias.

Between Less and More, Nam June Paik

On the final page, Fulvio Irace elaborates on boredom as an enabler of balance, after providing a brief genealogy that locates the origins of *noia* in the literary work of Gerardo Patecchio in the thirteenth century. In "Between Less & More: Boredom," Irace describes the condition as a "composition of popular origin consisting in a review of everything which causes trouble"—"the sublime art of rhetoric which, in the dialectic of passions, welds the difference in the arc of affinities!"[34] Boredom confronts enjoyment, thus demonstrating the existence of both poles and promoting their identification and qualitative differentiation, an extension of Roland Barthes's assertion that "you can't get rid of boredom with a gesture of irritation or liberation"; to clarify, Irace quotes at length from "The Gifted Braid" (1815) by Lorenzo Pignotti:

> Love, which knows where to find Boredom, rapidly unfolds its gilded wings ... at last he comes to a superb palace, which he enters, to see Boredom seated between Pomp and Ceremony ... The Goddess keeps not a single form, not a single colour; at each instant everything changes like a cloud at the mercy of the wind ...

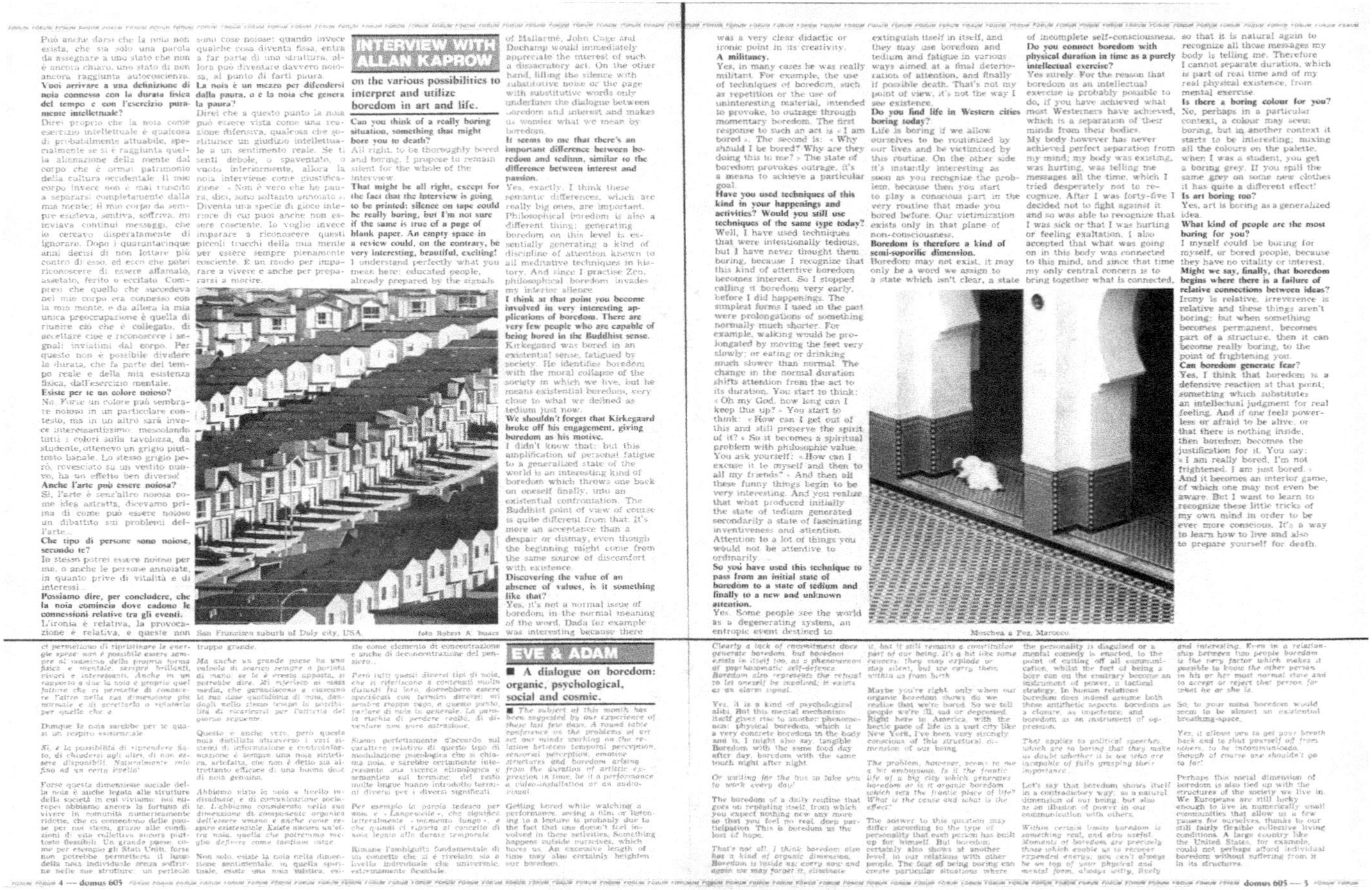

Figure 14.2 Second spread of "Boredom," *Domus* 605 (April 1980).

> Languidly reclining ... she yawns, heavy are her eyes with sleep; she keeps getting up and sitting down ... she desires, but hovers uncertain and irresolute among her cravings; she sighs, but without knowing for what object.[35]

As a goddess of change, Boredom is agitated, swaying from one extreme to another only to become dissatisfied with each destination. She does not personify frustrated desire but the desire for desire, creating demands impossible to satisfy and so perpetuating the illusion that they can be assembled in the future. To Irace, the pursuit of fulfillment entails the yearning for equilibrium, which could be formulated as a plain arithmetic locution in which a minus or a plus can decide what is boring and what is not. If this were possible, then boredom could be identified rapidly in architecture. Nevertheless, the question of which configurations are predisposed to the condition would arise—does it germinate from moderate subtraction or excessive multiplication? "From the indifferent repetition of rationalist housing or the Californian camouflages of some village aesthetic? The absoluteness of systematically 'quality-less' architecture or the sign-redundancy of the banquet of qualities?" As a historiographical reply, Irace configures boredom as the division between the modern and the postmodern, affirming decisively—referencing Venturi tacitly—that since less is no more any longer, then "less is a bore!"[36]

In the concluding subsection, Restany stages an encounter with Nam June Paik. Presented as a photo-novel shot by Harry Shunk, the story is set as a happenstance in an urban setting during winter, sequentially moving to an interior space that seems to be Paik's studio in New York (Figure 14.3). Although the photographs show a sequence of activities that would have taken a long time to occur, the dialogue reads as a fluid and succinct conversation:

> **PR**   Boredom! Who knows it?
>
> **NJP**   Aristocrats know.
>
> **PR**   Aristocrats can be rich in mind, too.
>
> **NJP**   Then they know to use boredom as a tip of spirit.
>
> **PR**   This is a Zen idea.
>
> **NJP**   Montaigne's and Duchamp's, too.
>
> **PR**   Boredom could be death, or even worse, bad taste.
>
> **NJP**   Boredom is not a cleaned up environment.[37]

In eight lines, boredom is posed as an agent of social and intellectual difference, a spiritual and philosophical principle common in both the West and the East, an existential and aesthetical concern, ultimately a condition of space—entropic, unclean, and un-modern. The discontinuous variety of historical, cultural, and ideological precedents operates and interacts in the present, demanding distributed rather than chronological interest. According to Paik, who had elaborated on the condition in 1976, boredom stems from the relationship between "INPUT-time and OUTPUT-time." While the second refers to

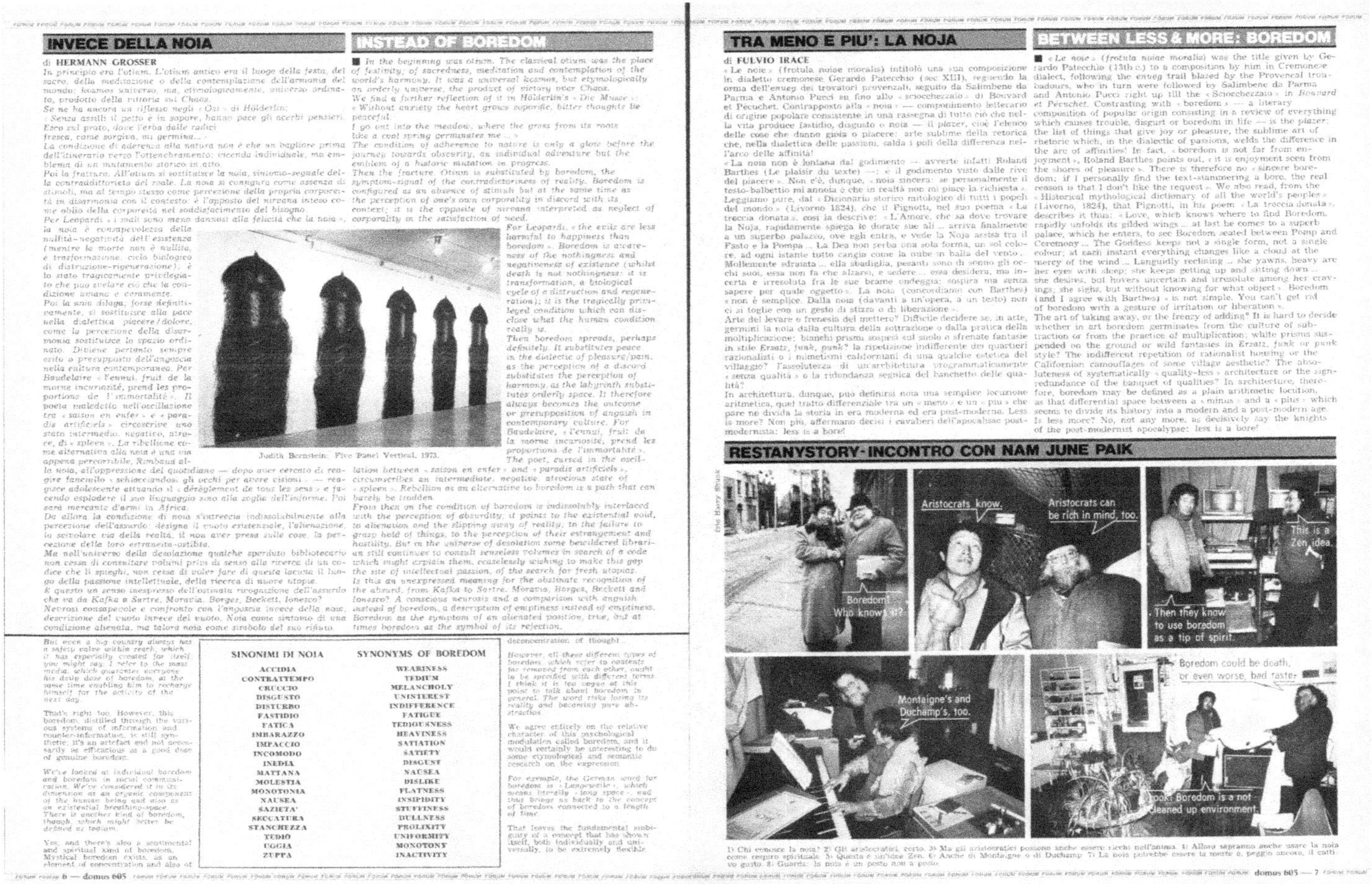

INVECE DELLA NOIA

di HERMANN GROSSER

INSTEAD OF BOREDOM

Judith Bernstein: Five Panel Vertical, 1973.

SINONIMI DI NOIA	SYNONYMS OF BOREDOM
ACCIDIA	WEARINESS
CONTRATTEMPO	TEDIUM
CRUCCIO	MELANCHOLY
DISGUSTO	UNINTEREST
DISTURBO	INDIFFERENCE
FASTIDIO	FATIGUE
FATICA	TEDIOUSNESS
IMBARAZZO	HEAVINESS
IMPACCIO	SATIATION
INCOMODO	SATIETY
INEDIA	DISGUST
MATTANA	NAUSEA
MOLESTIA	DISLIKE
MONOTONIA	FLATNESS
NAUSEA	INSIPIDITY
SAZIETA'	STUFFINESS
SECCATURA	DULLNESS
STANCHEZZA	PROLIXITY
TEDIO	UNIFORMITY
UGGIA	MONOTONY
ZUPPA	INACTIVITY

TRA MENO E PIU': LA NOJA

di FULVIO IRACE

BETWEEN LESS & MORE: BOREDOM

RESTANYSTORY · INCONTRO CON NAM JUNE PAIK

foto Harry Shunk

1) Chi conosce la noia? 2) Gli aristocratici, certo. 3) Ma gli aristocratici possono anche essere ricchi nell'anima. 4) Allora sapranno anche usare la noia come respiro spirituale. 5) Questa è un'idea Zen. 6) Anche di Montaigne o di Duchamp. 7) La noia potrebbe essere la morte o, peggio ancora, il cattivo gusto. 8) Guarda: la noia è un posto non a posto.

Figure 14.3 Third spread of "Boredom," *Domus* 605 (April 1980).

the objective duration of an event, the first denotes its subjective experience, susceptible to compression or extension; for instance, the survivors of air crashes or ski accidents who claim to have recollected their whole life in a flashback, or Proust who isolated himself in a cork-lined room to ponder over a childhood moment. To the artist, boredom gestures simultaneously to these two dimensions of time as sources of information that the brain has to process and edit in order to promote further stimulation, like a "metamorphosis (not only in quantity, but also in quality)."[38] The interrelation between experience and memory advances gradually from the output-time of the exterior environment towards greater moments of input-time in interiority. As elaborated through his work in video art, Paik suggests that simultaneity, pixilation, and techniques of temporal lag induce boredom, as an eternal present that denies the future and abjures the past.

The Most Normal State

The "Forum" avoids prescriptive associations between boredom and architectural forms, pursuing its relevance rather than its appearance. The condition is equally negative and positive, defensive and aggressive, unintentional and deliberate, precarious and advantageous, biological and political—"the most normal state."[39] In all instances, as argued in the entries through the manifold quotations and references, boredom insinuates that inhabitation is an analytical action. Since the modernist proposal of perfect harmony cannot be achieved, then the postmodernist project is to expose incongruences and fractures through architecture and design. Consequently, as in the Proust Armchair, the "banal objects," and the Groninger Museum, the construction of artefacts for dwelling and daily use ought to simulate conditions of heterogeneity and fragmentation, as reflections of the new metropolis. In this realm, boredom is in constant development; if the condition depends on modernity, then its evolution is bound to vary according to the maturity of the era. While the linear everyday life of the turn of the nineteenth century was planned according to the activities of capitalist production, Mendini and Restany anticipate a reality of multiplicity in which the many offerings of the environment coexist, aided and reliant on technological omnipresence and its capacity to connect distant locations, confirming the parallelism of the virtual and the actual. Following Jameson, who remarks how the art of Paik challenges the viewer by tendering many screens demanding attention, the "Forum" requires the reader to accept all the entries as monitors projecting information, at once and randomly, "something for which the word collage is still only a very feeble name."[40]

Aligned with the postmodern search for variety, the fragments of the section show that the logic of multiplicity defies both coincidence and any absorption with a sole object of attention as meaningful and productive, utilizing the overlapping of personalities as a means to promote simultaneity and tension. By composing a totality of conglomerating pieces, Mendini and Restany capitalize on the capacity of the individual to organize dispersion, supported by the split attention of boredom. Architecture thus turns into a source of memory, mind-wandering, and daydreaming, structuring a type of knowledge that guides everyday life and surpasses the simple desire for distraction or the compilation of data—partly like Proust's "mémoire involontaire" that actualizes the past in the present, partly like Henri Bergson's "mémoire pure" that invokes the past to rehash the present.[41]

CHAPTER 15
SERVITUDE AND LIBERALISM: RUSSELL KIRK

> Our ridicules are kept in the back-ground—
>   Ridiculous enough, but also dull;
> Professions too are no more to be found
>   Professional; and there is nought to cull
> Of folly's fruit: for, though your fools abound,
>   They're barren and not worth the pains to pull.
> Society is now one polish'd horde,
> Form'd of two mighty tribes, the *Bores* and *Bored*.
>
> Lord Byron, Don Juan (1823)

Since the popularization of boredom, the accusation of "being boring" has served as a social differentiator. As early as 1823, Lord Byron grouped modern society into "one polish'd horde," subdivided into "the *Bores* and *Bored*"; similarly, in 1893, Oscar Wilde penned a character to theatrically affirm that "it is absurd to divide people into good and bad," since "people are either charming or tedious"; and acknowledging the power of suffusing social encounters with boredom, in 1931, Hilaire Belloc composed "A Guide to Boring," with techniques and recommendations for how to "bore the enemy" to maintain distance.[1] The categorization is elitist and dismissive, denoting that those who find others boring have access to privileges that cannot be shared, a lifestyle that entails a particular sense of belonging and ideological affiliation. However, due to its relational essence and dependence on personal appreciation, "being boring" is immune to political contestation. It is a passive-aggressive indictment—at once comic and tragic as well as trivial and serious, objectively unverifiable, lacking the promise of epistemic gain but with palpable effects and implications.[2]

The same attitude was adopted by Russell Kirk in "The Architecture of Servitude and Boredom," an essay published in the spring of 1982 in the conservative journal *Modern Age*. To the political theorist and cultural critic, "with great buildings or with small, the architecture of our mass-age, in this latter half of the twentieth century, has been wondrously boring." In the United States and the United Kingdom, the built environment of the post-World War II era is described as a misstep of liberal governments and their disregard for religious beliefs, moral values, and social distinction. These principles, coercive and mutually dependent agents of all the variations of non-conservatism, including socialism, fascism, and even neo-conservatism, produce boring buildings that impose boredom on their inhabitants, influencing their behavior. "Featureless," "grim," and "unskilfully constructed" architecture marks political domination and the impossibility of social significance of the inhabitants forced to occupy it, installing subjugation, unrest, and ultimately violence and crime.[3] In addition, Kirk avows, the refusal of urban planning to integrate and preserve monuments of the past impels seclusion and the abandonment of public affairs; instead of invigorating communality, the spaces constructed by non-conservative systems of power curtail civic possibilities.

Without Classes, Faith, or Historical Consciousness

In 1956, diagnosing a crisis in the American and English literary production after the Victorian period, Kirk defined boredom as the result of the conviction that, in modernity, life is not worth living and the world is not worth dwelling in. The condition is presented as a pattern of conduct imposed by industrialism, functionalism, and "the ideas which men hold about themselves."[4] Due to these origins, it "descends upon the masses from above," positing the blame in "the shapers of national destinies and the philosophers in the Academy." Social boredom constitutes the ultimate residue of a filtering process of the ideas of liberal leaders, moving from the political, intellectual, and monumental to the cultural, emotional, and quotidian. For Kirk, the expressions of society are not the reflection of its "mood" but the "cause and forerunner of the mood of society"; for instance, "literature thrives in an age of variety" but "it sickens in a time of uniformity" due to "a dearth of important writers, and a dearth of intelligent readers." In a circular manner, the masses suffer but also spread boredom:

> A society which looks upon men as mere production-and-consumption units of interchangeable value cannot understand the subtle shadings of personality and rank of a different sort of age. The springs of the imagination thus are dried up. For a time, satire can exist by pointing out the decay of faith and heroism and love and variety; but when even the memory of these themes fades, then satire, too, comes to an end. Then boredom triumphs in life and in art.
>
> . . .
>
> Will all of us labor under a profound depression of spirits (in part conscious, in part below the level of consciousness) because of the boring and servile architecture about us? And will the society now taking form in America resign itself to a parallel barrenness of soul and mind, under a political domination of unimaginative and complacent bureaucrats?[5]

Influenced by the conservatism of T. S. Eliot, Kirk asserts that class differentiation is essential to avoid social deterioration.[6] Although "conscious believers in religious truth will labour within any society to achieve charity and justice," the drive to compete among individuals instigates moral progression and advancement, enforcing "continuity and coherence in the civil social order."[7] Nonetheless, the discord between the aristocracy and the middle and lower classes turns unhealthy when it is the outcome of the liberal attempts to achieve equality and atomize responsibility; if everyone would perform identically then routinization and monotony would surface. The utopia of egalitarianism threatens with perpetuating a state of sameness in which all efforts would be directed to overcome the generic and interchangeable. To Kirk, boredom is equivalent to a space without social division, faith, ethical concerns, and historical consciousness. It can be identified as an individual complaint in "the Hellenistic world, in imperial Roman life before the triumph of Christianity, perhaps in the Byzantine era," but its presence in modernity is one of the "frightening symptoms of social fatigue."[8] This "grimy secular world of uniformity, suspicious of beauty, contemptuous of belief," is ruled "by an 'élite' of dull positivists and behaviorists and technicians, knowing no standards or aspirations but those of their own narrow trade."[9] Their base is an inadequate educational system that provides access to the same information and knowledge to everyone, regardless of their capacities and interests, fostering "academic collectivism" rather than "academic communities."[10] Since everyone is instructed in an indistinguishable manner, the possibilities of spawning difference diminish, promoting individualistic ambition. From the doctrine of equality of opportunity comes "mediocrity and boredom," components of a collective malaise concerned with the pursuit of material distraction and immediate pleasure—"people cut off from tradition, social sympathy, and the hope of posterity, wretched social insects caught in the trap of self, men and women bored with pleasure, bored with people, bored with life."[11] In the case of the built environment, social boredom manifests in the destruction of "our ancient edifices to make ready the ground upon which the barbarian nomads of the future will encamp in their mechanized caravans."[12]

Cleveland, Detroit, London

Boredom becomes evident in the qualities of the new architecture that replaces old buildings. As a method of assessment, Kirk implies that in the same manner that crime and unrest can be recorded and quantified through statics, the configurations and materials of boring architecture can be recognized and categorized, surpassing subjective perception. First, as a basic condition, the phenomenon is urban. Second, regarding aesthetics, boring edifices feature repetition, lack of ornamentation, and incongruous scales. And third, in terms of history, their presence interferes with the continuum of tradition. Epitomized in the rectilinear shapes and rigid surfaces of the International Style and Brutalism, this architecture is ugly because it does not relate to the human reality and its need for expression; instead of inducing creativity, the architecture of "practical knowledge" engenders disquiet, exhaustion, and frustration, "leaving man in torment."[13]

Kirk maintains that the architecture of boredom in the United States was a consequence of the egalitarian project of the "Great Society," designed by President Lyndon B. Johnson in the 1960s to reduce poverty and racial injustice. Recalling his visits to downtown Cleveland, Kirk observes how the aim to homogenize society through the creation of work opportunities in urban centers had resulted in the erection of economic

Boredom, Architecture, and Spatial Experience

follies that ignore the history of architecture (Figure 15.1). Despite the efforts to preserve certain structures of the past—such as the Cuyahoga Building, a late nineteenth-century structure in Chicago style, restored in 1979 but demolished in 1982 for the construction of the BP America skyscraper—the juxtaposition of the distant past and the immediate present, without intercession, was unsuccessful in highlighting the presence of public and religious nodes; the visual obstruction of important monuments had created unattractive scenarios:

> A few hundred yards in front of us, St John's College, the last handsome stone complex to be erected in Cleveland, has been pulled down to make way for an insurance company's skyscraper, now being erected. (It is one of the mysteries of urban America today that despite a glut of office space downtown, brand-new office towers continue to shoot up mushroom-like, often with public subsidies involved.) St John's Cathedral is being hidden from view by very tall featureless glass-and-steel office buildings.[14]

Accompanied by the decoration of squares and open spaces with "junk sculpture," the "long vistas of boredom" configured by orthogonal streets and avenues, preferred by modernist planning, propel desertion. After working hours, Cleveland seems moribund, a wasteland. For Kirk, since the possibilities of sociability in the public realm become minimal, the seclusion in residential spaces turns into the typical mode of inhabitation. Yet the traditional house—semi-detached or detached, with a porch and a backyard,

Figure 15.1 Construction of parking behind City Hall, Cleveland (1973). Photograph by Bernie Noble, from the Cleveland Press Collections. Courtesy of the Michael Schwartz Library Special Collections, Cleveland State University.

symbolic of family values passed through generations—had been replaced by high-rise apartments. While some urban dwellers, "cliffdwellers," adopted the lifestyle imposed by this architecture, others were pushed towards the outskirts, consolidating suburbia and slums.[15] The displaced population, primarily minority groups in under-privileged circumstances, were forced to live in new developments designed as low-income projects, changing not only their way of living but also the popular idea of the architecture of home—from long-lasting, unique, of the best quality possible, expanding horizontally next to others, to urgent, mass-produced, unrefined, and stacked on top or placed below others.

For Kirk, Detroit was another case of the architecture of boredom. Anticipating its decline and bankruptcy in 2013, the city is portrayed as "tasteless" and "in decay" despite the efforts to revitalize its economy and achieve prosperity through urban modernization. For example, the ambitiously named Renaissance Centre, a complex of seven interconnected towers conceived by Henry Ford II and designed by John Portman, finished in 1981, required the demolition of several eighteenth- and nineteenth-century structures of civic importance, including the City Hall. Although a selection of pieces of the past were preserved in the surroundings, they became overshadowed, their relationship with the city unarticulated; the Wayne County Courthouse was engulfed by tall buildings and its entrance space eliminated. Crucially, Kirk remarks that the architectural obliteration of Detroit was the result of political and economic interests antithetical to the liberal claims of equality, as in the clearance of Poletown, a district inhabited, since the 1870s, by Eastern European immigrants and their descendants. It was carried out in 1981 owing to the coalition of the mayor, planning officers, and even religious authorities; more than 1,100 homes, two schools, a hospital, and many churches were replaced by a General Motors plant (Figure 15.2), offering only repetitive labor in exchange:

> So Poletown is gone; and the decent people of small means who lived there have been shuffled off to the architecture of boredom and servitude. You may be sure they'll not spend their declining years in any Renaissance Centre. Again, the power of eminent domain and plenty of public money were involved in this successful assault on community. Are people treated more arbitrarily, with greater disregard of their rights in property, in a socialist dictatorship?[16]

Exposing the architecture of boredom as a phenomenon of liberalism, Kirk notes that the social and racist unrest in the United Kingdom in 1981 "arose in one the ugliest and most boring of the county-council public housing schemes, afflicted by a ghastly monotony."[17] In his view, the architecture built or rebuilt by the welfare system was "shoddy and badly designed." In the City of London, the damage caused by German bombs during World War II cleared spaces into which buildings of "nasty grey concrete" were erected, marking fissures in the flow of history. Consequently, the architecture that contributed to the gradual appearance of the British Empire, mainly the image of power extending harmoniously from St. Paul's Cathedral to the Tower of London, became

Figure 15.2 Poletown General Motors plant, Detroit, Michigan (1986). BL004030. Michigan Bell Telephone Company Photographs, Bentley Historical Library, University of Michigan.

diminished by large-scale structures incapable of establishing formal and symbolic connections with the pre-Roman origins of the city; the imposition of the modern substituted "the old picturesque confusion" with "a new ugly confusion." A paramount instance is the Barbican Estate, designed by Chamberlain, Powell and Bon Architects and built from 1965 to 1982, with multiple programs, constituting "a failure of intellect and imagination," "a disgrace to England," and an "embarrassing atrocity" not even befitting of a communist regime. Its Brutalist qualities—the rough texture of the exposed concrete, the elevated walkways, the modular composition, the interior public spaces that confront the surrounding towers—confirmed the critic's belief that modern buildings compose "an architecture of sham: the outward symbol of a society which, despite all its protestations of being 'free' and 'democratic', rapidly sinks into servility."[18]

Kirk depicts modern buildings as authoritarian. They minimize not only history but also the scale of its inhabitants, as intimidating structures due to their bigness. Moreover, once architectural projects are executed, the possibility of financial gain reverts and governmental interest vanishes; not only are constructions left to deteriorate but social disorder also unfolds. To Kirk, this is a predictable cycle that explains the connection between overall decline, architectural impoverishment, and the aim of non-conservative systems to secure hegemony by inflicting timid behavior, "an ennui formerly characteristic only of senescent peoples."[19] In the architecture of boredom, there is "no leaven of diversity," "nothing whatsoever that wakes the imagination or satisfies the memory."[20] Far from being proper of any geography, the lack of "imaginative building" extends to all those societies controlled by liberalism—"Germany, France, Italy, or Scandinavia. Everywhere it is the architecture of the mass-age, so far as lodging goes; and the architecture of the bureaucrats' epoch, so far as public buildings are in question."[21]

Planning to Thrive

In a speech delivered to the 48th Conference of the American Institute of Planners in 1965, Kirk insisted that the efforts of the discipline "must be concerned primarily with the person, and how he thrives under a plan; with the republic (or the public interest), and what sort of society arises from grand designs."[22] As such, urban planning and architecture require a moral imagination that insists on the reverential preservation of the beliefs and configurations of the past. By extending the unique features of each city, the universal can be avoided, turning the local and permanent rather than the global and fashionable into the interesting, with abundant identity: "when all interesting architecture has fallen into the limbo of lost things, presumably the rising generation will raise no objection to the architecture of servility and boredom, because they will know no alternative. Desire will have starved to death."[23]

Therefore, innovation for the sake of economic progression constitutes not progress but a distraction that threatens the achievement of personal wellbeing, the prerequisite for the formation of healthy communities. Practitioners of urban planning and architecture ought to search novelty only if it compliments what has already been validated as meaningful, taking into account the limits of design; Kirk cautions, quoting Eliot, "one thing to avoid is *universalized* planning; one thing to ascertain is the limits of the plannable."[24] By implication, the integrity of planners and their capacity to compensate for errors must be tested. If all actions are to be designed, then what is to become of those realities that escape utilitarianism, including "religion, the higher learning, the sense of beauty, the life of family and traditional community, the sense of historic continuity that distinguishes a nation from a mere mob of individuals?"[25]

To tackle the determinism of planning, the critic prescribes four laws of urban and architectural design, inspired by a letter he received from a "conservatively inclined" college student in Oklahoma.[26] The frustrated correspondent listed four causes of the decadence in the built environment of the United States. The first was the low and simplistic quality of the architecture of the International Style, represented by the work of "Paul Rudolph, Louis I. Kahn, Gordon Bunshaft, and the Eastern boys."[27] The second constituted the vast size of modern cities, which endanger human culture by materializing the dystopian visions of "the Brave New Worlds that our periodicals display," such as the extensive projections of Paolo Soleri for City of Mesa.[28] The third was the threat of the automobile and the railway infrastructure to "make civilization obsolete," destroying historical centers, fragmenting the countryside, and facilitating the immigration of minorities.[29] And the fourth condemned the ambitions of real estate ventures as "the great makers of slumurbia, responsible for the concentration of skyscrapers ... defended as part of a free economy." To remedy these problems, Kirk's first recommendation is the adoption of human scale, basing all architecture in the corporeal features of its users, in an organic manner. The second is the nurturing of "the sensation of home" through the strengthening of "neighbourhoods, voluntary associations, old landmarks and historic monuments," opting for restoration and rehabilitation. The third is the control of speculative developments, since all edifices and public spaces ought to serve the common good and not be primarily concerned with financial gain. And the fourth is the re-activation of civic activity through buildings capable of welcoming "long-established customs, habits, and political institutions of a community."[30]

These overarching suggestions are not directed exclusively to planners and architects. Notably, they require incorporation across the whole apparatus of production, from authorities and investors to builders and manufacturers of materials. Rendering the consumer passive but unveiling architecture as the sequence of activities that create the built environment in political association, Kirk relates ideology to design and construction. If the principles are liberal, then architecture creates the purely modern, as a self-regarding project that depends on financial wealth and power. If the values are conservative, then architecture adopts and prolongs the formations of the past, strengthening tradition and nurturing the communal. To avoid the architecture of boredom, all agents ought to provide "permanence and security of territory, 'a place of one's own' ... one of the deepest longings of humankind."[31]

Poetry against Boredom

Echoing Lord Byron's, Wilde's, and Belloc's classification of society into the boring and the bored, Kirk identified the architecture of boredom as an expression of social and political disparity. On the one hand, he characterized human occupation according to emotional response, unveiling the influence of governmental power in everyday inhabitation—those who dwell in spaces constructed by liberalism suffer boredom and thus become servile. On the other, the critic posed the built environment as fundamentally politicized, charged with ideological connotations that become evident in the design and location of architecture—the center is privileged but prone to the boredom of urban agitation while the periphery is disadvantaged and vulnerable to the boredom of suburban dormancy. In "The Architecture of Boredom and Servitude," not only is the built environment conceived through social relations and material negotiations, but also society is constituted through architecture and spatial practices.[32]

If the political informs architecture, if architecture affects society, and if society is political, then boredom discloses governmental systems as either ineffective in procuring welfare, or unconcerned with the public and eager to levy its power. Accordingly, modern architecture is either a failure if it lacks the qualities to guarantee security and represent society, or a success if it induces subservient behavior. To Kirk, the condition creates difference through indifference, provoking cycles of passive enthrallment and active insurrection that distract rather than evolve, emphasizing the importance of everyday life by insisting on overcoming its triviality.[33] Inescapable in modernity—"the Age of the Common Man"—the burden of having nothing to do but having the means to pursue the interesting is demarcated by the consumption of the unattractive, followed by acts of transgression.[34] The architecture of boredom—"prefabricated bungalows, all quite alike inside and out"—has diverted efforts to create religious and civic monuments— "handsome state buildings."[35] Subsequently, since "mankind can endure anything except boredom," foreseeable unrest and violence arise in its inhabitants to counteract the surrounding apathy, provoking "suicide, violence, unnatural vices, drunkenness, addiction to narcotics, and even revolution."[36]

As part of this culture of servitude and subordination, the architecture of boredom is unidirectional, incapable of suggesting anything beyond its functionalism. For Kirk, these buildings are "shoddy," "badly designed," "featureless," "bare," "grim," "nasty," "dangerous," "perilous," "impoverished," and "grey"; they are inelegant and costly, irritated by the decay no expense can prevent.[37] Even if the new could be transformed into a positive source of collective life, modern architecture conspires against the possibility of establishing tradition by being transient. Instead of conserving "what remains of the better taste of other times," "we build cinder-block drugstores, glass office buildings and fiber-board ranch-type shanties full of gadgets intended to turn obsolete within two years."[38] Moreover, as Kirk observes in York, the high speed of the cycle of making, consuming, and discarding modern architecture contributes to the absence of social memory, generating impatience since the present becomes the only preoccupation—the population has become "indifferent, often hostile, to religion of any sort: to the Mysteries they prefer the carnalities of the cinema and the cheap press; more and more, as even the doctrinaire social planner and the aggressive logical positivist are coming to admit, these people draw upon the moral capital of England's yesterday."[39]

To replenish the reserve of the past, equally exhausted and ignored by liberalism, Kirk advocates the implementation of poetry in every aspect of life. Elegiac and rhythmical literature, an expression of "genius," "imagination," and "boldness," embeds the principles and values of conservatism and of everything that is permanent.[40] As an instrument of the governing elites, poetry serves to promote convictions "derived from some other source than pure reason."[41] Because architecture is a medium of representation and communication, then its configurations have to be understandable and meaningful, inspiring feeling before enforcing thinking. Particularly in the case of public buildings that accommodate official institutions but require restrictive access, façades have to be stimulating and aspirational, capable of depicting the canonical and cultured in order to infuse faith in the system. For Kirk, the clarity, rationalism, and functionalism of modernity—extensions of the "cold hearts and smug heads" of "the men of the Enlightenment"—generates an architecture of regular organization that lacked any mystery or venerability. "Efficiency and Progress and Equality" is a deceitful motto that replaces "all those fascinating and lovable peculiarities of human nature and human society which are products of prescription and tradition"; as he confessed in his autobiography of 1963, revealing his pre- rather than post-modern temperament, "I would have given any number of neo-classical pediments for one poor battered gargoyle."[42]

CHAPTER 16
CHARLES JENCKS, REM KOOLHAAS, AND THE GENERIC

As an adjective, *generic* denotes "belonging to a genus or class; applied to a large group or class of objects; general"; and as a noun, it refers to manufactured products that are "not special; not brand-name; in plain, cheap packaging."[1] While the former usage dates to the late seventeenth century, the latter appeared in the early 1950s in the pharmaceutical industry, and by the mid-1970s its meaning had widened to indicate any collection of objects of similar characteristics. In 1977, at the same time the generic emerged as a popular category, Charles Jencks formulated the Ivan Illich Law of Diminishing Architecture, named after the philosopher who asserted that uncontrolled growth can be counterproductive. Included in *The Language of Post-Modern Architecture*, the law states that "for any building type there is an upper limit to the number of people who can be served before the quality of the environment falls" and "economies of scale go into reverse," similar to the effects of "the size of animals, jumbo jets and cocktail parties."[2] Jencks originally formulated it as a comment on the modernist commitment to bigness and the capitalist endeavor to create standardized buildings, which were both out of scale and capable of producing financial gain quickly. However, in 2002, in an article titled "How Big is Bad?" for *The Architectural Review*, with an explicatory graph, the critic overtly linked the law to boredom, seeing it as an effect of the generic. "The idea behind the Law," he wrote, "is that, given enough computer time, you could calculate the numbing repetition of elements in a building, and whether they were yesterday's clichés, and thus produce a rough measure of boredom." In particular, this connection is evident in the architecture of "Supermodernism (as the Dutch call it) or generic architecture (as Koolhaas terms it)."[3]

Unlike the negative connotations of these elaborations—Jencks confesses to "hate boredom" but admits that "Rem occasionally convinces me that it could be interesting"—Rem Koolhaas constructs the relationship between bigness, the generic, and boredom as "a theoretical domain" with the "potential to reconstruct the Whole, resurrect the Real, reinvent the collective, reclaim maximum possibility."[4] Although bigness, which many designers must produce, challenges authorship and erases the modernist request to express on the outside the program of the inside, this hyper-architecture allows many concurrent spaces, escaping the determinism of planning and the duty to animate the entirety of a building. While discussions with a psychological tone affirm that the generic in architecture contests the human necessity for complexity, the underlying intuition in Koolhaas's "The Generic City" (1995) is that the capacity of architecture to produce boredom is reassuring and needed. After the high stimulation produced by modernism and postmodernism—"in a kind of shrill register"—the built environment of the twenty-first century requires sedation, absence, and evacuation rather than agitation, presence, and congestion.[5] The generic operates as a negative provocation, defined by vast but neutral architecture capable of smoothing unfunded and exhausted expectations, reducing excitement, and de-fetishizing history.

In the accounts by Jencks and Koolhaas, in which they implicitly ponder how the experiential and the emotional occur in the production of the built environment, boredom acts as tiredness, oscillating from the personal encounter with spaces and edifices to the professional practice of architecture and its conceptualization. For Jencks, the condition is exemplified by the sensibility of Koolhaas, the quintessential bored architect and architect of boredom, who "fears and hates and repulses boredom" yet is "attracted by it, ... typical of the moderns."[6] Nevertheless, the architect is interested not in the precise measurement of the condition but in its critical possibilities. Boredom in the generic is an opportunity for respite and creation, since "the subject should not spend all the attention in architecture ... but the subject can be inspired by serenity and regularity."[7] It permits the consideration of other pressing concerns, turning the non-specific and universal into the locus of the transcendental—for Koolhaas, "the generic *must* mean something."[8]

Generic Individualism

In December 2015, Jencks delivered the lecture "Generic Individualism—the Reigning Style of Our Time—and Its Discontents" at The Bartlett School of Architecture. He noted that structures of the same formal principles—the generic—but with minor geometric variations—the individual—dominate the marketplace of late capitalism, a premise he illustrated by looking at the recent architectural developments in Singapore and at other iconic buildings around the world. This architecture is large—in both height and breadth—and tends to incorporate curves that twist its appearance, designs that its makers claim to be experientially immersive. Planned by large-scale architectural firms, generic individualism is ideologically contradictory since its results differ from the principles that their architects defend. For instance, the "regular and unified beauty" of the urban parametricism of Zaha Hadid Architects, intended to be applied globally to contribute to urban cohesion, instead only intensifies local difference due to its newness. And projects like One Hyde Park Plaza (2011) in London by Rogers Stirk Harbour + Partners are "antisocial and retrograde," abandoned by its wealthy owners who purchased units as investments, despite the ethos of social responsibility proclaimed by Richard Rogers. For Jencks, these arrangements eliminate history and break with tradition, ethics, and, above all, context. In his view, the bigness of generic individualism cannot be considered an integral part of any urban fabric; paraphrasing Koolhaas, "it exists rather than coexists, the subtext is fuck context."[9]

In the address, Jencks referred to the graph of the Ivan Illich Law. The two coordinates establish, in a mathematical fashion, a quantifiable correlation between bigness and boredom (Figure 16.1). The horizontal axis, labeled "quality," ranges from "worse, more

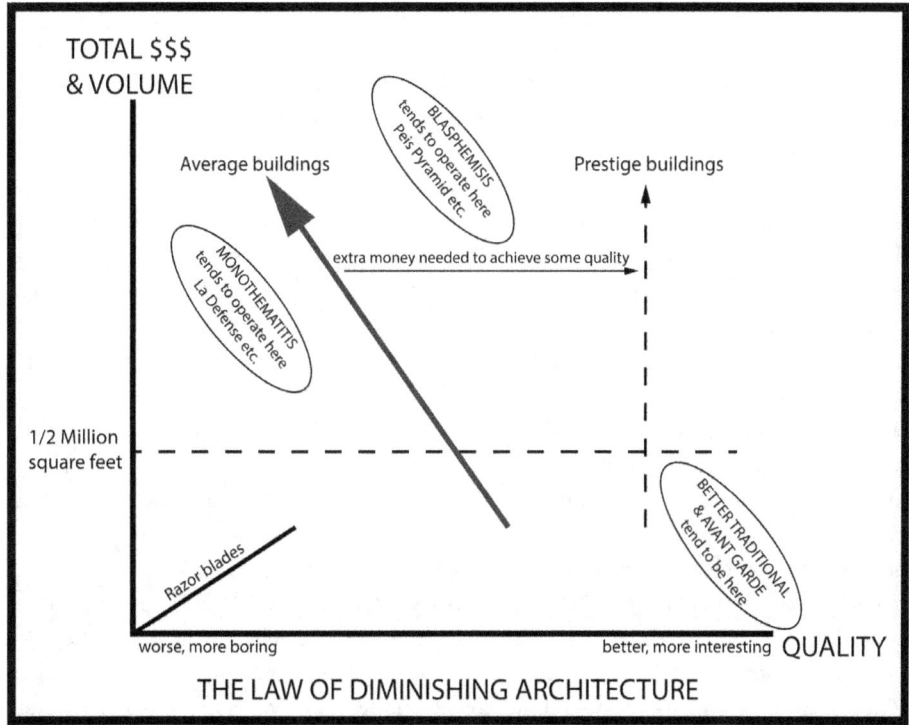

Figure 16.1 Graph of the Ivan Illich Law of Diminishing Architecture (2002). Courtesy of Charles Jencks.

boring" at the far left to "better, more interesting" at the far right, while the vertical is the range of "total $$$ and volume," the lowest at the bottom. A third of the way up the vertical axis, at half a million square feet, is a horizontal dotted line indicating the point at which structures become "big," and a vertical dotted line well along the "quality" axis on the right is labeled "prestige buildings"; below the half million square feet mark and to the right of the prestige marker, the "better traditional & avant-garde" buildings "tend to occur." A red upward arrow, beginning from the lower far right in the high-quality range, points to the upper left, near the top range of total money and volume, indicating that "average buildings" begin to appear along a spectrum of diminishing quality and increasing volume and cost. The arrow warns that buildings are approaching "average" quality, further broken into two types of "average buildings." The first is "monothematitis"—a term borrowed from William L. MacDonald to refer to the iteration of Roman architecture—with the example of the La Défense development (1958–), and the second is "blasphemisis," such as the pyramidal additions to the Louvre Museum by I. M. Pei (1989), both in Paris.[10]

According to Jencks, the Ivan Illich Law was informed by cultural critiques in the late 1960s that castigated repetitious modernism, including literature—"with Norman Mailer condemning modern architecture as 'empty landscapes of psychosis'"—and philosophy—"with Ivan Illich attacking the bureaucracy of the National Health Service in Britain."[11] Illich, a twentieth-century Roman Catholic priest and philosopher, who proposed dismantling the education system to eliminate the routinization of everyday life, questioned the allegation that unmeasured progress in the mechanisms of modernization contributes to better conditions of living. To him, the pursuit of a technique beyond its limits can be detrimental since it encourages over-consumption, caused by dis-economies that tend to failure and the incapacity to keep in mind the primary intentions of the system.[12] The dependence on "unchecked industrial development made in the name of an ideology of indefinite energy consumption" carries with it "the boredom of narrow horizons and the stifling oppression of a world closed in on itself."[13] Instead, Illich advised the testing of design in terms of degrees of ambition and contrivance, encouraging moral criticism of the modern production of goods and services for profit.

Jencks, seeking an association with these observations, affirms that his detection of the relationship between architectural bigness, the generic, and boredom is not one of a judgment of taste culture but rather a comment on the reigning economic and political circumstances. As agents of the financial sector, architects have to respond to the demands of investors to appeal rapidly to the market, and so they rely on the clarity and directness of clichés. Jencks points out that like Walt Disney, "who said, 'no one ever has gone broke, gone bankrupt, underestimating the taste of the American public,'" "you aim to the belly, pretty low, below the belly if you can, you aim at sex organs, and you don't go broke." Or Philip Johnson, "who was aware that boring modernism was sold out to corporate America. He was the biggest sell out to corporate America; in 1985, he had over 2 billion dollars' worth of work." As a political instrument, the architecture of bigness is related to totalitarianism. The phenomenon can be traced to Rome, "when the city hit a million people, sometime around the first century, when Augustus and the fascists took over." To strengthen their power, each emperor, one after the other, constructed fora as spaces for discussion controlled by the Senate, "like American Presidents who build libraries to themselves, and once you go to Rome, you might as well go to Egypt."[14]

As a recurrent pattern in civilization, the creation of bigness and the generic is complicit with governmental hegemonies—size and repetition is a strategy by which to intimidate the masses. The resulting boredom is foreseeable; it possesses the characteristics of an unspoken regulation that affects all members of society. To Jencks, the role of twentieth-century politics is to produce a monoculture that derives from socioeconomic and environmental deprivation, turning people into regulated habitués of the same references. "Every dictator around the world, without exception, produces rubbish, clichés," says Jencks in an interview in 2014—"if you are a dictator, you have to be boring. Take Mussolini, he was an anarchist, then a syndicalist, then a socialist and then a fascist." With the same trajectory of opposing the status quo to gain popular acceptance but without establishing jurisdictional conventions, liberalism had nurtured a capitalist system that fostered predictable behavior and an unreflective sentimentality. These qualities are evident in the routines of the "organization man" of the 1950s, described as "men in grey flannel suits who lived in Westport, Connecticut, commuting every day to New York ... working in large impersonal offices filling up the city."[15]

theory

Norman Foster enjoys running a big firm of architects, and designing big things for Big Japan. But New York City has enjoyed for the world's biggest skyscrapers: the Flatiron building, Woolworth's, Chrysler, Empire State and WTC. J. Corbusier did no like the idea, Bolshevik "hipness", Rem Koolhaas has also made a virtue, and partial theory, from this concept and it is the new architects who does not search for big communications. 'Make no small plans', they whisper to themselves, recalling the Modernist injunction of Daniel Burnham as he devised the grand layout for Chicago by the lake.

Small may be beautiful, as E.F. Schumacher opined in the 1970s (or 'quite beautiful' as Ian Hamilton Finlay rephrased it it one of his ironic concrete poems) but it is hard to live up to the ideal. Richard Rogers confessed in a *New Yorker* shuffle over 30 years ago, like all the careerists in suffer, but like the issues, progressing to topic of architects aspire to grapple with big issues, production realities soon pushed him over the limit. For the country as a whole, it is very hard to resist the economic pressure to become bigger, to grow one's way out of social problems, most obviously the immiseration of the poor. Zero population growth is a very sensible policy as far as ecology is concerned, but no government will pursue it for political reasons.

Moreover, there is the Modernist ideological commitment to bigness. Big government, big labour unions, big economies of scale have many justifications, but consider only one, the paradigm of the razor blade. As modern designers liked to point out, the more razor blades manufactured, the better each one gets. Before Gillette pursued this paradigm, the quality of a blade was deter-

mined, roughly, by precision-cutting and constant sharpening. A rich man could (in) his barber to home and grind away until his blades were manufactured to justify the investment in new tooling equipment, then all the poor could shave more quickly, cheaply and closer in the skin than the richest man in the world. QED, the bigger the production-run, the better the quality of each razor blade. The same was true of the Model A Ford, the mass-produced house (so Le Corbusier said), and free teeth on the health service (as Cedric Price used to say).

Yet a moment's thought about the actual state of national health gives one pause. There are limits to growth and economies of scale, a point reached when bigger means worse. Think of a jet faster than Concorde, or a building taller than 120 storeys. The paradigm of the razor blade is not a model for all productive activity. Some activities are improved up to a point, but then who can see or whom the point is reached, who can say how big becomes too big?

Law of diminishing architecture

In the mid-70s, I tried to wrestle with this question and formulated a Law of Diminishing Architecture', after the man who discovered counter-productive growth in other fields, and framed it as follows: 'For any building type, there is an upper limit to the number of people who can be served before the quality of the environment falls'. With knots sprouting up in London it was quite obvious. When 3000 tourists swarmed together for lunch, as sight-seeing, as they did in some large

How Kong's forest of clusters conjures the bigness almost beyond bearing?

HOW BIG IS BAD?

Bigness, it seems, is one of the unavoidable characteristics of modern culture: the global market and ever-increasing populations seem to demand bigger and bigger buildings. Charles Jencks argues that bigness almost inevitably leads to boredom and anomie.

Moscow hotels, then the quality of the food, or the experience of Red Square, was somewhat diminished; that is, when compared with either of quality or the experience of a group. In 1973 it appeared that this limit inherent in large numbers. The Mall in the Gary Hamaco Sir, the stereotype of 'the societesque', dramatised a truth. With large impersonal offices filling up the cities, ennui might be caused by corporate downscaling, or microsaphic faces that matched their own (as in a cliche of journalism at the time). Or, perhaps, boredom was caused by the speed at which mega-buildings were dropped onto a rich, unsuspecting site. Either how, might if were architecture into what was called the *dumb-lot*.

Big 25 years later other reasons, including economic determinants, seem more compelling than psychological ones. The evidence of the underclass rule is obvious to anyone flying over a growing downtown, or walking down Sixth Avenue in New York, or looking past Hong Kong's waterfront: proof too pacific to deny. But why should big usually mean boring, why shouldn't the Modernist hope, that mass-production can increase quality, be true?

With most large buildings there appears to be a kind of Richter scale measuring the numbers. Once a certain critical mass is reached is likely to be twice as important, and the analogue beyond at every surface so any for every extra $10 million dollars spent on a building. So the $50 million dollar, 40-storey skyscraper, compared to a $20 million, 20-storied one, is likely to be 16 times as dull. There are exceptions, and these figures are ridiculously precise, in order to make a point: money and size are measurable, dullness is not. But the idea behind the law is that, given enough computer time, you could calculate the numbing repetition of elements in a building, and whether they were yesterday's cliches, and thus produce a rough measure of boredom. If you graph the tendencies they produce a curve similar to many distributions found in nature and culture, called the power law.

'A rough measure of boredom.' Jencks's graph of the law of diminishing architecture.

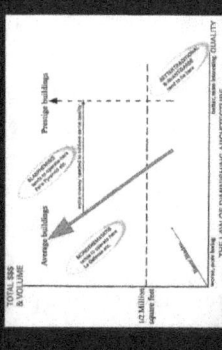

Dumb Boxes, Expensive Prestige

Since its inception, the Ivan Illich Law has been revived and reiterated verbatim, not only in the seven editions of *The Language of Post-Modern Architecture* but also in other writings by Jencks, explained through different projects.[16] In 2002, he referred to the Potsdamer Platz development in Berlin (1995–2001) as a case of bigness and monotony (Figure 16.2). Planned by Hilmer & Sattler with Renzo Piano and the participation of Arata Isozaki, Rafael Moneo, Richard Rogers, and other renowned architects, on a site destroyed during World War II and then bisected by the Berlin Wall, the buildings are "both stereotyped and overblown" despite "some good ecological intentions and contextual theory, some pleasant urban spaces and detailing." The Daimler-Benz Tower is deemed "an insult" to the surroundings, "inept in its massing and endless repetition"; its orange terracotta cladding fails to reconcile the height of the tower with the small scale of the adjacent structures.[17] Wondering how distinguished architects could have created such questionable configurations, Jencks concludes that the modernist paradigm of standardization and mass production as means to improve design is responsible for the mistaken belief that quantity can increase quality, proof that the Law of Diminishing Architecture cannot be avoided if the system does not change.

Grouped under the typology of the "dumb box," these structures are the result of programmatic arrangements, unconcerned with expression, history, context, or even thematic articulation. Acting as neutral and repetitive backdrops that enable commercial transactions, they respond to the capitalist values of the companies behind their speculative development—only four corporations in the case of Potsdamer Platz, the largest building site in Europe during its construction.[18] For Jencks, bigness leads inevitably to dumbness. Although he maintains both that it is impossible to ascertain when big becomes too big and that boredom cannot be measured in itself, once boredom is paired with the size of buildings and their cost, then a power law appears; "a kind of Richter Scale," "ridiculously precise," "sadly, very powerful," capable of numerically and graphically exposing a curve of interrelation:

> Over a threshold of about a half-a-million square feet, every skyscraper ten floors higher than the next is likely to be twice as uninspired, and the same goes, beyond a certain point, for every extra $10 million dollars spent on a building. So the $60 million dollar, 60-storey skyscraper, compared to a $20 million, 20-storied one, is likely to be 16 times as dull.[19]

In 1990, in "Between Kitsch and Culture," published in *Architectural Design* and reprinted in the sixth edition of *The Language of Post-Modern Architecture*, Jencks remarked that while the Law of Diminishing Architecture had been ignored for over fifteen years, it remained valid. He mentioned that "since it now looks true beyond reasonable doubt, I will ask the reader's indulgence for repeating it: 'for any building type there is an upper limit to the number of people who can be served before the quality of an environment falls.'" In this version, adding the experience of users to the equation, bigness is described by comparing the buildings for Disney (1990) in Burbank by Michael Graves with the World Financial Center (1988) in New York by Cesar Pelli. Despite the inclusion of pop iconography in the first and the simplicity of the second, both projects appear totalizing instead of pluralistic, "not very interesting" due to their "super-controlled atmospheres."[20] Jencks concedes that the glass surfaces by Pelli are "intelligent wallpaper"—a good example of repetition—and that the interiors by Graves constitute "an interesting handling of what could be called colour-field architecture"—imaginative and different.[21] However, the result is populistic and unsurprising rather than clever and capable of sustaining attention. As part of the Disney experience, the 758 bedrooms of the Swan Hotel and the 1,510 units of the Dolphin Hotel—together costing more than a third of a billion of US dollars—"are not much better or worse than the average, gargantuan Sheraton which is their equal in cost and type: impersonal, efficient and bland in service." Their bigness appears inadequate to their function; "one needs grand functions for the grandiosity to feel right—something like the naval battles staged on false lakes, as the Romans and Florentines used to put on behind their similarly Herculean palazzi."[22]

First illustrated through big hotels and the rise of mass tourism in London in the 1970s, the effects of architectural bigness become evident in the poor quality and impassive facilities offered by the capitalist system. Enormous hotels not only produce "staff shortages and absenteeism" but also attract more visitors, causing management problems, such as having to move tourists "from one ambience to the next in a smooth and continuous flow."[23] Reflecting on the law and its relation to modernism, Jencks recalls that "it happened that when I was writing this, I had been with my wife to the Rossiya Hotel in Moscow." The building by Dmitry Chechulin—opened in 1967, the largest in Europe until its closure and demolition in 2006—"was designed to beat American capitalism, in which 6000 people could eat lunch at the same time and—believe me—the food tasted like that."[24] To him, the same rationale applies to large architectural offices that create big buildings. Design suffers due to the lack of personalization and the high speed of production that enforces the rationalization of taste, based on statistical averages of style. In these projects, architects, clients, and final users are multiple, transient, and anonymous; "in short, buildings today are nasty, brutal and too big because they are produced for profit by absentee developers, for absentee landlords for absent users whose taste is assumed as clichéd."[25]

Contradicting his assertion that "too big is too big, whatever the approach," Jencks maintains that "prestige" can be achieved in the architecture of bigness if enough resources can be secured to produce high quality.[26] Unlike the disciplined use of technology advocated by Illich—an askesis that would not permit bigness—more money supposes the capacity of hiring more professionals, having more time to develop projects, reflecting on the desired outcomes, and selecting better materials for construction. For Jencks, this scenario of intellectual and economic affluence can contribute decisively to the production of "architecture" rather than the "zero-rated creativity of building," with features that "include the very things that define the art of architecture; a new concept, light and space dynamics, ornament and structural expression, sculptural gesture, and innovation."[27] Prestige buildings, which avoid simplicity, thus can never be boring for "they have more interesting shapes, they have variation, they have meaning, they have luxury and they have choice. Not all those are psychological, experiential things."[28] In the revival of the Law of Diminishing Architecture in 2002, the critic presented prestige in bigness through the Hong Kong Bank (1985) by Norman Foster. In 2014 and 2015, he added the internationally acclaimed CCTV Headquarters (2012) and The Interlace (2013), both by Koolhaas; like "the tallest building in the world at any moment," these cases are exceptions, corroborating "the general truth all the more: they are very rare."[29]

Cosmological Boredom

Notwithstanding these architectural concerns—with modernism and postmodernism, with history and crisis, with monotony and variety—for Jencks, the ultimate relationship between bigness, boredom, and the interesting is a condition of the universe, at both micro and macro scales. At the micro level, the critic generalizes protons, omitting details and in a pseudo-scientific tone, as being "like other protons, every proton is like every other proton, protons are incredibly boring if they are protons." But if their symmetry is altered, then they turn noteworthy by becoming something else. By extension, at the macro level, in a leap towards the definitive bigness of the cosmological, the origin of the universe is posed as "super-symmetrical" until the Big Bang broke its symmetry, and "every time it breaks symmetry the universe becomes more interesting, which is interesting architecturally." Jencks evokes the postmodern agenda of diversity and mobilizes the epistemological need of science to find difference in natural phenomena, saying that the interesting is better than the boring "from an intellectual and perceptual point of view because there's more sensitivity in experience":

> Everything has become better since the Big Bang. For the last 13.8 billion years, it's getting more interesting all the time. Because chemistry is evolving, matter is evolving. How many elements are there? There is 92 in the table, right? But the first 50 were created in supernova and then they stopped creating and then it had another generation of supernova, so for the first billion years there was only 50 or 40 elements, up to iron. Then they all had to be recooked and create the next 40, up to uranium, and in the last 20 years we have bombarded these uranium atoms and we have created 118 elements. Look at Mars, at any planet except Earth. They only have 500 or so of these minerals species. How many minerals are there? There's 4700 minerals on Earth. In Mars, probably 500. In Mercury, probably 100. Would you live on Mercury?[30]

Claiming to challenge Copernicus and Albert Einstein who affirmed that the universe is isotropic and homogenous—"everywhere the same, in your terms and my terms ... boring"—Jencks avows that it is full of fundamental processes that constantly create alteration, "like an asteroid hitting us." The search for the interesting caused him to also become a landscape architect whose work is based on the theory of the asymmetrical universe; he contends that "everybody is going crazy, all the physicists and cosmologists—I am talking about the top people—are in a tailspin because the recent 2013 evidence of the Planck satellite shows that the universe looks like what I am building."[31]

The Boring City

Compared to the factuality that appeals to Jencks, the discussions by Koolhaas about bigness, the generic, and boredom emerge as literary stories rather than as analytical arguments. The Big Bang does not trace the origin of the universe but rather the emergence in the late nineteenth century of "a generation of conceptual breakthroughs and supporting technologies" that propelled the construction of large and extra-large buildings—"an architectural Big Bang."[32] In this genealogy, the novel systems of horizontal and vertical transportation, telecommunication and the production of materials, electricity and the control of interior environments are constructs that enable original ideations of architecture. For Koolhaas, the capacity to build vast structures establishes an ideological discourse, without a manifesto, that constantly requires higher levels of complexity and the dissociation of architecture from exhausted narratives and previous aesthetic aspirations.[33] Simply due to size, bigness creates generic spaces rather than specific architecture, no longer needing the city but becoming the city, breaking any urban tissue as well as the correspondence between form and function. It has the capacity of containing hybrid programs and multiple environments that affect experience, fostering moments of retreat and concentration—not as polarities but as persistent tranquility.

"The Generic City" occupies the last part of the "Extra Large" section of *S,M,L,XL* (1995). Written a year before its publication, it is divided into seventeen sections, with numbered subsections, but no paragraph separations. Although intersected by the Dictionary that runs throughout the book, the text appears as a continuous sequence of thoughts—like a monologue written in the informative tone of medication pamphlets, with precautions, indications, and possible side effects. Additionally, a series of photographs taken by Koolhaas introduce and close the essay, in full spreads. Shot in movement, from the interstitial infrastructure of transportation, the images are blurry and of unidentified cityscapes, almost without human presence. These components provide a context about an existing situation, which—like boredom—cannot be remedied or enhanced since any intervention gives rise to the awareness of its existence, jeopardizing its attributes.

As a metaphor, "The Generic City" describes the architectural and spatial equivalent of late twentieth-century boredom. Both are ambiguous and ambivalent, critical and manifold, products of wealthy economies that problematize significance, transcendence, and the possibilities of transgression. Their emergence remains in the present and keeps only the material of the past that can be logically understood and put to use. Far from being averted, the boredom of the Generic City is a desired state of desiring the common, as Koolhaas defines it in the "Dictionary," in a confessional way:

BOREDOM

But the most exhausting thing of all is boredom.

BOREDOM

If my interest in the banal architecture of the 1950s and 1960s, the derivatives of Ernesto Rogers and Richard Neutra, seems a somewhat boring source, I can only answer that to die of boredom is not so bad.

BORING

The thing that everybody finds out about me once they really get to know me is just how terrifically boring I am, and how I aspire to being boring, I'm sure eventually it will turn everybody off of me because my dream in life is to wear sweats and go to the mall.

BORING

I like boring things.[34]

Lack and Neutrality

Resonating with the definition of generic medications—brandless, unrefined, having disposed of the unnecessary, but with the needed strength and capacity for performance—Koolhaas affirms that "the great originality of the Generic City is simply to abandon what doesn't work." It provides the essential, without idealism, as "the post-city being prepared on the site of the ex-city." Therefore, despite the volumetric presence of generic architecture, and when compared to traditional architecture, it constitutes lack—of identity, public engagement, centrality, and the construction of history as a source of meaning. Instead of difference and character, blankness is procured by intentional and multinational homogenization. Instead of commonality and ethical obligation, anomie, social fragmentation, and political disinterest reign, not only prompting the abandonment of public life but also validating a modern sociology based on individualism. Instead of the hierarchical distinction between center and periphery, typical of the imperialist polis, in the Generic City everywhere is equally relevant or irrelevant since the importance of location is given by the user in constant transit through a system of impartial flow. Instead of the construction of history to understand the past and present, the preoccupation with time and its passing becomes dominant, turning memories into a source of material for distraction and entertainment through simulation without nostalgia, ready to be consumed.[35] Ultimately, as Antonio Negri observes, poetry is surmounted in the Generic City, no longer in need of preservation or restoration since the new does not need to be enhanced by the old.[36]

Carefully planned but thriving and failing unpredictably, the Generic City comprises airports and skyscrapers, the two dominant typologies. The first responds to the widespread condition of movement and travel. As suggested by Koolhaas, echoing

Heidegger's elaboration of boredom as the search for home in the world, this migration can be geographical but also spatial and ontological, defining inhabitation through the concurrence of the physical aspects of exteriority, the interactions with the virtual and the privacy of interiority. Despite their ubiquity and identical function, airports are "among the most singular characteristic elements of the Generic City, its strongest vehicle of differentiation." Superficially, they feature aesthetical variations to be recognized, "like a drastic perfume demonstration, photomurals, vegetation, local costumes give a first concentrated blast of the local identity (sometimes it is also the last)."[37] These hubs of dynamism resemble national theme parks, constantly increasing in size through architectural additions that offer services unrelated to travel, similar to the immobile centers of traditional cities.

As the second typology, skyscrapers move from the horizontality of the airport to the exclusively vertical. They can exist anywhere—"in a rice field, or downtown"—with the same interior configuration. Because the Generic City originated in Asian capitals close to the Equator that require protection from extreme weather, skyscrapers are sealed in flat surfaces, with mechanisms to control light and temperature, like standing capsules. Designed in a free style, their most convoluted expressions depend on standardized curtain-wall structures adhering to hidden metallic or concrete columns and beams, with regular glass panels repeated endlessly and joined by semi-fluid sealants. Dissimilar to the utopian optimism of Paul Scheerbart in the early twentieth century, for whom crystalline buildings would avoid sterile environments, glass membranes "turn each building into a mixture of a straightjacket and oxygen tent," with "the appearance of intellectual rigor through the liberal application of a transparent spermy compound that keeps everything together by intention rather than design—a triumph of glue over the integrity of materials."[38]

Also defined by the engineering of glass, the architecture of airports, skyscrapers, hotels, and other typologies incorporate atria, giving the Generic City its distinctive postmodern character and constituting fifty-one percent of the volume of buildings. They are controlled and hermetic voids that create entrances and welcome "the cave-dweller in its relentless provision of metropolitan comfort," nulling the variations of nature.[39] Unlike the nineteenth-century arcades that softened the encounter between interior and exterior, these extensive vestibules are accessed directly from the transportation facilities, usually located in the underground. Like petri dishes, the suspension of the environment restricts interpersonal relations, favoring individual movement amidst the omnipresence of the redundant—space matters inasmuch as it provides facilities for self-absorption, without external interference.

To minimize presence and heighten subjective experience, the aesthetics of the Generic City are dominated by subtle gradations of reflectivity. In addition, the colors are neutral, "an explosion of beige" that, to Koolhaas, resembles unaroused genitalia, "metallic-matte aubergine, khaki-tobacco, dusty pumpkin." Within these parameters, there are interesting and boring buildings, both connected to the architecture of Mies van der Rohe. The interesting is exemplified by the unevenness of the Friedrichstadt tower (1921), and the boring by the regularity of the volumes produced thereafter:

This sequence is important: obviously, after initial experimentation, Mies made up his mind once and for all against interest, for boredom. At best, his later buildings capture the spirit of the earlier work—sublimated, repressed?—as a more or less noticeable absence but he never proposed "interesting" projects as possible buildings again. The Generic City proves him wrong: its more daring architects have taken up the challenge Mies abandoned, to the point where it is now hard to find a box.[40]

Far from being ugly and homogenous, the architecture of the Generic City is essentially beautiful and diverse. Yet then variety is the norm, perceived as repetitive and monotonous. Referring to Gorky's description of Coney Island as "varied boredom," Koolhaas declares that "variety cannot be boring" and "boredom cannot be varied"; however, the "infinite variety of the Generic City comes close, at least, to making variety normal: banalized in a reversal of expectation, it is repetition that has become unusual, therefore, potentially, daring, exhilarating."[41] Similarly, the proliferation of the new does not disturb. If the act of creating something that did not exist before can be overlooked, then the construction of the architecturally neutral can be achieved. In an interview in 2012, Koolhaas asserts through the existentialism of Robert Musil, "it is about not having properties. I think it can be done. *Der Mann ohne Eigenschaften* [*The Man without Qualities*, 1940] is a very important book for me."[42]

Smooth Space, Calm but Eerie

In this domain—"big enough for everybody"—experience focuses on the present and architecture never matures. The built environment "self-destructs and renews" and thus becomes "equally exciting—or unexciting—everywhere." According to Koolhaas, this lack of traits affects users, who appear physically attractive as well as "even-tempered, less anxious about work, less hostile, more pleasant." Opposed to the destructive and addictive behavior associated with boredom, such as the hostility and crime that is spurred by the dystopian architecture of J. G. Ballard, the stillness of the Generic City, where transgression has been regulated and commercialized, does not lead to violence. Delinquency and risk can be safely practiced, since "the most popular sites ... are the ones once most intensely associated with sex and misconduct. Innocents invade the former haunts of pimps, prostitutes, hustlers, transvestites, and to a lesser degree artists." Due to these commodities, experiential boredom is reduced, enforcing "weak and distended sensations, few and far between emotions," without extremes or urgencies.[43]

This space is coherent, unified and regular, open and flat like "a clearing in the forest." Its flow "*sedates*," induces "a *hallucination of the normal*," and produces the same effects of tranquilizing drugs. Koolhaas attests—seemingly immune to this torpor—that "the dominant sensation of the Generic City is an eerie calm: the calmer it is, the more it approximates the pure state." This quietude is achieved via the strengthening of movement in the infrastructure of travel. Highways and airports become actualized versions of boulevards, arcades, and plazas, mediated by technology or the attitude of busyness and promoting the construction of networks with dispersed but unified nodes of arrival and departure—"in fact surprisingly sensual, a utilitarian pretense entering the domain of *smooth* space." The fleshly quality is deceivingly inorganic, sexualized but unresponsive, in drowsy rest. As a system, the smooth space of the Generic City arranges encounter rather than objectification, fostering pre-modern nomadism where trajectory is more important than destination and continuous variation reigns over formal immobility. Though appearing neutral to its consumers, this immersive fluidity muffles authoritarian governments, turning architecture and space into political accomplices in the procurement of a dazed population easy to govern. For Koolhaas, "very often, the regime has evolved to a surprising degree of invisibility, as if, through its very permissiveness, the Generic City resists the dictatorial."[44]

In Transit

Jencks and Koolhaas imply that boredom in architecture is symptomatic of transition, a manifestation of a process of readjustment and modification. On the one hand, the critic awaits new technologies and an economic bonanza that will produce big structures of high quality, marking the beginning of another stylistic period. On the other, the architect expects a state of equilibrium that will allow a future that would resist excess and promote a non-hierarchical flow of spaces. Although these suggestions remain in the architectural as solipsistic affirmations, only referring to the social and political to identify the generic, they coincide with the portrayal of postmodernity, or supermodernity, as a circumstance of movement.

The bigness and impersonality condemned by the Ivan Illich Law and the characterlessness of the Generic City echo the anthropological identification of "non-places" by Marc Augé, developed during the early 1990s. Epitomized by airports and traveling, these architectures are part of a generalized production of spatial conditions that insist on the present, without historical meaning and devoid of possibilities for communal engagement, best described through an automobile advertisement—"the irresistible wish for a space of our own. A mobile space which can take us anywhere. A space where everything is to hand."[45] According to Augé, while "places" offer the possibilities of establishing relations, "historical and concerned with identity," "non-places" cannot because they are abstract and generic, easy to iterate, closer to the notion of "space" and the cultural expressions of the late twentieth century.[46] Contrasting with the conflict of early modernism with the past, supermodernity has solved history by dissolving it, assuming its impossibility to provide existential significance, and thus overlooking any symbolism in previous architecture. Whereas old places need to be "listed, classified, promoted to the status of 'places of memory', and assigned to a circumscribed and specific position," new spaces require signs, texts, ideograms, and maps that indicate prohibitions and conventions. The recent typologies are concerned with minimizing the range of experience so the built environment can be easily regulated:

> A world where people are born in the clinic and die in hospital, where transit points and temporary abodes are proliferating under luxurious or inhuman conditions (hotel chains and squats, holiday clubs and refugee camps, shantytowns threatened with demolition or doomed to festering longevity); where a dense network of means of transport which are also inhabited spaces is developing; where the habitué of supermarkets, slot machines and credit cards communicates wordlessly, through gestures, with an abstract, unmediated commerce; a world thus surrendered to solitary individuality, to the fleeting, the temporary and ephemeral.[47]

Aligned with the positivism of the Ivan Illich Law, Augé maintains that supermodernity could be quantified through its non-places—"with the aid of a few conversions between area, volume and distance"—by adding all the space that transportation systems, commercial and leisure facilities, and the network of satellite communication occupy.[48] Different from the aesthetics of the Generic City, the physical attributes of the built environment are not the exclusive determinants of non-places since they do not exist in pure form. Instead, they fluctuate and tangle together depending on how they are inhabited and, in particular, narrated. Every space is vulnerable to becoming a place in the same manner that every place can turn into a non-place, as Augé asserts by referencing Maurice Merleau-Ponty: "the space could be to the place what the word becomes when it is spoken: grasped in the ambiguity of being accomplished, changed into a term stemming from multiple conventions, uttered as the act of one present."[49] By implication, in the case of Jenks, the boredom derived from the unwanted neutrality of bigness can be altered through speech and writing as well as discourse and theory, turning its low quality into an index of an alternate reality. With the same means, in the case of Koolhaas, the boredom of the generic can be emphasized to procure flow and smooth spaces. In both, naming boredom—directing attention to it—turns the condition into an interesting presence, a positive something that is endangered if it becomes conscious, susceptible of being transformed through language but impossible to be treated architecturally.

CHAPTER 17
JORGE SILVETTI AND SYLVIA LAVIN: UNAMUSED MUSES AND LYING FALLOW

In contemporary architectural parlance, the interesting and the boring have become interrelated, being almost interchangeable. To say "it's interesting" can constitute an interjection when there is nothing to communicate; it can be the point of entry into a discussion, or it can ultimately denote boredom. When "it's interesting" means "it's boring," the euphemism is critical, its ambiguity requiring explanation, so that it conveys not a subjective valuation but a defendable argument. However, the lack of clarity may be intentional—to gain time to say something else, to elucidate on what might actually be of attraction, or to gauge if it is worth disclosing what is considered undeserving of attention. The expression is often heard in socio-professional gatherings and during reviews at exhibitions and in university studios, all opportunities for ritualized examination. Moreover, the way in which "it's interesting" is received by the listener, such as another architect or professor, depends on who says it; although informal, it entails authority. To be accepted as a valid and solid judgment, "it's interesting" not only relies on the knowledge and reputation of the person making the assessment, but also necessitates a twofold justification. It calls for a description of what the speaker perceives as contradictory and repetitive as well as relevant and motivating. The indictment must also conclude by stipulating how what has been identified as negative—equally interesting and boring—possesses the potential for offering the positive, turning the analytical into the creative.

Critiques of the interesting are necessary to elaborate on the boring, and critiques of the boring are fundamental to detect the interesting. Jorge Silvetti, in "The Muses Are Not Amused: Pandemonium in the House of Architecture" (2002), and Sylvia Lavin, in "Lying Fallow" (2013), explore this correlation by surveying and evaluating the architectural production of the decade prior to their publication. The first was delivered as a Walter Gropius Lecture at Harvard University Graduate School of Design. Although it does not refer to boredom explicitly, the argument exposes deficiencies in the architecture of the 1990s; for Silvetti, it lacked significance, the potential to be prolonged as future reference, and the capacity to excite academia. The second was a commission from the editorial board of *Log* to commemorate its tenth anniversary; Lavin, describing the field of architecture during the first years of the twenty-first century as flat, in a state of repose, and hopefully in preparation for important production, diagnoses boredom as the reigning condition of the time. Both Silvetti and Lavin are distinguished educators, active in the evaluation of architecture and with an international presence, and their elaborations, emerging from within academia, discuss architecture as a practice with its own codes, not autonomous but intertextual, in charge of leading the configurations of the built environment. As if to provoke, the authors omit any exhaustive scrutiny of specific cases, including only images to accompany their claims. Silvetti projected more than 200 photographs and drawings in the background, varying from architectural projects to modern art and himself playing the piano.[1] Lavin used a sequence of photographs of the Serpentine Pavilions in London, from 2002 to 2013.

Silvetti and Lavin reveal that the relationship between the boring and the interesting is a systemic preoccupation and a fluid component of the discipline. The purpose of identifying boredom, unlike the triumphant acknowledgment of prizes, publications, and exhibitions, is to correct and educate, an indication that the trajectory of action ought to be reassessed. Through the accusation of being boring—possibly the most definitive affront among architects—modifications are considered that would turn boring to interesting, meanwhile implicitly composing a new set of unwanted conditions, though left unmentioned because memory cannot be total. Resonating with Michel Foucault's definition of examination as the mixture of hierarchical scrutiny and individual judgment, the power of boredom in architecture derives from its simplicity and its capacity to be universally understood.[2] In the appraising circles of the discipline, it acts as a critical method that patrols against what is regarded as superfluous, regularizing by searching for its opposite.

Assessing Goddesses

In an interview in 2015, Silvetti clarified that the title "The Muses Are Not Amused: Pandemonium in the House of Architecture" is suggestive rather than literal; in his view, the classical goddesses of inspiration "were nervous actually, and upset, . . . not amused."[3] The metaphor, a rhetorical strategy but "with its limitations," not only captures attention and establishes the tone of the lecture, but it also relates to the understanding of architecture as a discipline, "a territory and a certain specificity . . . worthy of exploration, particularly in good schools of architecture where we are concerned, above all, with education and the advancement of knowledge." In this realm of "Architecture with capital A," the muses are not bored nor do they constitute the cause of boredom. Instead, they are dissatisfied with the ideas and ideologies behind the production of architecture, with the academics and practitioners and their techniques to generate form. According to Silvetti, "form is the fundamental and specific thing" that architects "imagine and produce" but which has been neglected in teaching and learning processes, risking creativity and "turning the architect into a dazed observer of seductive wonders."[4]

To explore this condition in the period, bracketed by the victorious irruption of the Guggenheim Museum Bilbao in 1997 and the violent consequences of September 11, 2001, Silvetti identifies four stylistic, parallel, trends of architectural innovation. The first is *programism*, defined as the derivation of "an overenthusiastic embrace of the otherwise healthy revisitation of the idea of 'program' (as opposed to 'function')," in which graphic representations, drawn from neutral data, are transformed into buildings, with little alteration. For Silvetti, programism is not only vague, since statistical information can be obtained from anywhere, but it also potentially relieves architects of their creative responsibility. Represented by the superposition of spaces of the Stack Attack (1997) project for a vertical park in the Netherlands by MVRDV, this approach is described as worn out and outdated, an echo of the naiveté of the design of the 1960s and "discredited methodological doctrines of the recent past, such as those of the Pattern Language or General Systems theories."[5] The results are tautological and insensitive, requiring further imagination and relevant knowledge about the history of architecture to overcome their misguided pragmatism and lack of intellectual profundity.

The second style is *thematization*, a term borrowed from marketing and advertising, coined to identify and typify theme parks. Its main attribute is the desire to control the vocabulary, syntax, and message of architecture; according to Silvetti, thematization is deterministic and misleading, since it aims "to conjure up something that cannot be present, either because it exists only in the past, in memory, or in literary fiction or because, while contemporaneous, it exists in some exotic, far-off, or inaccessible place." Like the modern cycle of the interesting turning boring, the shortening of the space between the expectations of users and the encounter with the environment results in momentary, delusional, and meaningless pleasure. Where the experience of programism is characterized by apathy and aloofness, this second trend appeals to the engaging and experiential, employing recognizable precedents and clichés that promise the instatement of bygone or alternative values and their routines, but offering only mimesis and parody. An example of mimesis is Marie Antoinette's hameau at Versailles, designed as "the outpost retreat of the queen, where she and her guests could relieve their boredom and indulge in the silly game of acting like peasants." Instances of parody are projects similar to Las Vegas, which organize a public realm that relies on the simultaneous use of varied topics that are not re-enacted but exaggerated and lampooned. In architecture, mimesis and parody are both contestable since their construction implies the reconstruction of political, social, and cultural values, informing the behavior of users. As used by "extreme contextualism" and "the most recalcitrant excesses of New Urbanism," "thematization for living not only suppresses disbelief but also posits amnesia as the necessary condition to permit moralistic prescription of the way of life it wants to enforce."[6]

The third trend constitutes the *blobs* that emerged in the early 1990s. Short-lived but dominant, they appeared as body-snatchers that exposed the novel ability of architects to produce configurations that did not have any citations of the past. Their production relied on the automatism of the digital, challenging authorship and the capacity to attach cultural meaning to the new and the possibility to initiate alternate traditions. As "shapeless creatures, seemingly from outer space or some bad intestinal condition," blobs problematize the cycle of creation and consumption. They presented a feast of what had not been seen yet, too quick and precise to be synchronized with the attendant processes of cultural description. To Silvetti, these pioneering forms suddenly created a "frightening abyss" that probed desire by tacitly asking "Who wants that?"—"we make Blobs because we can ... Both their proliferation and quick fall into benign indifference today (by 2002 the whole thing had subsided in both magazines and schools) speak clearly about their fascinating but somewhat misguided pursuit." As architectural manifestations of the nostalgia for the future of the 1990s, blobs exposed the swing of the stylistic pendulum that favored the nostalgia for the past during the 1970s and 1980s. However, the euphoria for the next is not limitless and thus has the same probabilities of becoming "just as ridiculous and debilitating" as the yearning for history. In this interplay of temporalities, blobs created perplexity, turning into "vehicles of more esoteric referents," such as "biological analogues to architecture, followed by processes, international flows, then more abstract manifestations such as statistical data." This liberalism, humorously but tellingly epitomized in the sinuous landscape of the playground of the Teletubbies, heightened conservative strategies to generate "simpler, historical" architecture, demanding the intelligent evaluation of references.[7]

The final trend Silvetti identifies is *literalism*. Rather than being a formal set of principles, it is the labeling of formlessness with concrete attributes—"for example: a meaningless blob, when seen as liquid, suggests a flow; when seen as viscous, suggests adaptability; and when seen as a malleable solid, suggest flexibility." Illustrated by the dissolution of figure and ground of the proposal for the Yokohama Port Terminal (1994) in Japan by UN Studio, Silvetti states that "the mindless embracing of such tempting liquid-viscous-plastic formal intimations as the actual formal architectural solutions" is incapable of solving urban and social problems. Antithetical to the efforts of postmodernism to reinstate communication in architecture, literalism lacks creativity and significant complexity, remaining superficial while stubbornly contending that architecture can be factually organic. Buildings that pretend to be broken, old, flowing, or folding are the result of the direct transposition of metaphors, not only neglecting the orthodox language of architecture but also ignoring the fact that the built environment is immobile. Although literary figures can serve to portray and enrich architectural form, they cannot replace it. As posed in "The Muses Are Not Amused," literalism is dangerously weakening because of its easiness and forbearance; any form can be attached to any moniker as long as it provokes public response, that "domain par excellence of the one-liner."[8]

For Silvetti, the detection and naming of the four trends, "an odd grouping of heterogeneous 'architectures' that nevertheless share common traits," allowed him to advance a temporary conclusion.[9] Programism, thematization, blobs, and literalism endanger creativity in architecture due to their determination to ramble out of the discipline, looking for foreign quotations and atypical allusions in order to assume them uncritically. Therefore, when scrutinized, their outcome appears dilettante despite their compelling representations and use of technology. The efforts of architects employing these trends seem minimal, as if practitioners would be bored with architecture, losing their status as originators and thereby preferring to be intermediaries—"the midwife, as Colin Rowe would have said." This adopted role avoids "the knowing, willing, acting agent in the creation of architectural form," and conceptualizes the discipline as "the marriage of other agents, external and independent of the architect."[10]

Silvetti compares the architectural circumstances of the 1990s to the baroque of the seventeenth and eighteenth centuries; this parallelism is "a paradox indeed, since the baroque is associated with an excess of consciously controlled form production based on a precedent, namely, the classical language of architecture." Both periods are outlined by the closeness of architecture to strategies of rhetoric, the production of instances of entertainment and popular consumption, and the testing and blurring of the limits between the arts, evidenced in the attempts to congeal movement. The use of these techniques, allies against the portrayal of buildings as inert and stationary, aimed to produce wonder, a moment of doubt that takes the beholder out of the familiar, amusing and diverting attention from everyday concerns with both gentility and vulgarity. Like programism, thematization, blobs, and literalism, the will of the baroque to achieve the impossible—the freezing of action—is disclosed as arrogant because of the desire to attain narrative climax. Yet the architecture of the 1990s inverted the order of Architecture as Art into Art as Architecture, with the sole purpose of distracting and gratifying through the provision of surprise. For Silvetti, this travesty, "where boredom enters in my picture," has produced another crisis of confusion in the discipline, "mostly prevalent in academia, journalism, and museums, between two conditions in which architecture finds itself performing absolutely different roles, one as the support of artistic ideas and another as the inspiration for buildings, but most of the time without realizing on what stage it is actually standing."[11]

Theory to Form

In the postscript written for the publication of "The Muses Are Not Amused," Silvetti not only reconsiders the muses as inadequate authorities to guide the production of architecture—"Erato, Clio, Euterpe, Melpomene, and the rest are old ladies who long ago lost their credibility as art changed"—but also emphasizes theory as an instrument for design. The intellectual elaborations of architecture are differentiated from pure autonomy or stifling historicism that might cause stagnation, being an aspect of the discipline that contributes to the analysis and understanding of its intricacies while informing its production. Through theory, architecture ought to be self-reflective and refer to its fundamental principles, "without denying the 'intertextuality' and cultural 'contamination' that we so much appreciate now," "not as a figurative source for architecture but as the operative cultural mechanism with which architecture cannot avoid interaction."[12] When asked if the task of these dialogues is to assist in the creation of form and how can they provide criticality to design, Silvetti stresses that it is not "about helping in a direct way—giving a methodology is not the solution." Instead, architectural thought should create "an atmosphere ... that somehow is always focused on the design process and creativity, helping architects to think better. That is what, in the best moments, it did." To the architect, people are currently bored with theory and criticism—"an important hypothesis that I cannot prove"; they are responding to a historical shift in their interaction with design, as if there were two generational approaches:

> The first group, with truly active practitioners, use the project to anchor speculative thinking, such as Peter Eisenman. Then there are the theoreticians, such as Jeffrey Kipnis and Sanford Kwinter, who come from philosophy and from other disciplines.

I find them, particularly Sanford, incredibly intelligent and amazing to talk to. But I think, in the end, their discourse has not finally helped anything. They have not pushed a line or a way of thinking that has changed or helped clarify this more. Of course, one talks to a person of that calibre and you always learn something, but it is not a very substantial part of what we do or think today. It just became very unproductive.[13]

The first generation of theorists and critics goes back to leading thinkers and practitioners prior to the 1970s, a moment in academia and specialized media dedicated to the speculation about architecture in terms of design. For Silvetti, this glorious era was embodied by Colin Rowe and Aldo Rossi, who were vigorously involved in the discourse and creation of architecture; however, that exchange of concepts and forms "does not exist anywhere anymore, ... everybody had at that time different ideas." Contrastingly, the second generation is homogeneous, focusing on similar themes, self-indulgent and incapable of gluing the discourse, even in renowned schools. The field has become divided: "all the talk about multidisciplinary is not true. People are not talking to each other anymore because everybody is talking about what they do. It could be very good, but there is nothing that holds it together." The theory of recent times is indifferent not only to the basic concerns of the assembly of architecture but also to its pedagogy. From experience, Silvetti, a Harvard professor, affirms that "students do not care about it (I do not necessarily take students' feelings as definers—they need to be criticized too—but they tell you something about the interests of the period), and students' attention do not lie." The reigning boredom with theory and criticism derives from its separation from the language of design—diagramming, drawing, and building—and the increasing tendency to ignore that critical thinking is part of the project and that it is rooted in the act of design. For Silvetti, the problem resides in the slowness of theory that cannot keep up with the pace of technological development and the demands of the market. Furthermore, desynchronized with the long processes of the construction of architecture, the constant and quick change of trends does not permit insightful judgment:

We change from fashion to fashion according to what new programs come in. . . . That is a real problem—the fast introduction into the process of methods of producing or generating form. "The Muses," and all kinds of other things that I have been doing or saying, have to do with trying to accommodate this new situation, which is inevitable. We are still figuring out how to re-integrate them in the process of design, because when you go into practice it is another story. . . . Whether it applies or helps you with your boredom, I do not know. But that is how I contextualize my thinking, particularly of that moment.[14]

Observing the Field

Unlike Silvetti, Lavin, in an interview of 2014, admits to being interested in boredom. Although she does not consider herself an expert in it, she acknowledges its significance, as both a theoretical construct and an instrument for historical investigation. In her view, "the idea of overexposure leads to the inability to grasp details and that produces a sensation that we call boredom. That has been part of the literature of the avant-garde, and I find that very interesting." In "Lying Fallow," boredom is normalized as a stage required before creation, a moment of distracted attention that forces the reconsideration of forgotten aspects, "which is good, and I think that is what I was really arguing for in that piece." When questioned about the title in relation to Kierkegaard's original metaphor of boredom as "a field lying fallow," Lavin confesses to not being aware of it while writing, asserting that the essay was produced intuitively—"it was nothing very fancy ... At my age, I start to forget what I know."[15]

This empirical approach suggests that boredom is individual and critical as well as dependent on experience and expertise. In *Kissing Architecture* (2011), Lavin describes her visit to the Museum of Modern Art in New York after the addition of 1997 by Yoshio Taniguchi, perceiving boring bustle and boring architecture. As a canonical institution, MoMA appears contradictory, since "the very home of good architectural design" had created "a series of buildings that is each more boring than the last"—"stupefying" in the case of the intervention of 1984 by Cesar Pelli. The architecture of the additions also resonate with Clement Greenberg's belief that modernity ought to provide neutrality in order to favor cognition, negating affect.[16] Similar to the etymology of boredom as a space of too much as well as of too little, the outmoded banality of the infrastructure of MoMA acts as a blank vessel that contrasts with progressive exhibitions. However, the duality does not liberate the visitor from encountering a space of abstraction, no longer radical or utopian but rather corporative; Lavin compares it to a generic airport, where circulation prevails and lack of movement becomes an obstacle:

> A continuous movement of people, goods, and images ties the museum together. The trajectory begins in the street, where most visitors' time is spent waiting in a slow-moving line. After money has been paid and each person has squeezed through the narrow turnstile, a space that seems generous by comparison invites visitors to move more quickly up the stairs, through the atrium, which we now know has 7,354 meters of space, to the once again more controlled upward motion of the escalator. When they finally arrive in a gallery, the pace picks up even further. No one can actually stop to look for long.[17]

The Key to Invention

Boredom and the observation of the boring require distance from whatever causes boredom or is considered boring. This separation, which is personal yet at the same time negates any involvement with the object of appraisal, ensures criticality and is thus ideal for the assembly of discourse. Throughout "Lying Fallow," boredom is undesired but not negative. It poses contemporary architecture as a field whose flatness is twofold: nothing of interest has happened until now, while what is happening right now lacks clarity.

These two topographies share "the same quality of total uniformity," grouped under boredom, "a kind of umbrella term, to describe what in fact were two different phenomena, but in relation to which I had a similar reaction."[18] The condition provides space for thinking and reconsideration, as an historical plane, "with more room," that precedes radical change and nurtures new sensibilities—"if boredom, like frustration, is the key to invention, more boredom now will lead to more invention in the future."[19]

To Lavin, boredom is not an existential ennui; rather, happy boredom is the outcome of the last thirty years of architectural production, defined by the critical turn and the digital revolution. Both forces surpass the influence of exemplary and celebrated figures since they are systemic and collective, "what George Kubler called the shape of time." As part of this context, boredom signals a common sensibility and the absence of structural change. This flatline does not entail low quality but rather stasis in the core principles of architecture, in the logic of thinking about architecture, and in its techniques; consequently, formal sameness becomes an index, not only in professional practice but also in the work of students, proving that the condition is widespread, derived from mainstream culture rather than endemic in the discipline. For Lavin, "when Peter Zumthor's proposed building for LACMA, Jürgen Mayer's Metropol Parasol, SANAA's Serpentine Pavilion, and virtually every first-year design student project have exactly the same parti, discrimination seems futile and repetition and replication are revealed as the rule." The lack of difference produces no interest, neither for critics nor for practitioners nor for the general public; it fails to introduce paradigms, which is why "today, architecture, as such and as a whole, despite and maybe even because of the interest of particular individual buildings and the goodness of everybody's intentions, is, well, boring."[20]

Furthermore, Lavin acknowledges, boredom is a concern in the evaluation of architecture, as in the theoretical work of Henry-Russell Hitchcock and Reyner Banham, which denounced duplication in the production of the mid-twentieth century. For Hitchcock, the standardization that informed and inspired the modernist production of architecture had not surpassed the orderly use of modules and grids, and hence propelled the formulaic construction of "bureaucratic architecture," a different route from the work of "geniuses" dedicated to conceiving the unique and inimitable.[21] In turn, Banham identifies parallel trends of boredom and interest in the confrontation of the architecture of tradition with the landscape of technology, helping him to take stock of the configurations of the built environment. Through these observations of the past, Lavin detects boredom in the discipline to decipher her own boredom with the architecture of the present, which she illustrates with the photographs of the Serpentine Pavilions but without reference to them. The lack of attention to the series does not suggest that each object may be boring but rather that their serialization has become boring, as a part of the system of professional practice in the United Kingdom. The role of each pavilion is rigidly defined, unchangeable, and no longer worthy of her consideration. Boredom is "axiomatically non-definitive," not inherent in the object; Lavin describes "a dynamic between an object and a subject and particular historical circumstances, which produces an affect that we call boring.... At certain moments, X object in relation to X subject will be boring, and under other conditions it will not be boring."[22]

Resistance as Method

In "Lying Fallow," boredom is a modus of inspection capable of initiating research, a "Carpe Taedium" that Lavin recommends to her doctoral students.[23] She has become attentive to aspects and material that once were considered "very boring," like a set of "the most boring kind of drawings that you can possibly imagine, ... terrible from any traditional point of view." In her work, boredom generates questions, like curiosity does, about reasons for the existence or the creation of conditions that have not received scholarly attention, exposing how perception and response have evolved in the history of the field. Like a boomerang that depends on the original force of propulsion to travel and return, the exploration and elucidation of the boring requires the intent to turn the boring into the interesting, finding something interesting to make it interesting. For Lavin, boredom opens possibilities of finding connections by locating her presence in a moment of uneventfulness, which enables her to trace the possibilities of action, "in a non-literary way and non-immaterial way and a non-authoritative way," to "just track who goes where, what do they do, what do they buy, where does it go." However, if the outcome—the interesting—is overexposed, then it becomes boring again:

> I was just at the AA [Architectural Association] the other day. I was asked to give a lecture in relation to a little collection of essays that they have just published for me. The expectation was that I could say something about this book, and kind of being excited about it. But I could barely bring myself to say anything about it, and the part of the lecture in which I was speaking about it was boring to me. I am sure it must have been boring to the audience. One of the reasons was not that I found the material boring but rather I just didn't think that I had anything more to say about it. Every thought I could possibly have was in that book.[24]

As a personal reaction rather than a theoretical formulation, she finds that mindless reiteration is a sign of exhaustion; it may be "a quantitative thing—on any topic, I only have so much to say," as in the case of lecturing, when oral narration turns into an uneventful recitation, without possibility for further elaboration. Nonetheless, boredom is different from exhaustion since it can lead to discovery. Lavin admits pursuing the first and fighting the second, rejecting emotional or intellectual unproductivity: "I am resistant to exhaustion, but I do not know why.... If boredom is an entropic decay of interest, is decay the same as completion? I think not. I think entropy does not really allow for that." She likes to lecture when she is "still thinking out loud, when the problem is unresolved in my mind," and so she dismisses the possibility of being jaded with the field. For her, jading connotes failure of the object to impress and insensitivity of the perceiver to respond, which arouse the suspicion of deception or disappointment, "like if you were a better architect, it would still be of interest, or if you were a better critic, you would find something to say."[25]

Not Interested

In both "The Muses Are Not Amused" and "Lying Fallow," the insinuations, denunciations, and confessions of boredom—finding architecture boring or being bored by its production—uncover the flow from interest to disinterest as a negotiation rather than a dichotomy. As implied by Silvetti in the classification of programism, thematization, blobs, and literalism, what may appear stimulating and captivating can turn unsatisfactory if formal creation remains on the surface and is only concerned with the novel. To him, boredom has to do with "a culture that is so much geared by consumption" that "we need new forms fast, and they don't last long."[26] As Lavin notes in her encouragement to architects to persevere in the "minorly interesting things they are doing" and "tolerate the ennui," what may appear as boring and mundane can become the point of entry into the unnoticed. In her view, "boredom does its work on attention in small steps, slowly and steadfastly," prompting invention and the recasting of architecture; it is a force of waiting, "available to those who are ready to seize it."[27] The verdicts of Silvetti and Lavin coincide: the field is insufficient and boring—like Giedion's identification of "confusion and boredom" in the 1950s and 1960s—a judgment that they argue through observation and in architectural terms, without socioeconomic or political contextualization. In addition, they rely on their academic credentials to expose, in a controversial but authoritative manner, a negative condition by suggesting and utilizing boredom as a rhetorical trope.

Silvetti and Lavin avoid the dissection of particular cases. Their methodology transgressively desists from using the conventions of documentation and archival research favored by contemporary architectural history and theory.[28] At first glance, their explications resemble opinions, but they transcend the personal through the wide appeal of their assertions; every reader has experienced that inescapable boredom, either within or outside of the field. The case of study thus becomes a set of overarching circumstances, which permits general inspection and the consequent recommendation of systemic corrections and adjustments. Lavin warns that many schools of architecture, "modelled on the marketplace and the convention center, big schools where more or less anything goes if students will pay for it," will "alter the world through their long, slow, and incremental effects."[29] Silvetti cautions against the illusion that architects are not accountable for the creation of form, since the digital underscores the process rather than the creative input; if that were true, "then one could accept the designer for the responsibility for the form without being responsible for the process," but in fact, he says, "the form is the result of the process, and so the process is what counts."[30]

The unamused muses and the field lying fallow appear to entertain not the question of why creation has not changed but rather why the production of late has failed to provide opportunities for positive elaboration, as if theoretical knowledge constitutes the teleology of architecture. For Silvetti and Lavin, architectural invention is a process of making that requires interpretation, judgment, and the attribution of value. Echoing Roland Barthes's claim that "to be bored means that one cannot produce the text," cannot "open it out, *set it going*," their diagnoses derive from the incapacity to establish and consume relationships of significance.³¹ Even though both educators remain alert to and enthusiastic about the emergence of noteworthy architecture, their boredom with the recent past implies disinterest in the present, a simultaneous listlessness and nimbleness that entail not a reluctance to keep investigating and generating discourse but rather the critical questioning of the system of architectural production. With a modern sensibility that refuses to accept boredom as a permanent condition, the undertone of their elaborations resonates with the nervous disquiet of Joseph Brodsky—"a school is a factory is a poem is a prison is academia is boredom, with flashes of panic"³²—and the irascible impatience of Lydia Davis:

> I don't want to be bored by someone else's imagination. Most people's imagination just isn't very interesting—you can guess where the author got this idea and that idea. You can predict what will come next before you finish reading one sentence. It all seems so arbitrary.
>
> . . .
>
> I feel like saying: Please spare me your imagination, I'm so tired of your vivid imagination, let someone else enjoy it. That's how I'm feeling these days, anyway, maybe it will pass.³³

EPILOGUE
ARCHITECTURES OF BOREDOM

The interdependence between boredom and architecture is at the core of modernity. As a constituent of political, cultural, and socioeconomic processes, the condition is inherent in the production, experience, and reception of the built environment, a factor indispensable to the discipline. Although the provision of optimal conditions for inhabitation—a modern motto, related to physical and mental wellbeing—constitutes an attempt to avoid boredom, the disaffection with what already exists continues to stimulate the capitalist creation of what has not yet been seen, entailing speculative investments that demand technological innovation. Despite this ubiquitous influence, boredom in architecture is either discussed as a social problem that ought to be resolved by providing places for gregariousness and entertainment, or treated as a subjective denunciation of formal repetition and inadequate design. In 2016, inadvertently following this dichotomy, the Venice Biennale of Architecture, "Reporting from the Front," curated by Pritzker laureate Alejandro Aravena, featured circumstances that were considered boring in the past, particularly during the economic boom of the 1990s and early 2000s. Across the exhibitions were buildings of the everyday and of low quality, presented as urgent and emergent problems, including structures that have been left incomplete and abandoned due to the financial crisis, the effects of global warming, and conflict resulting from inequality and totalitarian governance.[1] From Taiwan to Spain via a detour to Chile, these dysfunctions, still immune to the verdicts of history and the solutions of the future, are fixed in the present. By becoming objects of attention, they are the new interesting, and the production of the previous generation is thus tacitly relegated to the position of the new boring.

Boredom can therefore be understood as a condition of space across many architectures, which by being infused with boredom turn into fabrications of ephemerality and consilience rather than of permanency and teleology. Within the domain of boredom, three spaces appear, each related to the relationship between the bored sufferer and the boring environment, and each with specific sensibilities and levels of complexity. The first space relates to the individual, the "I" that encounters boredom directly, in isolation, regardless of the encircling busyness. "I'm bored" can only be uttered as an assertion of individuality; it articulates the distance between exteriority and interiority and thus contributes to the awareness of the parallel existence of both realms. The second space is a social differentiator, the "they" that establishes groups with cultural idiosyncrasies and ideological affiliations, dependent on the other to exist. "They're bored" and "they're boring" are speculations that require an exterior context to acquire validity; this "they" navigates the immediate environment to return to the individual with new intelligence, possibly enlightening. The third space is communal, the "we" that shares the same fundamental circumstances in the modern era, whether consciously recognized or not.

"We're bored" is a diagnosis, of the past and the present, and a call to action that requires emotional and intellectual cooperation; this enforces the collective inhabitation of the interstices that have escaped planning, nurturing experimentation.

Rather than excluding each other, these three spaces of boredom coexist in continuous slippage and dynamism. Like the weather, dust, or fog, using W. Benjamin's and Heidegger's metaphors, they invade every aspect of the production of the environment, interlacing the material with the intangible and the spatial with the temporal. Due to this topological interrelation, "I am," "they are," and "we are bored" paradoxically divide and bond, confuse and clarify, and displace and restore. Their architectures may be as empty and sparse as the impossible fantasies of a locus communis noted by Marx in the factory workers of the nineteenth century, or as full and luxuriant as the ostensibly boring buildings of Oran described by Camus.

I'm Bored

As a monitor of behavior that also informs it, boredom can have lasting effects. It can safeguard the individual from danger while helping to define lifetime goals and interests. Le Corbusier, who complained of enduring the condition during his early encounters with architecture, at the age of twenty wrote in a diary entry after an excursion to Vienna in 1907: "sad day; no purpose whatever; mortal boredom; one rages, one rears up, one is a tiny angry god in solitary combat against this mocking inert mass, the inexorable *indifference* of the big city." With the same splenetic tone in a letter of 1910 to his parents, while he was an apprentice in the studio of Peter Behrens, he complained:

> Each day begins by opening a big hole in front of me and dropping me into it because I thought I wasn't being an idiot, which I am, and in a way that's disgustingly and unacceptably unfair. Of course it's my own fault, but my sickness is right there, mocking me, frustrating me. You no longer understand such a creature, my dear parents, nor do I. I've given up—first victory, or already a first defeat: trying to analyse why. It's all summed up in a single word of two syllables: Boredom.[2]

The "I'm bored" of a young Le Corbusier surfaces as the need for change and the attempt to identify the meaningful. To become manifest, either during or after, and to demarcate its zone of operation, boredom borrows from other proximate phenomena. Despite the specificity of its expressions—architecture, in the case of Le Corbusier, who reacts to the developments of the early twentieth century—boredom resists interpretative closure. It begins as one theme and morphs into another, challenging the capacity of narration of the individual and leaving marks. When put together by the bored "I," they fail to compose identifiable trajectories, or significant stories, that might allow the existential encounter with architecture. Though when seen by the interested "they" and "we," the marks turn into nodes of biographical axes, providing a sense of direction.

"I'm bored" depends on self-theorization, a personal but indefinite attempt to rationalize the distance between the demands of sentiments and thoughts and the requisites of society. As Siegfried Kracauer reflected in 1924, after having observed the crowded stadia and picture palaces in Berlin, boredom is more than the outcome of banality; it is also a critical rejection to the modern environment. In his view, being bored is "the only proper occupation, since it provides a kind of guarantee that one is, so to speak, still in control of one's own existence." The failure to acknowledge boredom amidst the culture of entertainment indicates its success in annihilating the space of the "I": "if one were never bored, one would presumably not really be present at all and would thus be merely one more object of boredom."[3] This heightened individuality has the capacity to generate doubt about the futile propositions of modernity and the apathy propelled by capitalism. Kracauer's prophylactic to evade unnecessary and unproductive entanglements with the superficial is seclusion, which will stimulate introspection and self-absorption instead. This alternate boredom permits the confrontation and reconnection with that which is desired, in intensity and extensity; conquering the determinism imposed by media and the cycle of work and leisure thus allows genuine inhabitation to be regained.

They're Bored

Boredom cannot exist separated from other conditions or set of concepts. The presence of the other and the possibility of difference must therefore be acknowledged, but difference is accompanied by ideological implications. In the debate of 1982 between Christopher Alexander and Peter Eisenman on "the contrasting concepts of harmony in architecture," Alexander proposes to agree that Chartres is "a great building," attempting to establish a common ground for discussion. Yet Eisenman replies, "I think it is a boring building ... for me, is one of the least interesting cathedrals." He continues to explain his rejection of Alexander's assessment of Chartres with an anecdote: "in fact, I have gone to Chartres a number of times to eat in the restaurant across the street—had a 1934 red Mersault wine, which was exquisite—I never went into the cathedral. The cathedral was done *en passant*. Once you've seen one Gothic cathedral, you have seen them all."[4] Too antagonistic to be accidental, Eisenman's boredom dismisses Alexander's knowledge and sensibility, an implicit accusation that Alexander had not paid adequate attention to the building, the stylistic period, or even the whole history of the discipline.

Eisenman's expressions of "they're boring" and "I'm interesting" infringe aggressively upon the "I'm interested" of Alexander. When asked to pick another building to dissect together, he makes another irrefutable claim in choosing the Palazzo Chiericati by Andrea Palladio, which possesses intellectuality, he says; "it makes me feel high in my mind, not in my gut." For Alexander, Eisenman's withdrawal of feelings not only require specialized attention—"if this weren't a public situation, I'd be tempted to get into this on a psychiatric level"—but also constitute a symptom of the rejection of everything emotional about modern architecture, a negation of the intangible forces that "have governed the formation of buildings over the last 2000 years or so." Reproving and correcting, Eisenman answers by declaring that "the panicked withdrawal of the alienated self was dealt with in Modernism—which was concerned with the alienation of the self from the collective."[5] Again, Eisenman's response diminishes the likelihood of positive engagement, indicating not only his unwillingness to be associated with any tradition but also his lack of interest in collaboration. This projective boredom operates as criticality and selectivity, morphing into a seemingly debilitated capacity for establishing affinity; it is a dynamic protection against the risk of losing uniqueness.

As in the ripostes of Eisenman to Alexander, the need for recognition of "they're bored" implicates morality, since the possibility of caring for something or someone necessitates more than self-interest. Unlike the religiosity of acedia and the secularity of despair, where not even the desire for desire can exist, in amorality, boredom opens the way for a hope for diversity and for finding mutual pursuits with others.[6] "They're bored" tests the limits of respect; who and what is considered bored and boring indicates degrees of tolerance for contiguous convictions. Far from providing strict regulations, the space of "they" guides practices and codes of behavior, imbuing social relations with affection and knowledge while responding to the environment—positively through creation and preservation or negatively through obliteration and neglect.

We're Bored

The boundless interiority of "I'm bored" and the exterior limitations of "they're bored" differ from "we're bored," which introduces a sense of community that is based on the principles of progress and the monetary transactions of capitalism. It is a shared and unreserved condition, without a set of positive values or prescribed rituals to be performed in its name. Its location in the present, between that which happens and that which fails to occur, creates a space of immersion in which "we're bored" is unmentioned and unmentionable but nevertheless lends structure to that which is communicable and communicated, such as the safety, predictability, and punctuality found in the most developed cities in the Western world. Responding to the release of the 2015 update of the World Happiness Report commissioned by the United Nations, two articles, published in well-established periodicals, explored the relationship between the best standards of livability and boredom. In the Gulliver section of *The Economist*, in the article by B. R. titled "Boring Cities: Torporville," the author calls the phenomenon an "intractable problem" of cities that strive to become "nicer places in which to live"; however, "the more they succeed the less interesting they become."[7] In the *Financial Times*, in "Why the 'Happiest' Cities Are Boring" by John Kay, boredom is a communal construction resulting from the overarching aims of modern planning heralded by Le Corbusier; in Canada, for instance, "boringness isn't intrinsic" but is a "cherished project" of its inhabitants.[8]

In these accounts, cities such as Geneva, Toronto, and even New York and London are depicted as characterless, offering only experiential sameness. B. R. and Kay assert that these sites want for the possibility of the unexpected, adventure, and the excitement of risk; neutral and uninspiring architecture perpetuates an isotropic and stable everywhere. To Kay, in contemporary New York, "the streets feel safe and the once dysfunctional underground system seems to work as well as any metro in any big city. Both above and below ground the city has become, not to put too fine a point on it, pleasant." And in London, "the Tube is now far safer and more reliable than it ever was.... Going for a night out in Brixton or Shoreditch, once a daring pursuit, is no longer the edgy experience it once was."[9] This homogeneity of functionality and peaceful coexistence is "nice but not fun," easy to navigate and preferable to the "grime and danger" of the 1980s but without a significant here nor there.[10] However, the unifying and idealized portrayal of these architectures, generic and gentrified centers for the administration and accumulation of the concrete abstractness of money, is tailored to the affluence of the intended audience of the two publications. Unintentionally, both reporters confirm that boredom is a relationship that escapes irrefutable definitions and representations; it is the space of "we" that does not depend merely on buildings. Instead, the modern built environment is one of its many components, structuring and structured by the condition as well as attending and attended by the negotiations between interiority and exteriority.

As the opinion pieces in *The Economist* and the *Financial Times* attest, the pervasiveness of "we're bored" cannot be objectively grasped but can be reflected upon and acted out. In line with the search for the ethical in Kierkegaard, the need for a leader in Heidegger, and the nexus of the mass individual in A. Benjamin, mutual boredom entails a call for awakening that necessarily involves the concern with the design and dwelling of the world. In modernity, while the respect for "I'm bored" establishes the lay morality of "they're bored," the task of "we're bored" is to reclaim existential interest through collective experience, amidst the specificity of modern architecture, generating social commitment and environmental responsibility.

I Am, They Are, and We Are Bored

If seen historically, the spaces of "I am," "they are" and "we are bored" signal different phases of the development of the modern era and its built environment, circumscribed within the recurrent cycles of economic prosperity and decline. "I'm bored" resonates with the experience of the long nineteenth century, characterized by a state of spatial and temporal in-betweenness. The negotiations of the urban and the rural through the creation and consolidation of railways, roads, and commerce routes accentuated the loss of previous systems of belief and meaning. In consequence, the expectations of the individual came into question, inducing confusion. As Kierkegaard observed with resentment, history became "real and true" because it was "lived" as boredom and redundancy: "Wretched fate! In vain you paint your furrowed face like an old harlot, in vain you make a racket with your fool's bells. You bore me, it's always the same, idem per idem. No variation, always a rehash."[11] In turn, "they're bored" extends to the social and informs the nascent comprehension of the city as primary nature. In the twentieth century, despite the emergence of many expressions of a boredom that is the dearth of what is not attained, a boredom that is anomie and a threat to memory, the architecture and infrastructure of the urban became a source of fascination, fostering utopias of sameness and illusions of an absolute geography. For Heidegger, the inexorable immersion in this duality of passive anonymity and superficial action had endangered the development of humanity with the world as a whole, ignoring philosophy and hence producing boredom, the defining quality of "the spiritual space—if one may say such a thing—in which we move."[12] To this generalized circumstance, "we're bored" reacts by acknowledging the impossibility of transcendence. It encourages variety and multiplicity as well as transgression, responses evident in the fragmentary structures of the modern metropolis as well as in the virtual spheres of the post-metropolis. Amidst this entanglement of cause and effect—in the corporeal, emotional, and intellectual—A. Benjamin rescues boredom as a historical mood that becomes "a nexus of operations" and delineates the contemporaneous subjectivity, its architectures, and the interconnection with other temporalities.[13]

The unbearable boredom of a young Le Corbusier, the limits established by the boredom of Eisenman upon Alexander, and the privileged boredom of *The Economist* and the *Financial Times*, rather than being exceptional cases, simply constitute more episodes in the continuing story of the modern built environment. They corroborate the rifeness of the condition while exposing its intricate variations throughout time, carrying remnants of the past with indifference but always saturated with the possibilities of an indeterminate future. This extended modernity—superficially and profoundly bored, outlined by boredom—escapes the peril of a total architectural homogenization driven by a common intellectuality, since it depends on individual experience and the cultural sensibility of creators and users. Even if architectural configurations may become nearly identical with or perfectly different from each other, the way in which they are encountered will vary, prompting relationships and actions—in interiority and exteriority, morally and ethically—that form functional and malleable spaces of inhabitation and appropriation, affirmation and revolt.

NOTES

Introduction

1. Titled *Noia* in Italian, the novel has also been translated as *The White Canvas*. Alberto Moravia, *Boredom*, trans. Angus Davidson (New York: New York Review of Books, 1999), 8–9. With the same rapidity, in 1979, Anton Zijderveld divided Western history into three periods of boredom, culminating with the philosophy of Georg W. F. Hegel: "The boredom caused by Roman imperialism had been driven away by Christianity. . . . The Protestant has left the beauty and holiness of the Middle Ages, and is ever more immersed in the dreariness of the routines of everyday life. There he can only experience boredom—a very pervasive boredom which could only be driven out by a third religion or world view, succeeding the world-views of the *Imperium Romanum* and the Roman Catholic Church. Hegelianism, we may assume, was the most suitable candidate." Anton Zijderveld, *On Clichés: The Supersedure of Meaning by Function in Modernity* (London: Routledge and Kegan Paul, 1979), 79–80.

2. Fredric Jameson, *Postmodernism, or, the Cultural Logic of Late Capitalism* (London: Verso, 1991), 303.

3. Emil Cioran, *Tears and Saints*, trans. Ilinca Zarifopol-Johnston (Chicago: The University of Chicago Press, 1995), 86. Also for Cioran, history—the recording and classification of preliminary events—is the result of our fear of boredom. *History and Utopia*, trans. Richard Howard (New York: Seaver, 1987), 109.

4. Charles Nuckolls explains the difference: "in depression, so much energy is required to inhibit the aggressive (but forbidden) impulse that the person is drained of vitality. Boredom is the opposite side of the same coin. In boredom the impulse remains energetic—hence the feeling that one should be 'doing something'—but it cannot be satisfied because its real object, being forbidden, eludes identification." Charles Nuckolls, "Boring Rituals," *Journal of Ritual Studies* 21, no. 1 (2007): 42–3.

5. Quoted in Wolf Lepenies, *Melancholy and Society* (Cambridge: Harvard University Press, 1992), 108, from Maine de Biran, *Journal I* (February 1814–December 1816).

6. However, Peter Toohey asserts that boredom is an umbrella-like concept, encompassing several similar conditions, such as acedia, melancholia, and nausea. Peter Toohey, *Boredom: A Lively History* (New Haven: Yale University Press, 2011), 136.

7. For Patricia Spacks, "the expanding definition of boredom in our time means that by now one might argue that virtually every word currently written speaks of the condition in one way or another." Patricia Meyer Spacks, *Boredom: The Literary History of a State of Mind* (Chicago: University of Chicago Press, 1996), ix.

8. Friedrich Schlegel, "Athenaeum Fragments," in *Philosophical Fragments*, trans. Peter Firchow (Minneapolis: University of Minnesota Press, 1991), 18.

9. Maurice Blanchot, *The Infinite Conversation*, trans. Susan Hanson (Minneapolis: University of Minnesota Press, 1993), 242.

10. Barbara Dalle Pezze and Carlo Salzani, *Essays on Boredom and Modernity* (Amsterdam: Rodopi, 2009), 24.

Notes to pp. 3–7

11. Martin Heidegger, *The Fundamental Concepts of Metaphysics: World, Finitude, Solitude*, trans. William McNeill and Nicholas Walker (Bloomington: Indiana University Press, 2001), 77.

12. Walter Benjamin, "Boredom, Eternal Return," in *The Arcades Project*, trans. Howard Eiland and Kevin McLaughlin, ed. Rolf Tiedemann (Cambridge: Belknap, 1999), 104.

13. Henri Lefebvre, *Introduction to Modernity: Twelve Preludes*, trans. John Moore (London: Verso, 1995), 353.

14. Psychology and psychoanalysis do not elaborate on the growth of the phenomenon in the last 200 years; as Barbara Dalle Pezze and Carlo Salzani assert, "the medicalization of boredom lacks any sense of history and does not explain it as a social and historical phenomenon characteristic of modernity." Pezze and Salzani, *Essays on Boredom and Modernity*, 15.

15. Fernand Braudel, *A History of Civilizations* (London: Allen Lane/Penguin, 1994), 34–5. Alison and Peter Smithson observe, "it has always taken a very long time for a useful thing to become an idea—to acquire formal value ... to have a place amongst other ideas ... to become capable of being defined, adjusted, perfected, rejected, re-perfected in the mind—often almost to the point of losing the practical intention of the original thing. ... Things become ideas only very slowly; what we now call *space* and think about without too much difficulty—the space between buildings conceived as out-of-doors salons and corridors—did not crystallize as idea until the time of Nancy, the mid-eighteenth century." Alison and Peter Smithson, *Without Rhetoric. An Architectural Aesthetic 1955–1972* (London: Latimer New Dimensions, 1973), 56, 59 (italics in original).

16. For most economists, this theory is interpretative rather than scientific.

17. According to Søren Kierkegaard, "language has time as its element; all other media have space as their element." Therefore, the expression of boredom might be more accurate in literature due to its temporal characteristic. For Lars Svendsen, in the study of boredom "literature is a great deal more illuminative than quantitative sociological or psychological studies." And for Elizabeth Goodstein, literary texts are fundamental, because "in representing boredom, they depict its sociological and philosophical significance as intertwined." Søren Kierkegaard, *Either/Or: A Fragment of Life*, trans. Alastair Hannay (London: Penguin Books Limited, 2004), 79; Lars Svendsen, *A Philosophy of Boredom*, trans. John Irons (London: Reaktion, 2005), 28; Elizabeth Goodstein, *Experience without Qualities: Boredom and Modernity* (Stanford: Stanford University Press, 2005), 15.

18. Kierkegaard, *Either/Or*, 227.

19. A previous print use appears in *The Albion*, a British newspaper. Cryptically, it wrote in 1829: "Neither will I follow another precedental mode of boredom, and indulge in a laudatory apostrophe to the destinies which presided over my fashioning." In Wijnand Van Tilburg, "Leprosy of the Soul? A Brief History of Boredom," *The Conversation* (2020), https://theconversation.com.

20. Maxim Gorky, "Boredom," *The Independent Magazine* (1907), 310.

21. Albert Camus, "The Minotaur, or the Stop in Oran," in *The Myth of Sisyphus and Other Essays*, trans. Justin O'Brien (New York: Vintage Books, 1955), 130.

22. Sigfried Giedion, *Space, Time and Architecture. The Growth of a New Tradition* (Cambridge: Harvard University Press, 1967), xxxii.

23. Andrew Benjamin, "Boredom and Distraction: The Moods of Modernity," in *Walter Benjamin and History*, ed. Andrew Benjamin (London: Continuum, 2005), 166.

24. Russell Kirk, "The Architecture of Servitude and Boredom," *Modern Age* 26, no. 2 (1982): 114, 115.

Chapter 1

1. Aldous Huxley, "Accidie," in *Mass Leisure*, ed. Eric Larrabee and Rolf Meyersohn (Glenco: The Free Press, 1958). Historical accounts of boredom are inconclusive due to the impossibility of stabilizing its essence and comprehensively encompassing its cultural development. See, for example, Reinhard Kuhn, *The Demon of Noontide: Ennui in Western Literature* (Princeton: Princeton University Press, 1976); or Toohey, *Boredom*, cxx.

2. In a space dominated by the consecration of nature and the predominance of civil and religious architecture, mythical expressions surfaced to denote concern with absence and repetition. In the *Timaeus* (c. 360 BC), Plato portrays the distance between the actual and the ideal, the human and the divine, as a realm mediated by desire—deified in Eros, a god of yearning and lack. The secular equivalent ἅλυς and its verbal forms appeared at the same time to designate irritation and impatience with unwanted repetition. Among the numerous Latin counterparts—including *fastidium, otium, satietas, vacare, fatigo, defatigo, defetiscor, torpor, languidus, desidia, inertia, ineptia, piget, hebes, obtundo, molestus, odiosus, odium*, and *vexo—horror loci* and *taedium vitae* signified exhaustion with the attempt to find satisfactory spaces to inhabit. The first appears in writings by Lucretius and Horace as the ailment of fictional characters who rush aimlessly between landscapes and villages only to become discontented with every destination, experiencing restlessness, unsettledness, and a displeasure in limits. The second is present in the work by Seneca and ranges from a momentary distress to a chronic discontent with the world, questioning the capacity of the surroundings to provide existential meaning. As a literary figure, horror loci conveys not psychological characteristics but philosophical preoccupations with dynamism and stasis. Plato, *Timaeus* (The Gutenberg Project, 2008), http://www.gutenberg.org/files/1572/1572-h/1572-h.htm; Peter Toohey, "Some Ancient Notions of Boredom," *Illinois Classical Studies* 13, no. 1 (1988): 160; Kuhn, *The Demon of Noontide*, 23.

3. Evagrius Ponticus was an ascetic monk of the fourth century who qualified acedia as demonic. He is credited with developing the first list of eight capital sins, giving acedia the longest treatment. However, in the following century, acedia—indifference—was merged with *tristitia*—sadness—to create *sloth*, reducing the list to seven sins. Ibid., 44.

4. Huxley, "Accidie," 15, 16, 20. Many historians and philosophers connect acedia with boredom, including Michael Raposa and Lars Svendsen. However, Nicholas Lombardo, in his interpretation of Thomas Aquinas and emotions that concurs with Walter Benjamin, argues that acedia is not an equivalent of boredom: "Perhaps the most obvious dissimilarity is that, in popular understanding, boredom denotes a psychological state that does not *by definition* imply moral defect, while *acedia* is a vice and does imply moral defect.... Consequently, it seems more accurate to say that *acedia* is a cause of boredom, and perhaps the preeminent cause, but that it is neither identical with boredom nor its only possible cause." Nicholas Lombardo, *The Logic of Desire. Aquinas on Emotion* (Washington D.C.: The Catholic University of America Press, 2011), 197 (italics in original); Walter Benjamin, "On the Concept of History," in *Selected Writings: Volume 4, 1938-1940*, ed. Howard Eiland and Michael Jennings (Cambridge: Belknap, 2006), 391.

5. Thomas Aquinas, *Summa Theologica, Secunda Secundae* (The Gutenberg Project, 2006), http://www.gutenberg.org/cache/epub/18755/pg18755.html Q. 35, Art. 3.

6. Robert Burton, H. Jackson, and W. H. Gass, *The Anatomy of Melancholy* (New York: New York Review of Books, 2001), part I, section II, member II, subsection VI, 244; part II, section II, subsection III, 65.

7. Matthew Green, *The Spleen and Other Poems* (European Libraries, 1796), https://archive.org/stream/spleenandotherp01stotgoog#page/n5/mode/2up. An earlier description by George Cheney defines spleen as a "generalised gloom," often blamed on the bad weather of England. George Cheney, *The English Malady: Or, a Treatise of Nervous Diseased of All Kinds, as Spleen,*

Vapour, Lowness of Spirits, Hypocondriacal, and Hysterical Distempers, Etc. (London: G. Straham, 1733), 194–9.

8. Huxley, "Accidie," 17.
9. Ibid. Thomas Weiskel affirms that "[Edmund] Burke began his treatise by laying down a premise that the passions are never engaged by the familiar. Boredom masks uneasiness and intense boredom exhibits the signs of the most basic of modern anxieties, the anxiety of nothingness, or absence." Thomas Weiskel, *The Romantic Sublime: Studies in the Structure and Psychology of Transcendence* (Baltimore: Johns Hopkins University Press, 1976), 18.
10. Huxley, "Accidie," 17. According to Seán Healy, Charles Baudelaire introduced the term *spleen* into French "to do justice to the exalted quality of his own ennui." And according to Jacques Le Goff, Baudelaire coined the term *modernity* in the article "The Painter of Modern Life" (1860-3). Derived from the French *mode* and coinciding with the temporal qualities of boredom, it denotes a concern with the present. Seán Healy, *Boredom, Self, and Culture* (Rutherford: Fairleigh Dickinson University Press, 1984), 29; Jacques Le Goff, *History and Memory* (New York: Columbia University Press, 1992), 40.
11. Michael Raposa describes ennui as "boredom coloured by melancholy," while Jack Barbalet affirms that boredom "is not a feeling of acceptance of or resignation toward a state of indifference, as ennui is." Michael Raposa, *Boredom and the Religious Imagination* (Charlottesville: University of Virginia, 1999), 34; Jack Barbalet, "Boredom and Social Meaning," *The British Journal of Sociology* 50, no. 4 (1999): 634–5.
12. Huxley, "Accidie," 17; Patrice Petro, *Aftershocks of the New: Feminism and Film History* (New Brunswick: Rutgers University Press, 2002), 61.
13. Huxley, "Accidie," 18.
14. The Russian скука carries the connotation of a whining sound as well as of sorrow. Terence Wade, *Russian Etymological Dictionary* (Bristol: Bristol Classical Press, 1996), 200.
15. "Boredom," in *The Oxford English Dictionary*, ed. James A. H. Murray et al. (Oxford: Clarendon Press, 2001), 414.
16. Robert K. Barnhart and Sol Steinmetz, *Chambers Dictionary of Etymology* (Edinburgh: Chambers, 1988), 108; Eric Partridge, *Origins: A Short Etymological Dictionary of Modern English* (London: Routledge and Kegan Paul, 1966), 54; Walter W. Skeat, *An Etymological Dictionary of the English Language* (Oxford: Clarendon, 1953), 108.
17. Walter Skeat arrives at the same connotation by referring to a line in Shakespeare's *Henry VIII* (c. 1613): "At this instant He bores me with some trick." Skeat, *An Etymological Dictionary of the English Language*, 108.
18. *The Oxford English Dictionary* relies on the correspondence between politician George Selwyn and socialite George Williams and the Earls of March and Carlisle to date the earliest use of *bore* and *to bore* in the sense of "to be tiresome or dull." In the letters from 1766 to 1768, the terms express the preoccupation of the writers with being perceived as monotonous and repetitive. Before *boredom* became popular, the short-lived *boreism* and *borism* designated "the characteristic behaviour of bores" and "the practice of being a bore." "Boredom," 414; J. Jesse and G. Selwyn, *George Selwyn and His Contemporaries, with Memoirs and Notes* (London: R. Bentley, 1843), 24, 52, 55, 62, 86, 88, 90, 95, 110, 243.
19. The earliest letter with the term *boredom* dates from July 22, 1844, to painter Daniel Maclise. Charles Dickens, *Letters 1833–1856* (London: Charles Scribner's Sons, 1879), 124.
20. *The Letters of Charles Dickens: 1832–1846* (London: The Nonesuch Press, 1938), 333.
21. "Interesting," in *The Oxford English Dictionary*, ed. James A. H. Murray, et al. (Oxford: Clarendon Press, 2001), 1100.

22. Partridge, *Origins*, 187; Pezze and Salzani, *Essays on Boredom and Modernity*, 11.
23. Ibid.; Spacks, *Boredom*, 116.
24. Roland Barthes, *The Pleasure of the Text* (New York: Hill & Wang, 1975), 26. Boredom is a recurrent theme in the work by Barthes. In 1979, a year before his death, he complained of boredom due to his incapacity to fulfil or transcend desire. Describing a scene with one his lovers, he wrote in his diary: "I asked him to come and sit beside me on the bed during my nap; he came willingly enough, sat on the edge of the bed, looked at an art book; his body was very far away—if I stretched out an arm toward him, he didn't move, ... he soon went into the other room. A sort of despair overcame me. ... How clearly I saw that I would have to give up boys, because none of them felt any desire for me, and I was either too scrupulous or too clumsy to impose my desire on them; that this is an unavoidable fact, averred by all my efforts of flirting, that I have melancholy life, that, finally, I'm bored to death by it." *Incidents*, trans. Richard Howard (Berkeley: University of California Press, 1992), 79.
25. In Greek antiquity, Eros entailed desire as well as lack. Diotima of Mantinea pointed out in *The Symposium* (c. 385-370 BC) that "desire is a bastard got by Wealth on Poverty and ever at home in a life of want." Similarly, Seán Healy has described boredom as "psychic anorexia," the refusal to be nurtured by the environment. Anne Carson, *Eros the Bittersweet* (London: Dalkey Archive Press, 1998), 5-10; Healy, *Boredom, Self, and Culture*, 60.
26. Matthias Schirren, *Bruno Taut. Alpine Architektur. Eine Utopie* (Berlin: Prestel, 2004), 72.
27. Le Corbusier, *Towards a New Architecture* (London: The Architectural Press, 1982), 15.
28. Quoted in Erwin Panofsky, *Perspective as Symbolic Form*, trans. Christopher Wood (New York: Zone Books, 1991), 29-30, from Ernst Cassirer, *Philosophy of Symbolic Forms*, vol. 2: "Mythical Thought," trans. Ralph Manheim (New Haven: Yale University Press, 1955), 83-4.
29. Panofsky, *Perspective as Symbolic Form*, 31, 42-4.
30. A compilation of references on boredom by Henri Lefebvre can be found in "The Black Sun of Boredom: Henri Lefebvre and the Critique of Everyday Life" (Laurentian University, 2012) by Patrick Gamsby. For Lefebvre, the qualities of the urban are not confined to the scale of the city; they spread across all the landscape produced by the network of human activity. Cities constitute epicenters of boredom, reaching as far as communication and transportation allow. Iain Borden, "Beyond Space. The Ideas of Henri Lefebvre in Relation to Architecture and Cities" (unpublished: The Bartlett, UCL, 2006), 18.
31. Lefebvre, *Introduction to Modernity*, 117, 118 (italics in original), 119.
32. Ibid., 124. Analogous to the identification of two types of boredom, Lefebvre distinguishes everyday life from the everyday. Whereas the former refers to the meaningful experience of existence—permeated by myths and values—the latter constitutes the repetitive, fragmentary, and routinized—void and impossible to resolve. The boredom of the modern everyday "evades the grip of forms," but it is accentuated by forms programmed as desire and change: "production anticipates reproduction; production produces change in such a way as to superimpose the impression of speed onto that of monotony. Some people cry out against the acceleration of time, others cry out against stagnation. They're both right." *Everyday Life in the Modern World*, trans. by Sacha Rabinovitch (New Brunswick: Transaction, 1984), 182; "The Everyday and Everydayness," *Yale French Studies*, no. 37 (1987): 10.

Chapter 2

1. Braudel, *A History of Civilizations*, 389; Robert Heilbroner, *Beyond Boom and Crash* (New York: Norton, 1978), 64.

2. In nineteenth-century translations of *The Thoughts of Blaise Pascal*, weariness is treated as equivalent to *ennui*, while twentieth-century versions use *boredom*. Blaise Pascal, *The Thoughts of Blaise Pascal*, trans. Paul C. Kegan (London: Bell, 1899), 34, 35.
3. Braudel, *A History of Civilizations*, 340.
4. Georg W. F. Hegel, *Philosophy of Mind: Being Part Three of the Encyclopaedia of the Philosophical Sciences*, trans. William Wallace and A. V. Miller (Oxford: Clarendon Press, 1971), 69.
5. Arthur Schopenhauer, *The Essays of Arthur Schopenhauer: The Wisdom of Life* (The Gutenberg Project, 2004), http://www.gutenberg.org/cache/epub/10741/pg10741.html.
6. *The World as Will and Representation*, vol. 1 (London: Courier Dove, 2012), 313. For Schopenhauer, intellectual reflection and creativity invigorate and enlighten "the multifarious phenomena of self and nature," not only providing a critical apprehension of the world in relation to the inwardness of the individual but also overcoming the "vague longing" akin to boredom. *The Essays of Arthur Schopenhauer: The Art of Literature and the Art of Controversy* (Overland Park: Digireads.com, 2010), 89.
7. Friedrich Nietzsche, *The Anti-Christ*, trans. H. Mencken (New York: Cosimo, 2005), 69; quoted in Leslie Paul Thiele, "Postmodernity and the Routinization of Novelty: Heidegger on Boredom and Technology," *Polity* 29, no. 4 (1997): 494–5, from Friedrich Nietzsche, *On the Genealogy of Morals*, trans. Walter Kaufmann and R. Hollingdale (New York: Vintage, 1967), 97. Nietzsche affirms that boredom exists in modern life because the sources of its suppression no longer exist. If in pre-modern times, morality and religion prevented boredom, then in the modern era these means of suppression have been drained of their power. Philip Kain, "Nietzsche, the Kantian Self, and Eternal Recurrence," *Idealistic Studies* 34, no. 3 (2004): 233.
8. Friedrich Nietzsche, *The Gay Science: With a Prelude in German Rhymes and an Appendix of Songs*, ed. Bernard Williams, trans. Josefine Nauckhoff and Adrian del Caro (Cambridge: Cambridge University Press, 2001), 273–4 (italics in original). To Nietzsche, "for thinkers and all sensitive spirits, boredom is that disagreeable 'windless calm' of the soul that produces a happy voyage and cheerful winds. They have to bear it and must wait for its effects on them. Precisely this is what lesser natures cannot achieve by any means. To ward off boredom at any cost is vulgar, no less than work without pleasure." Ibid., 57.
9. Nikolai Kondratieff, *The Long Wave Cycle* (New York: Richardson & Snyder, 1984), 68, 70, 75.
10. Heilbroner, *Beyond Boom and Crash*, 12, 64, 70.
11. For a comprehensive history of cotton and its role in modernity, see Sven Beckert, *Empire of Cotton: A Global History* (New York: Vintage Books, 2015).
12. Braudel, *A History of Civilizations*, 376; Lars Svendsen, *Fashion: A Philosophy*, trans. John Irons (London: Reaktion, 2006), 19, 113, 172. According to Bernard Rudofsky, fashion "is engineered and controlled change; fashion and boredom are mutually dependent." Bernard Rudofsky, *Behind the Picture Window* (Oxford: Oxford University Press, 1955), 199.
13. Quoted in Braudel, *A History of Civilizations*, 376.
14. Ibid., 25–6, 330–1. According to Braudel, "*proletariat* was included in the French Academy's Dictionary in 1828. *Mass*, in the singular and especially in the plural, became the key words … *Socialist* and *Socialism* came into general use in the 1830s. So too did *Communism*, in the vague sense of economic and social equality.… The word *capitalism* was used by Louis Blanc in his *Organization of Work* (1848–50) and by [Pierre-Joseph] Proudhon in 1857; it appeared in the Larousse dictionary in 1867.… Less successful new words included 'bourgeoisism' and 'collectism.'" Ibid., 390–1.

15. For Braudel, this is "an age-old phenomenon, present in all materially advanced societies in the past. But there is no denying that in the nineteenth century it greatly intensified, causing a good deal of heart-searching." Ibid.; Heilbroner, *Beyond Boom and Crash*, 31–2.
16. Karl Marx and Friedrich Engels, *Capital*, vol. 1, trans. Ben Fowkes (London: Penguin Books, 1976), 548; Marx, "Production, Consumption, Distribution, Exchange (Circulation)," in *Grundrisse* (London: Penguin, 1973), 18 (italics in original).
17. Francis Galton, "The Measure of Fidget," *Nature* 32 (1885): 174. In *The Expression of the Emotions in Man and Animals* (1872), Charles Darwin, Galton's cousin, did not include boredom.

Chapter 3

1. Charles Baudelaire, "Spleen," in *Poems of Baudelaire*, ed. Roy Campbell (New York: Pantheon Books, 1952), 99–102.
2. According to Alastair Hannay, Kierkegaard was a character estranged from the society of his time. He only traveled four times to Berlin, and spent most of his life inside his small apartment in Copenhagen. Theodor Adorno called him "the flâneur who promenaded in his room." Alastair Hannay, "Introduction," in Søren Kierkegaard, *Either/Or: A Fragment of Life* (London: Penguin Classics, 1992), 16; Theodor W. Adorno, *Kierkegaard: Construction of the Aesthetic*, trans. Robert Hullot-Kentor (Minneapolis: University of Minnesota Press, 1989), 41.
3. The terms "inwardness" and "outward spheres" are taken from *Kierkegaard: Construction of the Aesthetic* (1933) by Adorno. Jameson corroborates this division later in the twentieth century: "their work [that of modern authors and artists] was said to represent a new 'inward turn' and the opening up of some new reflexive deep subjectivity: the 'carnival of interiorized fetishism', [György] Lukács once called it." Jameson, *Postmodernism*, 311.
4. Kierkegaard, *Either/Or*, 27. To Hannay, "it was the spirit of philosophy itself, incarnate in Hegel, that Kierkegaard was out to destroy, and in order to break with Hegel he could not resort to the discursive and systematic methods of the Hegelians themselves.... Kierkegaard was thus able to put his native literary talent to the edifying task of regenerating ethics in the ordinary-life situations that make up a human life." Hannay, "Introduction," 10.
5. Kierkegaard, *Either/Or*, 179, 180, 182.
6. Lore Huhn and Philipp Schwab, "Kierkegaard and German Idealism," in *The Oxford Handbook of Kierkegaard*, ed. John Lippitt and George Pattison (Oxford: Oxford University Press, 2013), 83. Kierkegaard pioneered the use of the Danish *kedsomhed*, decisively locating the condition in the modern era. In Old Danish, the equivalent of *boredom* is *kjedsommelighed*, *kjedsommeligheben*; and *boring* is *kjedsommelige*, *kjedsommelig*. Søren Kierkegaard, *Enten-Eller: Et Livs-Fragment / Udgivet Af Victor Eremita* (Kjøbenhavn: C. A. Reitzel, 1843).
7. Kierkegaard, *Either/Or*, 142, 74, 85–6.
8. Ibid., 479.
9. Only in its first edition did it appear as two separate volumes, giving the public the option of reading the first or the second or both manuscripts, in any order. It was published as one volume in the second edition of 1849. Hannay, "Introduction," 3.
10. Farhang Erfani, "Sartre and Kierkegaard on the Aesthetics of Boredom," *Idealistic Studies* 34, no. 3 (2004): 304, 307.

11. Kierkegaard, *Either/Or*, 47, 53, 46.
12. Ibid., 66, 78, 67–8.
13. Ibid., 227.
14. Hannay explains existence as "something like 'standing out from,' from the Latin prefix *ex* ('out of') and the verb *sistere* ('to stand, place, set'). Existential writers, including Kierkegaard himself in later work, draw on this sense to distinguish the form of *human* being from that of other kinds of entity. Human being is a kind of 'rising up out of' the world of things, which involves a questioning about those things and also a questioning about what to make of human being in particular cases. Here, however, Kierkegaard is exploiting the original sense to make a distinction *within* human being, according to which woman can only 'rise up out of the world' with the help of the man, implying a sense of 'existence' in which woman-being does not yet amount to 'existence' but is only 'being' (for-another)." Hannay, "Introduction," 626–7 (italics in original).
15. Kierkegaard, *Either/Or*, 43.
16. To George Pattison, "to say 'I am bored' is not to report an inner state but is to say 'This task, this society, this world is not worth my attention.'" George Pattison, "Boredom," in *Kierkegaard and the Quest for Unambiguous Life: Between Romanticism and Modernism* (Oxford: Oxford University Press, 2013), 67.
17. William McDonald, "Kierkegaard's Demonic Boredom," in *Essays on Boredom and Modernity*, ed. Barbara Dalle Pezze and Carlo Salzani (New York: Rodopi, 2009), 63.
18. Kierkegaard, *Either/Or*, 228, 441.
19. Ibid., 229.
20. In Kierkegaard's view, the English are paradigmatic in this respect: "occasionally you meet an English traveller, however, who is an incarnation of this talent, a heavy immovable groundhog whose linguistic resources are exhausted in a single-syllable word, an interjection with which he signifies his greatest admiration and most profound indifference, because in the unity of boredom admiration and indifference have become indistinguishable." Ibid., 230, 231, 238.
21. Ibid., 232, 233 (italics in original). In late nineteenth-century France, *dromomania* was the name given to the pathology of endless traveling.
22. Ibid., 239–40.
23. *The Concept of Anxiety: Kierkegaard's Writings VIII*, trans. Reidar Thomte (Princeton: Princeton University Press, 1987), 132–3; *Either/Or*, 520 (italics in original).
24. Ibid., 528, 439, 559.
25. Ibid., 173.
26. Ibid., 473, 453, 389, 54.

Chapter 4

1. Although in early English versions *ennui* appears as *dullness*, in later ones it is translated as *boredom*. An example of the first is *The Red and the Black*, trans. C. K. Scott Moncrieff (New York: The Modern Library, 1926).
2. Stendhal writes, "When the prince had finished his siege of Kehl, he said to Julien, 'You look like a Trappist, you are carrying to excess that principle of gravity which I enjoined upon you

in London. A melancholy manner cannot be good form. What is wanted is an air of boredom. If you are melancholy, it is because you lack something, because you have failed in something. ... That means showing one's own inferiority; if, on the other hand you are bored, it is only what has made an unsuccessful attempt to please you, which is inferior. So realise, my dear friend, the enormity of your mistake.'" Stendhal, *The Red and the Black*, trans. Horace Samuel (London: Kegan Paul, Trench, Trubner & Co., 1916), 402–3.

3. Ibid., 428.
4. Lee Anna Maynard separates idleness from restlessness, relating the first to the beautiful and the second to the sublime. Based on *A Philosophical Reading into the Sublime and Beautiful* (1757) by Edmund Burke, she connects the boredom of women to "female beauty dependent on stasis and confinement." On the other hand, the male realm is sublime since it entails "movement." Furthermore, Maynard subdivides the boredom of women according to two typologies identified in *A Vindication of the Rights of Woman* (1792) by Mary Wollstonecraft. The first constitute the "fine ladies," always idle and waiting. The second are the "patient drudges," constantly restless and helping others. Lee Anna Maynard, *Beautiful Boredom. Idleness and Feminine Self-Realization in the Victorian Novel* (Jefferson: McFarland & Company, 2009), 7, 29.
5. According to Barbara Edwards, "It is thought that she [Catherine Gore] was able to enter the novel writing market because her husband [Captain Charles Gore] knew of publishers who were willing to publish his travel writings." Barbara Edwards, "Catherine Gore" (Sheffield Hallam University, 1998), http://extra.shu.ac.uk/corvey/corinne/1Gore/BioGore.html.
6. Although silver fork novels lost their popularity after the 1830s, Gore kept writing in the same style until 1858. This coincided with the emergence of a popular culture based on print media. According to Patricia Anderson, the appearance of *The Penny Magazine* in 1832 in London marks this era. Winifred Hughes, "Elegies for the Regency: Catherine Gore's Dandy Novels," *Nineteenth Century Literature* 50, no. 2 (1995): 190; Patricia Anderson, *The Printed Image and the Transformation of Popular Culture, 1790–1860* (Oxford: Clarendon Press, 1991).
7. April Kendra, "Catherine Gore and the Fashionable Novel: A Reevaluation" (University of Georgia, 2003), 5. Contrasting with the seriousness attributed to the novels by Jane Austen, in a letter of probably 1831, Gore confessed to be "a reader of rubbish long before I became a writer of it," and her obituary in the *Times* named her "the best novel writer of her class and the wittiest woman of her age." R. A. Gettmann, *A Victorian Publisher: A Study of the Bentley Papers* (Cambridge University Press, 2010), 71; John Franceschina, "Introduction," in *Gore on Stage*, ed. John Franceschina (New York: Garland Publishing, 1999), 1; *Times* (London: February 4, 1861).
8. Catherine Gore, *Women as They Are, or the Manners of the Day*, vol. 1 (London: Henry Colburn and Richard Bentley, 1830), 64; vol. 2, 112; vol. 3, 223; vol. 2, 43.
9. Hughes, "Elegies for the Regency: Catherine Gore's Dandy Novels," 195, 6, 25.
10. Gore, *Women as They Are*, vol. 1, 14, 122–3.
11. Most likely by a male reviewer. "Mrs's Gore Women as They Are; or, the Manners of the Day," *The Edinburgh Review* 51 (1830): 445, 447. For Mary Astell, in *A Serious Proposal for the Ladies, for the Advancement of their True and Greatest Interest* (1701), time should neither "be buried in Idleness, nor lavish'd out in unprofitable concerns ... for a stated portion of it being daily paid to GOD in Prayers and Praises, the rest shall be imploy'd in innocent, charitable, and useful Business." Quoted in Maynard, *Beautiful Boredom*, 27.
12. "Mrs's Gore Women as They Are; or, the Manners of the Day," 445–6, 447.
13. Ibid. Laurie Langbauer, *Novels of Everyday Life: The Series in English Fiction 1850–1930* (Ithaca: Cornell University Press, 1999), 81.

Notes to pp. 33–40

14. Onomatopoeic of "little field."
15. Gore, *Women as They Are*, vol. 1, 120–1, 51–2 (italics in original).
16. Ibid., 1, 51–2; Lauren Berlant, *The Female Complaint* (Durham: Duke University Press, 2008), viii; Allison Pease, *Modernism, Feminism, and the Culture of Boredom* (Cambridge: Cambridge University Press, 2012), 19.
17. Gore, *Women as They Are*, vol. 3, 159.
18. Ibid.
19. Ibid., vol. 1, 124–5.
20. Gore continued to explore themes of boredom and amusement, publishing *The Diary of a Désennuyée* in 1936.
21. In addition, Dickens uses the expression "bored to death" five times to describe the boredom of Lady Dedlock, onomatopoeic of "dead lock" or "death lock."
22. Charles Dickens, *Bleak House* (New York: The Modern Library, 2002), 215, 385.
23. In "The Streets—Night" (1836), Dickens highlights these qualities: "But the streets of London, to be beheld in the very height of their glory, should be seen on a dark, dull, murky winter's night, when there is just enough damp gently stealing down to make the pavement greasy, without cleansing it of any of its impurities." *Sketches by Boz* (Boston: Houghton, Mifflin and Company, 1894), 50.
24. Dickens was well aware of the nature of serial publication. In his letters as editor of *Household Words* (1850–9) and *All the Year Round* (1859–70), he often gave advice on the technical requirements of writing publications in parts. Lance Schachterle, "Bleak House as a Serial Novel," *Dickens Studies Annual* 1 (1970): 212–13.
25. Alice Van Buren Kelley, "The Bleak Houses of *Bleak House*," *Nineteenth Century Fiction* 25, no. 3 (1970): 253.
26. Dickens, *Bleak House*, 4.
27. Ibid., 383–4, 616.
28. Ibid., 83, 861.
29. Ibid., 152.
30. Ibid., 387, 393–4.
31. Ibid., 705, 745.
32. Ibid., 775, 857.
33. The theme of "bleakness" in architecture has been recently readdressed in architectural theory and history. See, for example, Timothy Brittain-Catlin, *Bleak Houses: Disappointment and Failure in Architecture* (Cambridge: MIT Press, 2014), and Owen Hatherley, *A New Kind of Bleak: Journeys Through Urban Britain* (London: Verso Books, 2012).
34. As Gianni Vattimo affirms in *The End of Modernity* (Baltimore: J. Hopkins University Press, 1985), 7.
35. These two novels can be considered pioneers of modernist literature. For Allison Pease, literary works of the late nineteenth and early twentieth centuries are "full of bored characters, from the obvious ones such as the unnamed narrator of Charlotte Gilman Perkins's short story 'The Yellow Wallpaper' (1892) or T. S. Eliot's typewriter girl in *The Waste Land* (1922) to less obvious ones such as Nella Larsen's Helga Crane in *Quicksand* (1928), Virginia Woolf's Rachel Vinrace in *The Voyage Out* (1915), or Connie Chatterley in D. H. Lawrence's *Lady Chatterley's Lover* (1915)." For Maynard, earlier works of female boredom, particularly *Jane Eyre* (1847) by Charlotte Brontë, *Middlemarch* (1874) by George Eliot, and *The Portrait of*

a Lady (1882) by Henry James, elide "major events ... on which conventional (physical) action relies and turning the attention instead to the plane of mental or psychological action." Pease, *Modernism, Feminism, and the Culture of Boredom*, 1; Maynard, *Beautiful Boredom*, 119.

Chapter 5

* This chapter is a revision of "Boredom and Space: Blunting and Jading as the Causes of Change in Architecture." *The Journal of Architecture*, 20:5, 831–8, October 2015, DOI: 10.1080/13602365.2015.1092461. With the permission of Taylor & Francis Ltd.
1. Otto Fenichel, "On the Psychology of Boredom," in *Organization and Pathology of Thought*, ed. David Rapapport (New York: Columbia University Press, 1951), 349–51.
2. Quoted in ibid., 349.
3. Wölfflin, *Renaissance and Baroque*, trans. Kathrin Simon (Ithaca: Cornell University Press, 1992), 73.
4. Adolf Göller, "What Is the Cause of Perpetual Style Change?," in *Empathy, Form, and Space: Problems in German Aesthetics 1873–1893*, ed. Harry Mallgrave and Eleftherios Ikonomou (Santa Monica: Getty Publication Programs, 1993), 202, 224.
5. Georg Simmel, "The Metropolis and Mental Life" (Blackwell Publishing, 1971), 11–12, http://www.blackwellpublishing.com/content/BPL_Images/Content_store/Sample_chapter/0631225137/Bridge.pdf.
6. Mark Jarzombek, *The Psychologizing of Modernity: Art, Architecture, and History* (Cambridge: Cambridge University Press, 2000), 38.
7. Quoted in ibid., 50, from Robert Vischer, *Kunstgeschichte und Humanismus* (Stuttgart: Goschen, 1880), 3.
8. Quoted in Jarzombek, *The Psychologizing of Modernity*, 59, from Theodor Lipps, "Einfühlung und ästhetischer Genuss," *Die Zukunft*, no. 54 (1906): 100–12.
9. Lipps, quoted in C. K. Ogden, I. A. Richards, and James Wood, *The Foundations of Aesthetics* (New York: Lear Publishers, 1925), 66–7.
10. Robert Vischer introduced the term in his doctoral dissertation *On the Optical Sense of Form: A Contribution to Aesthetics* (1873).
11. Quoted in Harry Francis Mallgrave, *The Architect's Brain: Neuroscience, Creativity, and Architecture* (Chichester: Wiley-Blackwell, 2010), 77, from Robert Vischer, *Uber das optische Formgefuhl* (Leipzig: Herrmann Credner, 1873).
12. "On the Optical Sense of Form: A Contribution to Aesthetics," in *Empathy, Form, and Space: Problems in German Aesthetics 1873–1893*, ed. Harry Francis Mallgrave and Eleftherios Ikonomou (Santa Monica: Getty Publication Programs, 1993), 104–5.
13. Mallgrave, *The Architect's Brain*, 78.
14. Göller was particularly concerned with beauty—"*an inherently pleasurable, meaningless play of lines or of light and shade*"—as the ultimate goal of architecture. Göller, "What Is the Cause of Perpetual Style Change?," 195 (italics in original).
15. Quoted in Jarzombek, *The Psychologizing of Modernity*, 41, from Heinrich Wölfflin, "Theodor Lipps, Raumästhetik und geometrisch-optische Täuschungen," *Kunstchronik: Wochenschrift für Kunst und Kunstgewerbe* 9 (1898): 292–3.
16. Heinrich Wölfflin, "Prolegomena to Psychology of Architecture," in *Empathy, Form, and Space: Problems in German Aesthetics 1873–1893*, ed. Harry Francis Mallgrave and Eleftherios Ikonomou (Santa Monica: Getty Publication Programs, 1993), 151.

17. Wölfflin, *Renaissance and Baroque*, 77–8.
18. Quoted in John Onians, *Neuroarthistory: From Aristotle and Pliny to Baxandall and Zeki* (New Haven: Yale University Press, 2007), 116, from Heinrich Wölfflin, "Prolegomena zu einer Psychologie der Architektur," in *Kleine Schriften 1886-1933* (1946), 31.
19. Wölfflin, *Renaissance and Baroque*, 73.
20. Onians, *Neuroarthistory*, 119.
21. Mallgrave, *The Architect's Brain*, 89.
22. Wölfflin, *Renaissance and Baroque*, 85–7.
23. Originally delivered at the Stuttgart Technische Hochschule. Onians, *Neuroarthistory*, 108.
24. Adolf Göller, *Die Entstehung der architektonischen Stilformen: Eine Geschichte der Baukunst nach dem Werden and Wandern der Formgedanken* (Stuttgart: Konrad Wittwer, 1888).
25. Mallgrave, *The Architect's Brain*, 82.
26. Göller, "What Is the Cause of Perpetual Style Change?," 202. The metaphor of memory as a process of imprinting has been constant in art history. In *A Treatise of the Images of Christ, and of His Saints* (1567), Nicolas Sanders describes how knowledge "engraves" images in the mind from information provided through sensorial experience. Stuart Clark, *Vanities of the Eye: Vision in Early Modern European Culture* (Oxford: Oxford University Press, 2007), 168–9.
27. Onians, *Neuroarthistory*, 115.
28. Göller, "What Is the Cause of Perpetual Style Change?," 204, 194–5.
29. Ibid., 217, 206.
30. Sigfried Giedion, *Constancy, Change and Architecture* (Cambridge: Harvard University Press, 1961), 3.
31. Malcolm Quantrill and Bruce Webb, *Constancy and Change in Architecture* (College Station: Texas A&M University Press, 1991), xiv.

Chapter 6

* This chapter is a revision of "On Boredom: The Blurred Spaces of Maxim Gorky's Coney Island." First published in *Sensing Architecture: Essays on the Nature of Architectural Experience*, edited by Owen Hopkins, Royal Academy Digital, 2017. With the permission of the Royal Academy of Arts.

1. Rem Koolhaas, *Delirious New York: A Retroactive Manifesto for Manhattan* (New York: Monacelli Press, 1994), 32, 29.
2. Gorky, "Boredom," 310, 317.
3. Ibid., 309.
4. Tovah Yedlin, *Maxim Gorky: A Political Biography* (Westport: Praeger, 1999), 67; Alexander Kaun, *Maxim Gorky and His Russia* (New York: B. Blom, 1968), 569.
5. "Riot of Enthusiasm Greets Maxim Gorky," *The New York Times* (1906), http://query.nytimes.com/mem/archivefree/pdf?res=F40C1EFD3A5A12738DDDA80994DC405B868CF1D3; Kaun, *Maxim Gorky and His Russia*, 569.
6. Yedlin, *Maxim Gorky*, 70.

7. "Gorky and Actress Asked to Quit Hotels," *The New York Times* (1906), http://query.nytimes.com/mem/archivefree/pdf?res=F60616FF3C5A12738DDDAC0994DC405B868CF1D3.
8. Yedlin, *Maxim Gorky*, 72–3; "Aldine Club Luncheon without Maxim Gorky," *The New York Times* (1906), http://query.nytimes.com/mem/archivefree/pdf?res=F10914FB3A5A12738DDDA00994DC405B868CF1D3.
9. Yedlin, *Maxim Gorky*, 73.
10. "Maxim Gorky's Disillusion," *The New York Times* (1906), http://query.nytimes.com/mem/archivefree/pdf?res=FB0610FA3A5A12738DDDAE0994DC405B868CF1D3.
11. Norman Otis, "Maxim Gorky a Disappointed Man," *The New York Times* (1906). Years later, in an article for the Russian newspaper *XX vek*, Gorky regarded the episode as an expression of the ideology of the upper sector of bourgeois society, not proper of the United States but typical of middle-class morality. Yedlin, *Maxim Gorky*, 75, from Gor'kii, *Sobraine sochinenii*, vol. 23, 392–3.
12. Gorky, "Boredom," 311.
13. As Schopenhauer writes, "In middle-class life boredom is represented by the Sunday, just as want is represented by the six weekdays." Schopenhauer, *The World as Will and Representation*, vol. 1, 313.
14. Gorky, "Boredom," 314, 317.
15. John Kasson, *Amusing the Million: Coney Island at the Turn of the Century* (New York: Hill & Wang, 1978), 108; A. P. Mohun, "Designed for Thrills and Safety: Amusement Parks and the Commodification of Risk, 1880–1929," *Journal of Design History* 14 (2001): 304. In addition to amusement parks such as those on Coney Island, other architectural typologies emerged through modernity with the intention of discharging social and emotional tension, including cinemas, museums, and other cultural and educational facilities. Josef Pieper, *Leisure as the Basis of Culture*, trans. Alexander Dru (New York: Random House, 1963), 69; George Ritzer, "The Disenchanted Kingdom," *The Sun* 2002, 13. Sharon Zukin observes that "although Coney Island never had racial covenants or Jim Crow laws and black families used the beach at least as early as 1880, day-trippers tended to cluster separately, by race and ethnicity, along the shore." Sharon Zukin et al., "From Coney Island to Las Vegas in the Urban Imaginary: Discursive Practices of Growth and Decline," *Urban Affairs Review* 33, no. 5 (1998): 641–2.
16. Theodor Adorno differentiated "leisure" from "free time" and from "spare time," affirming that the first "denoted the privilege of an unconstrained, comfortable life style, hence something qualitatively different and far more auspicious—and it indicates a specific difference, that of time which is neither free nor spare, which is occupied by work, and which one could designate as heteronomous. Free time is shackled to its opposite." Theodor Adorno, *The Culture Industry. Selected Essays on Mass Culture* (London: Routledge, 1991), 162, 64. Margaret Mead observes the same in "The Pattern of Leisure in Contemporary American Culture," in *Mass Leisure*, ed. Eric Larrabee and Rolf Meyersohn (Glencoe: Free Press, 1958), 12.
17. Gorky, "Boredom," 311.
18. The blasé attitude is predominantly a rational response, belonging to the brain—a protective organ—which creates intellectual mechanisms to comprehend and articulate "those rapidly shifting stimulations of the nerves which are thrown together in all their contrasts." For Simmel, the anonymous city exerted a dramatic new power on its inhabitants, accentuating the regular pace of everyday life. Simmel, "The Metropolis and Mental Life," 14; Kevin Aho, "Simmel on Acceleration, Boredom, and Extreme Aesthesia," *Journal for the Theory of Social Behaviour* 37, no. 4 (2007): 451.

19. Gorky, "Boredom," 310.
20. Ibid., 309, 311.
21. Ibid.
22. Ibid., 317. Similar to the attackers of Arina, a character in "Out of Boredom," a short story by Gorky written in 1897, also translated as "For Want Something to Do," in *Maxim Gorky. Collected Works in Ten Volumes* (Moscow: Progress Publishers, 1978).
23. Gorky, "Boredom," 311–12, 316. The essence of these architectural containers echoes the etymological origins of the term "boredom" in Russian. Скука, recorded in dictionaries since 1704, derives from the onomatopoeic ку, in reference to the cuckoo, the solitary bird without a nest of its own. Wade, *Russian Etymological Dictionary*, 200. In Coney Island, the impossibility of synchronizing inwardness with the outward world produces homesickness. In modernity, the struggle to find a place to dwell in the city, capable of responding to the inner structure and desires of the individual, is chronic and unresolved. Being out of home flattens every space and every experience, and leisure becomes meaningless.
24. Gorky, "Boredom," 316.
25. "Gorky on Coney," *The New York Times* (1907), http://query.nytimes.com/mem/archivefree/pdf?res=F10914FB3A5A12738DDDA00994DC405B868CF1D3.
26. In 1967, Paul Hoffman, a reporter from *The New York Times*, described Coney Island as a "city in miniature," not because of its architectural and urban features but because of its problems: "youth riots, slums, public housing complexes and the racial minorities that were assigned to live there, and anti-poverty programs." Quoted in Zukin et al., "From Coney Island to Las Vegas in the Urban Imaginary: Discursive Practices of Growth and Decline," 632, from Paul Hoffman, "Coney Island's Slums and Tidy Homes Reflect Big City Problems," *The New York Times* (1967), 29.
27. "Gorky on Coney."
28. Quoted in Yedlin, *Maxim Gorky*, 67, from *Letters of Gorky and Andreev: 1891–1912*, 85.
29. Koolhaas, *Delirious New York*, 30, 68, 70.

Chapter 7

1. This passage is from the 1927 translation of *Towards a New Architecture* (1923). A more accurate translation of the sentence "L'homme et la femme modernes s'ennuient chez aux; ils vont au dancing" would be "The modern man and woman are bored at home; they go dancing," changing the emphasis from a space to an activity. Le Corbusier, *Towards a New Architecture*, trans. Frederick Etchells (London: The Architectural Press, 1982), 11–14; *Vers Une Architecture* (Paris: Flammarion, 2005), 94.
2. Clement Greenberg, "Avant-Garde and Kitsch," in *Modern Culture and the Arts*, ed. James Hall and Barry Ulanov (New York: McGraw-Hill, 1967), 153.
3. To Marshall Berman, "there is a mode of vital experience—experience of space and time, of the self and others, of life's possibilities and perils—that is shared by men and women all over the world today. I will call this body of experience 'modernity'.... In the twentieth century, the social processes that bring this maelstrom into being, and keep it in a state of perpetual becoming, have come to be called 'modernization'.... Over the past century, these visions and values have come to be loosely grouped together under the name of 'modernism.'" Marshall Berman, *All That Is Solid Melts into Air: The Experience of Modernity* (London: Verso, 1983), 15–16.

4. For Albert Hirschman, "All the heroic virtues were shown to be forms of mere self-preservation by Hobbes, of self-love by Rochefoucauld, or vanity and of frantic escape from real self-knowledge by Pascal. The heroic passions were portrayed as demeaning by Racine after having been denounced as foolish, if not demented, by Cervantes." In addition, "by the early eighteenth century we find Shaftesbury defining interest as the 'desire of those Conveniences, by which we are well provided for, and maintained'... David Hume similarly uses the terms 'passion of interest' or the 'interested affection' as synonyms for the 'avidity of acquiring goods and possessions' or the 'love of gain.'" Albert Hirschman, *The Passions and the Emotions* (Princeton: Princeton University Press, 1977), 11, 15, 32, 37; quotes from Anthony Ashley-Cooper, Earl of Shaftesbury, *Characteristic of Men, Manners, Opinions, Times* (Indianapolis: Bobbs-Merrill, 1964. 1711), 332; and David Hume, *A Treatise of Human Nature* (1739), book III, part II, section II.

5. Quoted in Hirschman, *The Passions and the Emotions*, 134, from John Maynard Keynes, *The General Theory of Employment. Interest and Money* (London: Macmillan, 1936), 374.

6. Hirschman cites Montesquieu and Hume. From the latter, "avarice, or the desire of gain, is a universal passion which operates at all times, in all places, and upon all persons." And from the former, "it is almost a general rule that wherever the ways of man are gentle (*moeurs douces*) there is commerce; and wherever there is commerce, there the ways of men are gentle. ... Commerce ... polishes and softens (*adoucit*) barbarian ways as we can see every day." Quoted in Hirschman, *The Passions and the Emotions*, 54, 60, from Hume, *Essays Moral, Political, and Literary*, ed. T. H. Green and T. H. Grose (London: Longmans, 1898), 176; and Montesquieu, *Esprit des lois*, XX, I.

7. Hirschman, *The Passions and the Emotions*, 65, 132 (italics in original), 135.

8. Jean-Paul Sartre, *Nausea*, trans. Lloyd Alexander (London: Hamish Hamilton, 1962), 105.

9. Ernest Mandel, *Late Capitalism* (London: Verso, 1978), 46, 47.

10. Braudel, *A History of Civilizations*, 8.

11. Mandel, *Late Capitalism*, 57; Kondratieff, *The Long Wave Cycle*, 93 (italics in original).

12. Mandel, *Late Capitalism*, 131.

13. Braudel, *A History of Civilizations*, 395.

14. Neurasthenia was originally identified in 1880 by George Beard, an American neurologist. Symptoms included "twitchiness, punctuality and busyness and which led to any number of emotional and physical ailments including 'dyspepsia, headaches, paralysis, insomnia, and anesthesia.'" However, the term *neurasthenia* did not prove useful in Europe. Aho, "Simmel on Acceleration, Boredom, and Extreme Aesthesia," 450-1. In the same line, Bertrand Russell identified modern boredom as proper to urban populations, impeding happiness and making life "hot and dusty and thirsty, like a pilgrimage in the desert." Bertrand Russell, "Boredom and Excitement," in *The Conquest of Happiness* (New York: Bantam Books, 1968), 43.

15. Anne Stiles, "Go Rest, Young Man," *Monitor on Psychology* 43, no. 1 (2012): 32. Pease remarks, "In the 1910 *Autobiography of a Neurasthene*, written by a female doctor, the narrator notes that the passivity of women's lives makes them particularly susceptible to neurasthenia: 'This anxious watching and waiting did me no good. But after all what is a woman's life, whether wife, mother, or that of a doctor, but watching and waiting ... I have watched and waited every blessed minute of my life and I suppose I shall end it all by watching and waiting for death. It is a woman's life.'" Quoted in Pease, *Modernism, Feminism, and the Culture of Boredom*, 25, from Margaret Cleaves, *Autobiography of a Neurasthene: As Told by One of Them and Recorded by Dr. Margaret A. Cleaves* (Boston: R.G. Badger, 1910), 40-1.

16. Braudel, *A History of Civilizations*, 384-5.

17. One of the earliest records with this description of war appears in *Current History and Forum*, vol. 1 (New York: *The New York Times*, 1915), 979.
18. Paul Emmons and Andreea Mihalache, "Architectural Handbooks and the User Experience," in *Use Matters: An Alternative History of Architecture*, ed. Kenny Cupers (New York: Routledge, 2013), 48.
19. Quoted in Caterina Cardamone, "Classical Tradition in Josef Frank's Writings" (unpublished: Université Catholique de Louvain-la-Neuve, 2015), from Josef Frank, *Aesthetische Weltanschauung* (Hermann Czech archive: post 1945?), f. 26.
20. Walter Sobotka, *Principles of Design. A Retrospect* (1970), 384–5.
21. Ibid. Correspondence of Josef Frank with Walter Sobotka, October 1958.
22. Ibid., 410–11, 85.
23. *Boredom at Work: The Empty Life* (Oklahoma State Department of Health, 1961).
24. *Boredom at Work: The Search for Zest*. In 1973, the Volvo Kalmar Assembly system was developed to allow the workers to be involved in the production of a complete automobile. Other strategies include designer uniforms, ambiance music, personalized cubicles, group activities, and outings. For Heilbroner, this is better exemplified in the practices of Japanese companies that "begin the day with mass calisthenics and singing, and provide lessons in flower arranging for their female employees," also guaranteeing lifetime employment to create commitment and belonging. Heilbroner, *Beyond Boom and Crash*, 33.
25. Ralph Greenson was a pioneer of Freudian psychoanalysis in California, having Tony Curtis, Frank Sinatra, Vivien Leigh, and Marilyn Monroe among his patients. Ralph Greenson, "On Boredom," *Journal of the American Psychoanalytic Association* 1, no. 1 (1953).
26. Heron, "The Pathology of Boredom," 53.
27. Ibid., 54.
28. Ernest Schachtel, *Metamorphosis: On the Development of Affect, Perception, Attention, and Memory* (New York: Basic Books, 1959), 232–4, 354–5.
29. Quoted in Heron, "The Pathology of Boredom," 56, from Christopher Burney, *Solitary Confinement* (1951).
30. Gordon Pask, "A Comment, a Case History and a Plan," in *Cybernetics, Art, and Ideas*, ed. Jasia Reichardt (Greenwich: New York Graphic Society, 1971), 77, 80.
31. Quoted in Molly Wright Steenson, "Architectures of Information: Christopher Alexander, Cedric Price, and Nicholas Negroponte & MIT's Architecture Machine Group" (Princeton University, 2014), 148; from John Frazer, Letter to Cedric Price (January 11, 1979), Generator document folio DR 1995:0280:65. Cedric Price Archives, Canadian Centre for Architecture, Montreal.
32. Susan Sontag, *As Consciousness Is Harnessed to Flesh: Journals and Notebooks, 1964–1980* (New York: Farrar, Straus and Giroux, 2012), 144. In 1967, referring to Michelangelo Antonioni, Samuel Beckett, and William S. Burroughs, Sontag affirmed that "the charge of boredom is really hypocritical. There is, in a sense, no such thing as boredom. Boredom is only another name for a certain species of frustration." *Against Interpretation* (New York: Dell Publishing, 1967), 303.
33. *As Consciousness Is Harnessed to Flesh*, 145.
34. Ina Blom writes that Fluxus wondered "How can you claim attention for something that defies any attempt to focus for any long period of time that breaks all the rules of communication?" Ina Blom, "Boredom and Oblivion," in *The Fluxus Reader*, ed. Ken Friedman (London: Academy Editions, 1998).

35. While the pop art of Warhol attempted to create the boring since "the more you look at the same exact thing, the more meaning goes away, and the better and emptier you feel," the Fluxus elaborations of Dick Higgins elevated boredom as an instrument of "environmentalism" and the creation of "intensified spaces" to allow the reconnection with "events as events." Quoted in Svendsen, *A Philosophy of Boredom*, 104, from Andy Warhol, *The Philosophy of Andy Warhol*, 27; Dick Higgins, "Boredom and Danger," *The Something Else Newsletter* 1, no. 9 (1968): 1–6.

36. Susan Sontag, "Notes on 'Camp'" (Georgetown University, 1964), 2, http://faculty.georgetown.edu/irvinem/theory/Sontag-NotesOnCamp-1964.html. According to Thomas Oden, the incapacity "to have a keen sensitivity to one's environment" becomes manifest in boredom. The experience of this condition is characterized by the perception of the present as devoid of "potential or actual value actualisation." In a diagram of "the structure of boredom," Oden locates the bored individual in between the memory of the guilt of the past and the anxiety of the imagination of the future, susceptible to "emptiness" if the immediate environment is insufficient or to "meaninglessness" if religious idols are irrelevant. Thomas Oden, *The Structure of Awareness* (Nashville: Abingdon Press, 1969), 13, 190, 195.

37. Sontag, "Notes on 'Camp,'" 9. Also writing during the economic boom of the early 1960s, Herbert Marcuse affirmed that the risk of the material wealth of the industrial society is the emergence of the "one-dimensional man," an individual caught in between "the rational and the irrational," not knowing how to "promote the art of life." Herbert Marcuse, *One-Dimensional Man* (Boston: Beacon Press, 1964), 247, 256, 257. In 1963, the same year that Betty Friedan published *The Feminine Mystique* to denounce boredom as an epidemic of American women, "a trio of housewives in Van Nuys, Calif., developed a remedy: a center for adult education called Everywoman's Village, which, LIFE explained, 'offers familiar cures for advanced cases of housewife boredom.'" Eliza Berman, "How a California School Cured 'Advanced Causes of Housewife Boredom,'" *Time* (2015), http://time.com/4000588/school-for-bored-housewives.

38. Robert Venturi, *Complexity and Contradiction in Architecture* (London: The Architectural Press, 1966), 16, 17.

39. Robert Venturi, Denise Scott Brown, and Steven Izenour, *Learning from Las Vegas: The Forgotten Symbolism of Architectural Form* (Cambridge: MIT Press, 1972), 101, 103, 102 (italics in original). In *Architecture as Signs and Systems* (2004), Venturi and Scott Brown include boredom as one of the aspirations of "mannerist architecture that acknowledges and accommodates the complexity and contradiction of today," and mannerism is defined as "a boredom with rules from knowing them so well." Robert Venturi and Denise Scott Brown, *Architecture as Signs and Systems: For a Mannerist Time* (Cambridge: Belknap, 2004), 75–7, 212.

40. Heilbroner, *Beyond Boom and Crash*, 78.

41. Guy Debord, "On the Passage of a Few Persons through a Rather Brief Unity of Time," *Bureau of Public Secrets* (1959), http://www.bopsecrets.org/SI/debord.films/passage.htm.

42. Quoted in Pease, *Modernism, Feminism, and the Culture of Boredom*, 73, from Guy Debord, "Perspectives for Conscious Alterations of Everyday Life," in *Situationist International Anthology*, ed. Ken Knabb (Berkeley: Bureau of Public Secrets, 1981), 71.

43. Ivan Chtcheglov, "Formulary for a New Urbanism," *Bureau of Public Secrets* (1953), http://www.bopsecrets.org/SI/Chtcheglov.htm.

44. Andy Medhurst, "What Did I Get?," in *Punk Rock: So What?*, ed. Roger Sabin (London: Routledge, 1999), 228.

45. Jon Savage argues that the entire Punk style "spoke of boredom" and became "a theatrical expression of boredom's prison … Boredom described the expansive, occluded, utopian politics that built up at the Sex Pistols' core … everyone involved with the Sex Pistols instinctively realized boredom's spatial aspect and used its rhetoric as a key." Jon Savage, "The Great Rock 'N' Roll Swindle," in *Impresario: Malcolm Mclaren and the British New Wave*, ed. Paul Taylor (Cambridge: MIT University Press, 1988), 48. Boredom in Punk was also popularized by The Clash; in "London's Burning" (1979), they sing: "London's burning with boredom now." The Clash, *London's Burning, The Clash* (London: CBS, 1977).
46. Designed by the Situationist-inspired art director Jamie Reid.
47. Heilbroner, *Beyond Boom and Crash*, 14; Braudel, *A History of Civilizations*, 491, 489, 492.
48. Heilbroner, *Beyond Boom and Crash*, 69, 81.
49. For Freya Matthews, "the miasma of boredom that has descended on environmentalism in recent years—the sense that, though important, environmentalism is a kind of societal chore, a bleak responsibility settling ever more heavily on the shoulders of younger and future generations." Freya Matthews, *Reinhabiting Reality: Towards a Recovery of Culture* (Albany: State University of New York Press, 2005), 68. According to George Monbiot, "our survival in the modern economy requires the use of few of the mental and physical capacities we possess. Sometimes it feels like a small and shuffling life. Our humdrum, humiliating lives leave us, I believe, ecologically bored." George Monbiot, "Our Ecological Boredom," *The New York Times* (2015), http://www.nytimes.com/2015/01/19/opinion/our-ecological-boredom.html?_r=0.

Chapter 8

1. In Heidegger's work, boredom appears for the first time in an address titled "The Concept of Time," delivered at the Marburg Theological Society in July 1924. In this lecture, the philosopher affirms that time can never become boring since its essence is to move forward; therefore, it "never becomes long because it originally has no length." This position is reversed in *The Fundamental Concepts of Metaphysics*. Heidegger's examination of boredom was imparted under the effects of the publication of *Being and Time* (1927), his magnum opus, and after he had finished a successful period of teaching at the University of Marburg. In 1928, the forty-year-old philosopher returned to Freiburg, his alma mater, to take up the chair vacated by his former teacher, Edmund Husserl. The lectures of 1929–30 coincided with a moment of intellectual progression, institutional change, and physical readjustment to a new place of living. The house in Freiburg, in which he lived until 1971, was built during the summer of 1928 in order to be ready for occupation in the winter. This relocation must have been characterized by waiting, making new acquaintances, and traveling—ideal situations, all developed in the lectures as typologies of boredom, to concatenate the experience of time to the qualities of the environment, without the particularities of any determined place. The transcription of the lectures was supervised by Heidegger. It was published in German in 1983 and it was translated into English in 1995. Goodstein, *Experience without Qualities*, 280; Adam Sharr, *Heidegger's Hut* (Cambridge: MIT Press, 2006), 87.
2. Heidegger, *The Fundamental Concepts of Metaphysics*, 1.
3. In March 1966, in a speech delivered on the celebration of the sixtieth birthday of Eugen Fink, a friend and former student, Heidegger posed the essence of philosophy as the possibility "to attain the matter of thinking." This concern, however, is endangered by the dissipation of philosophy into independent sciences, and by the manipulation of philosophy by different sciences. Following Nietzsche, to avoid the objectification proper to science and the

disappearance of philosophy under a "technical world-civilization," he prescribes poetry as a remedy since Western thinking derives from Greek poets. Opposed to boredom, his call is for a way of reasoning capable of opening "the time-play-space for poetising, so that through the poetising word there may again be a wording world." Ibid., 367–9.
4. Ibid., 82, 180 (italics in original).
5. For Heidegger, modern philosophy began with the principles laid out by Descartes in *Meditations on First Philosophy* (1641). Ibid., 2, 43.
6. Quoted in ibid. 5, from Novalis, *Schriften*, vol. 2 (Jena: J. Minor, 1923), 179, Frg. 21.
7. Heidegger, *The Fundamental Concepts of Metaphysics*, 5.
8. Ibid., 55 (italics in original).
9. In translations of Heidegger's work, the German *Stimmung* is rendered as *mood* as well as *attunement*. For example, Michael Zimmerman and Paul Thiele translate it as *mood*, while William McNeill and Nicholas Walker translate it as *attunement*. The former term refers to "mode" which denotes manner, kind, and limit, and the latter means "being in tune with," a state of synchronization. In both cases, *Stimmung* constitutes the tone that surpasses "merely psychological 'colorations' projected onto things." Michael E. Zimmerman, *Heidegger's Confrontation with Modernity: Technology, Politics, and Art* (Bloomington: Indiana University Press, 1990), 141.
10. For Heidegger, the study of attunements cannot be achieved through objective enquiry, observation, or psychological methods. If they are turned into objects of scientific analysis, their essential qualities are "precisely destroyed, or at least not intensified, but weakened and altered." Heidegger, *The Fundamental Concepts of Metaphysics*, 60–1.
11. Jonathan McKenzie, "Governing Moods: Anxiety, Boredom, and the Ontological Overcoming of Politics in Heidegger," *Canadian Journal of Political Science Association* 41, no. 3 (2008): 574; Parvis Emad, "Boredom as Limit and Disposition," *Heidegger Studies* 1, no. 1 (1985): 67.
12. Heidegger, *The Fundamental Concepts of Metaphysics*, 67 (italics in original). This coincides with the contemporary classification by neuroscience of boredom as a mood. Antonio Damasio, *Looking for Spinoza: Joy, Sorrow, and the Feeling Brain* (Orlando: Harcourt, 2003), 43.
13. Heidegger, *The Fundamental Concepts of Metaphysics*, 60. Writing about Nietzsche, Heidegger affirms that "the will can appeal to ways and means for suppressing the bad mood, but it cannot directly awaken or create a countermood: for moods are overcome and transformed always only by moods.... Mood is never merely a way of being determined in our inner being for ourselves.... Mood is precisely the basic way in which we are outside ourselves." Quoted in Thiele, "Postmodernity and the Routinization of Novelty: Heidegger on Boredom and Technology," 498, from Martin Heidegger, *Nietzsche*, vol. 1: "The Will to Power as Art," trans. D. Krell (New York: Harper and Row, 1979), 99.
14. *The Fundamental Concepts of Metaphysics*, 60.
15. Ibid., 63, 67, 78–9, 81 (italics in original).
16. According to Jean-Luc Marion, "boredom distinguishes itself just as much from nihilism and negation as from anxiety: it does not value, nor depreciate; it does not fight, nor predicate; it does not lack beings, nor suffer the assault of the nothing. ... One should much rather understand it as a radical uninterest: the one who yields to boredom and henceforth proceeds from it hates *(est mihi in odio)* because nothing makes any difference for him *(nihil interest mihi)*; indifference to things provokes their undifferentiation; nothing distinguishes them, since between them and the one who is bored there is nothing; there is nothing among them

because there is nothing between them and whoever is bored. The suspension of the world does not manifest any Being-in-the-world but the dissolution of worldhood itself." Jean-Luc Marion, *Reduction and Givenness: Investigations of Husserl, Heidegger, and Phenomenology*, trans. Thomas Carlson (Evanston: Northwestern University Press, 1998), 191.

17. Heidegger, *The Fundamental Concepts of Metaphysics*, 69, 71, 76. Heidegger advocates the philosophical interpretation of the contemporary conditions of the individual, based on the implications of the fusion of Greek philosophy with Christian thought in *The Will to Power* (1901) by Friedrich Nietzsche. "Soul and spirit" are conceptualized as "specific fundamental orientations" that relate to the "Dionysian" and the "Apollonian." While the first is qualified as "sensuousness and cruelty," "the enjoyment of productive and destructive energy," and "constant creation," the second is posed as an "illusion," "the *eternity* of beautiful form," and "the aristocratic legislation '*thus it shall be always!*'" Both resonate with boredom: the Dionysian as a condition of eternal return, and the Apollonian as the inhabitation of a temporal threshold, in between past and future. Ibid., 73; Friedrich Nietzsche, *Der Wille zur Macht. Gesammelte Werke*, vol. 19 (Munich: Musarionausgabe, 1920), 336ff; *The Will to Power*, trans. W. Kaufmann and R. J. Hollingdale (New York: Random House, 1968), 520ff, 359f, 1049 (italics in original).

18. Heidegger, *The Fundamental Concepts of Metaphysics*, 77 (italics in original).

19. Goodstein, *Experience without Qualities*, 291.

20. Situatedness integrates cultural, social, and political circumstances and therefore is historically specific. It is descriptive rather than prescriptive, in constant actualization. Jeff Malpas, *Heidegger's Topology: Being, Place, World* (Cambridge: MIT Press, 2006), 43.

21. Heidegger, *The Fundamental Concepts of Metaphysics*, 82, 83, 86 (italics in original).

22. Ibid., 87–8. For Heidegger, the identification of three typologies of boredom is neither objective nor definite. The graduation of intensities does not intend to be a progressive scale of boredoms in which the first is the cause of the second, and the second is an indispensable step to the third. Conversely, the two first typologies of boredom are echoes of the third, which is the closest to the temporal essence of Dasein. Ibid., 156–67.

23. Ibid., 92.

24. Ibid., 99 (italics in original).

25. Ibid., 109.

26. Ibid., 111, 113, 114 (italics in original). For Graham Harman, the second type of boredom is "especially relevant to the modern world, in which everyone tries to become involved with everything, leaving no one with enough time for anything. Everyone is too busy for anything essential." Graham Harman, *Heidegger Explained: From Phenomenon to Thing* (Chicago: Open Court Publishing, 2007), 87.

27. Heidegger, *The Fundamental Concepts of Metaphysics*, 124, 125, 128 (italics in original).

28. Ibid., 134.

29. Kevin Aho, *Heidegger's Neglect of the Body* (Albany: State University of New York Press, 2009), 115.

30. Heidegger, *The Fundamental Concepts of Metaphysics*, 134–5, 136 (italics in original). According to Peter Watson, Heidegger "hated all cities" and "elevated his hatred of city life to an entire philosophy." Peter Watson, *A Terrible Beauty: A History of the People and Ideas That Shaped the Modern Mind* (London: Weidenfeld & Nicolson, 2000), 233.

31. Heidegger, *The Fundamental Concepts of Metaphysics*, 134, 137, 143, 146 (italics in original). Heidegger corroborates these ideas by referring to the German term for boredom. *Langeweile*

is posed as "the while [Weile]" that "becomes long [lang]," "not the time of the clock or chronology, but the lengthening or shortening of time proper." *The Fundamental Concepts of Metaphysics*, 152. For Martha Gabriel, "the word Langeweile means 'a long while' conveying that in boredom, time loses its measure." Martha Gabriel, "Boredom: Exploration of a Developmental Perspective," *Clinical Social Work Journal* 16, no. 2 (1988): 157.

32. Heidegger, *The Fundamental Concepts of Metaphysics*, 149 (italics in original). Heidegger emphasizes that the "moment of vision" is different from the enlightenment posed by Kierkegaard since both entail dissimilar understandings of time: "He [Kierkegaard] clings to the ordinary concept of time, and defines the 'moment of vision' with the help of 'now' and 'eternity'. ... Time as within-time-ness knows only the 'now', it never knows a moment of vision." Quoted in Vincent McCarthy, "Martin Heidegger: Kierkegaard's Influence Hidden and in Full View," in *Kierkegaard and Existentialism*, ed. Jon Stewart (London: Ashgate, 2011), 104, from Martin Heidegger, *Sein und Zeit* (Halle: Niemeyer, 1927), 338.

33. Heidegger, *The Fundamental Concepts of Metaphysics*, 162–3, 161–2, 163–4 (italics in original). For Heidegger, since the condition is not attached to any particular object, space, or event, there is no way to know if "man has in the end become boring to himself" or "whether contemporary people become bored by particular things or become more bored than in other epochs." Ibid., 161–2.

34. This terror has been interpreted by Miguel de Beistegui as Heidegger's intent to ground Nazism: "Can Heidegger really have genuinely seen in Nazism the possibility of freeing the essence of Dasein and of constituting it in an authentic community? I believe so." Miguel de Beistegui, *Thinking with Heidegger: Displacements* (Bloomington: Indiana University Press, 2003), 62–3, 77–8.

35. Richard Polt, "Heidegger in the 1930s: Who Are We?," in *The Bloomsbury Companion to Heidegger*, ed. Francois Raffoul and Eric S. Nelson (London: Bloomsbury Academic, 2013), 40.

36. Heidegger delves into this difference in the essay "On the Essence of Ground" (1928). Heidegger, *The Fundamental Concepts of Metaphysics*, 175–6.

37. Ibid., 176–7 (italics in original). On the topic of "man and animal," Giorgio Agamben provides a summary of Heidegger's elaboration on boredom. Giorgio Agamben, *The Open: Man and Animal*, trans. Kevin Attell (Palo Alto: Stanford University Press, 2004).

Chapter 9

* This chapter is a revision of "Oran, the Capital of Boredom." Copyright © 2018. From *Reading Architecture: Literary Imagination and Architectural Experience*, edited by Angeliki Sioli and Yoonchun Jung. New York: Routledge. With the permission of Taylor and Francis Group, LLC, a division of Informa plc.

1. According to Ernest Mandel, the failure of modernism in countries like Algeria is due to the fact that "the mass population existed outside the realm of capitalist commodity production. The slow displacement of pre-capitalist relations of production led to the increasing immiseration of the indigenous population, which became willing to sell its labour-power at ever lower prices in order to be able to bear at least part of the ever more oppressive burden of ground-rent, usury and taxes." This is different from countries such as Australia or New Zealand where "the whole population was incorporated from the outset into the capitalist production of commodities." Mandel, *Late Capitalism*, 364.

2. Albert Camus, *The Plague*, trans. Stuart Gilbert (London: Penguin, 2001), 5.

3. *The Outsider*, trans. Joseph Laredo (London: Penguin, 1983), 26.

4. According to Patrick McCarthy, Camus and his friends "walked in the square near the cathedral and through the old Spanish town [Oran] ... they disliked the rich businessmen and were friendly with the small shopkeepers and the artisans." Patrick McCarthy, *Camus. A Critical Study of His Life and Work* (London: Hamish Hamilton, 1982), 36–7.
5. Albert Camus, "The Minotaur, or the Stop in Oran," 130.
6. As posed by Camus in *The Myth of Sisyphus* (1942).
7. McCarthy, *Camus*, 274; John Lambeth, "The Figure of the Labyrinth in 'Le renégat' and 'La Pierre qui pousse,'" in *A Writer's Topography: Space and Place in the Life and Works of Albert Camus*, ed. Jason Herbeck and Vincent Grégoire (Leiden: Brill, 2015), 217.
8. Camus, "The Minotaur," 133.
9. Leo Stan, "Albert Camus: Walled within God," in *Kierkegaard and Existentialism*, ed. Jon Stewart (Surrey: Ashgate, 2011), 68.
10. Camus, "The Minotaur," 121, 120.
11. Georges Bataille, *Visions of Excess*, ed. Allan Stoekl, trans. Allan Stoekl, Carl Lovitt, and Donald Leslie (Minneapolis: University of Minnesota Press, 1985), 175.
12. Camus imagines Descartes: "I go out walking every day amid the confusion of a great crowd, with as much freedom and tranquillity as you could do on your garden paths. ... Descartes, planning to meditate, chose his desert: the most mercantile city of his era." Camus, "The Minotaur," 115–16, 119, 120.
13. Ibid., 121, 119.
14. Ibid., 120. In "Notes of a New Town" (1962), Lefebvre uses a similar analogy to describe "N," the city of pure boredom: "This community has shaped its shell, building and rebuilding it, modifying it again and again according to its needs. Look closely and within every house you will see the slow, mucous trace of this animal which transforms the chalk in the soil around it into something delicate and structured: a family." Lefebvre, *Introduction to Modernity*, 116.
15. Camus, "The Minotaur," 120, 129–30, 120.
16. Ibid., 130, 120, 121.
17. Ibid., 116, 117, 121.
18. In the available digital records, only the last name Wolf appears as the architect of the building. "Maison du Colon" (Musée de l'Histoire vivante, 2015), http://www.museehistoirevivante.com/expovirtuelle/Algerie/ImgAlg/Chapitre3/Oran/popMaisonDuColon20.htm.
19. Executed by Fernand Belmonte.
20. Philip Dine, "Shaping the Colonial Body," in *Algeria & France, 1800–2000: Identity, Memory, Nostalgia*, ed. Patricia Lorcin (Syracuse: Syracuse University Press, 2006), 41; Camus, "The Minotaur," 126.
21. Ibid., 127.
22. In reference to the animals that lived in the area until its foundation in 902. "Histoire de la ville d'Oran" (Oran-DZ, 2015), http://www.oran-dz.com/ville/histoire.
23. Camus, "The Minotaur," 128.
24. Ibid., 129.
25. Ibid., 116.
26. As explained by Heidegger in *The Fundamental Concepts of Metaphysics*, 98. According to Herbert Morris, Camus must have been familiar with the philosophy of Heidegger. Christian Parreno, "Interview with Herbert Morris" (2014).

27. Camus, "The Minotaur," 147.
28. Ibid., 117, 118, 120.
29. Ibid., 122, 130.
30. The boxing presented by Camus resonates with the differentiation from wrestling posed by Roland Barthes, almost two decades later. For Barthes, "boxing is a Jansenist sport, based on a demonstration of excellence." Roland Barthes, *Mythologies* (London: Vintage Classics, 2000), 15.
31. Dine, "Shaping the Colonial Body," 41.
32. As Barthes points out, "the logical conclusion of the contest does not interest the wrestling-fan, while on the contrary a boxing-match always implies a science of the future." Barthes, *Mythologies*, 16.
33. Camus, "The Minotaur," 122.
34. At the time that Camus was writing, *fondouk* was also used as "a derogatory term used by the pieds-noirs [people of European ancestry who lived in French Algeria] to refer to a 'native' rabble." Dine, "Shaping the Colonial Body," 41.
35. Camus, "The Minotaur," 122, 124, 126.
36. Ibid., 129.
37. The essay was published in an anthology titled *Summer*. According to Douglas Johnson, "when Camus was in Oran, one of his favourite companions was Pierre Galindo. Through him Camus learned of an incident on the beach at Bouisseville which took place in August 1939, when members of 'la bande Galindo' found themselves jostled by two Arabs and one of them was attacked with a knife." Douglas Johnson, "The First Man of France." *Prospect* (1996), http://www.prospectmagazine.co.uk/arts-and-books/thefirstmanoffrance.
38. Camus, "The Minotaur," 114. Camus visited Oran in 1942, after his departure from Algeria in 1940. McCarthy, *Camus. A Critical Study of His Life and Work*, 164; Robert Zaretsky, *Albert Camus. Elements of a Life* (Ithaca: Cornell University Press, 2010), 126.
39. Camus, "The Minotaur," 114. Resonating with this latency, Camus wrote in 1937 that "any country where I am not bored is a country that teaches me nothing." "Death in the Soul," in *Lyrical and Critical Essays*, trans. Ellen Conroy Kennedy (New York: Alfred A. Knopf, 1968), 44.

Chapter 10

1. Giedion, *Space, Time and Architecture*, x. In the foreword of *Mechanization Takes Command*, Giedion writes the same about the origins of *Space, Time and Architecture*: "I attempted to show the split that exists in our period between thought and feeling." The book normalizes mechanization as "an agent, like water, fire, light. It is blind and without direction of its own. It must be canalized … Being less easily controlled than natural forces, mechanization reacts on the senses and on the mind of its creator." *Mechanization Takes Command. A Contribution to Anonymous History* (New York: W. W. Norton & Company, 1975), v, 714.
2. Giedion notes, "The demand for *shaping the emotional life* of the masses is still out of the picture. It is *regarded as unessential* and most of it is in the hand of speculators." "The Need for a New Monumentality," in *New Architecture and City Planning*, ed. Paul Zucker (New York: Philosophical Library, 1944), 549, 561 (italics in original), 550, 558–9, 550.

3. In *Mechanization Takes Command*, Giedion exposes the negative effects of monotonous labor through the depiction of *Modern Times* (1936) by Charlie Chaplin. However, he also defends the assembly line by comparing it to the need of the stability of home: "Henry Ford (1922) tells of a worker who had to perform a particularly monotonous task, actually one single motion of the hand. At his request, he was moved to another position, but after a few weeks he asked to be put back in his old job. Here Henry Ford hits on a phenomenon known to every urbanist who has slum-dwellers to resettle: No matter how primitive and unsanitary conditions may be, a certain number will always be found who refuse to leave their slum for new houses, and who prefer by far their old and familiar conditions." *Mechanization Takes Command*, 124–5, in reference to *My Life and Work* (1922) by Henry Ford; "The Need for a New Monumentality," 551.
4. Ibid., 551–2. Giedion's interest in the everyday becomes evident in *Mechanization Takes Command*, subtitled *A Contribution to Anonymous History*. He writes, "For the historian there are no banal things." *Mechanization Takes Command*, 3.
5. "The Need for a New Monumentality," 553, 555.
6. For Giedion, the building of the League of Nations was a case of "moral cowardice reflected in its architecture." Ibid., 553 (italics in original).
7. Giedion says art institutions, for example, do not understand the emotional life of the public. This promotes disconnection between artists and reality, which results in disengaging art. Ibid., 557, 568; *Architecture, You and Me. The Diary of a Development* (Cambridge: Harvard University Press, 1958), 68.
8. "The Need for a New Monumentality," 565–6.
9. *Space, Time and Architecture*, x.
10. Ibid., xxxii.
11. Ibid. This definition of playboy architecture resonates with the character of the seducer in *Either/Or* by Kierkegaard, concerned with the pleasure of the present rather than with the significance of the processes of existence.
12. Ibid., xxxiii. Karsten Harries updates at the end of the twentieth century: "If Giedion had hoped that this turn to 'playboy-architecture' would prove a passing fad, such hope went disappointed. Today, as we approach the end of both the century and the millennium, the 'romantic orgy' he deplored shows no sign of abating." Karsten Harries, *The Ethical Function of Architecture* (Cambridge: MIT Press, 1997), 6.
13. Giedion, *Space, Time and Architecture*, xxxiii.
14. Ulrich Franzen, "Outspoken Briton Dislikes U.S. Modern Architecture," in *Douglas Putnam Haskell Papers* (Columbia University Libraries, 1961).
15. Douglas Haskell, "In the Forum," *Architectural Forum* (1961), 79.
16. Reservations could be made at the offices of the Architectural League, 115 East 40th Street. "The New Forces in Architecture," in *Architectural League of New York Records, 1880s–1974* (Archives of American Art, Smithsonian Institution, 1961).
17. "Architecture—Fitting and Befitting," *Architectural Forum* (1961), 86. A year after the symposium, August Heckscher published *The Public Happiness*, which delved into social boredom, loneliness, and alienation. Informing his ideas on boring architecture, Robert Venturi references this work in *Complexity and Contradiction in Architecture* (1966). August Heckscher, *The Public Happiness* (New York: Atheneum, 1962). Now called the Century Foundation, the institution, founded in 1919, conducts "timely, non-partisan research and policy analysis that informs citizens, guides policymakers, and reshapes what

18. For the public, doors opened at 7.30 pm so tickets could be exchanged for reserved tickets by 8.15 pm.
19. In the records of the League, José A. Fernández consistently appears as the chairman and Ulrich Franzen as co-chairman. However, in the report by the *Architectural Forum*, Franzen is credited as chairman. "Architecture—Fitting and Befitting," 86. Cutler was also an architect at Skidmore, Owings & Merrill.
20. In some internal communications, it also appears as "Art Market in Our Society."
21. "Architecture—Fitting and Befitting," 86.
22. Ibid. The records of the League show that there were almost no concessions in the tickets—even the co-chairman paid the entrance fee. In addition, the records contain an organized typewritten list of attendants at the beginning of the series, in October 1960, only to become less systematic and to disappear by the end. Kathryn Farell was in charge of the tickets.
23. Haskell, "In the Forum," 79.
24. The list of people who purchased tickets also included Paul F. Basile, William Callahan, Miriam W. Code, Justine I. Cohen, Philip Grove, Charles Gissel, J. W. Green, R. P. Harlow, Donald P. Herzig, Lori Hodges, John Hogan Jr., Sylvan L. Joseph Jr., Helen Ketchum, W. Noffke, Leo. A. Novick, George Okunis, Kay Olson, J. R. Osbourne, Gordon L. Schenck, Bernard J. Rosen, C. Rother, Mel Solomon, Robert L. Thorson, and Kathleen Walsh.
25. Franzen, "Outspoken Briton Dislikes U.S. Modern Architecture." In an undated document of the League promoting the event, it appears as "Shaw of Architecture."
26. Ibid.
27. The description is undated and it might have been used as part of the invitation for the cocktail reception and dinner.
28. Haskell, "In the Forum," 79.
29. The "Art in Our Society" symposium was not included, probably because it did not focus on architecture. "Architecture—Fitting and Befitting," 86.
30. The complete speech by Johnson was included in an anthology of 1979. Philip Johnson, "The International Style—Death or Metamorphosis," in *Writings*, eds. Peter Eisenman and Robert A. M. Stern (New York: Oxford University Press, 1979). In an undated description, it is affirmed that the event was going to be "taped for later use on East and West coast radio stations." A tape that might contain Banham's complete speech rests in the Douglas P. Haskell archive, in the Avery Architectural & Fine Arts Library, Department of Drawings & Archives, Columbia University, Box 116, Item "3/30 League/*Forum* lecture, Johnson and Banham, 1 side only." At the time of writing, the material was not available to the public.
31. The photograph of Johnson is by Tommy Weber, photographer for *Time*. No credit is given to the photograph of Banham, which suggests that it might have been provided by himself or his publisher.
32. Philip Johnson and Jeffrey Kipnis, "A Conversation around the Avant-Garde," in *Autonomy and Ideology. Positioning an Avant-Garde in America*, ed. R. E. Somol (New York: The Monacelli Press, 1997), 47; "Architecture—Fitting and Befitting," 87.
33. Succinctly, Johnson affirmed that "it was obvious it [the International Style] was a style. It was obviously different from the individualist work before the war." Philip Johnson, "International Style—Death or Metamorphosis," in *Philip Johnson Papers* (New York: Museum of Modern Art Archive, 1961), 1.

Notes to pp. 95–98

34. "Architecture—Fitting and Befitting," 87.
35. Johnson wrote in 1994, "I was a devoted disciple of Mies... but then I got bored with it." In Stanley Abercrombie, "A Few Good Buildings: Reading the Obituaries of Philip Johnson," *The American Scholar* 74, no. 2 (2005): 118; "Architecture—Fitting and Befitting," 87 (italics in original).
36. Ibid.
37. According to his wife, the trip was "the realisation of a longheld dream." Mary Banham, "The 1960s," in Reyner Banham, *A Critic Writes: Essays by Reyner Banham*, eds. Mary Banham, Sutherland Lyall, Cedric Price, and Paul Barker (Berkeley: University of California Press, 1996), 47.
38. "Re: Reyner Banham," in *Douglas Putnam Haskell Papers* (Avery Architectural & Fine Arts Library. Columbia University Libraries, 1961).
39. Other information was provided as well: "Reyner Banham was born in Norwich, England 1922 of lineage of both technical and esthetic [sic] bents: one grandfather was an engineer; the other a wood engraver. After a mixed technical and grammar school education he was apprenticed as an aero engine technician. He has a bachelor's degree in the history of art from the Courtauld Institute, University of London where he later taught (or, as Banham apparently puts it, 'he was engaged in teaching juvenile delinquents').... He has been a regular contributor to the *Architectural Review*; to *Covilta Delle Macchina* in Rome, the *Mirador* in Buenos Aires; and the *Art News* in London. He is literary advisor to the *Architects Journal*, and the architectural correspondent to the *New Statesman* in London. He is now full time on the staff of the *Architectural Press*. (It was not clear whether he is still connected with all of the other publications listed above.)" In addition, details of his visit were included: "Mr. Coti at Praeger was interested in knowing when Banham would be here—'they might like to arrange some other things' for him. (Franzen's secretary says he arrives night of March 29—lecture is March 30—and will probably stay two or three weeks—with a stay at Carbondale where he is going to lecture. Says she, it is very difficult to get any definite plans from Banham; but apparently he won't stay here more than two or three weeks because he is teaching in London and must get back for that)." Ibid.
40. "Architecture—Fitting and Befitting," 87.
41. Ibid.
42. Giedion remarked that "these studies have required more than ten years." *The Eternal Present* was the result of research trips to France, Spain, Mesopotamia, and Egypt, followed by teaching at the Federal Institute of Technology, Zurich, Harvard, and the A. W. Mellon Lectures in the Fine Arts at the National Gallery of Art, Washington D.C. Giedion, *Constancy, Change and Architecture*, 6.
43. *The Eternal Present: The Beginnings of Art. A Contribution on Constancy and Change* (New York: Bollingen Foundation, 1962), 7.
44. *Constancy, Change and Architecture*, 22, 24.
45. Ibid., 4.
46. Ibid., 6.
47. *Architecture and the Phenomena of Transition* (Cambridge: Harvard University Press, 1971), 1, 2.
48. *Constancy, Change and Architecture*, 30.
49. In *Architecture and the Phenomena of Transition*, Giedion identifies three space conceptions, all dominated by verticality as the aspect that differentiates the prehistorical and pre-architectural form the historical and architectural: "*The first space conception: architecture as

space-radiating volumes. . . . The first space conception was that of the first high civilizations: Mesopotamia and Egypt. . . . The pyramids and the Parthenon both stand as volumes in space." "*The second space conception: architecture as interior space*. Roman, Medieval, Renaissance, and Baroque architecture, with all their stylistic differences, adhered to the same space conception." "*The third space conception: architecture as both volume and interior space*. In the twentieth century it was the painters who introduced the new space conception. This was in conscious opposition to the restless superficiality of painting and architecture in the late nineteenth century and to the Art Nouveau." *Architecture and the Phenomena of Transition*, 2–5 (italics in original).

50. *Constancy, Change and Architecture*, 29.
51. Ibid., 30, 7–8.

Chapter 11

1. Aldous Huxley, "Los Angeles, a Rhapsody," in *Writing Los Angeles: A Literary Anthology*, ed. David Ulin (New York: Library of America, 2002), 61.
2. Simone de Beauvoir, "America Day by Day," in ibid., 349; James M. Cain, "Paradise," in ibid., 125.
3. Charles Bukowski, *Post Office* (London: Ebury Publishing, 2011), 72.
4. Reyner Banham, "L.A.: The Structure Behind the Scene," *Architectural Design* 41(1971): 230. According to Nigel Whiteley, "Banham initially found the city 'incomprehensible', but changed his mind for three reasons. First, he got familiar with the city; second, he wanted to like Los Angeles; and third, because the city represented a 'fit environment for human activities in the Second Machine Age.'" Nigel Whiteley, *Reyner Banham: Historian of the Immediate Future* (Cambridge: MIT Press, 2002), 225, 228.
5. Echoing the illustrations commissioned by Banham of François Dallegret for "A Home Is Not a House" (1965). In the essay, individual, family, and social life are enclosed within a traveling bubble inflated upon demand. Reyner Banham, "A Home Is Not a House," *Art in America* 2 (1965): 70–9.
6. Quoted in Hadas Steiner, "The Architecture of the Well-Serviced Environment," *ARQ: Architectural Review Quarterly* 9, no. 2 (2005): 133, from *Archigram 3: Expendability* (1963). Probably the most adamant opponent of boredom in architecture, Peter Cook describes the condition as "a despicable enemy." In an interview of 2014, he stated: "I hate the architectural position that edifies boredom, which says 'this is right' or 'this is good.' . . . In my mind, boredom goes with all that is tedious, do-good, politically correct, healthy food, don't do anything naughty, don't speak too loudly. To all that stuff, I say 'fuck them!'" Christian Parreno and Ingrid Lønningdal, "From Anonymity to Boredom to Creativity," *Architecture and Culture*, (2020), DOI: 10.1080/20507828.2020.1792217.
7. Banham, "L.A.: The Structure Behind the Scene," 230.
8. *Los Angeles: The Architecture of Four Ecologies* (London: Penguin, 1971), 23.
9. According to Kevin Starr, "as early as 1542, sailing into San Pedro Bay, Juan Cabrillo noticed how the smoke from Native American fires, hanging in the air, stretched horizontally across the Los Angeles plain. Indeed, the Native American name for this plain was the Valley of Smokes." Kevin Starr, *Golden Dreams: California in an Age of Abundance, 1950–1963* (New York: Oxford University Press, 2009), 259–60.

10. Los Angeles was founded in 1781. The name in Spanish is "El Pueblo de Nuestra Señora la Reina de los Ángeles del Río de Porciúncula." *California: A History* (New York: Random House Publishing Group, 2007), 37.

11. The approach is both visionary and primitivist. Banham theoretically contributes to the establishment of the notion of sustainability, adding to the efforts carried out until that moment by Buckminster Fuller. In addition, Banham aligns himself with the 1960s American acknowledgment of architecture as a primal human need, stressing that the relationship with nature is a universal and timeless circumstance that has defined civilizations, as exposed in the exhibition "Architecture without Architects," curated by Bernard Rudofsky at MoMA in 1964. According to Michael Osman, Banham's "turn to ecology took place in the mid-1960s, when he began to treat buildings as tools used by humans to produce environmental conditions for their own benefit and pleasure." Michael Osman, "Banham's Historical Ecology," in *Neo-Avant-Garde and Postmodern: Postwar Architecture in Britain and Beyond*, ed. Mark Crinson and Claire Zimmerman (New Haven: Yale University Press, 2010), 232.

12. As Alison and Peter Smithson note, "Los Angeles is fine in many respects, but it lacks legibility—that factor which ultimately involves identity, and the whole business of the city as a comprehensible extension of oneself. The layout of Los Angeles and the form of its buildings do not indicate places to stop and do things in. What form it has is in its movement pattern, which is virtually an end in itself." Smithson, *Ordinariness and Light. Urban Theories 1952-1960 and Their Application in a Building Project 1963-1970* (London: Faber and Faber, 1970), 182.

13. According to Georges Teyssot, "the word comfort in English derives from the French *confort*, originally referring to moral or psychological comfort. Thus welfare and 'feeling well' had an initial moral meaning. It was only during the eighteenth century that comfort acquired its modern meaning, indicating material and technological circumstances that enabled physical 'well-being.'" Georges Teyssot, "Boredom and Bedroom: The Suppression of the Habitual," *Assemblage*, no. 30 (1996): 46, 49.

14. Banham, *Los Angeles*, 38-9, 25.

15. Ibid., 61.

16. It was carved in the 1920s and has been altered by renowned artists and architects, including Frank Gehry, Hodgetts and Fung, George Stanley, and Lloyd Wright.

17. Banham, *Los Angeles*, 111.

18. Ibid., 112-13.

19. The house was originally built as a movie set in the Irvin Willat Film Studio in Culver City. In 1934, it was moved to Beverly Hills and converted to a private residence.

20. Banham, *Los Angeles*, 112-13.

21. Ibid., 124, 106.

22. Ibid., 134, 139.

23. Ibid., 161.

24. *Reyner Banham Loves Los Angeles* (London: BBC, 1972).

25. *Los Angeles*, 169.

26. Ibid., 169-72, 161. Watts was well connected to the rest of the city by trains until the first half of the twentieth century. When the Pacific Electric gradually stopped operating, it became "nowhere." "L.A.: The Structure Behind the Scene," 229. Robert Lambert affirms that in the face of leisure, "the alternatives are clear: boredom and civil disorder—Watts times a thousand." Robert Lambert, "The Forty-Year Coffee Break," *The English Journal* 55, no. 6 (1966): 771.

27. Banham, *Los Angeles*, 111; "L.A.: The Structure Behind the Scene," 229.
28. Sigmund Freud, *Psychopathology of Everyday Life*, trans. Abraham Arden Brill (London: Unwin, 1914), 167. In "Beyond the Pleasure Principle," Freud writes, "*Protection against* stimuli is an almost more important function for the living organism than *reception* of stimuli. The protective shield is supplied with its own store of energy and must above all endeavour to preserve the special modes of transformation of energy operating in it against the effects threatened by the enormous energies at work in the external world—effects which tend towards a levelling out of them and hence towards destruction." "Beyond the Pleasure Principle," in *Standard Edition of the Complete Psychological Works* (London: The Hogarth Press, 1955), 27 (italics in original).
29. *Psychopathology of Everyday Life*, 167.
30. Banham, *Los Angeles*, 172–3.
31. Ibid., 209–10, 161.
32. Ibid., 35, 88–90, 215. Unlike J. G. Ballard, who in *Crash* (1973) describes the simultaneous condemnation and acclamation of roads as opportunities for boredom and transgression: "We had entered an immense traffic jam. From the junction of the motorway and Western Avenue to the ascent ramp of the flyover the traffic lanes were packed with vehicles, windshields leaching out the molten colours of the sun setting above the western suburbs of London. Brake-lights flared in the evening air, glowing in the huge pool of cellulosed bodies. Vaughan sat with one arm out of the passenger window. He slapped the door impatiently, pounding the panel with his fist. To our right the high wall of a double-decker airline coach formed a cliff of faces. The passengers at the windows resembled rows of the dead looking down at us from the galleries of a columbarium. The enormous energy of the twentieth century, enough to drive the planet into a new orbit around a happier star, was being expended to maintain this immense motionless pause." J. G. Ballard, *Crash* (London: Harper Perennial, 2008), 124.
33. Heidegger, *The Fundamental Concepts of Metaphysics*, 77.
34. Banham, *Los Angeles*, 216. According to Starr, "Los Angeles experienced its first smog attack in July 1940, followed by a second attack in September 1942. A third attack—brought on, it was later determined, by increased automotive traffic during a streetcar strike—came in July 1943 and reappeared in September. The smog attack of September 8, 1943, subsequently known as Black Wednesday, brought the city to a standstill." Starr, *Golden Dreams*, 259–60.
35. Banham, *Los Angeles*, 5, 216. Banham learned to drive "in order to read Los Angeles in the original." For Tom Wolfe, automobiles in Los Angeles "are an inspiration, if you will, a wonderful fantasy extension of the curved line, and since the car in America is half fantasy anyway, a kind of baroque extension of the ego." Tom Wolfe, *The Kandy-Kolored Tangerine-Flake Streamline Baby* (New York: Farrar, Straus and Giroux, 2009), 89.
36. As David Brodsly comments, "driving provides a scheduled opportunity to do nothing. The freeway commute is Los Angeles' distinctively urban form of meditation." Quoted in Iain Borden, *Drive. Journeys through Film, Cities and Landscapes* (London: Reaktion, 2013), 153, from David Brodsly, *L.A. Freeway: An Appreciative Essay* (Berkeley, 1981), 41. To Iain Borden, "In *America*, Baudrillard speaks of driving as 'a spectacular form of amnesia' where not only is 'everything to be obliterated' but also, and tellingly, where 'everything is to be discovered.'" Bordern, *Drive*, 153, from Jean Baudrillard, *America* (London, 1988), 5.
37. Banham, *Los Angeles*, 122. However, in *Reyner Banham Loves Los Angeles*, he suggests that driving can produce a sense of being lost: "When you are there in the traffic in Central Boulevard, you can be pretty estranged and nervous." *Reyner Banham Loves Los Angeles*.
38. As a creative counterpart of the monotonous monumentality of the freeways, the architecture of "The Style that Nearly . . ." exposes a diverse yet compact expression of buildings only possible in Los Angeles. Typified by the Eames house (1949) by Charles Eames, the Case Study house

(1950) by Raphael Soriano, and the Hale house (1951) by Craig Ellwood, they feature "experimental" design, "not merely odd works of architectural genius but a whole consistent style." Insinuating that the transgressive force of boredom not only produces accident and entropy but also high resolution, Banham portrays the residences as detailed, innovative, and unpretentious. They constitute genuine efforts to provide a way of dwelling that responds to the environment, not being the result of formal manipulations or representational ambitions. The steel structures and use of other materials are "unmonumental" and of "exact location," particularly if "compared with Mies's and Johnson's work back East." Resonating with the plains and climate of Los Angeles, horizontality, transparency, and spaces in between inside and outside prevail; their purity tends towards the ascetic, contrasting with the extroversion of the commercial architecture and their compelling signs. Banham, *Los Angeles*, 207–9.

39. Banham, *Los Angeles*, 235, 236. According to Nigel Whiteley, Banham's concern with *une architecture autre* was at its most intense in the 1950s. The expression appeared for the first time in an article titled "The New Brutalism" for *The Architectural Review*, published in December 1955. Analogous to *un art autre*, formulated by Michel Tapié in 1952, it reconsidered four areas: "a revision of architectural Modernism; technology; popular culture; and the New Brutalism." Nigel Whiteley, "Banham and 'Otherness': Reyner Banham (1922–1988) and His Quest for an Architecture Autre," *Architectural History* 33 (1990): 189 (italics in original).

40. Banham, *Los Angeles*, 237, 238.

41. Peter Plagens, "Los Angeles: The Ecology of Evil," *Artforum* 11 (1972): 68, 67, 73, 76, 70, 69.

42. Ibid., 69, 68, 74.

43. Ibid., 69, 90.

44. Ballard writes, "As I eased my feet on to the control pedals I was aware of all these drivers, of the volumes their bodies had occupied, their assignations, escapes, boredom that pre-empted any response of my own." Ballard, *Crash*, 44.

45. Plagens, "Los Angeles: The Ecology of Evil," 70, 72. For a comprehensive study of the smog problem in the city in the 1960s, see Barry Commoner, "Los Angeles Air," in *The Closing Circle: Nature, Man and Technology* (New York: Alfred A. Knopf, 1971).

46. Quoted in Plagens, "Los Angeles: The Ecology of Evil," 72, from Liza Williams, *Up the City of the Angels* (New York: Putnam, 1971), 47–8.

47. Plagens, "Los Angeles: The Ecology of Evil," 76.

48. Quoted in ibid., from Richard Neutra, *Life and Shape* (New York: Appleton-Century-Crofts, 1962), 266.

49. As Cees Nooteboom observes, "it may be something that passes if you are here longer, but on some street corners, at some hours, in some 'settings', I have the irresistible feeling that I am acting in a movie, am an extra in a scene that somewhere means something entirely different." Cees Nooteboom, "Autopia," in *Writing Los Angeles: A Literary Anthology*, ed. David Ullin (New York: Library of America, 2002), 572.

50. In contrast to the legends of modernism, such as Frank Lloyd Wright and Le Corbusier. In "A Home Is Not a House," Banham affirms that architecture is "the art of creating monumental spaces." Banham, "A Home Is Not a House," 70, 73. Furthermore, in a review of *Motel of the Mysteries* (1979) by David Macaulay, Banham suggests that the great outdoors can inflict boredom: "it smells of the study and the lamp, not of those boring, sweaty, interminable miles of dust and sun glare between Denver and Topeka in high August, or that feeling that there is no escape from Nebraska, on which so many travellers comment." "The Haunted Highway," *New Society* 52 (1980): 299.

51. Jameson, *Postmodernism*, 38–9, 42, 43.

Chapter 12

1. Niels Prak, *The Visual Perception of the Built Environment* (Delft: Delft University Press, 1977), 59. According to Prak, the need for variety "is more difficult to demonstrate than the need for food or sexual contacts, for the last two needs are directed at objects," whereas the first "is directed at a *relation* between objects or settings." Ibid., 60 (italics in original).
2. Richard Smith observed in 1981 that only forty academic papers on boredom were published between 1926 and 1979, fewer than one per year. Lesley Kenny, "Boredom Escapes Us: A Cultural Collage in Eleven Storeys" (University of Toronto, 2009), 124, citing Richard Smith, "Boredom: A Review," *Human Factors* 23, no. 3 (1981): 338.
3. For Jameson, "a certain spatial turn has often seemed to offer one of the more productive ways of distinguishing postmodernism from modernism proper, whose experience of temporality—existential time, along with deep memory—it is henceforth conventional to see as dominant of the high modern." Jameson, *Postmodernism*, 154, 163, 72.
4. Prak, *The Visual Perception of the Built Environment*, 69, 67.
5. Prak points out that "the criticism of architects of monotonous buildings is thrown in relief when it is easily compared to [Abraham] Moles' (1971) criticism of light music. According to Moles, light music is easily enjoyed because it has such a low information-content. We catch on to it because of its many redundant elements: a simple melody, a few chords, many repetitions. But these same elements start to bore us after we have heard the same piece a few times over." Ibid., 71.
6. Quoted in Kenny, "Boredom Escapes Us," 13, from Brian O'Doherty, *Object and Idea: An Art Critic's Journal 1961–1967* (New York: Simon and Schuster, 1967), 237; quoted in Hannah Richardson, "Children Should Be Allowed to Get Bored, Expert Says," *BBC News* (2013), http://www.bbc.com/news/education-21895704.
7. Russell, "Boredom and Excitement," 43.
8. Quoted in Paul Kennedy, "The Motorcycle Is Yourself," *CBC* (2015), http://www.cbc.ca/radio/ideas/the-motorcycle-is-yourself-1.2914205; William Ralph Inge, *The End of an Age and Other Essays* (New York: The MacMillan Company, 1949), 216.
9. For instance, Andreas Elpidorou, "The Bright Side of Boredom," *Frontiers in Psychology* 5 (2014): 1–4; J. Barbalet, "Boredom and Social Meaning," *The British Journal of Sociology* 50, no. 4 (1999): 631–46; Wijnad Van Tilburg and Eric Igou, "On Boredom and Social Identity: A Programmatic Meaning-Regulation Approach," *Personality and Social Psychology Bulletin* 37, no. 12 (2012): 1679–91; Shane Bench and Heather Lench, "On the Function of Boredom," *Behavioral Sciences* 3, no. 3 (2013): 459–72.
10. Quoted in Richardson, "Children Should Be Allowed to Get Bored, Expert Says"; Sandi Mann, "Does Boredom Bring Out Our Creative Flair?," *Huffington Post* (2013), http://www.huffingtonpost.co.uk/sandi-mann/does-boredom-bring-out-out-creative-flair_b_2447393.html (italics in original).
11. Elpidorou, "The Bright Side of Boredom," 2, 4 (italics in original).
12. The literature in psychology that covers these different manifestations is extensive and recent. For example, N. LePera, "Relationships between Boredom Proneness, Mindfulness, Anxiety, Depression, and Substance Use," *New School Psychology Bulletin* 8, no. 2 (2011): 15–25; Yael K. Goldberg et al., "Boredom: An Emotional Experience Distinct from Apathy, Anhedonia, or Depression," *Journal of Social and Clinical Psychology* 30, no. 6 (2011): 647–66; Kimberley B. Mercer and John D. Eastwood, "Is Boredom Associated with Problem Gambling Behaviour? It Depends on What You Mean by 'Boredom,'" *International Gambling Studies* 10, no. 1 (2010):

91–104; Eric R. Dahlen et al., "Boredom Proneness in Anger and Aggression: Effects of Impulsiveness and Sensation Seeking," *Personality and Individual Differences* 37, no. 8 (2004): 1615–27; S. J. Vodanovich, "Psychometric Measures of Boredom: A Review of the Literature," *The Journal of Psychology* 137, no. 6 (2003): 569–95; Steven J. Kass, Stephen J. Vodanovich, and Anne Callender, "State-Trait Boredom: Relationship to Absenteeism, Tenure, and Job Satisfaction," *Journal of Business and Psychology* 16, no. 2 (2001): 317–27; J. Sommers and S. J. Vodanovich, "Boredom Proneness: Its Relationship to Psychological—and Physical—Health Symptoms," *Journal of Clinical Psychology* 56, no. 1 (2000): 149–55; Hope M. Seib and Stephen J. Vodanovich, "Cognitive Correlates of Boredom Proneness: The Role of Private Self-Consciousness and Absorption," *The Journal of Psychology* 132, no. 6 (1998): 642–52; Frederick T. L. Leong and Gregory R. Schneller, "Boredom Proneness: Temperamental and Cognitive Components," *Personality and Individual Differences* 14, no. 1 (1993): 233–9; S. Ahmed, "Psychometric Properties of the Boredom Proneness Scale," *Perceptual Motor Skills* 71, no. 3 (1990): 963–6; A. Blaszczynski, N. McConaghy, and A. Frankova, "Boredom Proneness in Pathological Gambling," *Psychological Reports* 67, no. 1 (1990): 35–42; R. Farmer and N. D. Sundberg, "Boredom Proneness—the Development and Correlates of a New Scale," *Journal of Personality Assessment* 50, no. 1 (1986): 4–17.

13. Jeff Ferrell, "Boredom, Crime, and Criminology," *Theoretical Criminology International Journal* 8, no. 3 (2004): 287–302; *Reclaim the Streets* (2013), http://rts.gn.apc.org/sp'96/society.htm.

14. In a case that combines terrorism, war, and the risk of death, trucker Toshifumi Fujimoto cures the boredom of his job—a daily drive from Osaka to Tokyo or Nagasaki carrying goods—by traveling to zones of conflict to experience them directly, as a tourist. After visiting Yemen in 2014 and Cairo in 2013, he visited Aleppo in 2015, entering the country clandestinely from Turkey, to join the Free Syria Army, experience combat, and take photographs to post on social media. Fujimoto declares, "it fascinates me, and I enjoy it . . . I'm not afraid if they shoot at me or that they might kill me. I'm a combination of samurai and kamikaze." AFP, "Bored Japanese Trucker Gets Kicks from Syria 'War Tourism,'" *Al Arabiya News* (2013), http://english.alarabiya.net/articles/2013/01/03/258384.html.

15. As covered by the media, boredom is the most powerful recruiting tool of terrorists, attracting uneducated young groups with reduced possibilities of attaining a modern "ordinary life"—as in Yemen, where unemployment rises to fifty percent. On the internet, experiences similar to those of video games and extreme sports are presented as meaningful; *Time* reports, "young women schooled on Disney princess DVDs join ISIL dreaming of, in the words of one recruit's tweet, 'doing a Mulan' and going out disguised as a man on the battlefield." According to the magazine, this phenomenon echoes "the dangerous mix of anxiety and boredom" that Europe experienced in the first half of the twentieth century. Quoting *Defying Hitler* (2000) by Sebastian Haffner, a memoir about growing up in Germany in the interwar period, Carla Power compares the "emptiness of boredom" and "the yearning for 'salvation' through alcohol, through superstition, or best of all, through a vast, overpowering, cheap mass intoxication" with the offerings of terrorism. In her view, "for kids raised in the mall and online, reared to believe that 'choice' is their birth-right but who have watched their choices dwindle after the economic crash, ISIL might just be the cheap mass intoxication they're looking for." Carla Power, "Terrorists' Most Powerful Recruiting Tool: Boredom," *Time* (2015), http://time.com/3857035/terrorists-recruiting-tool/.

16. According to the International Centre for the Study of Radicalisation and Political Violence of King's College London, in the Middle East a significant number of local rebels abandon the cause because the expectation of gaining access to better living conditions—including luxury goods and cars—does not materialize. Meanwhile, those militants of Western background tend to leave due to the boredom with shortages of electricity, internet connection, and basic services. Peter E. Neumann, "Victims, Perpetrators, Assets: The Narratives of Islamic State Defectors" (ICSR, 2015), http://icsr.info/wp-content/uploads/2015/09/ICSR-Report-Victims-Perpertrators-Assets-The-

Narratives-of-Islamic-State-Defectors.pdf. In 2014, according to *Le Figaro*, some of the French fighters in Syria asked for advice on how to return. They complained of not participating in a noble battle—"I've basically done nothing except hand out clothes and food," "I help clean weapons and transport dead bodies from the front," "they make me do the washing up," "they want to send me to the front, but I don't know how to fight," "my iPod doesn't work anymore here. I have to come back." Marie-Amélie Lombard-Latune, "Des recrues de Daech demandent à leurs avocats de préparer leur retour en France," *Le Figaro* (2014), http://www.lefigaro.fr/actualite-france/2014/11/30/01016-20141130ARTFIG00191-des-recrues-de-daech-demandent-a-leurs-avocats-de-preparer-leur-retour-en-france.php.

17. Jorg Kustermans and Erik Ringmar, "Modernity, Boredom, and War: A Suggestive Essay," *Review of International Studies* 37, no. 4 (2011): 1778. For further elaboration on the role of boredom as an experience of war, see Linda Åhäll and Thomas Gregory, *Emotions, Politics and War* (London: Taylor & Francis, 2015).

18. Nico Lambrechts, "Successful Banker Jumped to His Death from No 1 Poultry Building," *The Telegraph* (2012), http://www.telegraph.co.uk/news/9616861/Successful-banker-jumped-to-his-death-from-No-1-Poultry-building.html; Natalie Evans, "City Roof Fall Horror: Businesswoman Plunges 80ft to Her Death from Restaurant Roof Terrace in Front of Horrified Commuters," *The Mirror* (2012), http://www.mirror.co.uk/news/uk-news/businesswoman-plunges-80ft-to-death-from-restaurant-1306018.

19. Samuel Osborne, "Coq D'argent: Man Wrote 'I Have Cracked' on Phone before Becoming Sixth Person to Fall to Death from London Roof Garden," *Independent* (2016), http://www.independent.co.uk/news/uk/home-news/coq-dargent-man-wrote-i-have-cracked-on-phone-before-becoming-sixth-person-to-fall-to-death-from-a7000721.html.

20. Alexandre Kojève taught philosophy at the École pratique des hautes études in Paris during the 1930s and retired to work as a bureaucrat in the European Economic Community, affirming that nothing else could be achieved in philosophy. Fukuyama describes him as "a brilliant Russian émigré ... While largely unknown in the United States, Kojève had a major impact on the intellectual life of the continent. Among his students ranged such future luminaries as Jean-Paul Sartre on the Left and Raymond Aron on the Right; post war existentialism borrowed many of its basic categories from Hegel via Kojève." Francis Fukuyama, "Have We Reached the End of History?" (RAND Corporation, 1989), http://www.rand.org/pubs/papers/P7532.html., 1, 3, 4.

21. Ibid., 4, 2. For Fukuyama, these expressions include not only the abolition of "slavery and the slave trade" and the extension of "the franchise to workers, women, blacks, and other racial minorities, etc." but also war. He elaborated further in 1992, "Boredom with peace and prosperity has had far graver consequences in the past. Take, for example, the First World War. The origins of this conflict remain to this day complex, much-studied, and controversial. Interpretations of the causes of the war, including German militarism and nationalism, the progressive breakdown of the European balance of power, the increasing rigidity of the alliance system, the incentives placed on pre-emption and offense by doctrine and technology, and the stupidity and recklessness of individual leaders, all contain elements of the truth. But in addition, there was another intangible but crucial factor leading to war: many European publics simply wanted war because they were fed up with the dullness and lack of community in civilian life." *The End of History and the Last Man* (London: Penguin Books, 1992), 330–1.

22. In China, the third plenum of the Tenth Central Committee in 1978 began to decollectivize agriculture, reducing the role of the state to a tax collector—as a universal homogeneous state—and allowing the infiltration and consumption of international goods, incentivizing work, and altering public taste. In the Soviet Union, the reforms of the perestroika of Mikhail

23. Ibid., 16, 17, 8, 9.
24. To Fukuyama, under liberalism, the only two forces that may not be solved are religion and nationalism. The rise of Christian, Jewish, and Muslim fundamentalism appears as counteraction to the "broad unhappiness with the impersonality and spiritual vacuity of liberal consumerist societies." However, in a circular manner, modern liberalism emerged as a result of the incapacity of pre-modern religious systems to provide unity and stability. Even though Islam offers a theocratic alternative, the doctrine "has little appeal" and "it is hard to believe that the movement will take on any universal significance." Ibid., 16, 17.
25. Ibid., 22–3. Jameson agrees, "But there is a deeper reason for the disappearance of the Great Writer under postmodernism, and it is simply this, sometimes called 'uneven development': in an age of monopolies (and trade unions), of increasing institutionalized collectivization, there is always a lag. Some parts of the economy are still archaic, handicraft enclaves; some are more modern and futuristic than the future itself." Jameson, *Postmodernism*, 307.
26. Fukuyama, "Have We Reached the End of History?," 23. In the book version of the essay, Fukuyama pairs "the end of history" with "the last man," a type of subjectivity characterized by boredom with the consumerist principles of liberalism: "To the extent that liberal democracy is successful at purging *megalothymia* from life and substituting for it rational consumption, we will become last men. But human beings will rebel at this thought. That is, they will rebel at the idea of being undifferentiated members of a universal and homogeneous state, each the same as the other no matter where on the globe one goes. They will want to be citizens rather than *bourgeois*, finding the life of masterless slavery—the life of rational consumption—in the end, boring." *The End of History and the Last Man*, 314 (italics in original).
27. "Have We Reached the End of History?," 23.
28. Following the economic elaborations by Branco Hovart. Heilbroner, *Beyond Boom and Crash*, 87–8, 70–1.
29. Pérez explains, "A new product appearing in the early phase of a new system has a more dynamic market life ahead than one introduced at its maturity phase. This happens for two main reasons. One is the exhaustion of the opportunity space of that particular system, so that the last innovations are likely to be very minor. For example, the long series of home electrical appliances in the early 20th Century began with the refrigerators and the washing machine and petered out with the electric can-opener and the electric carving knife. The other reason for decreasing market dynamism is the intense learning that occurs within the system and the externalities that result from it." Carlota Pérez, "Technological Revolutions and Techno-Economic Paradigms," *Technological Governance*, no. 20 (2009): 3–4, 7.
30. Ibid., 10, 8.
31. Heilbroner, *Beyond Boom and Crash*, 88–9.
32. As Heidegger asserts, "technology is the organization of a lack." Quoted in Thiele, "Postmodernity and the Routinization of Novelty," 504–5, from Martin Heidegger, *The End of Philosophy*, trans. J. Stambaugh (New York: Harper and Row, 1973), 107.
33. Orrin Klapp, *Overload and Boredom: Essays on the Quality of Life in the Information Society* (New York: Greenwood Press, 1986), 1, 2–3, 4, 7.
34. Svendsen, *A Philosophy of Boredom*, 88. For Sandi Mann, "technology is like junk food: there's no nutrition in it." Halls, "How You Can Use Boredom to Increase Happiness and Creativity," *GQ* (2016).

35. David Foster Wallace, *The Pale King* (New York: Little, Brown and Company, 2012), 85.
36. Bernard Cache, *Projectiles* (London: Architectural Association, 2011), 46, 60, 68.
37. Tony Judt, *Postwar. A History of Europe Since 1945* (London: Vintage, 2010), 580.
38. With irony, Judt also calls him "The Tallest Mast" and "The Visionary." Ibid., 624.
39. Ibid. (italics in original).
40. Quoted in Judt, *Postwar*, 535. According to Judt, "between 1973 and 1981 the British West Midland, home of small engineering firms and car plants, lost one in four of its workforce. The industrial zone of Lorraine, in north-east France, lost 28 percent of its manufacturing jobs. The industrial workforce in Lüneburg, West Germany, fell by 42 percent in the same years. When FIAT of Turin began its switch to robotization at the end of the 1970s, 65,000 jobs (out of total 165,000) were lost in just three years. In the city of Amsterdam, 40 percent of the workforce was employed in industry in the 1950s; a quarter century later the figure was just one employee in seven." Ibid., 459.
41. Ibid., 477, 544. Judt writes that "post-1945 rights talk thus concentrated on individuals. This too was a lesson of war. Even though men and women were persecuted in the name of their common identity (Jews, gypsies, Poles, etc.) they suffered as individuals; and it was as individuals with individual rights that the new United Nations sought to protect them." Ibid., 565.
42. Ibid., 773.
43. Heilbroner, *Beyond Boom and Crash*, 89; Nathan Mager, *The Kondratieff Waves* (New York: Praeger, 1987), 42.
44. Heilbroner, *Beyond Boom and Crash*, 89.
45. Paul Mason predicts that in the post-capitalist era, "the power of imagination will become critical. In an information society, no thought, debate or dream is wasted—whether conceived in a tent camp, prison cell or the table football space of a startup company." Paul Mason, "The End of Capitalism Has Begun," *The Guardian* (2015), https://www.theguardian.com/books/2015/jul/17/postcapitalism-end-of-capitalism-begun.

Chapter 13

1. Carlo Salzani, "The Atrophy of Experience: Walter Benjamin and Boredom," in *Essays on Boredom and Modernity*, ed. Barbara Dalle Pezze and Carlo Salzani (Amsterdam: Rodopi, 2009), 130. According to Joe Moran, "it is significant that he [W. Benjamin] never precisely defines 'boredom', and it is used in often contradictory senses in his work: it is both the ennui experienced by the fashionable dandies and boulevardiers of the city, and a more productive type of boredom which provides access to half-buried memories, missed historical opportunities and revolutionary possibilities." Joe Moran, "Benjamin and Boredom," *Critical Quarterly* 45, no. 1–2 (2003): 168.
2. A. Benjamin, "Boredom and Distraction," 156, 159.
3. W. Benjamin, "Boredom, Eternal Return," 105, 106.
4. A. Benjamin, "Boredom and Distraction," 157, 163, 164.
5. Quoted in ibid., 160 (italics in original), from Walter Benjamin, *Walter Benjamin: Selected Writings, 4: 1938–1940*, ed. Howard Eiland and Michael Jennings (Cambridge: Belknap, 2006), 268.

6. A. Benjamin, "Boredom and Distraction," 161, 63.
7. As W. Benjamin asserts, "the punishments of hell are always the newest thing going in this domain. What is at issue is not that 'the same thing happens over and over', and even less would it be a question here of eternal return. It is rather that precisely in that which is newest the face of the world never alters, that this newest remains, in every respect, the same.—This constitutes the eternity of hell. To determine the totality of its traits by which the 'modern' is defined would be to represent hell." Quoted in Salzani, "The Atrophy of Experience: Walter Benjamin and Boredom," 135, from Walter Benjamin, *The Arcades Project*, 544.
8. Quoted in W. Benjamin, "Boredom, Eternal Return," 115 (italics in original), from Friedrich Nietzsche, *The Will to Power*, trans. by Walter Kaufmann and R. J. Hollingdale (New York: Vintage Books, 1968), 35–6.
9. A. Benjamin clarifies, "ambivalence is not relativism. . . . The mass individual is the locus of ambivalence; the potentiality of the masses lies therein. The realization of that potential, however, should not be interpreted as a move from an ideological condition—a state of self-deception—towards truth." A. Benjamin, "Boredom and Distraction," 158, 159, 169.
10. W. Benjamin, "Boredom, Eternal Return," 119, 105.
11. "The Storyteller: Reflections on the Works of Nikolai Leskov," in *The Novel: An Anthology of Criticism and Theory 1900–2000*, ed. Dorothy Hale (Malden: Blackwell Publishing, 2006).
12. "On awakening the sleeper wishes to communicate the dream and yet all that is narrated is this boredom." A. Benjamin, "Boredom and Distraction," 162, 167.
13. E. H. Gombrich connects boredom with creation through doodling, exemplified in the sketches of Leonardo da Vinci and the automatic writing of André Breton. In his view, doodles constitute a "pleasure of boredom," as expressions "of the play instinct which never leaves us even when we grow up." E. H. Gombrich, "Pleasures of Boredom," in *The Uses of Images* (London: Phaidon, 1999), 213. In addition, the analogy of the cycle of boredom and the new as a threshold of creativity has appeared recently in mass media, usually as a recommendation to embrace the condition. See, for example, Johnnie Moore, "Boredom as the Threshold of Creativity" (2014), http://johnniemoore.com/boredom-as-the-threshold-of-creativity.
14. A. Benjamin, "Boredom and Distraction," 170, 168.
15. Ibid., 164–5, 170.

Chapter 14

1. Until his death in 2003. As an art historian, Restany was interested in new perceptual approaches resulting from modernity. According to Lisa Licitra Ponti, editor of *Domus* from 1948 to 1986, he supported New Realism: "It was Europe versus Pop, which came from America. This squabble with America was very interesting. But we published Restany because he was Restany, even if we didn't totally share his ideas—[the same thing as] when you publish a poet with whom you don't always share the same frame of mind but you, nevertheless, publish the poems." Beatriz Colomina, Craig Buckley, and Urtzi Grau, eds., *Clip, Stamp, Fold: The Radical Architecture of Little Magazines, 196x to 197x* (New York: Actar, 2010), 385.
2. Alessandro Mendini, "Dear Reader," *Domus* 602 (1980), 1; Ed Taverne, "Mendini's Farewell to Architecture," in *Alessandro & Francesdo Mendini! Philippe Starck! Michele De Lucchi! Coop Himelb(L)Au! In Groningen!*, ed. M. Martin, C. Wagenaar, and A. Welkamp (Groningen: Groninger Museum, 1996), 39.

3. In 2010, Mendini returned to *Domus* to produce eleven issues. The architect was chosen because of his interest in innovation—a priority in the ethos of the magazine—and his "ability to synthesize the fabric and history of both theory and practice in contemporary architecture." Under the slogan "a new utopia," Mendini explored "the history of grand transformations in architecture and design." In his view, the forces behind architectural production are "not so much ... of a technical nature, but rather humanistic and psychological: the ecology of exterior environments is preceded by that of interiors." Although the revamped magazine evoked memories of Mendini of the 1980s—the clever succession of articles and the provocative collocation of images—neither the "Forum" nor its composite outline returned. "Alessandro Mendini Returns to *Domus*," *Dezeen* (2010), http://www.dezeen.com/2010/02/23/alessandro-mendini-returns-to-domus.

4. Mendini, "Dear Reader," 1.

5. In reference to the madeleine scene from *In Search of Lost Time* (1913–22).

6. Stefano Casciani, "Interview with Alessandro Mendini," in Rem Koolhaas, Norman Foster, and Alessandro Mendini, *Colours: Rem Koolhaas/Oma, Norman Foster, Alessandro Mendini* (Basel: Birkhäuser, 2001), 239, 241–2.

7. Quoted in Taverne, "Mendini's Farewell to Architecture," 43.

8. Alessandro Mendini, "Towards an Architecture of Banality" (1979), http://www.ateliermendini.it/index.php?mact=News,cntnt01,detail,0&cntnt01articleid=251&cntnt01detailtemplate=AnniDett&cntnt01lang=en_US&cntnt01returnid=191; see Abraham Moles, *Le kitsch: l'art du Bonheur* (Paris: Mame, 1971).

9. Taverne, "Mendini's Farewell to Architecture," 43.

10. Renny Ramakers, *Droog Design: Spirit of the Nineties* (Rotterdam: 010 Publishers, 1998), 30–1.

11. Alessandro Mendini, "Universal Cosmetics" (1981), http://www.ateliermendini.it/index.php?mact=News,cntnt01,detail,0&cntnt01articleid=249&cntnt01detailtemplate=AnniDett&cntnt01lang=en_US&cntnt01returnid=189.

12. M. Marijke et al., "Alessandro Mendini, Walking the Tight-Rope between Art and Kitsch," *Elle Wonen* (1993).

13. Echoing Siegfried Kracauer's description of Berlin as "isolated events that assemble in a kaleidoscopic manner in a series of ever renewed images.... Whoever lives in Berlin long enough ends up not knowing where he is truly from. His existence is no longer shaped like a line but like a juxtaposition of dots." Quoted in Elie During, "Loose Coexistence: Technologies of Attention in the Age of the Post-Metropolis," in *Cognitive Architecture. From Biopolitics to Noopolitics. Architecture & Mind in the Age of Communication and Information*, ed. Deborah Hauptmann and Warren Neidich (Rotterdam: 010 Publishers, 2010), 270, from "Ein Film," originally published in *Frankfurt Zeitung*, February 4, 1925, reproduced in Siegfried Kracauer, *Kleine Schriften zum Film, 1921–1927* (Frankfurt: Suhrkamp Verlag, 2004).

14. Charles Jencks, "The Pleasure of the Architext," in *Alessandro & Francesdo Mendini! Philippe Starck! Michele De Lucchi! Coop Himelb(L)Au! In Groningen!*, ed. M. Martin, C. Wagenaar, and A. Welkamp (Groningen: Groninger Museum, 1996), 9.

15. This approach echoes Henri Bergson's affirmation that the beautiful cannot be "caused" and only be "suggested." Therefore, art ought to "impress" feelings rather than "express" them. Henri Bergson, *Time and Free Will: An Essay on the Immediate Data of Consciousness* (Mineola: Dover Publications, 2001), 16–17.

16. Alessandro Mendini, "Pieces of Dan's Body and Soul," in Dan Friedman, Jeffrey Deitch, Steven Holt, and Alessandro Mendini, *Dan Friedman: Radical Modernism* (London: Yale University Press, 1994), 194.

17. In the "Forum," the last name of the poet is not Houdar de la Motte but Lamoutte-Houdar. The last verse of the poem reads:

> It is a great pleasure that diversity.
> We are as we are.
> Give men the same spirit;
> You remove all the salt of society.
> One day boredom was born from uniformity.
>
> Antoine Houdart de La Motte, *Oeuvres*, vol. 9 (Paris: Prault, 1754)

18. Pierre Restany, "Forum: One Day Boredom Was Born from Uniformity," *Domus* 605 (1980), 2. *Domus* supported experimental and innovative work since the late 1960s, featuring the Radicals, "an emerging constellation of Italian and international artists and architects." Colomina, Buckley, and Grau, *Clip, Stamp, Fold*, 109.

19. Restany, "Forum: One Day Boredom Was Born from Uniformity," 2.

20. Ibid. For neuroscience, it is not possible to identify neural states of "rest" and "production," since the brain is always in motion. The functional and symbolic role of states of apparent aimless inactivity, such as "mind wandering" and "daydreaming," can no longer be referred to as "wasted" since they constitute moments of "diversified attention." According to Felicity Callard and Daniel Margulies, "the resting brain has been territorialized: it is conceptualized and materialised as a matrix that is constituted as perpetually productive, as intrinsically creative, and as thrown toward the future." Felicity Callard and Daniel Margulies, "The Industrious Suject: Cognitive Neuroscience's Revaluation of 'Rest,'" in *Cognitive Architecture. From Biopolitics to Noopolitics*, ed. Deborah Hauptmann and Warren Neidich (Rotterdam: 010 Publishers, 2010), 337.

21. "Forum: Eve & Adam," *Domus* 605 (1980), 4.

22. Ibid. 5. According to Peter Toohey, "if disgust protects humans from infection, boredom may protect them from infectious social situations: those that are confined, predictable, too samey for one's sanity." Toohey, *Boredom*, 15, 57.

23. Deborah Hauptmann and Warren Neidich, "Introduction," in *Cognitive Architecture: From Bio-Politics to Noo-Politics; Architecture & Mind in the Age of Communication and Information*, ed. Deborah Hauptmann and Warren Neidich (Rotterdam: 010 Publishers, 2010), 11.

24. "Forum: Eve & Adam," 5.

25. The repetition of weather echoes the relationship between sameness and desire described by Simone Weil: "Sameness is both the most beautiful and the most repulsive thing that exists. The most beautiful if it reflects eternity. The ugliest if it is a sign of something endless and unchangeable. Conquered time or infertile time. The symbol of beautiful sameness is the circle. The symbol of cruel sameness is the ticking of a pendulum." Quoted in Svendsen, *A Philosophy of Boredom*, 40, from Simone Weil, "The Power of Words," in *The Simone Weil Reader*, ed. George A. Panichas (1985).

26. W. Benjamin writes, "How fine the ironic overcoming of this attitude in the story of the splenetic Englishman who wakes up one morning and shoots himself because it's raining." W. Benjamin, *The Arcades Project*, 102.

27. "Forum: Eve & Adam," 5.

28. Allan Kaprow, "Forum: Interview with Allan Kaprow," *Domus* 605 (1980), 4.

29. Ibid. Kaprow's interest in the relationship between affections, time, and space was inspired by *Art as Experience* (1934) by John Dewey. In 1949, as a philosophy student, he wrote in the margins of a copy, "What is an authentic experience?" and "environment is a process of interaction." These concerns were influenced by principles of Zen Buddhism, popular in the post-war American generation of artists. According to Jeff Kelley, Kaprow never adopted Zen as a spiritual discipline, but after 1978, when he took personal guidance of a teacher on a daily

basis, he noticed "just how like certain aspects of Zen practice his works had actually become"—"the reduction of formalistic manoeuvres to nonsense; the heightened awareness of the present moment; methodism ... the willingness to let meanings drift through experience and then let them go." Jeff Kelley, *Childsplay: The Art of Allan Kaprow* (Berkeley: University of California Press, 2004), 200.

30. Kaprow, "Forum: Interview with Allan Kaprow," 4. Following these principles, Kaprow's work focused on the creation of spaces of possibilities. In 1965, he wrote, "The mood is growing among some younger architects to leave the contemporary 'neoclassic' style and to question the sacrosanct rectangle and arc which, with their variations, have dominated the shape of the art almost since its origins. Instead of a compass-and-ruler style, they are seeking one whose forms would emerge more from the feel of nature itself in all its variety and sense of the spontaneous and unplanned. When this happens, nature and architecture may truly ... become continuous." *Assemblage, Environment & Happening* (New York: Abrams, 1965), 151–2.

31. "Forum: Interview with Allan Kaprow," 5.

32. *Ticky-tacky*, a term included in the *Oxford English Dictionary* and credited to Malvina Reynolds, is a reference to the low-quality and low-cost material used in construction to make the development economically viable.

33. Hermann Grosser, "Forum: Instead of Boredom," *Domus* 605 (1980), 6.

34. Fulvio Irace, "Forum: Between Less & More," *Domus* 605 (1980), 7.

35. Quoted in ibid., from Lorenzo Pignotti, *La Treccia Donata: Poemetto Eroi-Comico* (Florence: Molini, Landi, e Comp., 1808).

36. Irace, "Forum: Between Less & More," 7.

37. Pierre Restany, "Forum: Restanystory—Encounter with Nam June Paik," *Domus* 605 (1980), 7.

38. Nam June Paik, "Video Art" (1976), http://nobetty.net/parsons_video/paik_inputoutput.pdf.

39. "Forum: Eve & Adam," 4.

40. Jameson, *Postmodernism*, 31.

41. Hauptmann and Neidich, *Cognitive Architecture*, 29.

Chapter 15

1. George Gordon Byron, *The Complete Poetical Works* (Oxford: Clarendon Books, 1986), 55 (italics in original); Oscar Wilde, "Lady Windermere's Fan," in *The Plays of Oscar Wilde* (Hertfordshire: Wordsworth, 2000), 168; Hilaire Belloc, "A Guide to Boring," in *A Conversation with a Cat* (Lepizig: Berbard Tauchnitz, 1931).

2. In this light, boredom appears similar to the mundane, which according to Simon During encompasses "those forms of life and experience that are not available for our moral or political or philosophical or religious or social aspirations and projects." Simon During, "Completing Secularism: The Mundane in the Neoliberal Era," in *Varieties of Secularism in a Secular Age*, ed. by Michael Warner, Jonathan Vanantwerpen, and Craig Calhoun (Cambridge: Harvard University Press, 2010), 113.

3. Kirk, "The Architecture of Servitude and Boredom," 114, 115; Bradley Birzer, *Russell Kirk: American Conservative* (Lexington: University Press of Kentucky, 2015), 145, 350. According to Kirk, "an ideology of Democratic Capitalism might be less malign than an ideology of

Communism or National Socialism or Anarchism, but it would not be much more intelligent or human." Quoted in *Russell Kirk*, 350, from Russell Kirk, "The Neoconservatives," in *Politics of Prudence* (Wilmington: ISI Books, 1993), 186-7.

4. "English Letters in the Age of Boredom," *Shenandoah* 7, no. 2 (1956): 3-15. In 1953, Kirk published an amended version of his doctoral dissertation under the title *The Conservative Mind*. Considered his magnum opus, it outlines six fundamental principles of conservative thinking. The first affirms the need for a "belief in a transcendent order, or body of natural law, which rules society as well as conscience," posing political problems as religious and moral concerns. The second refers to the need for "proliferating variety" in order to delve into the "mystery of human existence," opposed to "the narrowing uniformity, egalitarianism, and utilitarian aims of most radical systems." The third points to the conviction that a "civilized society requires orders and classes, as against the notion of a 'classless society.'" The fourth relates freedom to property, following the assumption that "economic levelling ... is not economic progress." The fifth questions any attempt to reconstruct society upon the abstract design of "sophisters, calculators, and economists." And the last acknowledges that change does not entail progress; however, "society must alter, for prudent change is the means of social preservation." The publication has seven editions—the last from 2001—and was reworked as the *Portable Conservative Reader* (1982) and transformed into ten principles in the *Politics of Prudence* (1993). They celebrate "permanent things," or "all that makes human life worth living, particularly the bedrock principles that have traditionally supported and maintained the health of society's central institutions: family, church and school." *The Conservative Mind: From Burke to Eliot* (Washington D.C.: Regnery 1986), 8-9.

5. Ibid.

6. For Kirk, Eliot's literary career constituted a "protest against the causes of ... boredom." In 1971, Kirk wrote a biography titled *Eliot and His Age: T. S. Eliot's Moral Imagination in the Twentieth Century*.

7. *Eliot and His Age: T. S. Eliot's Moral Imagination in the Twentieth Century* (Wilmington: ISI Books, 2008), 330-1.

8. As a proof of the increase of "social boredom," Kirk notes that, between 1937 and 1948, the crime in York had doubled. "York and Social Boredom," *The Sewanee Review* 61, no. 4 (1953): 666-7, 670.

9. *Eliot and His Age*, 285. This echoes the estrangement present in *The Waste Land* (1922) by Eliot:

> Trams and dusty trees.
> Highbury bore me. Richmond and Kew
> Undid me. By Richmond I raised my knees
> Supine on the floor of a narrow canoe.
> T. S. Eliot, *The Waste Land* (Philadelphia: Pennsylvania State University, 2000)

10. Kirk, "York and Social Boredom," 665. Writing about university education in the United States, Kirk affirmed that "multidiversity is a delusion. Apprenticeship, specialised training, part-time employment, and projects of the sort that William James called 'the moral equivalent of war' would be far better for most young people than four years of fun and games, or (more commonly) four years of sullen resentment, in a nominally liberal college or a nominally philosophical university." "Rebellion against Boredom," in *Seeds of Anarchy: A Study of Campus Revolution*, ed. Frederick Wilhelmsen (Dallas: Argus, 1969), 227, 235.

11. *Eliot and His Age*, 306; "York and Social Boredom," 667, 670.

12. Quoted in *Eliot and His Age*, 285, from T. S. Eliot, *Notes Towards the Definition of Culture* (London: Faber & Faber, 2010), 116.
13. In reference to John Henry Newman in *Discussions and Arguments on Various Subjects* (1885).Kirk, *The Conservative Mind*, 285.
14. Kirk, "The Architecture of Servitude and Boredom," 115.
15. Ibid., 114.
16. Ibid., 114, 118.
17. Ibid., 114. In 1952, Kirk planned to write a book on social boredom in the United Kingdom, titled *Vignettes of Welfare States*. The project was never realized. Birzer, *Russell Kirk*, 15.
18. Kirk, "The Architecture of Servitude and Boredom," 114, 120.
19. *The Conservative Mind*, 204.
20. "The Architecture of Servitude and Boredom," 118.
21. Ibid., 120.
22. Ibid., 116.
23. Gerald Russello, *The Postmodern Imagination of Russell Kirk* (Columbia: University of Missouri Press, 2007), 48; Kirk, "The Architecture of Servitude and Boredom," 119.
24. Quoted in "The Architecture of Servitude and Boredom," 116 (italics in original), from Eliot, *Notes Towards the Definition of Culture*, 117.
25. Quoted in Birzer, *Russell Kirk*, 400, from Russell Kirk, *Beyond the Dreams of Avarice* (Washington D.C.: Regnery, 1956), 215.
26. Kirk, "The Architecture of Servitude and Boredom," 116. In the same line of identifying problems and solutions, Alice Coleman exposes modern architecture as a case to be put on trial, asking, "What went wrong?" Her study of more than 100,000 dwellings in Britain is posed as evidence for the prosecution of the design and layout of modern estates. It links social malaise, from vandalism to alcoholism, to the architecture after World War II. Alice Coleman, *Utopia on Trial. Vision and Reality in Planned Housing* (London: Hilary Shipman, 1994).
27. Kirk, "The Architecture of Servitude and Boredom," 116. Gordon Bunshaft, as partner of Skidmore, Owings, and Merrill, designed the Lyndon B. Johnson Library in Austin, Texas. It opened in 1971.
28. Ibid., 116–17.
29. Ibid., 117. Kirk agrees with this, affirming that "our obsession with fast cars and our longing for the prestige of a suburban house have driven freeways remorselessly through a thousand living communities, destroying everything in their path, these appetites have drained leadership and money out of our cities, at the same time devouring the countryside through subdivisions, so that capitalistic America fulfils the prophecy of Marx that countryside and town must merge in one blur." Quoted in Birzer, *Russell Kirk*, 400, from Russell Kirk, "The Uninteresting Future," *Commonwealth* (1960), 248.
30. "The Architecture of Servitude and Boredom," 117.
31. Ibid.
32. For Doreen Massey, while the aphorism "space is a social construct" is proper to the 1970s, the idea that "the social is spatially constructed too" characterizes the 1980s. Doreen Massey, "Politics and Space/Time," in *Place and the Politics of Identity*, ed. Michael Keith and Steve Pile (London: Routledge, 1993), 145–6.
33. According to Laurie Langbauer, "boredom with the everyday points to it as the site of the ideological; this explained why the situationists were so vehemently against boredom.

'Boredom is counterrevolutionary,' they wrote in their journal, 'In every way.'" Laurie Langbauer, "The City, the Everyday, and Boredom: The Case of Sherlock Holmes," *Differences* 5, no. 3 (1993): 86, citing "The Bad Days Will End," *Situationist International* 7 (1962).

34. Quoted in Birzer, *Russell Kirk*, 397, from Russell Kirk, "Boredom Is the Deadly Enemy," *Ada Evening News* (1966), 9.
35. Quoted in Birzer, *Russell Kirk*, 397–8, from Kirk, "Boredom Is the Deadly Enemy," 9.
36. Ibid.; "Rebellion against Boredom," 31. In 1949, Kirk wrote to Bill McCann that "vice and indolence and bitter discontent are characteristics overwhelmingly general in our age. The more we look at these conditions, the more probable it appears that vice and indolence and discontent are scum upon a stagnant pool of social boredom and frustration." Quoted in Birzer, *Russell Kirk*, 145, from Russell Kirk, *A Program for Conservatives* (Chicago: Regnery, 1954), 103.
37. "The Architecture of Servitude and Boredom," 114, 115, 118, 119.
38. Quoted in Birzer, *Russell Kirk*, 400, from Kirk, "The Uninteresting Future," 247. For Kirk, TV and other media were also responsible for the rise of impatience: "Nor should we forget that young people between the ages of seventeen and twenty-one, in this year of Our Lord, have been fed the pabulum of television all their days. The TV producer must solve every personal or social problem within half an hour, or an hour at most; and students are indignant when the difficulties of the college, or the nation, or the world, are not resolved with equal celerity by the possessors of power. Man and society are perfectible on the flickering screen: surely we all would be utterly happy if only some wretched university president or some crepuscular military-industrial cabal were brought to heel." Kirk, "Rebellion against Boredom," 33.
39. "York and Social Boredom," 665. Referring to college protests in the late 1960s, Kirk observes that "War in Viet Nam [*sic*], Black Power, 'authoritarianism' at universities, opposition to the 'military-industrial complex', and other pretexts for students' rebellion are pretexts only. Really, the principal reason for discontent among college and university students is boredom: boredom among the better students because the modern American university offers too little for mind and conscience; boredom among the poorer students because they never should have enrolled at all." "Rebellion against Boredom," 26.
40. "The Architecture of Servitude and Boredom," 121.
41. Quoted in Russello, *The Postmodern Imagination of Russell Kirk*, 52, from Russell Kirk, *Redeeming the Time*, ed. Jeffrey Nelson (Wilmington: ISI, 1996), 131.
42. Quoted in Birzer, *Russell Kirk*, 404, from Russell Kirk, *Confessions of a Bohemian Tory: Episodes and Reflections of a Vagrant Career* (New York: Fleet, 1963), 23.

Chapter 16

1. "Generic," in *The Shorter Oxford English Dictionary*, ed. C. T. Onions (Oxford: Clarendon Press), 841; "Generic," in *Online Etymology Dictionary*, ed. Douglas Harper (2016), http://www.etymonline.com/index.php?term=generic.
2. Charles Jencks, *The Language of Post-Modern Architecture*, 3rd ed. (London: Academy, 1981), 3, 13; *Critical Modernism. Where Is Post-Modernism Going?* (London: Wiley-Academy, 2007), 211.
3. "How Big Is Bad?," *The Architectural Review* (2002), 67, 68.

4. Christian Parreno, "Interview with Charles Jencks" (2014); Rem Koolhaas and Bruce Mau, "Bigness or the Problem of Large," in *S,M,L,XL* (Rotterdam: 010 Publishers 1995), 510.
5. Christian Parreno, "Interview with Rem Koolhaas" (2012); Lieven de Cauter, *The Capsular Civilization. On the City in the Age of Fear* (Rotterdam: NAi, 2004), 15.
6. Parreno, "Interview with Charles Jencks."
7. "Interview with Rem Koolhaas." Jencks confesses that he has tried to discuss the Ivan Illich Law with Koolhaas, but the latter is not interested. Jencks, "Charles Jencks on the Power Law of Bad Architecture," *The Architectural Review* (2013), 32.
8. Koolhaas, "The Generic City," 1248 (italics in original); Cauter, *The Capsular Civilization*, 12.
9. Charles Jencks, "Generic Individualism—the Reigning Style of Our Time—and Its Discontents," *The Bartlett International Lecture Series 2015/16* (London: 2015). The original quote is, "it exists; at most, it coexists. Its subtext is *fuck* context." Koolhaas and Mau, "Bigness," 502 (italics in original).
10. Jencks explains, "I borrowed it from a historian of Roman architecture, William L. MacDonald. We were discussing the subject and he said, 'oh you mean monothematitis'. I said, 'spot on'. I was very taken by that. He was referring to Roman architecture that repeats, repeats, repeats the same—get a good idea and repeat it ad nauseum." Christian Parreno, "Interview with Charles Jencks."
11. Ibid. Jencks's quote by Mailer is from a 1963 article in which modern architecture is related to totalitarianism: "by dislocating us from the most powerful emotions of reality, totalitarianism leaves us further isolated in the empty landscapes of psychosis, precisely that inner landscape of void and dread which we flee by turning to totalitarian styles of life." Norman Mailer, "The Big Bite," *Esquire* 357 (1963), 24.
12. Carl Mitcham, "Ivan Illich: Critic of Professionalized Design," *Design Issues* 19, no. 4 (2003): 26.
13. Ivan Illich, *Energy and Equity* (New York: Harper & Row, 1974), 76.
14. Parreno, "Interview with Charles Jencks."
15. Ibid. The "organization man" is a reference to the observations on American society by David Riesman in *The Lonely Crowd* (1950).
16. In 2011, without referring to bigness or his Law of Diminishing Architecture, Jencks illustrated boredom with the Water Cube building for swimming sports, designed by PTW Architects for the Beijing Olympics of 2008. He affirmed that it "is a 'heroic Box' and, in a way, the ultimate postmodern oxymoron. Note the compressed opposites. Rippling cube, three-dimensional flatness, energetic boredom, ever-changing sameness and—because it culminates the 3000 years search for the minimal surface with maximal packing—The Wobbly Perfection! ... Is this complexity really cultural progress? From 1000 BC and the Platonic beehive of regular hexagons, we have evolved to this postmodern culmination—irregular regularity." Charles Jencks, *The Story of Post-Modernism* (London: Wiley 2011), 186. In 2014, clarifying that he is "a great fan of Rem and a very good friend," Jencks vehemently condemned De Rotterdam (2013), blaming the economic forces behind its production but also questioning the premises of the design: "when it was designed in 1989, that far back, the façades had different bay rhythms, and it had an interesting podium and an interesting sequence of space, but the developer got rid of everything. Why? Why? Why? Too big, too much programme." Parreno, "Interview with Charles Jencks."

17. Jencks, "How Big Is Bad?," 68.
18. Daimler-Benz, Sony Berlin, Herti, and ABB.
19. "How Big Is Bad?," 67.
20. "Post-Modernism between Kitsch and Culture," *Architectural Design* (1990), 29, 26; Parreno, "Interview with Charles Jencks."
21. "I think that more interesting wallpaper is better than less interesting wallpaper." Jencks affirms that he has discussed the law with Pelli, "who did not entirely agree." Ibid.; Jencks, "Charles Jencks on the Power Law of Bad Architecture," 32.
22. "Post-Modernism between Kitsch and Culture," 25–6.
23. *The Language of Post-Modern Architecture*, 13–14.
24. Parreno, "Interview with Charles Jencks."
25. Jencks, *The Language of Post-Modern Architecture*, 14.
26. "Charles Jencks on the Power Law of Bad Architecture," 32; "Post-Modernism between Kitsch and Culture," 29.
27. Jencks, "How Big Is Bad?," 68.
28. Parreno, "Interview with Charles Jencks."
29. The CCTV Headquarters was recognized as the Best Tall Building in 2013 by the Council of Tall Buildings and Urban Habitat. The Interlace, designed in collaboration with Ole Scheeren, was named Building of the Year in 2015 by the World Architecture Awards. Jencks, "How Big Is Bad?," 68.
30. Jencks clarifies, "every time I say universe I should say 'our universe' because we know that there might be multiple universes." Parreno, "Interview with Charles Jencks."
31. Ibid. Recent research from the University of Colorado affirms that "the Hubble expansion is isotropic to 7 per cent," suggesting that in the universe isotropy prevails but it does not entail symmetry. Jeremy Darling, "The Hubble Expansion Is Isotropic in the Epoch of Dark Energy," *MNRAS* 441, no. 1 (2014): 67–70; Michael Byrne, "New Measurements Confirm that the Universe Is Boring," *Motherboard* (2014), http://motherboard.vice.com/read/new-measurements-the-universe-is-boring.
32. Koolhaas and Mau, "Bigness," 498.
33. "The absence of a theory of Bigness—what is the maximum architecture can do—is architecture's most debilitating weakness. . . . Because there is no theory of Bigness, we don't know what to do with it, we don't know where to put it, we don't know when to use it, we don't know how to plan it." "Bigness," 509; Cauter, *The Capsular Civilization*, 20.
34. Rem Koolhaas and Bruce Mau, *S,M,L,XL* (Rotterdam: 010 Publishers, 1995), 70. These definitions can be traced to 1989, in a short article for *Design Book Review* in which Koolhaas affirms that "if my interest in the banal architecture of the 1950's and 1960's, the derivatives of Ernesto Rogers and Richard Neutra, seems a somewhat boring source, I can only answer that to die of boredom is not so bad. There were much worse architects than Neutra. But let's face it. I like that kind of architecture, and quite often it has been magnificently built. It has also at times reached a carefreeness and a freedom that interests me—not that I'm the only one to take an interest in it. But the question at stake is what Bruno Vayssière and Patrice Noviant have defined as 'statistic architecture': power architecture whose power is easy, that has moved without transition from the isolated experience to the series, from the series to repetition, and so on until you get sick of it. I'm trying to live with it but also to detach myself from it. And since nostalgia disturbs me, I'm trying more and more not to be modern, but to be contemporary." Rem Koolhaas, "Towards the Contemporary City,"

in *Theorizing a New Agenda for Architecture*, ed. Kate Nesbitt (New York: Princeton Architectural Press, 1996), 330.

35. "The Generic City," in *S,M,L,XL* (Rotterdam: 010 Publishers, 1995), 1252, 1256, 1257.
36. Antonio Negri, "On Rem Koolhaas," *Radical Philosophy* 154(2009): 48; Cauter, *The Capsular Civilization*, 14.
37. Koolhaas, "The Generic City," 1251.
38. Ibid., 1253, 1261.
39. Ibid., 1262. Cauter, *The Capsular Civilization*, 15.
40. Koolhaas, "The Generic City," 1260.
41. Ibid., 1262.
42. Parreno, "Interview with Rem Koolhaas."
43. Koolhaas, "The Generic City," 1250, 1262–3, 1257.
44. Ibid., 1250, 1254, 1260, 1261, 1255 (italics in original); Parreno, "Interview with Rem Koolhaas"; Lee Stickells, "Flow Urbanism: The Heterotopia of Flows," in *Heterotopia and the City. Public Space in a Postcivil Society*, ed. Michael Dehaene and Lieven de Cauter (London: Routledge, 2008), 255. The notion of "smooth space" was outlined by Gilles Deleuze and Félix Guattari in *A Thousand Plateaus: Capitalism and Schizophrenia* (1980).
45. Marc Augé, *Non-Places. Introduction to an Anthropology of Supermodernity*, trans. John Howe (London: Verso, 1995), 4.
46. To Augé, "the term 'space' is more abstract in itself than the term 'place', whose usage at least refers to an event (which has taken place), a myth (said to have taken place) or history (high places). It is applied in much the same way to an area, a distance between two things or points (a two-metre 'space' is left between the posts of a fence) or to temporal expanse ('in the space of a week'). It is thus eminently abstract." Ibid., 77–8, 82.
47. Ibid., 77–8, 96.
48. Ibid., 79.
49. Quoted in ibid., 80.

Chapter 17

1. Silvetti confesses that images "generate a lot of energy in my mind . . . and allow me to establish a narrative. . . . When I think, I have them in my mind. I do know that scholars do not need images, even architectural historians. . . . I think they are indispensable." Christian Parreno, "Interview with Jorge Silvetti" (2015).
2. Michel Foucault, *Discipline and Punish. The Birth of the Prison*, trans. Alan Sheridan (London: Penguin, 1979), 170.
3. Silvetti also delivered the lecture in Spanish, at the Universidad San Francisco de Quito, and the Pontificia Universidad Católica de Chile, with the title "Las musas no se divierten," which is closer to "The Muses Are Not Having Fun," a translation that fails to capture the same meaning of "The Muses Are Not Amused." Jorge Silvetti, "The 2002 Walter Gropius Lecture: A Note from Jorge Silvetti," in *Introductions: Jorge Silvetti*, ed. Rodolphe el-Khoury (Cambridge: Harvard University Graduate School of Design, 2004), 122; Parreno, "Interview with Jorge Silvetti."

4. Jorge Silvetti, "The Muses Are Not Amused: Pandemonium in the House of Architecture," in *The New Architectural Pragmatism*, ed. William Saunders (Minneapolis: University of Minnesota Press, 2007), 197, 176, 177.
5. Ibid., 178.
6. Ibid., 182.
7. Ibid., 184, 185, 186. *The Muses Are Not Amused: Pandemonium in the House of Architecture* (Cambridge: Harvard University Graduate School of Design, 2004), CD. The reference to the Teletubbies was not included in the print version of the lecture.
8. "The Muses Are Not Amused," 186–7, 188.
9. Ibid., 178, 188.
10. Parreno, "Interview with Jorge Silvetti"; Silvetti, "The Muses Are Not Amused," 188, 189.
11. Ibid., 189, 193.
12. "The Muses Are Not Amused," 197, 196. The lecture was revised for inclusion in *The New Architectural Pragmatism* (2007), edited by William Saunders.
13. Parreno, "Interview with Jorge Silvetti."
14. Ibid.
15. "Interview with Sylvia Lavin" (2014).
16. Sylvia Lavin, *Kissing Architecture* (Princeton: Princeton University Press, 2011), 15–16. Lavin references the following texts by Greenberg: "Modernist Painting" (1965), in *The New Art: A Critical Anthology*, ed. Gregory Battock (New York: E. P. Dutton, 1966), 100–11; "Towards a Newer Laocoon," in *Art in Theory, 1900–1990: An Anthology of Changing Ideas*, ed. Charles Harrison and Paul Wood (Oxford: Blackwell, 1992), 554–60; and "Avant-Garde and Kitsch," *Partisan Review* 6, no. 5 (Fall 1939): 34–49.
17. Lavin, *Kissing Architecture*, 18–19.
18. Parreno, "Interview with Sylvia Lavin." For Lavin, the difference between modernism and postmodernism is evident in the preference of Robert Venturi for the interesting and his indictment of Mies van der Rohe as a bore: "the only thing they had in common was that neither wanted to be bad. The aversion to being bad, even at the risk of becoming boring, may be their most significant and only shared legacy." Lavin, "Lying Fallow," *Log* 29 (2013): 17.
19. Ibid., 23, 24.
20. Ibid., 18, 19.
21. Ibid., 22.
22. Parreno, "Interview with Sylvia Lavin."
23. Lavin, "Lying Fallow," 24. The recommendation to her students was repeated in several sessions of the Ph.D. seminar that Lavin held in the fall of 2014.
24. Parreno, "Interview with Sylvia Lavin." When asked about the favoritism of American academia for the object and the archive, Lavin replied, "I would think that subjectivities are also things that one could think of as agents, and I would probably be apt to start thinking about things in terms of a field of agents. But I do think that post-structuralism in general found it difficult to address particularities, even in its critique of the universal and so forth. It had its own system for converting everything into a sign value.... I think that the shift in scholarship more broadly is to try to think about things in a less fundamentally semiotically driven way." Ibid.
25. Ibid.

26. "Interview with Jorge Silvetti."
27. Lavin, "Lying Fallow," 24.
28. As Foucault explains, "We should admit rather that power produces knowledge (and not simply by encouraging it because it serves power or by applying it because it is useful); that power and knowledge directly imply one another; that there is no power relation without the correlative constitution of a field of knowledge, nor any knowledge that does nor presuppose and constitute at the same time power relations." Foucault, *Discipline and Punish*, 27.
29. Lavin, "Lying Fallow," 23.
30. Parreno, "Interview with Jorge Silvetti."
31. To Barthes, "The reduction of reading to a consumption is clearly responsible for the 'boredom' experienced by many in the face of the modern ('unreadable') text." Roland Barthes, *Image, Music, Text*, trans. Stephen Heath (New York: Hill and Wang, 1978), 163 (italics in original).
32. Joseph Brodsky, *Less Than One: Selected Essays* (London: Penguin, 2011), 18.
33. Lydia Davis, "Not Interested," in *Can't and Won't* (London: Hamish Hamilton, 2014), 240, 241.

Epilogue

1. For example, the exhibition in the Central Pavilion featured the work of Maria Giuseppina Grasso as "resistance against the banality and mediocrity of the built environment," and David Chipperfield identified boredom as a social problem to confront in Sudan. In addition, the pavilion of Great Britain was dedicated to "Home Economics," the one of Spain to the "Unfinished," and the exhibition of Taiwan to "Everyday Architecture."
2. Quoted in Nicholas Weber, *Le Corbusier: A Life* (New York: Knopf, 2008), 52, 76 (italics in original).
3. Siegfried Kracauer, "Boredom," in *The Mass Ornament: Weimar Essays* (Cambridge: Harvard University Press, 1995), 332.
4. The debate took place at the Harvard University Graduate School of Design, on November 17, 1982. Christopher Alexander and Peter Eisenman, "Contrasting Concepts of Harmony in Architecture: The 1982 Debate between Christopher Alexander and Peter Eisenman," *Katarxis* 3 (1982), http://www.katarxis3.com/Alexander_Eisenman_Debate.htm.
5. Ibid.
6. According to Herbert Morris, "you can be bored and hope that something will come along and will make you feel alive. In despair, you have given up. That can be accompanied with such rage against your fate and the world that you do anything—violence can be expressed." Parreno, "Interview with Herbert Morris."
7. B. R., "Boring Cities: Torporville," *The Economist* (2015), http://www.economist.com/blogs/gulliver/2015/05/boring-cities.
8. The reference is from Jeet Heer, who wrote "Canadian boringness isn't intrinsic. 'It's something we work at, cherish and reward.'" John Kay, "Why the 'Happiest' Cities Are Boring," *Financial Times* (2015), http://www.ft.com/cms/s/2/1b915f0e-517b-11e5-b029-b9d50a74fd14.html.
9. B. R., "Boring Cities: Torporville."
10. In reference to Gertrude Stein, from a column by Jeremy Clarkson (the television presenter of *Top Gear*, a program dedicated to testing and driving fast cars) in the *Daily Telegraph*: "The thing is, though, I like Detroit because it's dangerous. As Gertrude Stein would have said:

'There's a there, there.' It's often argued that you never feel more alive than at the point of death and that is what makes Motor City so vibrant and zesty. When you know for sure there's a mugger round the next bend, you make the most of walking around it." The phrase by Stein is from *Everybody's Autobiography* (1937). Ibid.

11. Kierkegaard, *Either/Or*, 49.
12. Heidegger, *The Fundamental Concepts of Metaphysics*, 71.
13. A. Benjamin, "Boredom and Distraction," 156.

BIBLIOGRAPHY

Archival Sources and Interviews

Architectural League of New York Records, 1880s–1974. Archives of American Art, Smithsonian Institution, Washington D.C.
Douglas Putnam Haskell Papers. Avery Architectural & Fine Arts Library. Columbia University, New York.
Parreno, Christian. "Interview with Charles Jencks." 2014.
Parreno, Christian. "Interview with Herbert Morris." 2014.
Parreno, Christian. "Interview with Jorge Silvetti." 2015.
Parreno, Christian. "Interview with Rem Koolhaas." 2012.
Parreno, Christian. "Interview with Sylvia Lavin." 2014.
Philip Johnson Papers. Museum of Modern Art, New York.

Published Sources

Abercrombie, Stanley. "A Few Good Buildings: Reading the Obituaries of Philip Johnson." *The American Scholar* 74, no. 2 (2005): 117–20.
Adorno, Theodor. *Kierkegaard: Construction of the Aesthetic.* Translated by Robert Hullot-Kentor. Minneapolis: University of Minnesota Press, 1989.
Adorno, Theodor. *The Culture Industry. Selected Essays on Mass Culture.* London: Routledge, 1991.
AFP. "Bored Japanese Trucker Gets Kicks from Syria War Tourism." *Al Arabiya News* (2013). http://english.alarabiya.net/articles/2013/01/03/258384.html.
Agamben, Giorgio. *The Open: Man and Animal.* Translated by Kevin Attell. Palo Alto: Stanford University Press, 2004.
Åhäll, Linda, and Thomas Gregory. *Emotions, Politics and War.* London: Taylor & Francis, 2015.
Ahmed, S. M. S. "Psychometric Properties of the Boredom Proneness Scale." *Perceptual Motor Skills* 71, no. 3 (1990): 963–6.
Aho, Kevin. *Heidegger's Neglect of the Body.* Albany: State University of New York Press, 2009.
Aho, Kevin. "Simmel on Acceleration, Boredom, and Extreme Aesthesia." *Journal for the Theory of Social Behaviour* 37, no. 4 (2007): 447–62.
"Aldine Club Luncheon without Maxim Gorky." *The New York Times* (1906). http://query.nytimes.com/mem/archivefree/pdf?res=F10914FB3A5A12738DDDA00994DC405B868CF1D3.
Alexander, Christopher, and Peter Eisenman. "Contrasting Concepts of Harmony in Architecture: The 1982 Debate between Christopher Alexander and Peter Eisenman." *Katarxis* 3 (1982). http://www.katarxis3.com/Alexander_Eisenman_Debate.htm.
Anderson, Patricia. *The Printed Image and the Transformation of Popular Culture, 1790–1860.* Oxford: Clarendon Press, 1991.
Aquinas, Thomas. *Summa Theologica, Secunda Secundae.* The Gutenberg Project, 2006. http://www.gutenberg.org/cache/epub/18755/pg18755.html.
"Architecture—Fitting and Befitting." *Architectural Forum* (1961).
Atelier Mendini. "Committenze." http://www.ateliermendini.it/index.php?mact=News,cntnt01,detail,0&cntnt01articleid=16&cntnt01origid=59&cntnt01lang=en_US&cntnt01returnid=62.

Bibliography

Augé, Marc. *Non-Places. Introduction to an Anthropology of Supermodernity*. Translated by John Howe. London: Verso, 1995.
Ballard, J. G. *Crash*. London: Harper Perennial, 2008.
Banham, Mary. "The 1960s." In Reyner Banham, *A Critic Writes: Essays by Reyner Banham*, edited by Mary Banham, Sutherland Lyall, Cedric Price, and Paul Barker. Berkeley: University of California Press, 1996.
Banham, Reyner. "A Home Is Not a House." *Art in America* 2 (1965): 70–9.
Banham, Reyner. "L.A.: The Structure Behind the Scene." *Architectural Design* 41 (1971): 227–30.
Banham, Reyner. *Los Angeles: The Architecture of Four Ecologies*. London: Penguin, 1971.
Banham, Reyner. *Reyner Banham Loves Los Angeles*. London: BBC, 1972.
Banham, Reyner. *The Architecture of the Well-Tempered Environment*. London: Architectural Press, 1969.
Banham, Reyner. "The Haunted Highway." *New Society* 52 (1980): 297–9.
Barbalet, Jack. "Boredom and Social Meaning." *The British Journal of Sociology* 50, no. 4 (1999): 631–46.
Barnhart, Robert K., and Sol Steinmetz. *Chambers Dictionary of Etymology*. Edinburgh: Chambers, 1988.
Barthes, Roland. *Image, Music, Text*. Translated by Stephen Heath. New York: Hill and Wang, 1978.
Barthes, Roland. *Incidents*. Translated by Richard Howard. Berkeley: University of California Press, 1992.
Barthes, Roland. *Mythologies*. London: Vintage Classics, 2000.
Barthes, Roland. *The Pleasure of the Text*. New York: Hill & Wang, 1975.
Bataille, Georges. *Visions of Excess*. Translated by Allan Stoekl, Carl Lovitt, and Donald Leslie, edited by Allan Stoekl. Minneapolis: University of Minnesota Press, 1985.
Baudelaire, Charles. "Spleen." Translated by Roy Campbell. In *Poems of Baudelaire*, edited by Roy Campbell. New York: Pantheon Books, 1952.
Baudrillard, Jean. *America*. London, 1988.
Beauvoir, Simone de. "America Day by Day." In *Writing Los Angeles: A Literary Anthology*, edited by David Ulin. New York: Library of America, 2002.
Beckert, Sven. *Empire of Cotton: A Global History*. New York: Vintage Books, 2015.
Beistegui, Miguel de. *Thinking with Heidegger: Displacements*. Bloomington: Indiana University Press, 2003.
Belloc, Hilaire. "A Guide to Boring." In *A Conversation with a Cat*. Lepizig: Berbard Tauchnitz, 1931.
Bench, Shane, and Heather Lench. "On the Function of Boredom." *Behavioral Sciences* 3, no. 3 (2013): 459–72.
Benjamin, Andrew. "Boredom and Distraction: The Moods of Modernity." In *Walter Benjamin and History*, edited by Andrew Benjamin. London: Continuum, 2005.
Benjamin, Walter. "Boredom, Eternal Return." Translated by Howard Eiland and Kevin McLaughlin. In *The Arcades Project*, edited by Rolf Tiedemann. Cambridge: Belknap, 1999.
Benjamin, Walter. "The Storyteller: Reflections on the Works of Nikolai Leskov." In *The Novel: An Anthology of Criticism and Theory 1900–2000*, edited by Dorothy Hale. Malden: Blackwell Publishing, 2006.
Benjamin, Walter. *Walter Benjamin: Selected Writings, 4: 1938–1940*, edited by Howard Eiland and Michael Jennings. Cambridge: Belknap, 2006.
Bergson, Henri. *Time and Free Will: An Essay on the Immediate Data of Consciousness*. Mineola: Dover Publications, 2001.
Berlant, Lauren. *The Female Complaint*. Durham: Duke University Press, 2008.
Berman, Eliza. "How a California School Cured 'Advanced Causes of Housewife Boredom.'" *Time* (2015). http://time.com/4000588/school-for-bored-housewives/.

Bibliography

Berman, Marshall. *All That Is Solid Melts into Air: The Experience of Modernity.* London: Verso, 1983.

Birzer, Bradley. *Russell Kirk: American Conservative.* Lexington: University Press of Kentucky, 2015.

Blanchot, Maurice. *The Infinite Conversation.* Translated by Susan Hanson. Minneapolis: University of Minnesota Press, 1993.

Blaszczynski, A., N. McConaghy, and A. Frankova. "Boredom Proneness in Pathological Gambling." *Psychological Reports* 67, no. 1 (1990): 35–42.

Blom, Ina. "Boredom and Oblivion." In *The Fluxus Reader*, edited by Ken Friedman. London: Academy Editions, 1998.

Borden, Iain. "Beyond Space. The Ideas of Henri Lefebvre in Relation to Architecture and Cities." Unpublished: The Bartlett, UCL, 2006.

Borden, Iain. *Drive. Journeys through Film, Cities and Landscapes.* London: Reaktion, 2013.

Borden, Iain. "Space Beyond: Space and the City in the Writings of Georg Simmel." *The Journal of Architecture* 2 (1997): 313–35.

Boredom at Work: The Empty Life. Oklahoma State Department of Health, 1961.

Boredom at Work: The Search for Zest. Oklahoma State Department of Health, 1962.

Braudel, Fernand. *A History of Civilizations.* London: Allen Lane/Penguin, 1994.

Briton, Annie, and Martin J. Shipley. "Bored to Death?" *International Journal of Epidemiology*, no. 39 (2010): 370–1.

Brittain-Catlin, Timothy. *Bleak Houses: Disappointment and Failure in Architecture.* Cambridge: MIT Press, 2014.

Brodsly, David. *L.A. Freeway: An Appreciative Essay.* Berkeley, 1981.

Bukowski, Charles. *Post Office.* London: Ebury Publishing, 2011.

Burton, Robert, H. Jackson, and W. H. Gass. *The Anatomy of Melancholy.* New York: New York Review of Books, 2001.

Byrne, Michael. "New Measurements Confirm that the Universe Is Boring." *Motherboard* (2014). http://motherboard.vice.com/read/new-measurements-the-universe-is-boring.

Byron, George Gordon. *The Complete Poetical Works.* Oxford: Clarendon Books, 1986.

Cache, Bernard. *Projectiles.* London: Architectural Association, 2011.

Cain, James M. "Paradise." In *Writing Los Angeles: A Literary Anthology*, edited by David Ulin. New York: Library of America, 2002.

Callard, Felicity, and Daniel Margulies. "The Industrious Suject: Cognitive Neuroscience's Revaluation of 'Rest.'" In *Cognitive Architecture. From Biopolitics to Noopolitics*, edited by Deborah Hauptmann and Warren Neidich. Rotterdam: 010 Publishers, 2010.

Camus, Albert. "Death in the Soul." Translated by Ellen Conroy Kennedy. In *Lyrical and Critical Essays*, edited by Philip Thody. London: Vintage, 1968.

Camus, Albert. "The Minotaur, or the Stop in Oran." Translated by Justin O'Brien. In *The Myth of Sisyphus and Other Essays.* New York: Vintage Books, 1955.

Camus, Albert. *The Outsider.* Translated by Joseph Laredo. London: Penguin, 1983.

Camus, Albert. *The Plague.* Translated by Stuart Gilbert. London: Penguin, 2001.

Cardamone, Caterina. "Classical Tradition in Josef Frank's Writings." Unpublished: Université Catholique de Louvain-la-Neuve, 2015.

Carson, Anne. *Eros the Bittersweet.* London: Dalkey Archive Press, 1998.

Casciani, Stefano. "Interview with Alessandro Mendini." In *Rem Koolhaas, Norman Foster, and Alessandro Mendini, Colours: Rem Koolhaas/Oma, Norman Foster, Alessandro Mendini.* Basel: Birkhäuser, 2001.

Cassirer, Ernst. *Philosophy of Symbolic Forms*, vol. 2: "Mythical Thought." Translated by Ralph Manheim. New Haven: Yale University Press, 1955.

Cauter, Lieven de. *The Capsular Civilization. On the City in the Age of Fear.* Rotterdam: NAi, 2004.

Bibliography

Cheney, George. *The English Malady: Or, a Treatise of Nervous Diseased of All Kinds, as Spleen, Vapour, Lowness of Spirits, Hypocondriacal, and Hysterical Distempers, Etc.* London: G. Straham, 1733.

Chtcheglov, Ivan. "Formulary for a New Urbanism." *Bureau of Public Secrets* (1953). http://www.bopsecrets.org/SI/Chtcheglov.htm.

Cioran, Emil. *History and Utopia*. Translated by Richard Howard. New York: Seaver, 1987.

Cioran, Emil. *Tears and Saints*. Translated by Ilinca Zarifopol-Johnston. Chicago: The University of Chicago Press, 1995.

Clark, Stuart. *Vanities of the Eye: Vision in Early Modern European Culture*. Oxford: Oxford University Press, 2007.

Cleaves, Margaret. *Autobiography of a Neurasthene: As Told by One of Them and Recorded by Dr. Margaret A. Cleaves*. Boston: R.G. Badger, 1910.

Coleman, Alice. *Utopia on Trial. Vision and Reality in Planned Housing*. London: Hilary Shipman, 1994.

Colomina, Beatriz, Craig Buckley, and Urtzi Grau, eds. *Clip, Stamp, Fold: The Radical Architecture of Little Magazines, 196x to 197x*. New York: Actar, 2010.

Commoner, Barry. "Los Angeles Air." In *The Closing Circle: Nature, Man and Technology*. New York: Alfred A. Knopf, 1971.

Dahlen, Eric R., Ryan C. Martin, Katie Ragan, and Myndi M. Kuhlman. "Boredom Proneness in Anger and Aggression: Effects of Impulsiveness and Sensation Seeking." *Personality and Individual Differences* 37, no. 8 (2004): 1615–27.

Damasio, Antonio. *Looking for Spinoza: Joy, Sorrow, and the Feeling Brain*. Orlando: Harcourt, 2003.

Darling, Jeremy. "The Hubble Expansion Is Isotropic in the Epoch of Dark Energy." *MNRAS* 441, no. 1 (2014): 67–70.

Davis, Lydia. *Can't and Won't*. London: Hamish Hamilton, 2014.

Debord, Guy. "On the Passage of a Few Persons through a Rather Brief Unity of Time." *Bureau of Public Secrets* (1959). http://www.bopsecrets.org/SI/debord.films/passage.htm.

Dickens, Charles. *Bleak House*. New York: The Modern Library, 2002.

Dickens, Charles. *Letters 1833–1856*. London: Charles Scribner's Sons, 1879.

Dickens, Charles. *The Letters of Charles Dickens: 1832–1846*. London: The Nonesuch Press, 1938.

Dickens, Charles. *Sketches by Boz*. Boston: Houghton, Mifflin and Company, 1894.

Dine, Philip. "Shaping the Colonial Body." In *Algeria & France, 1800–2000: Identity, Memory, Nostalgia*, edited by Patricia Lorcin. Syracuse: Syracuse University Press, 2006.

During, Elie. "Loose Coexistence: Technologies of Attention in the Age of the Post-Metropolis." In *Cognitive Architecture. From Biopolitics to Noopolitics*, edited by Deborah Hauptmann and Warren Neidich. Rotterdam: 010 Publishers, 2010.

During, Simon. "Completing Secularism: The Mundane in the Neoliberal Era." In *Varieties of Secularism in a Secular Age*, edited by Michael Warner, Jonathan Vanantwerpen, and Craig Calhoun. Cambridge: Harvard University Press, 2010.

Edwards, Barbara. "Catherine Gore." Sheffield Hallam University, 1998. http://extra.shu.ac.uk/corvey/corinne/1Gore/BioGore.html.

Eliot, T. S. *Notes Towards the Definition of Culture*. London: Faber & Faber, 2010.

Eliot, T. S. *The Waste Land*. Philadelphia: Pennsylvania State University, 2000.

Elpidorou, Andreas. "The Bright Side of Boredom." *Frontiers in Psychology* 5 (2014): 1–4.

Emad, Parvis. "Boredom as Limit and Disposition." *Heidegger Studies* 1, no. 1 (1985): 63–78.

Emmons, Paul, and Andreea Mihalache. "Architectural Handbooks and the User Experience." In *Use Matters: An Alternative History of Architecture*, edited by Kenny Cupers. New York: Routledge, 2013.

Erfani, Farhang. "Sartre and Kierkegaard on the Aesthetics of Boredom." *Idealistic Studies* 34, no. 3 (2004): 303–17.

Evans, Natalie. "City Roof Fall Horror: Businesswoman Plunges 80ft to Her Death from Restaurant Roof Terrace in Front of Horrified Commuters." *The Mirror* (2012). http://www.mirror.co.uk/news/uk-news/businesswoman-plunges-80ft-to-death-from-restaurant-1306018.

Farmer, R., and N. D. Sundberg. "Boredom Proneness—the Development and Correlates of a New Scale." *Journal of Personality Assessment* 50, no. 1 (1986): 4–17.

Fenichel, Otto. "On the Psychology of Boredom." Translated by David Rapapport. In *Organization and Pathology of Thought*, edited by David Rapapport. New York: Columbia University Press, 1951.

Ferrell, Jeff. "Boredom, Crime, and Criminology." *Theoretical Criminology International Journal* 8, no. 3 (2004): 287–302.

"Forum: Eve & Adam." *Domus* 605 (1980).

Foucault, Michel. *Discipline and Punish. The Birth of the Prison*. Translated by Alan Sheridan. London: Penguin, 1979.

Franceschina, John. "Introduction." In *Gore on Stage*, edited by John Franceschina. New York: Garland Publishing, 1999.

Franzen, Ulrich. "Outspoken Briton Dislikes U.S. Modern Architecture." In *Douglas Putnam Haskell Papers*: Columbia University Libraries, 1961.

Freud, Sigmund. "Beyond the Pleasure Principle." In *Standard Edition of the Complete Psychological Works*, edited by James Stratchery. London: The Hogarth Press, 1955.

Freud, Sigmund. *Psychopathology of Everyday Life*. Translated by Abraham Arden Brill. London: Unwin, 1914.

Fukuyama, Francis. "Have We Reached the End of History?" RAND Corporation, 1989. http://www.rand.org/pubs/papers/P7532.html.

Fukuyama, Francis. *The End of History and the Last Man*. London: Penguin Books, 1992.

Gabriel, Martha. "Boredom: Exploration of a Developmental Perspective." *Clinical Social Work Journal* 16, no. 2 (1988): 156–64.

Galton, Francis. "The Measure of Fidget." *Nature* 32 (1885): 174–5.

Gamsby, Patrick. "The Black Sun of Boredom: Henri Lefebvre and the Critique of Everyday Life." Laurentian University, 2012.

"Generic." In *Online Etymology Dictionary*, edited by Douglas Harper, 2016. http://www.etymonline.com/index.php?term=generic.

Gettmann, R. *A Victorian Publisher: A Study of the Bentley Papers*. Cambridge University Press, 2010.

Giedion, Sigfried. *Architecture and the Phenomena of Transition*. Cambridge: Harvard University Press, 1971.

Giedion, Sigfried. *Architecture, You and Me. The Diary of a Development*. Cambridge: Harvard University Press, 1958.

Giedion, Sigfried. *Constancy, Change and Architecture*. Cambridge: Harvard University Press, 1961.

Giedion, Sigfried. *Mechanization Takes Command. A Contribution to Anonymous History*. New York: W. W. Norton & Company, 1975.

Giedion, Sigfried. *Space, Time and Architecture. The Growth of a New Tradition*. Cambridge: Harvard University Press, 1967.

Giedion, Sigfried. *The Eternal Present: The Beginnings of Art. A Contribution on Constancy and Change*. New York: Bollingen Foundation, 1962.

Giedion, Sigfried. "The Need for a New Monumentality." In *New Architecture and City Planning*, edited by Paul Zucker. New York: Philosophical Library, 1944.

Goldberg, Yael K., John D. Eastwood, Jennifer LaGuardia, and James Danckert. "Boredom: An Emotional Experience Distinct from Apathy, Anhedonia, or Depression." *Journal of Social and Clinical Psychology* 30, no. 6 (2011): 647–66.

Bibliography

Göller, Adolf. "What Is the Cause of Perpetual Style Change?" Translated by Henry Mallgrave and Eleftherios Ikonomou. In *Empathy, Form, and Space: Problems in German Aesthetics 1873–1893*, edited by Harry Mallgrave and Eleftherios Ikonomou. Santa Monica: Getty Publication Programs, 1993.

Göller, Adolf. *Die Entstehung der architektonischen Stilformen: Eine Geschichte der Baukunst nach dem Werden und Wandern der Formgedanken*. Stuttgart: Konrad Wittwer, 1888.

Goodstein, Elizabeth. *Experience without Qualities: Boredom and Modernity*. Stanford: Stanford University Press, 2005.

Gore, Catherine. *Women as They Are, or the Manners of the Day*, vol. 1–3. London: Henry Colburn and Richard Bentley, 1830.

"Gorky and Actress Asked to Quit Hotels." *The New York Times* (1906). http://query.nytimes.com/mem/archivefree/pdf?res=F60616FF3C5A12738DDDAC0994DC405B868CF1D3.

Gorky, Maxim. "Boredom." *The Independent Magazine* (1907).

Gorky, Maxim. "For Want Something to Do." Translated by Margaret Wettlin. In *Maxim Gorky. Collected Works in Ten Volumes*. Moscow: Progress Publishers, 1978.

"Gorky on Coney." *The New York Times* (1907). http://query.nytimes.com/mem/archivefree/pdf?res=F10914FB3A5A12738DDDA00994DC405B868CF1D3.

Green, Matthew. *The Spleen and Other Poems*. European Libraries, 1796. https://archive.org/stream/spleenandotherp01stotgoog#page/n5/mode/2up.

Greenberg, Clement. "Avant-Garde and Kitsch." In *Modern Culture and the Arts*, edited by James Hall and Barry Ulanov. New York: McGraw-Hill, 1967.

Greenson, Ralph. "On Boredom." *Journal of the American Psychoanalytic Association* 1, no. 1 (1953): 7–21.

Grosser, Hermann. "Forum: Instead of Boredom." *Domus* 605 (1980).

Hannay, Alastair. "Introduction." In Søren Kierkegaard, *Either/Or: A Fragment of Life*. London: Penguin Classics, 1992.

Harman, Graham. *Heidegger Explained: From Phenomenon to Thing*. Chicago: Open Court Publishing, 2007.

Harries, Karsten. *The Ethical Function of Architecture*. Cambridge: MIT Press, 1997.

Haskell, Douglas. "In the Forum." *Architectural Forum* (1961).

Hatherley, Owen. *A New Kind of Bleak: Journeys Through Urban Britain*. Verso Books, 2012.

Hauptmann, Deborah, and Warren Neidich, eds. *Cognitive Architecture: From Bio-Politics to Noo-Politics; Architecture & Mind in the Age of Communication and Information*. Rotterdam: 010 Publishers, 2010.

Healy, Seán. *Boredom, Self, and Culture*. Rutherford: Fairleigh Dickinson University Press, 1984.

Heckscher, August. *The Public Happiness*. New York: Atheneum, 1962.

Hegel, Georg Wilhelm Friedrich. *Philosophy of Mind: Being Part Three of the Encyclopaedia of the Philosophical Sciences*. Translated by William Wallace and A. V. Miller. Oxford: Clarendon Press, 1971.

Heidegger, Martin. *The Concept of Time*. Translated by William McNeill. Oxford: Blackwell, 1992.

Heidegger, Martin. *The Fundamental Concepts of Metaphysics: World, Finitude, Solitude*. Translated by William McNeill and Nicholas Walker. Bloomington: Indiana University Press, 2001.

Heilbroner, Robert L. *Beyond Boom and Crash*. New York: Norton, 1978.

Heron, Woodburn. "The Pathology of Boredom." *Scientific American* 196 (1957): 52–6.

Higgins, Dick. "Boredom and Danger." *The Something Else Newsletter* 1, no. 9 (1968): 1–6.

Hirschman, Albert. *The Passions and the Emotions*. Princeton: Princeton University Press, 1977.

"Histoire de la ville d'Oran". Oran-DZ, 2015. http://www.oran-dz.com/ville/histoire/.

Hughes, Winifred. "Elegies for the Regency: Catherine Gore's Dandy Novels." *Nineteenth Century Literature* 50, no. 2 (1995): 189–209.

Huhn, Lore, and Philipp Schwab. "Kierkegaard and German Idealism." In *The Oxford Handbook of Kierkegaard*, edited by John Lippitt and George Pattison. Oxford: Oxford University Press, 2013.

Huxley, Aldous. "Accidie." In *Mass Leisure*, edited by Eric Larrabee and Rolf Meyersohn. Glenco: The Free Press, 1958.

Illich, Ivan. *Energy and Equity*. New York: Harper & Row, 1974.

Inge, William Ralph. *The End of an Age and Other Essays*. New York: The MacMillan Company, 1949.

Irace, Fulvio. "Forum: Between Less & More." *Domus* 605 (1980).

Jameson, Fredric. *Postmodernism, or, the Cultural Logic of Late Capitalism*. London: Verso, 1991.

Jarzombek, Mark. *The Psychologizing of Modernity: Art, Architecture, and History*. Cambridge: Cambridge University Press, 2000.

Jencks, Charles. "Charles Jencks on the Power Law of Bad Architecture." *The Architectural Review* (2013).

Jencks, Charles. *Critical Modernism. Where Is Post-Modernism Going?* London: Wiley-Academy, 2007.

Jencks, Charles. "Generic Individualism—the Reigning Style of Our Time—and Its Discontents," *The Bartlett International Lecture Series 2015/16*. London, 2015.

Jencks, Charles. "How Big Is Bad?" *The Architectural Review* (2002).

Jencks, Charles. "Post-Modernism between Kitsch and Culture." *Architectural Design* (1990).

Jencks, Charles. *The Language of Post-Modern Architecture*. London: Academy, 1981.

Jencks, Charles. "The Pleasure of the Architext." In *Alessandro & Francesdo Mendini! Philippe Starck! Michele De Lucchi! Coop Himelb(L)Au! In Groningen!*, edited by M. Martin, C. Wagenaar, and A. Welkamp. Groningen: Groninger Museum, 1996.

Jencks, Charles. *The Story of Post-Modernism*. London: Wiley, 2011.

Jesse, J., and G. Selwyn. *George Selwyn and His Contemporaries, with Memoirs and Notes*. London: R. Bentley, 1843.

Johnson, Douglas. "The First Man of France." *Prospect* (1996). http://www.prospectmagazinne.co.uk/arts-and-books/thefirstmanoffrancee.

Johnson, Philip. "International Style—Death or Metamorphosis." In *Philip Johnson Papers*. New York: Museum of Modern Art Archive, 1961.

Johnson, Philip. *Writings*, edited by Peter Eisenman and Robert A. M. Stern. New York: Oxford University Press, 1979.

Johnson, Philip, and Jeffrey Kipnis. "A Conversation around the Avant-Garde." In *Autonomy and Ideology. Positioning an Avant-Garde in America*, edited by R. E. Somol. New York: The Monacelli Press, 1997.

Judt, Tony. *Postwar. A History of Europe Since 1945*. London: Vintage, 2010.

Kain, Philip. "Nietzsche, the Kantian Self, and Eternal Recurrence." *Idealistic Studies* 34, no. 3 (2004): 225–37.

Kaprow, Allan. *Assemblage, Environment & Happening*. New York: Abrams, 1965.

Kaprow, Allan. "Forum: Interview with Allan Kaprow." *Domus* 605 (1980).

Kass, Steven J., Stephen J. Vodanovich, and Anne Callender. "State-Trait Boredom: Relationship to Absenteeism, Tenure, and Job Satisfaction." *Journal of Business and Psychology* 16, no. 2 (2001): 317–27.

Kasson, John. *Amusing the Million: Coney Island at the Turn of the Century*. New York: Hill & Wang, 1978.

Kaun, Alexander. *Maxim Gorky and His Russia*. New York: B. Blom, 1968.

Kay, John. "Why the 'Happiest' Cities Are Boring." *Financial Times* (2015). http://www.ft.com/cms/s/2/1b915f0e-517b-11e5-b029-b9d50a74fd14.html.

Kelley, Alice Van Buren. "The Bleak Houses of *Bleak House*." *Nineteenth Century Fiction* 25, no. 3 (1970): 253–68.

Bibliography

Kelley, Jeff. *Childsplay: The Art of Allan Kaprow*. Berkeley: University of California Press, 2004.

Kendra, April. "Catherine Gore and the Fashionable Novel: A Reevaluation." University of Georgia, 2003.

Kennedy, Paul. "The Motorcycle Is Yourself." *CBC* (2015). http://www.cbc.ca/radio/ideas/the-motorcycle-is-yourself-1.2914205.

Kenny, Lesley. "Boredom Escapes Us: A Cultural Collage in Eleven Storeys." University of Toronto, 2009.

Keynes, John Maynard. *The General Theory of Employment. Interest and Money*. London: Macmillan, 1936.

Kierkegaard, Søren. *Either/Or: A Fragment of Life*. Translated by Alastair Hannay. London: Penguin Books Limited, 2004.

Kierkegaard, Søren. *Enten-Eller: Et Livs-Fragment / Udgivet Af Victor Eremita*. Kjøbenhavn: C. A. Reitzel, 1843.

Kierkegaard, Søren. *The Concept of Anxiety: Kierkegaard's Writings VIII*. Translated by Reidar Thomte. Princeton: Princeton University Press, 1987.

Kirk, Russell. *A Program for Conservatives*. Chicago: Regnery, 1954.

Kirk, Russell. *Beyond the Dreams of Avarice*. Washington D.C.: Regnery, 1956.

Kirk, Russell. "Boredom Is the Deadly Enemy." *Ada Evening News* (1966).

Kirk, Russell. *Eliot and His Age: T. S. Eliot's Moral Imagination in the Twentieth Century*. Wilmington: ISI Books, 2008.

Kirk, Russell. "English Letters in the Age of Boredom." *Shenandoah* 7, no. 2 (1956): 3–15.

Kirk, Russell. "Opportunity for Cities." *Ocala Star-Banner* (1965). http://news.google.com/newspapers?nid=1356&dat=19651115&id=Us1NAAAAIBAJ&sjid=tg4EAAAAIBAJ&pg=2035,676486.

Kirk, Russell. "Rebellion against Boredom." In *Seeds of Anarchy: A Study of Campus Revolution*, edited by Frederick Wilhelmsen. Dallas: Argus, 1969.

Kirk, Russell. *Redeeming the Time*. Edited by Jeffrey Nelson. Wilmington: ISI Books, 1996.

Kirk, Russell. *Confessions of a Bohemian Tory: Episodes and Reflections of a Vagrant Career*. New York: Fleet, 1963.

Kirk, Russell. "The Architecture of Servitude and Boredom." *Modern Age* 26, no. 2 (1982): 114–21.

Kirk, Russell. *The Conservative Mind: From Burke to Eliot*. Washington D.C.: Regnery, 1986.

Kirk, Russell. "The Neoconservatives." In *Politics of Prudence*. Wilmington: ISI Books, 1993.

Kirk, Russell. "The Uninteresting Future." *Commonwealth* (1960).

Kirk, Russell. "York and Social Boredom." *The Sewanee Review* 61, no. 4 (1953): 664–81.

Klapp, Orrin Edgar. *Overload and Boredom: Essays on the Quality of Life in the Information Society*. New York: Greenwood Press, 1986.

Kondratieff, Nikolai. *The Long Wave Cycle*. New York: Richardson & Snyder, 1984.

Koolhaas, Rem. *Delirious New York: A Retroactive Manifesto for Manhattan*. New York: Monacelli Press, 1994.

Koolhaas, Rem. "Towards the Contemporary City." In *Theorizing a New Agenda for Architecture*, edited by Kate Nesbitt. New York: Princeton Architectural Press, 1996.

Koolhaas, Rem, and Bruce Mau. *S,M,L,XL*. Rotterdam: 010 Publishers, 1995.

Kracauer, Siegfried. *The Mass Ornament: Weimar Essays*. Cambridge: Harvard University Press, 1995.

Kuhn, Reinhard. *The Demon of Noontide: Ennui in Western Literature*. Princeton: Princeton University Press, 1976.

Kustermans, Jorg, and Erik Ringmar. "Modernity, Boredom, and War: A Suggestive Essay." *Review of International Studies* 37, no. 04 (2011): 1775–92.

Lambert, Robert. "The Forty-Year Coffee Break." *The English Journal* 55, no. 6 (1966): 768–71.

Lambeth, John. "The Figure of the Labyrinth in 'Le renégat' and 'La Pierre qui pousse.'" In *A Writer's Topography: Space and Place in the Life and Works of Albert Camus*, edited by Jason Herbeck and Vincent Grégoire. Leiden: Brill, 2015.
Lambrechts, Nico. "Successful Banker Jumped to His Death from No 1 Poultry Building." *The Telegraph* (2012). http://www.telegraph.co.uk/news/9616861/Successful-banker-jumped-to-his-death-from-No-1-Poultry-building.html.
Langbauer, Laurie. *Novels of Everyday Life: The Series in English Fiction 1850–1930*. Ithaca: Cornell University Press, 1999.
Langbauer, Laurie. "The City, the Everyday, and Boredom: The Case of Sherlock Holmes." *Differences* 5, no. 3 (1993): 80–120.
Lavin, Sylvia. *Kissing Architecture*. Princeton: Princeton University Press, 2011.
Lavin, Sylvia. "Lying Fallow." *Log* 29 (2013).
Le Corbusier. *Towards a New Architecture*. Translated by Frederick Etchells. London: The Architectural Press, 1982.
Le Corbusier. *Vers Une Architecture*. Paris: Flammarion, 2005.
Le Goff, Jacques. *History and Memory*. New York: Columbia University Press, 1992.
Lefebvre, Henri. *Everyday Life in the Modern World*. Translated by Sacha Rabinovitch. New Brunswick: Transaction, 1984.
Lefebvre, Henri. *Introduction to Modernity: Twelve Preludes*. Translated by John Moore. London: Verso, 1995.
Lefebvre, Henri. "The Everyday and Everydayness." *Yale French Studies*, no. 37 (1987): 7–11.
Leong, Frederick T. L., and Gregory R. Schneller. "Boredom Proneness: Temperamental and Cognitive Components." *Personality and Individual Differences* 14, no. 1 (1993): 233–9.
Lepenies, Wolf. *Melancholy and Society*. Cambridge: Harvard University Press, 1992.
LePera, N. "Relationships between Boredom Proneness, Mindfulness, Anxiety, Depression, and Substance Use." *New School Psychology Bulletin* 8 (2011): 15–25.
Lombard-Latune, Marie-Amélie. "Des recrues de Daech demandent à leurs avocats de préparer leur retour en France." *Le Figaro* (2014). http://www.lefigaro.fr/actualite-france/2014/11/30/01016-20141130ARTFIG00191-des-recrues-de-daech-demandent-a-leurs-avocats-de-preparer-leur-retour-en-france.php.
Lombardo, Nicholas. *The Logic of Desire. Aquinas on Emotion*. Washington D.C.: The Catholic University of America Press, 2011.
Mager, Nathan. *The Kondratieff Waves*. New York: Praeger, 1987.
Mailer, Norman. "The Big Bite." *Esquire* 357 (1963).
"Maison du Colon" Musée de l'Histoire vivante, 2015. http://www.museehistoirevivante.com/expovirtuelle/Algerie/ImgAlg/Chapitre3/Oran/popMaisonDuColon20.htm.
Mallgrave, Harry Francis. *The Architect's Brain: Neuroscience, Creativity, and Architecture*. Chichester: Wiley-Blackwell, 2010.
Malpas, Jeff. *Heidegger's Topology: Being, Place, World*. Cambridge: MIT Press, 2006.
Mandel, Ernest. *Late Capitalism*. London: Verso, 1978.
Mandel, Ernest. *Long Waves of Capitalist Development: A Marxist Interpretation*. London: Verso, 1995.
Mann, Sandi. "Does Boredom Bring out Our Creative Flair?" *Huffington Post* (2013). http://www.huffingtonpost.co.uk/sandi-mann/does-boredom-bring-out-out-creative-flair_b_2447393.html.
Marcuse, Herbert. *One-Dimensional Man*. Boston: Beacon Press, 1964.
Marijke, M. et. al. "Alessandro Mendini, Walking the Tight-Rope between Art and Kitsch." *Elle Wonen* (1993).
Marion, Jean-Luc. *Reduction and Givenness: Investigations of Husserl, Heidegger, and Phenomenology*. Translated by Thomas Carlson. Evanston: Northwestern University Press, 1998.

Bibliography

Marx, Karl. *Capital*, vol. 1. Translated by Ben Fowkes. London: Penguin Books, 1976.
Marx, Karl. *Grundrisse*. London: Penguin, 1973.
Mason, Paul. "The End of Capitalism Has Begun." *The Guardian* (2015). https://www.theguardian.com/books/2015/jul/17/postcapitalism-end-of-capitalism-begun.
Massey, Doreen. "Politics and Space/Time." In *Place and the Politics of Identity*, edited by Michael Keith and Steve Pile. London: Routledge, 1993.
Matthews, Freya. *Reinhabiting Reality: Towards a Recovery of Culture*. Albany: State University of New York Press, 2005.
"Maxim Gorky's Disillusion." *The New York Times* (1906). http://query.nytimes.com/mem/archivefree/pdf?res=FB0610FA3A5A12738DDDAE0994DC405B868CF1D3.
Maynard, Lee Anna. *Beautiful Boredom. Idleness and Feminine Self-Realization in the Victorian Novel*. Jefferson: McFarland & Company, 2009.
McCarthy, Patrick. *Camus. A Critical Study of His Life and Work*. London: Hamish Hamilton, 1982.
McCarthy, Vincent. "Martin Heidegger: Kierkegaard's Influence Hidden and in Full View." In *Kierkegaard and Existentialism*, edited by Jon Stewart. London: Ashgate, 2011.
McDonald, William. "Kierkegaard's Demonic Boredom." In *Essays on Boredom and Modernity*, edited by Barbara Dalle Pezze and Carlo Salzani. New York: Rodopi, 2009.
McKenzie, Jonathan. "Governing Moods: Anxiety, Boredom, and the Ontological Overcoming of Politics in Heidegger." *Canadian Journal of Political Science Association* 41, no. 3 (2008): 569–85.
Mead, Margaret. "The Pattern of Leisure in Contemporary American Culture." In *Mass Leisure*, edited by Eric Larrabee and Rolf Meyersohn. Glencoe: Free Press, 1958.
Medhurst, Andy. "What Did I Get?" In *Punk Rock: So What?*, edited by Roger Sabin. London: Routledge, 1999.
Mendini, Alessandro. "Dear Reader." *Domus* 602 (1980).
Mendini, Alessandro. "Pieces of Dan's Body and Soul." In Dan Friedman, Jeffrey Deitch, Steven Holt, and Alessandro Mendini, *Dan Friedman: Radical Modernism*. London: Yale University Press, 1994.
Mendini, Alessandro. "Towards an Architecture of Banality." (1979). http://www.ateliermendini.it/index.php?mact=News,cntnt01,detail,0&cntnt01articleid=251&cntnt01detailtemplate=AnniDett&cntnt01lang=en_US&cntnt01returnid=191.
Mendini, Alessandro. "Universal Cosmetics." (1981). http://www.ateliermendini.it/index.php?mact=News,cntnt01,detail,0&cntnt01articleid=249&cntnt01detailtemplate=AnniDett&cntnt01lang=en_US&cntnt01returnid=189.
Mercer, Kimberley B., and John D. Eastwood. "Is Boredom Associated with Problem Gambling Behaviour? It Depends on What You Mean by 'Boredom.'" *International Gambling Studies* 10, no. 1 (2010): 91–104.
Mitcham, Carl. "Ivan Illich: Critic of Professionalized Design." *Design Issues* 19, no. 4 (2003): 26–30.
Mohun, A. P. "Designed for Thrills and Safety: Amusement Parks and the Commodification of Risk, 1880–1929." *Journal of Design History* 14 (2001): 291–306.
Monbiot, George. "Our Ecological Boredom." *The New York Times* (2015). http://www.nytimes.com/2015/01/19/opinion/our-ecological-boredom.html?_r=0.
Moran, Joe. "Benjamin and Boredom." *Critical Quarterly* 45, no. 1–2 (2003): 168–81.
Moravia, Alberto. *Boredom*. Translated by Angus Davidson. New York: New York Review of Books, 1999.
Motte, Antoine Houdart de La. *Oeuvres, Volume 9*. Paris: Prault, 1754.
"Mrs's Gore *Women as They Are; or, the Manners of the Day*." *The Edinburgh Review* 51 (1830): 444–62.
Negri, Antonio. "On Rem Koolhaas." *Radical Philosophy* 154 (2009): 48–50.

Neumann, Peter E. "Victims, Perpetrators, Assets: The Narratives of Islamic State Defectors." ICSR, 2015. http://icsr.info/wp-content/uploads/2015/09/ICSR-Report-Victims-Perpertrators-Assets-The-Narratives-of-Islamic-State-Defectors.pdf.
Nietzsche, Friedrich. *Human, All Too Human*. London: George Allen, 1934.
Nietzsche, Friedrich. *On the Genealogy of Morals*. Translated by Walter Kaufmann and R. Hollingdale. New York: Vintage, 1967.
Nietzsche, Friedrich. *The Anti-Christ*. Translated by H. Mencken. New York: Cosimo, 2005.
Nietzsche, Friedrich. *The Gay Science: With a Prelude in German Rhymes and an Appendix of Songs*. Translated by Josefine Nauckhoff and Adrian del Caro, edited by Bernard Williams. Cambridge: Cambridge University Press, 2001.
Nietzsche, Friedrich. *The Will to Power*. Translated by Walter Kaufmann and R. J. Hollingdale. New York: Vintage Books, 1968.
Nooteboom, Cees. "Autopia." In *Writing Los Angeles: A Literary Anthology*, edited by David Ullin. New York: Library of America, 2002.
Nuckolls, Charles. "Boring Rituals." *Journal of Ritual Studies* 21, no. 1 (2007): 33–48.
O'Doherty, Brian. *Object and Idea: An Art Critic's Journal 1961–1967*. New York: Simon and Schuster, 1967.
Oden, Thomas. *The Structure of Awareness*. Nashville: Abingdon Press, 1969.
Ogden, C. K., I. A. Richards, and James Wood. *The Foundations of Aesthetics*. New York: Lear Publishers, 1925.
Onians, John. *Neuroarthistory: From Aristotle and Pliny to Baxandall and Zeki*. New Haven: Yale University Press, 2007.
Osborne, Samuel. "Coq D'argent: Man Wrote 'I Have Cracked' on Phone before Becoming Sixth Person to Fall to Death from London Roof Garden." *Independent* (2016). http://www.independent.co.uk/news/uk/home-news/coq-dargent-man-wrote-i-have-cracked-on-phone-before-becoming-sixth-person-to-fall-to-death-from-a7000721.html.
Osman, Michael. "Banham's Historical Ecology." In *Neo-Avant-Garde and Postmodern: Postwar Architecture in Britain and Beyond*, edited by Mark Crinson and Claire Zimmerman. New Haven: Yale University Press, 2010.
Otis, Norman. "Maxim Gorky a Disappointed Man." *The New York Times* (1906).
Paik, Nam June. "Video Art." (1976). http://nobetty.net/parsons_video/paik_inputoutput.pdf.
Panofsky, Erwin. *Perspective as Symbolic Form*. Translated by Christopher Wood. New York: Zone Books, 1991.
Parreno, Christian and Ingrid Lønningdal. "From Anonymity to Boredom to Creativity." *Architecture and Culture* (2020). DOI: 10.1080/20507828.2020.1792217.
Partridge, Eric. *Origins: A Short Etymological Dictionary of Modern English*. London: Routledge and Kegan Paul, 1966.
Pascal, Blaise. *The Thoughts of Blaise Pascal*. Translated by Paul C. Kegan. London: Bell, 1899.
Pask, Gordon. "A Comment, a Case History and a Plan." In *Cybernetics, Art, and Ideas*, edited by Jasia Reichardt. Greenwich: New York Graphic Society, 1971.
Pattison, George. "Boredom." In *Kierkegaard and the Quest for Unambiguous Life: Between Romanticism and Modernism*. Oxford: Oxford University Press, 2013.
Pease, Allison. *Modernism, Feminism, and the Culture of Boredom*. Cambridge: Cambridge University Press, 2012.
Pérez, Carlota. *Technological Revolutions and Financial Capital: The Dynamics of Bubbles and Golden Ages*. Cheltenham: Edward Elgar, 2002.
Pérez, Carlota. "Technological Revolutions and Techno-Economic Paradigms." *Technological Governance*, no. 20 (2009): 185–202.
Petro, Patrice. *Aftershocks of the New: Feminism and Film History*. New Brunswick: Rutgers University Press, 2002.

Bibliography

Pezze, Barbara Dalle, and Carlo Salzani. *Essays on Boredom and Modernity*. Amsterdam: Rodopi, 2009.

Pieper, Josef. *Leisure as the Basis of Culture*. Translated by Alexander Dru. New York: Random House, 1963.

Pignotti, Lorenzo. *La Treccia Donata: Poemetto Eroi-Comico*. Florence: Molini, Landi, e Comp., 1808.

Plagens, Peter. "Los Angeles: The Ecology of Evil." *Artforum* 11 (1972): 67–76.

Plato. *Timaeus*. The Gutenberg Project, 2008. http://www.gutenberg.org/files/1572/1572-h/1572-h.htm.

Polt, Richard. "Heidegger in the 1930s: Who Are We?" In *The Bloomsbury Companion to Heidegger*, edited by Francois Raffoul and Eric Nelson. London: Bloomsbury Academic, 2013.

Power, Carla. "'Terrorists' Most Powerful Recruiting Tool: Boredom." *Time* (2015). http://time.com/3857035/terrorists-recruiting-tool/.

Prak, Niels. *The Visual Perception of the Built Environment*. Delft: Delft University Press, 1977.

Quantrill, Malcolm, and Bruce Webb. *Constancy and Change in Architecture*. College Station: Texas A&M University Press, 1991.

R., B. "Boring Cities: Torporville." *The Economist* (2015). http://www.economist.com/blogs/gulliver/2015/05/boring-cities.

Ramakers, Renny. *Droog Design: Spirit of the Nineties*. Rotterdam: 010 Publishers, 1998.

Raposa, Michael. *Boredom and the Religious Imagination*. Charlottesville: University of Virginia, 1999.

Restany, Pierre. "Forum: One Day Boredom Was Born from Uniformity." *Domus* 605 (1980).

Restany, Pierre. "Forum: Restanystory—Encounter with Nam June Paik." *Domus* 605 (1980).

Richardson, Hannah. "Children Should Be Allowed to Get Bored, Expert Says." *BBC News* (2013). http://www.bbc.com/news/education-21895704.

"Riot of Enthusiasm Greets Maxim Gorky." *The New York Times* (1906). http://query.nytimes.com/mem/archivefree/pdf?res=F40C1EFD3A5A12738DDDA80994DC405B868CF1D3.

Ritzer, George. "The Disenchanted Kingdom." *The Sun* (2002).

Rudofsky, Bernard. *Behind the Picture Window*. Oxford: Oxford University Press, 1955.

Russell, Bertrand. *The Conquest of Happiness*. New York: Bantam Books, 1968.

"Russell Kirk Foundation for Cultural Renewal." http://www.kirkcenter.org/.

Russello, Gerald. *The Postmodern Imagination of Russell Kirk*. Columbia: University of Missouri Press, 2007.

Salzani, Carlo. "The Atrophy of Experience: Walter Benjamin and Boredom." In *Essays on Boredom and Modernity*, edited by Barbara Dalle Pezze and Carlo Salzani. Amsterdam: Rodopi, 2009.

Sartre, Jean-Paul. *Nausea*. Translated by Lloyd Alexander. London: Hamish Hamilton, 1962.

Savage, Jon. "The Great Rock 'N' Roll Swindle." In *Impresario: Malcolm Mclaren and the British New Wave*, edited by Paul Taylor. Cambridge: MIT Press, 1988.

Schachtel, Ernest G. *Metamorphosis: On the Development of Affect, Perception, Attention, and Memory*. New York: Basic Books, 1959.

Schachterle, Lance. "Bleak House as a Serial Novel." *Dickens Studies Annual* 1 (1970): 212–24, 292–5.

Schirren, Matthias. *Bruno Taut. Alpine Architektur. Eine Utopie*. Berlin: Prestel, 2004.

Schlegel, Friedrich. *Philosophical Fragments*. Translated by Peter Frichow. Minneapolis: Uninversity of Minnesota Press, 1991.

Schopenhauer, Arthur. *The Essays of Arthur Schopenhauer: The Art of Literature and the Art of Controversy*. Overland Park: Digireads, 2010.

Schopenhauer, Arthur. *The Essays of Arthur Schopenhauer: The Wisdom of Life*. The Gutenberg Project, 2004. http://www.gutenberg.org/cache/epub/10741/pg10741.html.

Schopenhauer, Arthur. *The World as Will and Representation*, vol. 1. London: Courier Dove, 2012.
Seib, Hope M., and Stephen J. Vodanovich. "Cognitive Correlates of Boredom Proneness: The Role of Private Self-Consciousness and Absorption." *The Journal of Psychology* 132, no. 6 (1998): 642–52.
Sharr, Adam. *Heidegger's Hut*. Cambridge: MIT Press, 2006.
Silvetti, Jorge. "The 2002 Walter Gropius Lecture: A Note from Jorge Silvetti." In *Introductions: Jorge Silvetti*, edited by Rodolphe el-Khoury. Cambridge: Harvard University Graduate School of Design, 2004.
Silvetti, Jorge. "The Muses Are Not Amused: Pandemonium in the House of Architecture." In *The New Architectural Pragmatism*, edited by William Saunders. Minneapolis: University of Minnesota Press, 2007.
Silvetti, Jorge. *The Muses Are Not Amused: Pandemonium in the House of Architecture*. Cambridge: Harvard University Graduate School of Design, 2004. CD.
Simmel, Georg. "The Metropolis and Mental Life." Blackwell Publishing, 1971. http://www.blackwellpublishing.com/content/BPL_Images/Content_store/Sample_chapter/0631225137/Bridge.pdf.
Skeat, Walter W. *An Etymological Dictionary of the English Language*. Oxford: Clarendon, 1953.
Smithson, Alison and Peter. *Ordinariness and Light. Urban Theories 1952–1960 and Their Application in a Building Project 1963–1970*. London: Faber and Faber, 1970.
Smithson, Alison and Peter. *Without Rhetoric. An Architectural Aesthetic 1955–1972*. London: Latimer New Dimensions, 1973.
Sobotka, Walter. *Principles of Design. A Retrospect*. 1970.
Sommers, J., and S. J. Vodanovich. "Boredom Proneness: Its Relationship to Psychological—and Physical—Health Symptoms." *Journal of Clinical Psychology* 56, no. 1 (2000): 149–55.
Sontag, Susan. *Against Interpretation*. New York: Dell Publishing, 1967.
Sontag, Susan. *As Consciousness Is Harnessed to Flesh: Journals and Notebooks, 1964–1980*. New York: Farrar, Straus and Giroux, 2012.
Sontag, Susan. "Notes on 'Camp.'" Georgetown University, 1964. http://faculty.georgetown.edu/irvinem/theory/Sontag-NotesOnCamp-1964.html.
Spacks, Patricia Meyer. *Boredom: The Literary History of a State of Mind*. Chicago: University of Chicago Press, 1996.
Stan, Leo. "Albert Camus: Walled within God." In *Kierkegaard and Existentialism*, edited by Jon Stewart. Surrey: Ashgate, 2011.
Starr, Kevin. *California: A History*. New York: Random House Publishing Group, 2007.
Starr, Kevin. *Golden Dreams: California in an Age of Abundance, 1950–1963*. New York: Oxford University Press, 2009.
Steenson, Molly Wright. "Architectures of Information: Christopher Alexander, Cedric Price, and Nicholas Negroponte & MIT's Architecture Machine Group." Princeton University, 2014.
Steiner, Hadas. "The Architecture of the Well-Serviced Environment." *ARQ: Architectural Review Quarterly* 9, no. 2 (2005): 133–43.
Stendhal. *Le Rouge Et Le Noir*. Paris: Aubry, 1943.
Stendhal. *The Red and the Black*. Translated by C. K. Scott Moncrieff. New York: The Modern Library, 1926.
Stendhal. *The Red and the Black*. Translated by Horace Samuel. London: Kegan Paul, Trench, Trubner & Co., 1916.
Stickells, Lee. "Flow Urbanism: The Heterotopia of Flows." In *Heterotopia and the City. Public Space in a Postcivil Society*, edited by Michael Dehaene and Lieven de Cauter. London: Routledge, 2008.
Stiles, Anne. "Go Rest, Young Man." *Monitor on Psychology* 43, no. 1 (2012): 32.

Bibliography

Svendsen, Lars. *Fashion: A Philosophy*. Translated by John Irons. London: Reaktion, 2006.
Svendsen, Lars. *A Philosophy of Boredom*. Translated by John Irons. London: Reaktion, 2005.
Taverne, Ed. "Mendini's Farewell to Architecture." In *Alessandro & Francesdo Mendini! Philippe Starck! Michele De Lucchi! Coop Himelb(L)Au! In Groningen!*, edited by M. Martin, C. Wagenaar, and A. Welkamp. Groningen: Groninger Museum, 1996.
Teyssot, Georges. "Boredom and Bedroom: The Suppression of the Habitual." *Assemblage*, no. 30 (1996): 44–61.
"The New Forces in Architecture." In *Architectural League of New York Records, 1880s–1974*: Archives of American Art, Smithsonian Institution, 1961.
The Oxford English Dictionary. Oxford: Clarendon Press, 2001.
Thiele, Leslie Paul. "Postmodernity and the Routinization of Novelty: Heidegger on Boredom and Technology." *Polity* 29, no. 4 (1997): 489–517.
Tilburg, Wijnad Van, and Eric Igou. "On Boredom and Social Identity: A Programmatic Meaning-Regulation Approach." *Personality and Social Psychology Bulletin* 37, no. 12 (2012): 1679–91.
Toohey, Peter. *Boredom: A Lively History*. New Haven: Yale University Press, 2011.
Toohey, Peter. "Some Ancient Notions of Boredom." *Illinois Classical Studies* 13, no. 1 (1988): 151–64.
Van Tilburg, Wijnand. "Leprosy of the Soul? A Brief History of Boredom." *The Conversation* (2020). https://theconversation.com.
Vattimo, Gianni. *The End of Modernity*. Baltimore: J. Hopkins University Press, 1985.
Venturi, Robert. *Complexity and Contradiction in Architecture*. London: The Architectural Press, 1966.
Venturi, Robert, and Denise Scott Brown. *Architecture as Signs and Systems: For a Mannerist Time*. Cambridge: Belknap, 2004.
Venturi, Robert, Denise Scott Brown, and Steven Izenour. *Learning from Las Vegas: The Forgotten Symbolism of Architectural Form*. Cambridge: MIT Press, 1972.
Vischer, Robert. "On the Optical Sense of Form: A Contribution to Aesthetics." Translated by Harry Francis Mallgrave and Eleftherios Ikonomou. In *Empathy, Form, and Space: Problems in German Aesthetics 1873–1893*, edited by Harry Francis Mallgrave and Eleftherios Ikonomou. Santa Monica: Getty Publication Programs, 1993.
Vodanovich, S. J. "Psychometric Measures of Boredom: A Review of the Literature." *The Journal of Psychology* 137, no. 6 (2003): 569–95.
Wade, Terence. *Russian Etymological Dictionary*. Bristol: Bristol Classical Press, 1996.
Wallace, David Foster. *The Pale King*. New York: Little, Brown and Company, 2012.
Watson, Peter. *A Terrible Beauty: A History of the People and Ideas That Shaped the Modern Mind*. London: Weidenfeld & Nicolson, 2000.
Weber, Nicholas. *Le Corbusier: A Life*. New York: Knopf, 2008.
Weiskel, Thomas. *The Romantic Sublime: Studies in the Structure and Psychology of Transcendence*. Baltimore: Johns Hopkins University Press, 1976.
Whiteley, Nigel. "Banham and 'Otherness': Reyner Banham (1922–1988) and His Quest for an Architecture Autre." *Architectural History* 33 (1990): 188–221.
Whiteley, Nigel. *Reyner Banham: Historian of the Immediate Future*. Cambridge: MIT Press, 2002.
Wilde, Oscar. *The Plays of Oscar Wilde*. Hertfordshire: Wordsworth, 2000.
Wolfe, Tom. *The Kandy-Kolored Tangerine-Flake Streamline Baby*. New York: Farrar, Straus and Giroux, 2009.
Wölfflin, Heinrich. "Prolegomena to Psychology of Architecture." Translated by Harry Francis Mallgrave and Eleftherios Ikonomou. In *Empathy, Form, and Space: Problems in German Aesthetics 1873–1893*, edited by Harry Francis Mallgrave and Eleftherios Ikonomou. Santa Monica: Getty Publication Programs, 1993.

Wölfflin, Heinrich. *Renaissance and Baroque*. Translated by Kathrin Simon. Ithaca: Cornell University Press, 1992.
Yedlin, Tovah. *Maxim Gorky: A Political Biography*. Westport: Praeger, 1999.
Zaretsky, Robert. *Albert Camus. Elements of a Life*. Ithaca: Cornell University Press, 2010.
Zijderveld, Anton. *On Clichés: The Supersedure of Meaning by Function in Modernity*. London: Routledge and Kegan Paul, 1979.
Zimmerman, Michael E. *Heidegger's Confrontation with Modernity: Technology, Politics, and Art*. Bloomington: Indiana University Press, 1990.
Zukin, Sharon, Robert Baskerville, Miriam Greenberg, Courtney Guthreau, Jean Halley, Mark Halling, Kristin Lawler, et al. "From Coney Island to Las Vegas in the Urban Imaginary: Discursive Practices of Growth and Decline." *Urban Affairs Review* 33, no. 5 (1998): 627–54.

INDEX

Abell, Thornton 106
academia 19, 71, 171, 175–6, 181, 234 n.24
acedia 9, 10, 118, 186, 189 n.6, 191 n.3–4
Adam and Eve 26, 135
Adorno, Theodor W. 195 n.2, 201 n.16
Africa 3, 60, 77
airports 59, 61, 122, 166–7, 168, 177
Alberti, Leon Battista 43, 62
Alexander, Christopher 185–6, 188
Algeria 77, 82, 209 n.1, 211 n.38
amusement parks 6, 47, 50–3, 201 n.15
Andreeva, Maria 49–50
anomie 87, 108, 124, 166, 188
anxiety 10, 17, 36, 64, 87, 117, 192 n.9, 205 n.36, 207 n.16, 220 n.15
Aquinas, Thomas 9, 118, 191 n.4
Aravena, Alejandro 183
Archigram 101
Architectural Forum (journal) 89, 92
Architectural League of New York 6, 89, 92–3, 95, 99, 213 n.19
Armet and Davies 106
Art Nouveau 65, 215 n.49
Artforum (journal) 108
Astell, Mary 197 n.11
Athens 26, 78
atmospheres 37, 44, 70, 98, 111, 117, 132, 163, 175
atria 111, 112, 119, 167, 177
attunements 70, 207 n.9–10
   see also moods, *Stimmung*
Augé, Marc 169–70, 233 n.46

B. R. 186, 187
Babylon 1, 51
Ballard, J. G. 110, 168, 217 n.32, 218 n.44
Banham, Reyner 6, 7, 92–6, 99, 101–12, 178, 214 n.39, 215 n.4, 216 n.11, 218 n.38–9, 218 n.50
   Los Angeles: The Architecture of Four Ecologies 7, 101, 102, 106, 108, 111
Barbican Estate 152
Barthes, Roland 140, 180, 193 n.24, 211 n.30, 211 n.32, 235 n.31
Bataille, Georges 79
Baudelaire, Charles 10, 23, 129, 140, 192 n.10
Beard, George 203 n.14
Beauvoir, Simone de 101
Beckett, Samuel 64, 140, 204 n.32

Behrens, Peter 184
Belloc, Hilaire 147, 154
Belton, Theresa 117
Benjamin, Andrew 4, 7, 127–30, 187, 188, 224 n.9, 224 n.12
   "Boredom and Distraction: The Moods of Modernity" 7, 127–30
Benjamin, Walter 3, 7, 127–9, 136, 184, 191 n.4, 223 n.1, 224 n.7, 226 n.26
Bergson, Henri 145, 225 n.15
Berlin 162, 185, 195 n.2, 225 n.13
Berlin Wall 124, 162
Berman, Marshall 57–8, 202 n.3
Bernstein, Judith 140
Big Bang 164, 165
Biran de, Maine 2
Bismarck von, Otto 60
Blake, Peter 92
Blanchot, Maurice 2
Blanqui, Louis A. 129
blasé attitude 2, 51, 201 n.18
blasphemisis 159
   see also monothematitis
blobs 8, 173–4, 175, 180
blunting 6, 41, 43–4, 45
   see also jading
Bonaparte, Napoleon 88, 119
boredom
   aesthetic 24, 25, 28, 62, 135, 142
   communal 5, 8, 74, 128, 184, 186–7, 188
   etymology 11–12
   historical 5, 8, 19, 115, 119–20, 125, 129, 133, 188
   history 9–11, 191 n.2
   individual 5, 6, 8, 17, 23, 29, 39, 42–3, 63, 64, 70, 74, 111, 127, 136, 137, 144–5, 149, 177, 183, 184–5, 187, 188, 205 n.36–7
   social 5, 8, 9, 21, 33, 51, 71, 73–2, 75, 83, 107, 111, 117, 136, 142, 147, 148–9, 154–5, 183, 185–6, 188, 212 n.17, 228 n.8, 230 n.36, 235 n.1
Boredom at Work (film) 62–3
Borges, Jorge Luis 140
Borgia, Cesare 78
boringness 72, 115, 186, 235 n.8
BP America, Cleveland 150
Braudel, Fernand 4, 17, 18, 20, 60, 61, 62, 67, 194 n.14, 195 n.15
Bretecher, Claire 135

Index

Breuer, Marcel 92
Brezhnev era 123
Brighton Pavilion 104
Brixton 187
Brodsky, Joseph 181
Broggi, Carlo 88
Brooklyn 47, 50
Brown, Denisse Scott 65, 101, 205 n.39
Brown Derby Restaurant 65, 103
Browne, Hablot Knight (Phiz) 37
Brutalism 94, 149, 152, 218 n.39
Bukowski, Charles 101
Bunshaft, Gordon 153, 229 n.27
Burke, Edmund 192 n.9, 197 n.4
Burton, Robert 9
Byron, George Gordon 147, 154

Cache, Bernard 123
Caesars Palace 104
Cage, John 65, 135, 137
Cain and Abel 26
Cain, artist 82
Cain, James M. 101
California 67, 102, 106, 109, 112, 138, 142
Camus, Albert 6, 77, 79–85, 184, 210 n.4, 210 n.12, 210 n.26, 211 n.37–9
    "The Minotaur, or the Stop in Oran" 6, 77, 78, 82, 85
Canada 63, 186
capitalism 1, 4, 6, 7–8, 10, 11, 14, 19, 20, 21, 48, 51, 57, 58–9, 60, 61, 67–8, 71, 77, 88, 110, 111, 119–22, 125, 157–8, 160, 163, 183, 185, 186, 194 n.14, 209 n.1, 223 n.45, 227 n.3
    first cycle 19–21
    second cycle 21–2
    third cycle 60–1
    fourth cycle 61–6
    fifth cycle 120–3
Car and Driver (journal) 107
carpe taedium 179
Cassirer, Ernst 13
Catholicism 1, 120, 189 n.1
CCTV Headquarters 164, 232 n.29
Ceausescu, Nicolae 123
Chamberlain, Powell and Bon Architects 152
chaos 1, 18, 94, 138
Chartres Cathedral 185
Chaucer, Geoffrey 9
Chechulin, Dmitry 163
Cheney, George 191 n.7
Chichester, Daniel L. 62
Chiericati, Palazzo 185
China 61, 119–20, 221 n.22
Christianity 1, 17, 24, 149, 189 n.1, 208 n.17, 222 n.24
Chtcheglov, Ivan 66–7

Cioran, Emil 1, 189 n.3
City of Mesa 154
Cleveland 149–51, 150 (Figure 15.1)
clichés 87, 103, 140, 157, 160, 163, 173
Cocteau, Jean 135
Colin, Ralph E. 92
colonialism 20, 59
comfort 8, 13, 57, 102, 107, 118, 122, 167, 216 n.13
conduct books 31
Coney Island 6, 47–54, 168, 201 n.15, 202 n.23, 202 n.26
Congrés international d'architecture moderne (CIAM) 96
conservatism 50, 124, 147, 148, 154, 155, 174, 228 n.4
Cook, Peter 215 n.6
Coop Himmelb(l)au 134
Copenhagen 23, 26, 195 n.2
Copernicus 164
Crawford Manor 66
creativity 1, 7, 9, 10, 14, 26, 43, 58, 65, 89, 105, 108, 109, 112, 116, 117, 121, 123, 131, 134, 171, 172, 173, 175, 180, 194 n6, 224 n.13, 226 n.20
Critical Mass 117
Crystal Palace 12, 21
Cuba 61
Cutler, Robert W. 92, 213 n.19
Cuyahoga Building 150

Daimler-Benz Tower 162
Daly City 138
Darwin, Charles 195, n.17
Dasein, or being-in-the-world 70, 71, 74, 75, 76, 208 n.16, 208 n.22, 209 n.34
Davis, Lydia 181
Debord, Guy 66
Defence Research Board of Canada, 63
Descartes, René 17, 69, 78, 207 n.5, 210 n.12
desire 2, 9, 12–13, 14, 18, 24, 25, 29, 38, 52, 58, 59, 65, 94, 103, 115, 118, 128, 133, 142, 145, 153, 173, 186, 191 n.2, 193 n.24–5, 193 n.32, 203 n.4, 203 n.6
Detroit 151, 152 (Figure 15.2)
Dickens, Charles 5, 12, 29–30, 34, 37, 38, 39–40, 198 n.21, 198 n.23–4
    Bleak House 5, 12, 29, 30, 34, 35 (Figure 4.3), 36 (Figure 4.4), 37, 40
Disney, Walt 160
Disneyland 163, 220 n.15
displacement 72, 112, 118
distraction 1, 2, 25–6, 42, 47, 51, 53, 65, 77, 79, 84, 115, 117, 122, 123, 128, 145, 149, 153, 166
Doelger, Henry 138
Dolphin Hotel 163

Index

Domus (journal) 7, 131, 134, 139 (Figure 14.1), 141 (Figure 14.2), 143 (Figure 14.3), 224 n.1, 225 n.3, 226 n.18
Don Giovanni 24
Dreamland 47, 51
driving 107, 110, 217 n.35–7, 220 n.14, 235 n.10
Duchamp, Marcel 137, 142
dullness 34, 137, 192 n.18, 221 n.21
dumb box typology 7, 162
Durand, J. N. L. 88
Durham 33

Egypt 1, 82, 97, 98, 160, 214 n.42, 215 n.49
Einstein, Albert 164
Eisenman, Peter 175, 185–6, 188
Eliot, T. S. 148, 153, 198 n.35, 228 n.6, 228 n.9
Ellwood, Craig 102, 218 n.38
Elpidorou, Andreas 117
emotions 2, 11, 23–4, 33, 43, 47, 48, 70, 87, 98, 112, 168, 191 n.4, 231 n.11
empathy, or *Einfühlung* 41–3, 44, 116
engagement 2, 18, 42, 45, 64, 72, 77, 79, 135, 166, 169, 186, 187
Engels, Friedrich 20–1
England 26, 34, 37–8, 39, 40, 62, 96, 152, 155, 191 n.7, 214 n.39
Enlightenment 118, 156
ennui 10, 11, 29, 79, 110, 135, 153, 178, 180, 192 n.10–11, 194 n.2, 196 n.1, 223 n.1
environmentalism 68, 124, 205 n.35, 206 n.49
Eros 9, 24, 191 n.2, 193 n.25
eternal return 128, 129, 208 n.17, 224 n.7
ethics 24, 27–8, 67, 77, 129, 149, 166, 168, 188, 195 n.4
European Union 124
excitement 7, 12, 17, 18, 20, 22, 24, 51, 53, 63, 79, 84, 88, 101, 117, 125, 158, 187
exteriority 5, 18, 19, 22, 23, 24, 25, 29, 34, 70, 72, 74, 83, 87, 99, 112, 118, 127, 138, 167, 183, 187, 188
see also interiority
Eyck van, Aldo 134

fashion 18, 20, 89, 176, 194 n.12
Fenichel, Otto 41
Fernández, José A. 92, 213 n.19
Ferrell, Jeff 117
fidgeting 17, 22
Financial Times (newspaper) 186–7, 188
Flaubert, Gustave 78, 85, 134
Flegenheimer, Julien 88
Florence 78, 84
Fluxus 65, 204 n.34, 205 n.35
Fordice, James 31
Forum Design, Linz 133
Foster, Norman 164

Foucault, Michel 172, 235 n.28
Frampton, Kenneth 46
France 3, 60, 61, 82, 85, 125, 153, 223 n.40
Frank, Josef 61–2
Franzen, Ulrich 92, 213 n.19, 214 n.39
Frazer, John and Julia 64
French Revolution 1, 10, 119
Freud, Sigmund 105, 115, 204 n.25, 217 n.28
Friedan, Betty 205 n.37
Friedrichstadt tower 167–8
Fukuyama, Francis 7, 117, 119–20, 123, 221 n.20–1, 222 n.24, 222 n.26
Fuller, Buckminster 103, 216 n.11

Galindo, Pierre 85, 211 n.37
Galton, Francis 22
General Federation of Trade Union 60
General Motors plant, Detroit 151
Generator, project 64
generic 8, 11, 26, 79, 149, 157–8, 160, 165, 169, 170
Geneva 88, 187
George III, King 32
Germany 60, 62, 153, 220 n.15, 223 n.40
Gestalt 115
Giedion, Sigfried 6, 45, 87–94, 96–9
  Architecture, You and Me 88
  The Eternal Present 96–7, 214 n.42
  Mechanization Takes Command 87, 212 n.3
  "The Need for a New Monumentality" 87, 88
  Space, Time and Architecture 6, 46, 87, 99, 211 n.1
Giorgio, Francesco di 43
Gisborne, John 31
Glasgow 20
Glass House 65
God 1, 9, 17, 67, 70, 75, 197 n.11
Goethe, Johann von 23
Gogol, Nikolai 78
Göller, Adolf 6, 41–6, 98, 116, 199 n.14
Gombrich, E. H. 224 n.13
Gore, Catherine 5, 12, 29–34, 39, 40, 197 n.5–7, 198 n.20
  Women as They Are, or the Manners of the Day 5, 12, 29–34, 31 (Figure 4.1), 32 (Figure 4.2), 40
Gorky, Maxim 6, 47–53, 201 n.11, 202 n.22
  "Boredom" 6, 47–9, 48 (Figure 6.1), 49 (Figure 6.2), 53
Gothic 45, 67, 89, 185
graffitti 117
Grand Central Terminal, New York 97
Graves, Michael 163
Great White Fleet 61
Greece 87
Green, Matthew 10
Greenberg, Clement 57, 177, 234 n.16

255

Index

Greenson, Ralph 63, 204 n.25
Gregory, John 31
Griffith Park Observatory 105
Groninger Museum 133, 144
Grosser, Hermann 7, 131, 138, 140
Guggenheim Museum Bilbao 172
Guild House 66
Guimard, Hector 65

Haag, Ernest van den 92
Hansel and Gretel 104
Harries, Karsten 46, 212 n.12
Harrison & Abramovitz 62, 92
Harvard University Graduate School of Design 8, 45, 96, 171
Haskell, Douglas P. 92, 94
Haus der Deutschen Kunst 88
Healy, Seán 192 n.10, 192 n.25
Heckscher, August 92, 212 n.17
Hegel, Georg W. F. 5, 24, 45, 18, 23, 119, 189 n.1, 195 n.4, 221 n.20
Heidegger, Martin 3, 4, 6, 69–76, 97, 102, 127, 128, 187, 188, 206 n.3, 207 n.13, 208 n.17, 208 n.30, 209 n.32-3, 210 n.26
    The Fundamental Concepts of Metaphysics 6, 69, 206 n.1
Heilbroner, Robert 17, 19, 66, 67, 120, 121, 125, 204 n.24
Hellams, Alfred A. 62
Heron, Woodburn 63, 64
Hertzberger, Herman 134
Hilmer & Sattler 162
Hippocrates 9
Hirschman, Albert O. 58, 203 n.4, 203 n.6
Hitchcock, Henry-Russell 178
Hitler, Adolf 88
Hollywood Bowl 103, 216 n.16
home 6, 9, 17, 28, 38, 57, 61, 63, 67, 69–76, 102, 108, 112, 124, 127, 133, 138, 151, 154, 167, 202 n.23, 202 n.1, 212 n.3, 222 n.29
homesickness 6, 70, 202 n.23
Hong Kong Bank 164
Hood, Raymond 98
horizontality 44, 51, 79, 98, 105, 110, 118, 167, 218 n.38
horror loci 9, 191 n.2
House of the People, Bucharest 124
Hunt House 102
Huxley, Aldous 9–11, 101
Hyams, Leslie 92
hyperesthesia 42

idleness 14, 17, 29–30, 34, 37, 40, 197 n.4, 197 n.11
    see also restlessness
Illich, Ivan 157, 159–60, 163
    see also Ivan Illich Law of Diminishing Architecture

immigration 22, 57, 106, 151, 154
Industrial Revolution 3, 10, 17, 20, 72
Inge, William 117
International Style 6, 89, 94, 97, 99, 106, 149, 153, 213 n.33
interests 58–9, 60, 62, 67, 110, 119, 125, 128
    see also passions
interiority 5, 18, 19, 24–5, 29, 31, 34, 53, 70, 72, 73, 74, 83, 87, 99, 112, 127, 138, 144, 167, 183, 186, 187, 188
    see also exteriority
inwardness 23, 24, 27–8, 41, 43, 45, 47, 194 n.6, 195 n.3, 202 n.23
    see also outwardness
Irace, Fulvio 7, 131, 140, 142
Isaacs, Robert A. 138
Islamic State of Iraq and the Levant 118
Isozaki, Arata 162
Italy 50, 96, 131, 153
Ivan Illich Law of Diminishing Architecture 7, 157, 158, 159 (Figure 16.1), 162, 169, 170, 231 n.7
Izenour, Steven 65–6, 101

Jacobs, Jane 107
jading 41, 43, 45, 179
    see also blunting
Jameson, Fredric 1, 111, 112, 115, 144, 195 n.3, 219 n.3, 222 n.25
Janssen, Benno 88
Jencks, Charles 4, 7, 133, 134, 157–60, 162–5, 169–70, 231 n.7, 231 n.10, 231 n.16, 232 n.21, 232 n.30
    "How Big is Bad?" 157, 161 (Figure 16.2)
Johnson, Lyndon B. 149
Johnson, Philip 6, 65, 92, 93–5, 99, 160, 213 n.33, 214 n.35
Johnson, Samuel 119
Judt, Tony 123, 124, 125, 223 n.40–1

Kafka, Franz 140
Kahn, Louis I. 92, 153
Kant, Immanuel 68
Kaprow, Allan 7, 131, 135, 137–8, 226 n.29, 227 n.30
Kay, John 186–7
Keynes, John Maynard 58
Kierkegaard, Søren 4, 5, 23–8, 30, 127, 134, 177, 187–8, 190 n.17, 195 n.2, 195 n.4, 195 n.6, 196 n.14, 196 n.20, 209 n.32
    Either/Or: A Fragment of a Life 5, 23, 24, 25, 195 n.9, 212 n.11
Kipnis, Jeffrey 175
Kirk, Russell 7, 147–56, 227 n.3, 228 n.4, 228 n.6, 228 n.8, 228 n.10, 229 n.17, 229 n.29, 230 n.36, 230 n.38–9
    "The Architecture of Servitude and Boredom" 7, 147

Index

Klages, Ludwig 71
Klapp, Orrin 122
Klein, Yves 135
Kojève, Alexandre 119, 221 n.20
Kondratieff, Nikolai 4, 19, 59, 60, 61, 121
Koolhaas, Rem 4, 8, 47, 53–4, 157–8, 164, 165–70, 231 n.7, 232 n.34
   "The Generic City" 157, 165
Kootz, Samuel M. 92
Kracauer, Sigfried 185, 225 n.13
Kubler, George 178
Kwinter, Sanford 175

La Défense 125, 159
La Motte, Antoine Houdar de 13
Langeweile 11, 208 n.31
Las Vegas 104, 173
lassitude 2, 12, 42
Lavin, Sylvia 4, 8, 171–2, 176–81, 234 n.18, 234 n.23–4
   "Lying Fallow" 8, 171, 177, 179, 180
Le Corbusier 13, 57, 62, 65, 66–7, 96, 98, 107, 184, 186, 188, 218 n.50
League of Nations 88, 212 n.6
Lefebvre, Henri 3, 13–14, 193 n.30, 193 n.32, 210 n.14
Lefèvre, Camille 88
leisure 3, 10, 47, 51, 54, 57, 67, 122, 170, 185, 201 n.16, 202 n.23, 216 n.26
Leopardi, Giacomo 134
Lescaze, William 106
Levine, Jack 92
liberalism 20, 119–20, 123, 124, 151, 153, 154, 155, 160, 222 n.24, 222 n.26
Lipps, Theodor 41, 42, 43
literalism 8, 174, 175, 180
Liverpool 20
locus communis 21, 184
Log (journal) 171
Lombardo, Nicholas 191 n.4
London 12, 21, 30, 33, 37, 38, 40, 59, 79, 96, 104, 106, 108, 118–19, 124, 132, 151, 158, 163, 172, 187, 197 n.2, 197 n.6, 198 n.23, 206 n.45, 214 n.39, 217 n.32
London, Jack 49
Long Island 50
Los Angeles 7, 101–12, 109 (Figure 11.1), 132, 215 n.4, 215 n.9, 216 n.10, 216 n.12, 217 n.34–6, 218 n.38
Louvre Museum 125, 159
love 24, 140, 148, 203 n.4
Lucchi, Michele de 134
Luna Park 47, 48

MacDonald, William L. 159, 231 n.10
McGill University 63

Machiavelli, Niccolò 58
Mager, Nathan 60, 125
Mailer, Norman 159, 231 n.11
Maison du Colon 81–2, 81 (Figure 9.2)
Mallarmé, Stéphane 137
Mandel, Ernest 4, 59, 60, 209 n.1
Manhattan 47, 51, 52, 53
Mann, Sandi 117, 222 n.34
Marcuse, Herbert 205 n.37
Marie Antoinette 173
Marriott, Hugh 63
   see *Boredom at Work*
Martin, Albert C. 104
Marx, Karl 20–1, 59, 115, 119, 120, 184, 229 n.29
mass individual 7, 128, 187, 224 n.9
May 1968, Paris 66
Mayer, Jürgen 178
melancholy 1, 9–10, 52, 137, 192 n.11, 193 n.24, 196 n.2
Mellon Institute, Pittsburgh 88
mémoire involontaire 132, 145
mémoire pure 145
memory 2, 4, 27, 30, 44–5, 48, 79, 82, 84, 104, 105, 107, 129, 132, 134, 136, 144, 145, 148, 153, 155, 166, 169, 173, 188, 200 n.26, 205 n.36, 219 n.3, 223 n.1
Mendini, Alessandro
Merleau-Ponty, Maurice 170
Minotaur 6, 77, 79, 82, 83
Mitterrand, François 125
Modern Age (journal) 147
Modern Movement 95, 132
Moholy-Nagy, Sibyl 92, 107
Moles, Abraham 132, 219 n.5, 225 n.8
MoMA 92, 177, 216 n11
Moneo, Rafael 162
monothematitis 159, 231 n.10
   see also blasphemisis
monotony 2, 10, 12, 18, 28, 30, 40, 51, 62, 63, 65, 68, 77, 83, 101, 105, 115, 117, 124, 132, 135, 137, 149, 151, 162, 164, 193 n.32
moods 6, 19, 23, 24, 27, 44, 70, 207 n.13
   see also attunements, *Stimmung*
Moravia, Alberto 1, 140
Morris, Herbert 210 n.26, 235 n.6
Moscow 119, 163
Mourenx 14
Mozart, Wolfgang Amadeus 24
Musicolour 64
Musil, Robert 168
Mussolini, Benito 160
MVRDV 173

Nature (journal) 22
Navarrenx 14
Negri, Antonio 166

Index

Nénot, Henri Paul 88
Neohistoricism 94
Netherlands 173
neurasthenia 42, 60, 105, 203 n.14–15
Neutra, Richard 106, 110, 111, 112, 166, 232 n.34
new 7, 14, 44, 101, 111, 123, 127, 128–30, 133, 149, 155, 166, 168, 173, 224 n.13
  see also old
New Empiricism 97
New Urbanism 173
New York 47, 48, 49, 50, 52, 59, 62, 89, 92, 98, 108, 142, 160, 163, 177, 187
New York Herald (newspaper) 50
New York Public Library 97
Newton, Isaac 17
Niemeyer, Oscar 62
Nietzsche, Friedrich 18, 128, 129, 194 n.7–8, 206 n.3, 207 n.13, 208 n.17
No 1 Poultry Street 118–19
non-places 169–70
Norberg-Schultz, Christian 46
North Korea 61
North Vietnam 61
nostalgia 30, 120, 125, 166, 174, 232 n.34
Novalis 70

Occupy 117
Oden, Thomas 205 n.36
O'Doherty, Brian 117
Oklahoma State Department of Health 62
old 14, 152, 166
  see also new
Oliver, Henry 104
Oppenheim, Méret 131
Oran 6, 77–85, 78 (Figure 9.1), 184, 210 n.4, 211 n.37–8
organization man 160, 231 n.15
Organization of Petroleum Exporting Countries (OPEC) 67
otium 138, 191 n.2
outwardness, outward spheres 23, 24, 25–7, 43, 195 n.3
  see also inwardness

Paik, Nam June 7, 131, 135, 142, 144
Palladio, Andrea 131, 185
Panofsky, Erwin 13
Pantagruel 101
Paris 2, 3, 38, 59, 65, 66, 79, 97, 125, 127, 159
Pascal, Blaise 17–18, 20, 203 n.4
Pask, Gordon 64
passions 10, 58, 67, 140, 192 n.9, 203 n.4, 203 n.6
  see also interests
Patecchio, Gerardo 140
Paxton, Joseph 12
peace 118, 120, 221 n.21
  see also war

Pei, I. M. 92, 159
Pelli, Cesar 163, 177, 232 n.21
Pérez, Carlota 4, 121, 222 n.29
Perry, Grayson 117
Peshkova, Ekaterina 50
Petrescu, Anca 124
Philippines 61
Piano, Renzo 162
Pignotti, Lorenzo 140–1
Pirsig, Robert 117
Pisa, 84
Plagens, Peter 108–12
Plato 191 n.2
playboy architecture 89, 99, 212 n.11–12
Poletown 151
Ponticus, Evagrius 9, 191 n.3
Portman, John 112, 151
Potsdamer Platz 162
Prak, Niels 115, 116, 117, 219 n.1, 219 n.5
Price, Cedric 64, 65
programism 8, 172–3, 174, 175, 180
Protestantism 1, 189 n.1
Proust Armchair 132, 144
Proust, Marcel 132, 144, 145
Punk 67, 206 n.45

Quantrill, Malcolm 46
Queen Charlotte 32

Rabelais, François 101
Rauch, Cope and Lippincott 66
Reclaim the Streets 118
Regency era 10, 12, 19, 30, 34, 104
Renaissance 9, 44, 45, 108, 215 n.49
Renaissance Centre, Detroit 151
repetition 4, 9, 25, 26, 45, 51, 53, 62, 88, 111, 115, 122, 129, 130, 135, 137, 142, 149, 157, 160, 162, 163, 168, 183, 191 n.2, 226 n.25, 232 n.34
Restany, Pierre 7, 131, 134–5, 137, 142, 144, 224 n.1
restlessness 11, 17, 29–30, 34, 37, 40, 135, 191 n.2, 197 n.4
  see also idleness
Reynolds, Malvina 138, 227 n.32
Rockefeller Centre 92, 98
Rodia, Simon 105
Rogers, Ernesto 166, 232 n.34
Rogers, Richard 158, 162
Rohe, Mies van der 65, 167, 234 n.18
Romania 123
Romanticism 2, 10, 39, 71
Rome 160
Roosevelt, Theodore 60–1
Rossi, Aldo 176
Rossi, Tino 84
Rossiya Hotel 163

258

Index

Rostow, Walt 60
Rowe, Colin 174, 176
Royal Palace, Rabat 136
Rudolph, Paul 66, 92, 153
Russell, Bertrand 117, 203 n.14
Russia 1, 49, 50, 124
Russian Revolution 61

Saarinen, Aline 92
sameness 2, 3, 12, 21, 28, 30, 33, 52, 53, 58, 62, 67, 84, 103, 116, 117, 118, 119, 128, 129, 149, 178, 187, 188, 226 n.25, 231 n.16
SANAA 178
Sartre, Jean-Paul 59, 140, 221 n.20
Satie, Erik 65
Scandinavia 62, 153
Schachtel, Ernest 63-4
Scheerbart, Paul 167
Scheler, Max 71
Schindler, Rudolf M. 106, 112
Schlegel, Friedrich 2
Schopenhauer, Arthur 18, 20, 194 n.6, 201 n.13
Scientific American (journal) 63
Scully Jr., Vincent 92
September 11, 2001 172
Serpentine Pavilions 172, 178
servitude 21, 62, 124, 136, 151, 155
Sex Pistols 67, 206 n.45
Sert, Josep L. 92
Sheraton Hotel 163
Shoreditch 187
Shunk, Harry 142
Signac, Paul 132
Silvetti, Jorge 4, 8, 171-6, 180-1, 233 n.1, 233 n.3
 "The Muses are Not Amused, Pandemonium in the House of Architecture" 8, 171, 172, 174-6, 180, 233 n.3
Singapore 158
Situationism International 66, 67, 117, 229 n.33
skateboarding 117
skyscrapers 150, 154, 162, 166, 167
sleep 70, 127, 129, 133, 138, 224 n.12
Smithson, Peter and Alison 190 n.15, 216 n.12
socialism 20, 60, 62, 119, 147, 194 n.14, 227 n.3
Soleri, Paolo 154
Sontag, Susan 64, 65, 130, 204 n.32
Soviet Union 120, 221 n.22
Spadena House, or The Witch's House 104
Spain 61, 183, 214 n.42, 235 n.1
Spanish Colonial Revival 103
spatiality 2, 5, 13, 45, 64
Spengler, Oswald 71
spleen 10, 191 n.7, 192 n.10
Starck, Philippe 134
stasis 1, 24, 36, 72, 77, 118, 178, 191 n.2, 197 n.4
St Paul's Cathedral, London 151

Steeplechase 47, 51
Stendhal 29-30, 196 n.2
Stimmung 207 n.9
 see also attunements, moods
Stirling, James 118
stylistic variation 6, 44, 45, 98, 169, 174
suicide 9, 67, 110, 118-19, 155
Sunset Boulevard 65, 105, 110
supermodernism 157, 169-70
Swan Hotel 163
Sweden 3, 61, 62, 97

taedium vitae 9, 191 n.2
Taiwan 183, 235 n.1
Taniguchi, Yoshio 177
Taut, Bruno 13
technology 4, 13, 17, 47, 65, 66, 96, 102, 104, 121-3, 163, 169, 174, 178, 218 n.39, 221 n.21, 222 n.32, 222 n.34
Teletubbies 174, 234 n.7
temporality 26, 75, 82, 122, 219 n.3
terror 10, 53, 61, 75, 122, 123, 135, 209 n.34
terrorism 118, 120, 220 n.14-15
Thatcher, Margaret 124
The Architectural Review (journal) 157, 214 n.39, 218 n.39
The Economist (journal) 186, 187, 188
The Edinburgh Review (journal) 33
The Independent Magazine (journal) 47
The Interlace 164, 232 n.29
"The International Style—Death or Metamorphosis?" (symposium) 6, 89-94, 90 (Figure 10.1), 91 (Figure 10.2), 93 (Figure 10.3), 95 (Figure 10.4), 96, 99
The New York Times (newspaper) 50, 53
The New York World (newspaper) 50
thematization 8, 173, 174, 175, 180
ticky-tacky 105, 138, 227 n.32
Toffler, Alvin 122
Toronto 187
Tower of London 151
transgression 1, 14, 29, 84, 115, 118, 119, 133, 138, 155, 165, 168, 188, 217 n.32
Troost, Paul Ludwig 88
Twain, Mark 50

UN Studio 174
unemployment 22, 66, 67, 124, 220 n.15
uniformity 5, 59, 62, 94, 104, 111, 115, 120, 132, 134, 137, 148, 149, 178, 226 n.17, 228 n.4
United Kingdom 3, 7, 147, 151, 178
United Nations 62, 186, 223 n.41
United States of America 3, 7, 50, 60-1, 67, 77, 89, 97, 121, 147, 149, 153, 201 n.11, 228 n.10
UrbEx 117

Index

Vago, Joseph 88
Venice Biennale of Architecture 183
Venturi, Robert 65–6, 101, 142, 205 n.39, 212 n.17, 234 n.18
verticality 44, 51, 79, 98, 167, 214 n.49
Victorian era 31, 34, 38, 39, 148
Victory of Socialism Boulevard, Bucharest 124
Vienna 184
Vischer, Friedrich and Robert 42, 43, 199 n.10

waiting 2, 6, 11, 14, 40, 57, 71, 72–3, 77, 81, 84, 85, 110, 122, 180, 203 n.15
Wallace, David Foster 122
Walter Gropius Lecture 8, 96, 171
war 13, 61, 85, 118, 220 n.14, 221 n.21, 228 n.10
Warhol, Andy 65, 103, 109, 131, 133, 205 n.35
Water and Power Building, Los Angeles 104
Watts 105, 216 n.26
Wayfarers "Glass" Chapel 104
Wayne County Courthouse, Detroit 151
weather 3, 38, 72, 80, 98, 102, 103, 105, 106, 112, 127, 136, 167, 184, 191 n.7, 226 n.25
Webb, Bruce 46
Weber, Max 20

Westin Bonaventure Hotel 112
Westport 160
Wilde, Oscar 147, 154
Wiley House 65
Wills, H. W. 12
Wolf, architect 81, 210 n.18
Wölfflin, Heinrich 6, 41–6, 98, 116
World Financial Center, New York 163
World Happiness Report 186
World War I 61, 221 n.21
World War II 61, 151, 162
    post-World War II 7, 147, 229 n.26
Wright, Lloyd 104
Wurster, Catherine Baner 92

Yates, Brock 107
Yokohama Port Terminal 174
York 155
Yugoslavia 3

Zaha Hadid Architects 158
Zen 137, 142, 226 n.29
Ziegler, Leopold 71
Zumthor, Peter 178